Restoring Joy

THREE COMPLETE WORKS IN ONE VOLUME

Ordering Your Private World
Renewing Your Spiritual Passion
Rebuilding Your Broken World

GORDON MacDONALD

INSPIRATIONAL PRESS

NEW YORK

Previously published in three separate volumes as

ORDERING YOUR PRIVATE WORLD
© 1984, 1985 by Gordon MacDonald
RENEWING YOUR SPIRITUAL PASSION
© 1986, 1989 by Gordon MacDonald
REBUILDING YOUR BROKEN WORLD
© 1988, 1990 by Gordon MacDonald

This edition published by Inspirational Press in 1996.

Inspirational Press
A division of Budget Book Service, Inc.
386 Park Avenue South
New York, NY 10016

Inspirational Press is a registered trademark of Budget Book Service, Inc.

Published by arrangement with Thomas Nelson, Inc., Publishers.

Library of Congress Catalog Card Number: 95-81985

ISBN: 0-88486-137-6

Printed in the United States of America.

Contents

ORDERING YOUR PRIVATE WORLD

Acknowledgements

Except where otherwise indicated, all Scripture quotations in this book are from the *New American Standard Bible,* © 1960, 1962, 1963, 1968, 1971, 1972, 1973, 1975 and 1977 by the Lockman Foundation, and are used by permission.

Scripture quotations marked TLB are from *The Living Bible* (Wheaton, Illinois: Tyndale House Publishers, 1971) and are used by permission.

To the Grace Chapel family of Lexington, Massachusetts, my brothers and sisters, my co-laborers, my friends. Much of what this book is about, I learned from all of you.

I love you.

Contents

Foreword

In a few words, yet with penetrating wisdom, Gordon Mac-
Donald has invaded an arena of great conflict—our private
world—and addressed an issue of great concern—our need
for order. For years I have been saying that this man is a rich
and rare blend of personal intensity, scriptural integrity, and
practical insight. This book offers tangible proof of all three.
Having served many years as pastor and having traveled
thousands of miles to meet with and to minister to a broad
cross-section of humanity, the man has earned the right to be
heard. He thinks with the clear headed simplicity and ide-
alism of a prophet, he writes with a straight shooting realism
of a businessman, yet he has, deep within, the tender compassion of a shepherd. Best of all, Gordon MacDonald models his
message as well as he communicates it. With much enthusiasm I recommend this book to all of you who, like me, need
order in your private world.

Chuck Swindoll
Pastor and Radio Bible Teacher
"Insight for Living"

Preface:
Memo to the Disorganized

"I'm so disorganized!"
    "I can't get my act together!"
        "My inner life is a mess!"
            "My private life is a failure!"

I have heard words like these scores of times. In conversations over breakfast, in the study where I meet people in my capacity as a pastor, in the living room of my home.

The words do not always come from people whose lives are falling apart or who are on the verge of some disaster, either. They may be said by men or women who appear to be extremely productive and successful. The first few times I heard self-disclosures like these, I was shocked. Now, many years later, I know for a fact that personal organization is a universal human struggle.

In Western culture we produce huge numbers of books to help us organize our work, our calendars, our production schedules, our studies, and our careers. I have not seen much that speaks directly to the question of internal, or spiritual, organization. And that is where the problem is most acute.

The successful people I have met who are concerned about disorganization are usually talking about the private dimension of their lives. They usually have the public dimension quite well regulated. It's this private part of life where we know ourselves best of all: this is where self-esteem is forged, where basic decisions about motives, values, and commit-

7

ments are made, where we commune with our God. I call it *the private world*, and I like to refer to its ideal state as one of *order*.

I know something about the disorganization of the private world because, like many others, I have struggled with it all my life. And to bring order to my private world has been one of my greatest battles.

Because I have lived in the context of the Christian gospel my entire life, Jesus Christ has never been a stranger to me. That does not mean, however, that I have always understood His lordship. Even though I have usually followed Him, I have too often followed from afar.

To understand what He meant when He spoke of "abiding in me" and my "abiding in Him" was very difficult, for I am one of many who has not easily taken to commitment. It has not been a simple thing for me to perceive the process and the purposes by which Christ wants to "abide" (John 15:4) in my private world. Frankly, I was often frustrated when I saw people who found this matter of "abiding" to be a perfectly comprehensible matter and who appeared to make it work.

Slowly and sometimes painfully, I have discovered that to bring organization to the private world where Christ chooses to live is both a lifelong and a daily matter. Something within—the Bible calls it sin—resists both His residence and all of the resulting order. It prefers a disorder where wrong motives and values can be hidden away and drawn to the surface in unguarded moments.

This disorder is a matter of daily concern. When I was a child living in a home where our bedrooms were not carpeted, I was often fascinated by the dustballs that collected under my bed. It was a mystery to me as to where they came from. It seemed as if some mysterious force came during the night and littered the floor with those dustballs while I slept. Today I find dustballs in my private world every day. How they got there, I am not sure. But I have to keep ahead of them in the daily discipline of bringing order into my inner sphere.

Let me be perfectly clear that I base this entire treatment of order in one's private world on the principle of the indwelling Christ, who mysteriously but definitely enters our lives upon our personal invitation and commitment. Apart from the center point of personal choice to follow Him, most of the words in this book will disintegrate into meaninglessness. *To bring order to one's personal life is to invite His control over every segment of one's life.*

For me, the pursuit of internal organization has been a lonely struggle because, frankly, I have found there is almost a universal reluctance to be candid and practical about these affairs. Much preaching on these matters is done in lofty terms that leave the hearer moved emotionally but unable to move specifically. More than once I have read a book or listened to a presentation on getting the spiritual life together, agreed with every word, and then realized that the proposed process was elusive and indefinite. It has been a struggle for people like me who want definite, measurable ways of responding to Christ's offer to live within us.

Even though the struggle has been mostly a lonely one, there has been assistance when I needed it. Naturally, there has been help from Scripture and the teachings I have received within the Christian tradition. Encouragement has come from my wife, Gail (whose private world is remarkably well ordered), from a number of mentors who have surrounded me from my earliest years, and from a host of men and women whom I will never meet in this life because they are dead. But I have encountered them in their biographies, and I have been delighted to discover that many of them also wrestled with the challenge of ordering their private worlds.

When I started making some public remarks about the order of my private world, I was impressed with how many people immediately reacted: pastors, lay people, men and women in various positions of leadership. "Your struggle is my struggle," they would say. "Give me any tips you can."

The private world can be divided into five sectors. The first deals with what makes us function as we do—our motivation. Are we *driven* people, propelled by the winds of our times, pressed to conform or compete? Or are we *called* people, the recipients of the gracious beckoning of Christ when He promises to make us into something?

Another sector of our private world centers on what we do

with the limited amount of time we have in this life. How we allocate time for the purposes of personal growth and service to others is a key to our health as persons. The third sector is intellectual: what are we doing with our minds, that remarkable part of us capable of receiving and processing the truth about creation?

The fourth sector of our private world, I would suggest, is that of the spirit. I am not concerned about being particularly theological with my vocabulary when I suggest there is a special, intimate place where we commune with the Father in a way that no one else can appreciate or understand. This place of the spirit I call the garden of our private world.

Finally, within us is a sector that draws us to rest, to a Sabbath peace. This peace is different from the amusement found so often in the visible world about us. And it is so significant that I believe it should be recognized as a uniquely essential source of inner organization.

Among the many biographies I have studied is one on Charles Cowman, missionary pioneer in Japan and Korea. His life was a remarkable testimony to the nature of commitment and its personal cost. In his later years his health broke, and he was forced into early retirement. The fact that he could no longer actively preach and direct the work of his fellowship missionaries was a terrible burden. One of his friends said this of him:

> Nothing impressed me more than Brother Cowman's quiet spirit. I never saw him ruffled, although at times I saw him wounded until the tears fell silently over his cheeks. He was a sensitive, tender spirit, but his secret cross became his crown.[1]

Cowman was a man with a private world in order. Not only was his life organized in its public dimension, it was organized within.

That is what this book is all about. I will not hesitate to be as practical as I know how. I will talk a lot about my own personal experiences, not because I consider myself a worthy

1. Lettie B. Cowman, *Charles E. Cowman* (Los Angeles: Oriental Missionary Society, 1928), p. 175.

model of internal order, but because I see myself as a fellow-struggler with all those for whom this issue is important.

Where possible, I have reached into the Bible for stories and supporting insights. But I must add that I have not over-indulged in theological argument. I have written with the assumption that the person eager to maintain order in the private world has already taken the step of choosing to live in obedience to God. And I have also assumed a basic under-standing and agreement with the Christian way of life.

If you, the reader, find points of agreement with my treat-ment of this subject, then you may conclude as I have that much of the way we are teaching and preaching to one another these days may be seriously out of tune with spiritual reality. For I believe that some of the issues I have tried to unfold in the following pages are where life really simmers. Frankly, I do not think we hear enough about these issues. And I would be delighted if some of these thoughts, which come from my heart and are borrowed from other thinkers and writers, be-gin a dialogue among a few curious people.

Few authors write books alone. I certainly do not. In put-ting together my thoughts, I had not only the assistance of scores of authors who stimulated my thinking, but also the close and careful assistance of my wife, Gail, God's special gift to me, who read through version after version of these chap-ters, made innumerable comments in margins, and made me seek a greater level of realism and practicality.

To all those who think there is a more organized way to live within: join me on this bit of reflective adventure. At the end there may just be an opportunity for a deeper experience with God and an understanding of our mission in serving Him.

Memo to the Disorganized:

If my private world is in order, it will be because I am convinced that the inner world of the spiritual must govern the outer world of activity.

1

The Sinkhole Syndrome

The residents of a Florida apartment building awoke to a terrifying sight outside their windows. The ground beneath the street in front of their building had literally collapsed, creating a massive depression that Floridians call a sinkhole. Tumbling into the ever-deepening pit were automobiles, pavement, sidewalks, and lawn furniture. The building itself would obviously be the next to go.

Sinkholes occur, scientists say, when underground streams drain away during seasons of drought, causing the ground at the surface to lose its underlying support. Suddenly everything simply caves in, leaving people with a frightening suspicion that nothing—not even the earth beneath their feet—is trustworthy.

There are many people whose lives are like one of Florida's sinkholes. It is likely that at one time or another many of us have perceived ourselves to be on the verge of a sinkhole-like cave-in. In the feelings of numbing fatigue, a taste of apparent failure, or the bitter experience of disillusionment about goals or purposes, we may have sensed something within us about to give way. We feel we are just a moment from a collapse that will threaten to sweep our entire world into a bottomless pit. Sometimes there seems to be little that can be done to prevent such a collapse. What is wrong?

If we think about it for very long, we may discover the exis-

13

tence of an inner space—our private world—about which we were formerly ignorant. I hope it will become apparent that if neglected this private world will not sustain the weight of events and pressures that press upon it.

Some people are surprised and disturbed when they make such a self-discovery. They suddenly realize they have spent the majority of their time and energy establishing life on the visible level, at the surface. They have accumulated a host of good and perhaps even excellent assets such as academic degrees, work experience, key relationships, and physical strength or beauty.

There is nothing wrong with all of that. But often it is discovered almost too late that the private world of the person is in a state of disorderliness or weakness. And when that is true there is always potential for the sinkhole syndrome.

We must come to see ourselves as living in two very different worlds. Our outer, or public, world is easier to deal with. It is much more measurable, visible, and expandable. Our outer world consists of work, play, possessions, and a host of acquaintances that make up a social network. It is the part of our existence easiest to evaluate in terms of success, popularity, wealth, and beauty. But our inner world is more spiritual in nature. Here is a center in which choices and values can be determined, where solitude and reflection might be pursued. It is a place for conducting worship and confession, a quiet spot where the moral and spiritual pollution of the times need not penetrate.

The majority of us have been taught to manage our public worlds well. Of course, there will always be the undependable worker, the poorly organized homemaker, and the person whose social capacities are so immature that he becomes a drain on everyone around him. But most of us have learned to take orders, make schedules, and give directions. We know which systems best suit us in terms of work and relationship. We choose proper forms of leisure and pleasure. We have the capability to choose friends and make those relationships work well.

Our public worlds are filled with a seeming infinity of demands upon our time, our loyalties, our money, and our energies. And because these public worlds of ours are so visible, so real, we have to struggle to ignore all their seductions and demands. They scream for our attention and action.

The result is that our private world is often cheated, neglected because it does not shout quite so loudly. It can be effectively ignored for large periods of time before it gives way to a sinkhole-like cave-in.

The author Oscar Wilde was one who paid scant attention to his private world. William Barclay quotes Wilde's confession:

> The gods had given me almost everything. But I let myself be lured into long spells of senseless and sensual ease . . . Tired of being on the heights, I deliberately went to the depths in search for new sensation. What the paradox was to me in the sphere of thought, perversity became to me in the sphere of passion. I grew careless of the lives of others. I took pleasure where it pleased me, and passed on. I forgot that every little action of the common day makes or unmakes character, and that therefore what one has done in the secret chamber, one has some day to cry aloud from the house-top. I ceased to be lord over myself. I was no longer the captain of my soul, and did not know it. I allowed pleasure to dominate me. I ended in horrible disgrace.[1]

When Wilde writes, "I was no longer the captain of my soul," he describes a person whose inner world is in shambles, whose life is caving in. Although his words reach great heights of personal drama, they are similar to what many could say—many who, like him, have ignored their internal existence.

I believe that one of the great battlegrounds of our age is the private world of the individual. There is a contest that must be fought particularly by those who call themselves practicing Christians. Among them are those who work hard, shouldering massive responsibilities at home, at work, and at church. *They are good people, but they are very, very tired!* And thus they too often live on the verge of a sinkhole-like collapse. Why? Because although their worthwhile actions are very unlike those of Wilde, like him they become too public-

1. William Barclay, *The Letters to the Galatians and Ephesians* (Philadelphia: Westminster, 1976), p. 100.

world-oriented, ignoring the private side until it is almost too late.

Our Western cultural values have helped to blind us to this tendency. We are naively inclined to believe that the most publicly active person is also the most privately spiritual. We assume that the larger the church, the greater its heavenly blessing. The more information about the Bible a person possesses, we think, the closer he must be to God.

Because we tend to think like this, there is the temptation to give imbalanced attention to our public worlds at the expense of the private. More programs, more meetings, more learning experiences, more relationships, more busyness; until it all becomes so heavy at the surface of life that the whole thing trembles on the verge of collapse. Fatigue, disillusionment, failure, defeat all become frightening possibilities. The neglected private world can no longer hold the weight.

A man who has claimed Christian faith for more than ten years recently joined me on the sidelines of a soccer game in which our sons were playing. At halftime we took a stroll and inquired about each other. I asked him one of those questions that Christians ought to ask each other but feel odd in doing so.

I said, "Tell me how you're doing spiritually."

And he responded, "Interesting question! What's a good answer? Oh, I'm OK, I guess. I wish I could say I was growing or feeling closer to God. But the truth is that I'm sort of standing still."

I do not think I was out of line to pursue the matter because he gave me the impression he was genuinely interested in talking about this.

"Are you taking time regularly to order your inner life?"

He looked at me inquisitively. If I had said, "How's your quiet time?" he would have known exactly how to answer. That would have been measurable, and he could have responded in terms of days, hours and minutes, systems and techniques. But I had asked about the order of his inner life. And the key word is *order*, a word of *quality*, not quantity. And when he sensed that he showed discomfort.

"When does a guy ever get to order his inner life?" he

asked. "I've got work piled up to keep me going for the rest of the year. I'm out every night this week. My wife is after me to take a week's vacation. The house needs painting. So there's not too much time to think about ordering the inner life, as you put it."

He paused for a moment and then asked, *"What is the inner life anyway?"*

Suddenly I became aware that here was a professing Christian who had moved for years in Christian circles, had gained a Christian reputation for doing Christian things, but had never realized that underneath all the action and well-meaning noise there has got to be something solid, something dependable. That he saw himself as too busy to maintain an inner world, and that he was not sure he knew what it is anyway told me that he may have missed by a significant distance the central point of a life in touch with God. We had a lot to talk about.

Few people have had to wrestle with the pressures of a public world more than Anne Morrow Lindbergh, wife of the famous aviator. And she so jealously guarded her private world and wrote some insightful comments about it in her book *The Gift from the Sea:*

> I want first of all . . . to be at peace with myself. I want a singleness of eye, a purity of intention, a central core to my life that will enable me to carry out these obligations and activities as well as I can. I want, in fact—to borrow from the language of the saints—to live "in grace" as much of the time as possible. I am not using this term in a strictly theological sense. By grace I mean an inner harmony, essentially spiritual, which can be translated into outward harmony. I am seeking perhaps what Socrates asked for in the prayer from the Phaedrus when he said, "May the outward and inward man be one." I would like to achieve a state of inner spiritual grace from which I could function and give as I was meant to in the eye of God.[2]

Fred Mitchell, a leader in world missions, used to keep a motto on his desk that read, "Beware of the Barrenness of a

2. Anne Morrow Lindbergh, *The Gift from the Sea* (New York: Pantheon, 1955), pp. 23–24.

Busy Life." He too understood the potential collapse that follows when the inner world is ignored.

The Florida sinkhole is a physical picture of a spiritual problem with which many Western Christians must deal. As the pressure of life grows in the decades of the eighties and nineties, there will be more people whose lives resemble a sinkhole, unless they gaze inward and ask themselves, Is there a private world beneath the noise and action at the surface? A world that needs to be explored and maintained? Can strength and resilience be developed that will bear up under the pressure at the surface?

In a lonely moment in Washington when John Quincy Adams was overwhelmed by homesickness for his Massachusetts family, he wrote them a letter, addressing comments of encouragement and counsel to each son and daughter. To his daughter he wrote about the prospect of marriage and the kind of man she should choose to marry. His words reveal how highly he regarded an ordered private world:

> Daughter! Get you an honest man for a husband and keep him honest. No matter whether he is rich, provided he be independent. Regard the honor and moral character of the man, more than all other circumstances. *Think of no other greatness but that of the soul, no other riches but those of the heart.*(Italics added)[3]

Memo to the Disorganized:

If my private world is in order, it will be because I make a
daily choice to monitor its state of orderliness.

2

The View from the Bridge

A close friend was once an officer aboard a United States Navy nuclear submarine. He related to me an experience that happened one day while the sub was on duty in the Mediterranean. Many ships were passing overhead on the surface, and the submarine was having to make a large number of violent maneuvers to avoid possible collisions.

In the absence of the captain, my friend was duty officer, in charge of giving the commands by which the submarine was positioned at each moment. Because there was such a sudden and unusual amount of movement, the captain, who had been in his own quarters, suddenly appeared on the bridge asking, "Is everything all right?"

"Yes, sir!" was my friend's reply.

The captain took a quick look around and then started back out through the hatch to leave the bridge. As he disappeared he said, "It looks all right to me too."

That simple, routine encounter between a naval commander and one of his trusted officers provided me with a helpful picture of the order of one's private world. All around that submarine potential danger of collision was lurking. It was enough to make any alert captain show concern. But that danger was outside. Down deep inside the sub was a quiet place where there could be absolute control of the ship's destiny. And that was where the captain instinctively headed.

In that center of command there was not an ounce of panic; only a calm and deliberate series of actions being carried on by a highly trained crew of seamen doing their job. Thus when the commander appeared on the bridge to assure himself that everything was in order, it was. "Is everything all right?" he asked. Assured that it was, he looked about and agreed, "It looks all right to me too." He had gone to the right place and received the proper answer.

That is how the captain organized his sub. The appropriate procedures were practiced a thousand times when there was no danger. Thus, when it was time for action in a precarious situation, there was no need for the captain to panic. He could anticipate an excellent performance from the people on the bridge. When things are in order there, the submarine is secure no matter what the external circumstances. "It looks good to me too," says the captain.

But there have been cases in which those procedures have been ignored, perhaps left unpracticed. Then there can be disaster. Ships collide and sink, causing great loss. And so it is with human life when there is disorganization on the "bridge" of the inner world. The accidents that occur there have names like *burnout, breakdown,* or *blow-up.*

It is one thing for a person to make a mistake, or even to fail. We learn our best lessons of procedure and character under such conditions. But it is another thing to watch human beings disintegrate before our very eyes because there were no resources of interior support in the midst of the pressure.

The *Wall Street Journal* presented a series of articles entitled "Executive's Crisis," and one story featured Jerald H. Maxwell, a young entrepreneur who founded a successful hi-tech company. For a while he was considered to be a managerial and financial genius. But just for a while. Then there was a disintegration, a sinkhole collapse.

The day is etched into Jerald H. Maxwell's memory. His family will never forget it, either. To them it is the day he started weeping in his room, the day his exuberant self-confidence ended and his depression began, the day his world—and theirs—came tumbling down.

Maxwell had been fired! Everything fell apart, and he had no ability to handle the situation. The *Journal* continued:

> For the first time in his life, Mr. Maxwell was a failure, and it shattered him. His feeling of defeat led to an emotional break-down, gnawed away at the bonds between Mr. Maxwell and his wife and four sons and pushed him to the brink . . . "When things fell apart, they felt so bad I was ashamed," Mr. Maxwell recalls. He pauses and sighs, then goes on: "It says in the Bible that all you have to do is ask and you will receive Well I asked for death many times."[1]

Most of us have not asked for death as Maxwell did. But most of us have experienced the same pressure from the outer world, crowding in upon us to such an extent that we wondered if some sort of death was not imminent. During such moments we ask ourselves about the strength of our reserves—whether or not we can keep on going, whether it is worth it to keep pressing, whether it may be time to "cut and run." In short, we are not sure that there is enough spiritual, psychic, or physical energy to keep moving at the pace we are presently trying to maintain.

The key to all of this is to do what the captain of that submarine did. When there was a sense of violent turbulence all around, he headed for the bridge to determine whether or not things were in order. The answer, he knew, would be found nowhere else. And if everything was all right there, he knew he could retire to his quarters with confidence. The ship could handle the turbulent circumstances if everything was all right on the bridge.

One of my favorite Bible stories tells of the afternoon the disciples found themselves in a raging storm on the Sea of Galilee. Soon they were terrified and had lost all of their composure. Here were men who had fished this sea for years, who had their own equipment, and who must have seen such storms before. But for some reason, this time they were not able to handle the situation. Jesus, on the other hand, was asleep in the rear of the boat, and they ran to Him, furious that He seemed not to care that loss of life was a real threat.

1. "Executive's Crisis," *Wall Street Journal*, 12 March 1982, p. 1.

Perhaps we should at least credit them with knowing where to run.

After Christ had pressed peace into the storm, He asked the question that was central to all of their personal growth and development as spiritual leaders: "Where is your faith?" He could have asked in language I have been using, "Why isn't the bridge of your private world in better order?"

Why is it that for so many the answer to personal tension and pressure lies not in going to the bridge of life but rather in attempting to run faster, protest more vigorously, accumulate more, collect more data, and gain more expertise? We are of an age in which it seems instinctive to give attention to every cubic inch of life other than our inner worlds—the only place from which we can gain the strength to brave, or even beat, any outer turbulence.

Biblical writers believed in the principle of going to the bridge; they knew and taught that the development and maintenance of our inner worlds should be our highest priority. That is one practical reason that their work has transcended all times and cultures. For what they wrote they received from the Creator *who made us to work most effectively from the inner world toward the outer.*

One writer of Proverbs put the principle of the inner world in these words:

> "Watch over your heart with all diligence, for from it flow the springs of life" (Proverbs 4:23).

In one simple sentence the writer has conveyed to us a most amazing insight. What I call the "bridge," he calls the "heart." He sees the heart as a spring, and suggests that out of it can flow the energy, the insight, and the force that do not succumb to outer turbulence but rather overcome it. Keep the heart, he says, and it will become a wellspring of life from which you and others can drink.

But what does it mean to "keep" the heart? For one thing, the writer is obviously concerned that the heart be protected from influences outside itself that might jeopardize its integrity. The writer is also concerned about the strength and development of the heart in order to increase its capacity to bring order to one's life.

But even behind these possible lessons from the metaphor is the fact that keeping or guarding of the heart, the "bridge" of human life, is a deliberate and disciplined choice a man or woman must make. We must *choose* to keep the heart. Its health and productivity cannot be assumed; it must be constantly protected and maintained. Again, we need to remember what the captain of the submarine did when he felt something out of the ordinary going on: he immediately headed for the bridge. Why? Because he knew that that was the place in which all capability to face danger would be found.

In the New Testament, Paul made the same sort of observation when he challenged Christians to "not be conformed to this [outer] world, but be transformed by the renewing of your mind" (Romans 12:2).

J. B. Phillips translated Paul's words like this: "Don't let the world squeeze you into its mold."

The apostle set forth an ageless truth. He was directing that a right choice be made. Are we going to order our inner worlds so that they wil¹ create influence on the outer world? Or will we neglect our private worlds and thus permit the outer sphere to shape us? This is a choice we have to make every day of our lives.

This is an incredible thought. And it is the sort of insight that the terminated executive in the *Wall Street Journal* article had ignored. The evidence? His cave-in, when the world about him faced him with crushing pressure. He had no reserve of inner strength, no order to his private world.

Mary Slessor was a young single woman who left Scotland at the turn of the century to go to a part of Africa that was infested with disease and indescribable danger. But she had an indomitable spirit and kept going when lesser men and women broke down, ran, and never came back. Once, after a particularly draining day, she found herself trying to sleep in a crude jungle hut. Of that night she wrote:

I am not very particular about my bed these days, but as I lay on a few dirty sticks laid across and covered with a litter of dirty corn-shells, with plenty of rats and insects, three women and an infant three days old alongside, and over a dozen sheep and goats and cows outside, you don't wonder that I slept little. *But I had such a comfortable quiet night in my own heart.* (Italics added)[2]

Now that is the sort of thing we are thinking about when we address the question of order in our private world. Whether you call it the "bridge" in naval language or the "heart" in biblical language, the point is the same: there must be a quiet place where all is in order, a place from which comes the energy that overcomes turbulence and is not intimidated by it.

We will know that we have learned this significant principle when we come to the point where the development and maintenance of a strong inner world becomes the most important single function of our existence. Then in the moment when pressure rises and tension increases, we can ask, "Is everything all right?" And discovering that it is, we can say with the heart, "It looks all right to me, too."

2. James Buchan, *The Indomitable Mary Slessor* (New York: Seabury, 1981), p. 86.

Sector One

Memo to the Disorganized:

If my private world is in order, it will be because I recognize my proneness to operate according to schemes and patterns not made of God but fashioned by a disordered past.

3

Caught in a Golden Cage

The twelve men who followed Jesus Christ and ultimately founded His church were a strange group. There is not one of them (with the possible exception of John, whom I find to be likable and nonthreatening) I would have picked to lead a movement of the proportions of Christ's mission. No, I would not have picked them. But Jesus called them, and you know the result.

Frankly, some of those volunteers who were turned down by Jesus are more my style. They were go-getters; they knew a good thing when they saw it. They seem to have been bursting with enthusiasm. And He turned them down! Why?

Perhaps Jesus, with His extraordinary insight, looked into their private worlds and saw danger signs. Perhaps He saw *driven men,* out to make something of themselves. Maybe the very thing I like about them was the problem: they wanted to control the situation by saying when they would start and where they would go.

Perhaps (it's pure speculation) if they had come aboard we would have discovered that they had a lot more in their agendas than was apparent at first. We would have found that they were men with their own plans and schemes, goals and objectives. And Jesus Christ will not do mighty works in the private worlds of people who are so driven. He never has. He seems to prefer to work with people whom He calls. And that is why the Bible knows nothing of volunteers, only the called.

In an exploration of the inner sphere of the person, one has to begin somewhere, and I have chosen to begin where Christ appears to have begun—with the distinction between the *called* and the *driven*. Somehow He separated people out on the basis of their tendency to be driven or their willingness to be called. He dealt with their motives, the basis of their spiritual energy, and the sorts of gratification in which they were interested. He called those who were drawn to Him and avoided those who were driven and wanted to use Him.

How can you spot a driven person? Today it is relatively easy. Driven people show the marks of stress. Look for symptoms of stress, and you have probably found some driven men and women.

The contemporary world is giving a lot of attention to the subject of stress. Stress is a topic for books, for research, and the doctor's examination room virtually every time someone feels chest pains or stomach upset. Many people commit entire careers to its study. Scientists measure stress in laboratories by subjecting various materials to all sorts of pressure and temperature and vibration. Engineers monitor it in the frames and engines of automobiles and airplanes by driving or flying them under extreme conditions for thousands of miles. Stress in human beings is closely checked while people fly through space, sit in a pressure chamber at the bottom of the ocean, or face medical tests in a hospital examination lab. A man I know has developed a sensitive measuring device that traces brain waves and can tell the researcher the minute the subject of his study is over-stressed.

In the past decade it has become very apparent that many people in our society are under constant and destructive stress, as life for them reaches a pace that offers little time for any restorative rest and retreat. *Time* magazine reported:

> In the past 30 years, doctors and health officials have come to realize how heavy a toll stress is taking on the nation's well-being. According to the American Academy of Family Physicians, two-thirds of office visits to family doctors are prompted by stress-

related symptoms. At the same time, leaders of industry have become alarmed by the huge cost of such symptoms in absenteeism, company medical expenses and lost productivity.[1]

The article went on to say that the effects of stress are costing American business $50 to $75 billion a year, or more than $750 for every U.S. worker. Stress, *Time* says, "is a major contributor, either directly or indirectly, to coronary heart disease, cancer, lung ailments, accidental injuries, cirrhosis of the liver and suicide." And that is just the beginning.

What is behind all this? *Time* quotes Dr. Joel Elkes of the University of Louisville: "Our mode of life itself, the way we live, is emerging as today's principal cause of illness."

We are all aware that there is a kind of stress that is beneficial because it brings out the best in performers, athletes, or executives. But most of the attention presently being given to the subject centers on the kinds of stress that diminish human capacity rather than enhance it.

One fascinating study on stress has been conducted by Dr. Thomas Holmes. Holmes is known for his development of the famous Social Readjustment Rating Scale, or, as most of us know it, the Holmes Stress Chart. Holmes's stress chart is a simple measurement device that indicates how much pressure a person is probably facing and how close he may be to dangerous physical and psychic consequences.

After considerable research, various events common to all of us were assigned point totals by Holmes and his associates. Each point was called a "life-change unit." An accumulation of more than 200 of these units in any one year, Holmes suggests, could be the warning of a potential heart attack, emotional stress, or breakdown of the ability to function as a healthy person. The death of a spouse, for example, commands the highest number of "life-change" units, 100. Being fired from a job produces 47 points, while the acquisition of a new family member provides 39. Not all stress-producing events listed by Holmes are negative. Even positive and happy events such as Christmas (12 points) and vacations (13) create stress.

1. "Stress: Can We Cope?" *Time*, 6 June 1983, pp. 48–54.

My experience is that it is not unusual to talk with people whose point total is well beyond 200. A pastor, for example, comes to visit with me at my office. His point total, he tells me, is 324. His blood pressure is dangerously high; he suffers from constant stomach pains, he fears an ulcer, and he does not sleep well at night. On another day, I sit at breakfast with a young executive who admits that until recently his ambition had been to accumulate a million dollars before the age of 35. When he matches his present situation up against the Holmes Stress Chart, he is horrified to discover that his point total is 412. What do these two men from the business and religious world have in common?

These are what I call *driven* men. And their drive is costing them terribly—the point totals are simply a numerical indication of that fact. I use the word *driven* because it describes not only the condition in which they are pursuing life, but also because it is descriptive of the way many of the rest of us are not facing up to the reality of what we are doing to ourselves. Perhaps we are being driven toward goals and objectives without always understanding why. Or we may not be aware of the real cost to our minds, our bodies, and, of course, our hearts. By *heart* I mean the one written about in Proverbs 4:23, that fountainhead from which comes the energy of life.

There are lots of driven people doing very good things. Driven people are not necessarily bad folk, although the consequences of their drivenness may produce unfortunate results. In fact, driven people often make great contributions. They start organizations; they provide jobs and opportunities; they are often very bright and offer ways and means of doing things that benefit many other people. But nevertheless they are driven, and one worries about their ability to sustain the pace without danger to themselves.

Can driven people be spotted? Yes, of course. There are many symptoms that suggest a person is driven. Among the ones I see most often are these:

(1) *A driven person is most often gratified only by accomplishment.* Somewhere in the process of maturation this person discovers that the only way he can feel good about himself and his world is to accumulate accomplishments. This discov-

ery may be the result of formative influences at an early age; as a child, affirmation and approval may have been received from a parent or influential mentor only when something had been finished. Nothing of value may have ever been said until that task was completed. Thus the only way he could find love and acceptance was through accomplishment.

A psychology of achievement sometimes captures the heart in circumstances like that. A person begins to reason that if one accomplishment resulted in good feelings and the praise of others, then several more accomplishments may bring an abundance of good feelings and affirmations.

So the driven person begins to look for ways to accumulate more and more achievements. He will soon be found doing two or three things at one time, because that brings even more of this strange sort of pleasure. He becomes the sort of person who is always reading books and attending seminars that promise to help him to use what time he has even more effectively. Why? So that he can produce more accomplishments, which in turn will provide greater gratification.

This is the kind of person who sees life only in terms of results. As such he has little appreciation for the *process* leading toward results. This kind of person would love to fly from New York to Los Angeles at supersonic speed because to travel at ground speed and see the hills of Pennsylvania, the golden wheat of Iowa and Nebraska, the awesomeness of the Rockies, and the deserts of Utah and Nevada would be a terrible waste of time. Upon arrival in Los Angeles after a swift two-hour trip, this driven person would be highly irritated if the plane took four extra minutes to get into the gate. Arrival is everything to this accomplishment-oriented individual; the trip means nothing.

(2) *A driven person is preoccupied with the symbols of accomplishment.* He is usually conscious of the concept of power, and he seeks to possess it in order to wield it. That means that he will be aware of the symbols of status: titles, office size and location, positions on organizational charts, and special privileges.

There is generally a concern for one's own notoriety when in a state of drivenness. Who, the driven person wonders, knows about what I am doing? How can I be better connected with the "greats" of my world? These questions often preoccupy the driven person.

(3) *A driven person is usually caught in the uncontrolled pursuit of expansion.* Driven people like to be a part of something that is getting bigger and more successful. They are usually on the move, seeking the biggest and the best opportunities. They rarely have any time to appreciate the achievements to date.

The nineteenth-century English preacher Charles Spurgeon once said:

> Success exposes a man to the pressures of people and thus tempts him to hold on to his gains by means of fleshly methods and practices, and to let himself be ruled wholly by the dictatorial demands of incessant expansion. Success can go to my head and will unless I remember that it is God who accomplishes the work, that he can continue to do so without my help, and that he will be able to make out with other means whenever he wants to cut me out.[2]

You can see this unfortunate principle in the pursuit of some careers. But you can also see it in the context of spiritual activity, for there is such a thing as a spiritually driven person who is never satisfied with who he is or what he accomplishes in religious work. And of course this means that his attitude toward those around him is much the same. He is rarely pleased with the progress of his peers or subordinates. He lives in a constant state of uneasiness and restlessness, looking for more efficient methods, greater results, deeper spiritual experiences. There is usually no sign that he will ever be satisfied with himself or anyone else.

(4) *Driven people tend to have a limited regard for integrity.* They can become so preoccupied with success and achievement that they have little time to stop and ask if their inner person is keeping pace with the outer process. Usually it is not, and there is an increasing gap, a breakdown in integrity. People like this often become progressively deceitful; and they not only deceive others, they deceive themselves. In the at-

2. Cited in J. Oswald Sanders, *Spiritual Leadership* (Chicago: Moody, 1967), p. 23.

tempt to push ahead relentlessly, they lie to themselves about motives; values and morals are compromised. Shortcuts to success become a way of life. Because the goal is so important, they drift into ethical shabbiness. Driven people become frighteningly pragmatic.

(5) *Driven people often possess limited or undeveloped people skills.* They are not noted for getting along well with others. They were not born without the capacity to get along with others, but projects are more important to them than people. Because their eyes are upon goals and objectives, they rarely take note of the people about them, unless they can be used for the fulfillment of one of the goals. And if others are not found to be useful, then they may be seen as obstacles or competitors when it comes to getting something done.

There is usually a "trail of bodies" in the wake of the driven person. Where once others praised him for his seemingly great leadership, there soon appears a steady increase in frustration and hostility, as they see that the driven person cares very little about the health and growth of human beings. It becomes apparent that there is a non-negotiable agenda, and it is supreme above all other things. Colleagues and subordinates in the orbit of the driven person slowly drop away, one after another, exhausted, exploited, and disillusioned. Of this person we are most likely to find ourselves saying, "He is miserable to work with, but he certainly gets things done."

And therein lies the rub. He gets things done, but he may destroy people in the process. Not an attractive sight. Yet the ironic thing, which cannot be ignored, is that in almost every great organization, religious and secular, people of this sort can be found in key positions. Even though they carry with them the seeds of relational disaster, they often are indispensable to the action.

(6) *Driven people tend to be highly competitive.* They see each effort as a win-or-lose game. And, of course, the driven person feels he must win, must look good before others. The more driven he is, the larger the score by which he needs to win. Winning provides the evidence the driven person desperately needs that he is right, valuable, and important. Thus, he

is likely to see others as competitors or as enemies who must be beaten—perhaps even humiliated—in the process.

(7) *A driven person often possesses a volcanic force of anger*, which can erupt any time he senses opposition or disloyalty. This anger can be triggered when people disagree, offer an alternative solution to a problem, or even hint at just a bit of criticism.

The anger may not surface as physical violence. But it can take the form of verbal brutality: profanity or humiliating insults, for example. The anger can express itself in vindictive acts such as firing people, slandering them before peers, or simply denying them things they have come to expect, such as affection, money, or even companionship.

A close friend tells of sitting in an office with several working associates while the office manager, a woman who had worked for the company for fifteen years, made a plea for a week off to be with a sick baby. She made the mistake of responding tearfully when the boss refused her request. When he turned and saw her tears, he snarled, "Clean out your desk and get out of here; I don't need you anyhow." When she was gone he turned to the horrified onlookers and said, "Let's get one thing straight; you're all here for only one reason: to make me money. And if you don't like it, get out right now!"

Tragically, many good people who surround the driven person are more than willing to take the impact of such anger although it desperately hurts them, because they reason that the boss or the leader is getting things done, that he is being blessed by God, or that no one can argue with success. Sometimes the anger and its cruel effects are accepted simply because no one has either the courage or the ability to stand up to the driven person.

Recently a person who serves on the board of a major Christian organization told me of encounters with the executive director that included outbursts of anger studded with extraordinary profanity and demeaning language. When I asked why board members accepted this form of behavior, which was neither rare nor open to excuse, he said, "I guess we were so impressed with the way that God seemed to use him in his public ministry that we were reluctant to confront."

Is there anything else worth saying about the driven person, who by now appears to be entirely unlikeable? Yes, simply this:

(8) *Driven people are usually abnormally busy.* They are usually too busy for the pursuit of ordinary relationships in marriage, family, or friendship, or even to carry on a relationship with themselves—not to speak of one with God. Because driven people rarely think they have accomplished enough, they seize every available minute to attend more meetings, to study more material, to initiate more projects. They operate on the precept that a reputation for busyness is a sign of success and personal importance. Thus they attempt to impress people with the fullness of their schedule. They may even express a high level of self-pity, bemoaning the "trap" of responsibility they claim to be in, wishing aloud that there was some possible release from all that they have to live with. But just try to suggest a way out!

The truth is that the very worst thing that could happen to them would be if someone provided them with a way out. They really wouldn't know what to do with themselves if there were suddenly less to do. Busyness for the driven person becomes a habit, a way of life and thought. They find it enjoyable to complain and gather pity, and they would probably not want it any different. But tell a driven person that, and you'll make him angry.

This then is the driven person—not an entirely attractive picture. What often disturbs me as I look at this picture is the fact that much of our world is run by driven people. We have created a system that rides on their backs. And where that is true in businesses, in churches, and in homes, the growth of people is often sacrificed for accomplishment and accumulation.

Pastors who are driven men have been known to burn out scores of assistants and lay leaders because of their need to head organizations that are the biggest, the best, and the most well-known. There are business people who claim Christian faith and who have enjoyed a reputation for graciousness in the church, but who are ruthless in the office, pushing people and squeezing them for the last ounce of energy simply so that they themselves can enjoy the gratification of winning, accumulating, or establishing a reputation.

Recently a businessman became a Christian through the witness of a layman who is a good friend of mine. Not long after making his choice to follow Jesus Christ, he wrote a long letter to my friend who had guided him into faith. In it he described some of his struggles as the result of his driven condition. I requested permission to share part of the letter because it so vividly illustrated the driven person. He wrote:

Several years ago I was at a point of great frustration in my life. Although I had a wonderful wife and three beautiful sons, my career was going badly. I had few friends, my oldest son began getting into trouble—he started failing in school—I was suffering from depression, there was great tension and unhappiness in my family. At that time I had an opportunity to travel overseas where I stayed to work in a foreign company. This new opportunity was such an excellent one, financially and career-wise, that I made it number one in my life, forsaking all other values. I did many wrong (i.e., sinful) things to advance my position and success. I justified them as being of good consequence to my family (more money, etc.)—resulted in my lying to myself and my family and behaving wrongly in many ways.

Of course this was intolerable to my wife and she and my family returned to the U.S. I was still blind, however, to the problems that were within me. My success, my salary, my career—all moved upward. I *was caught in a golden cage* . . . [italics mine]

Although many wonderful things were happening outside me, inside I was losing everything. My capacity to reason and my capacity to decide were both weakened. I would evaluate alternatives constantly going over various options, always trying to pick the one that would maximize success and career. I knew in my heart that something was terribly wrong. I went to church, but the words there couldn't reach me. I was too caught up in my own world.

After a terrible episode with my family several weeks ago, I completely gave up my course of thinking and went to a hotel room for nine days to figure out what to do. The more I thought the more troubled I became. I began to realize how dead I really was, how so much of my life was dark. And worse than that, I could see no way out. My only solution was to run and hide, to start in a different place, to sever all connections.

This brutal description of a man on the bottom fortunately has a happy ending. For not long after his nine-day experience in a hotel room, he discovered the love of God and its capacity to engender dramatic change in his life. And a driven man turned into what we will call in our next chapter a *called man*. He got out of his golden cage.

In the Bible few men typify the driven man better than Saul, the first king of Israel. Unlike the previous story, which had a happy conclusion, this one has a miserable ending, for Saul never got out of his golden cage. All he did was heap increasing amounts of stress upon himself. And it destroyed him.

The Bible's introduction to Saul should be warning enough that the man had some flaws that, if not addressed within his inner world, would cause him quickly to lose personal control.

> There was a man of Benjamin whose name was Kish the son of Abiel, the son of Zeror, the son of Becorath, the son of Aphiah, the son of a Benjamite, a mighty man of valor. And he had a son whose name was Saul, a choice and handsome man, and there was not a more handsome person than he among the sons of Israel; from his shoulders and up he was taller than any of the people (1 Samuel 9:1–2).

Saul possessed three unearned characteristics at the beginning of his public life that had the potential to become assets or serious liabilities. Which they would be was his choice. And how Saul made those choices depended upon the daily order of his private world.

The three? First, wealth; second, an attractive appearance; and third, a physically large and well-developed body. All were attributes of a person's public world. In other words, the initial impression was that Saul was a better man than anyone around him. All three external marks commanded attention and gained him quick advantages. (Each time I think of Saul's natural gifts, I recall the bank president some years ago who said to me, "MacDonald, you could go a long way in the business world if you were about six inches taller.") And, most importantly, they provided him with a sort of charisma that made possible his achieving some early success without ever having to develop a heart of wisdom or spiritual stature. He was simply a fast starter.

As Saul's story unfolds in the biblical text we learn some other things about the man, things that could have either contributed to his success or become a part of his ultimate failure. We are told, for example, that he was good with words. When he was given a chance to speak before crowds, he was eloquent. The stage was set for a man to consolidate power and command recognition without ever having to develop any sense of a strong inner world first. And that was where the danger lay.

When Saul became king of Israel, he enjoyed too much immediate success. It apparently made him unaware that he had any limits to his life. He spent little time pondering his need for others, engendering a relationship with God, or even facing his responsibilities toward the people over whom he ruled. The signs of a driven man began to appear.

Saul became a busy man; he saw worlds he thought needed conquering. Thus when he faced an impending battle with the Philistines, Israel's great enemy of the day, and waited at Gilgal for Samuel the prophet to come and offer the necessary sacrifices, he grew impatient and irritable when the holy man did not arrive on time. Saul felt that his timetable was being compromised; he had to get on with things. His remedy? Offer the sacrifice himself. And that is exactly what he did.

The result? A rather serious breach of covenant with God. Offering sacrifice was the kind of thing prophets like Samuel did, not kings like Saul. But Saul had forgotten that because he saw himself as being too important.

From that time forward Saul found himself on a downhill track. "Now your kingdom shall not endure. The Lord has sought out for Himself a man after His own heart" (1 Samuel 13:14). This is how most driven men end.

Stripped of what blessing and assistance he had had from God up to this point, Saul's drivenness began to reveal itself even further. Soon all of his energies became consumed in holding onto his throne, competing with young David, who had caught the imagination of the people of Israel.

The Scriptures give several examples of Saul's explosive anger, which drove him to outrage as well as to moments of paralyzing self-pity. By the end of his life, he was a man out of control, seeing enemies behind every bush. Why? Because from the very beginning Saul had been a driven man, and he had never cultivated the order of his private world.

I wonder what Saul's point total would have been on Thomas Holmes's stress chart. I suspect it would have been up in the range of stroke and heart attack victims. But Saul never came to grips with his drivenness, either through something like a stress chart or by simply facing the inner rebukes God would have liked for him to have heard within his private world. Saul would not have lasted long among the twelve disciples Jesus picked. His own compulsions were far too strong. That which had driven him to grasp power and not let go, that which had caused him to turn on his closest supporters, and that which caused him to make a successive series of unwise decisions, finally led him to a humiliating death. He was the classic driven man.

To the extent that we see him in ourselves, we have work to do in our private worlds. For an inner life fraught with unresolved drives will not be able to hear clearly the voice of Christ when He calls. The noise and pain of stress will be too great.

Unfortunately, our society abounds with Sauls, men and women caught in golden cages, driven to accumulate, to be recognized, or to achieve. Our churches, unfortunately, abound with these driven people as well. Many churches are fountains gone dry. Rather than being springs of life-giving energy that cause people to grow and to delight in God's way, they become sources of stress. The driven man's private world is disordered. His cage may be lavishly golden. But it's a trap; inside there is nothing that lasts.

Memo to the Disorganized:

If my private world is in order, it will be because, having faced up to what drives me, I listen quietly for the call of Christ.

4
The Tragic Tale
of a Successful Bum

When the couple came into my office for the first of a series of visits, they sat in chairs as far apart from one another as possible. It was obvious that neither liked the other, at least at the moment. And yet the agenda was the saving of a marriage—theirs.

She was asking him to leave the home, I was told. When I asked her why, she said it was the only possible way there would be any peace or normal life for the rest of the family. There was no infidelity, no single issue. She simply wasn't prepared to live with him for the rest of his life, given his temperament and value system.

But he didn't want to leave. In fact he was shocked that she should have come to this conclusion, he said. After all, he was a faithful provider; their home was quite large and located in an upper-class neighborhood. The kids had everything they wanted. It was hard to figure out, he went on, why she would want to end the marriage. Besides, weren't they Christians? He'd thought all along that Christians didn't believe in divorce or separation. Would I please solve their problem?

The story slowly emerged. It became clear that I was visiting with one of those driven men and his wife. His drivenness was costing a marriage, a family, and his physical health. That the marriage was virtually dead I could see in their body language. That the family was in ruins I could deduce from their descriptions of the attitudes of the children. That his health was in jeopardy was obvious when he told me of a bundle of ulcers, migraine headaches, and occasional chest pains. The story continued to unravel.

Because he owned his business, he had the freedom to work his own hours: nineteen to twenty per day. And because he had such responsibilities, he was rarely at any function important to his children. He usually left the home before anyone was out of bed in the morning, and he rarely came home until the youngest of the children was already back in bed for the night. If he was present at a family meal, he tended to be sullen and preoccupied. It was not a rare occurrence for him to be called to the phone in the middle of supper and remain there for the remainder of the hour solving some problem or closing a sale.

In conflict, he admitted, he was given to explosive anger; in relationships he could be abrasive and intimidating. Put into a social situation he was usually bored with conversation and tended to withdraw and drink too much. When asked who his friends were, he could name no one except business associates. And when challenged as to things of importance apart from his work, he could think only of his sports car, his boat, and his skybox season tickets to the Red Sox—things, not people, all of which, ironically, he was usually too busy to enjoy anyway.

This was a man with almost no order at all in his private world. Everything was external. His life was, by his own admission, a bundle of activity and accumulation. He could never do enough; he could never earn enough to be satisfied. Everything had to get bigger, better, and more impressive. What was driving him? Could there ever be order to his private world?

After several conversations I began to gain some insight into the fantastic energy source that drove this man into a way of life that was destroying everything around him. In the midst of one of our talks, I asked him about his father. Suddenly his mood became dramatically altered. Anyone could have sensed that I had abruptly uncovered a deeply sensitive matter.

What slowly unfolded was a tale of extreme relational pain. His father, I learned, was a man given to extreme sarcasm and ridicule. He had regularly told his son, "You're a bum; you will always be a bum, nothing better!" It had been said so many times that the words had become emblazoned as if on a neon sign in the center of this young man's private world.

Here was a man, now in his early forties, who had unconsciously made a lifelong commitment. He had committed himself to disproving the label given to him by his father. Somehow he would demonstrate with unimpeachable evidence *that he was not a bum*. It became the essential preoccupation of his life without his ever really knowing it.

Since a state of "un-bumness" was equated with hard work, high income, and the status of wealth, these things formed the cluster of objectives for this driven man. He would show that he was a hard worker by owning a business and making it the best in that section of the Yellow Pages. He would make sure that it produced large sums of money for him, even if some of the money was "dirtied" by the way it was obtained. The large house, the sports car, the season tickets among the finest boxes at Fenway would all be measurable disclaimers of the paternal charge of "bumness." And thus it was that my visitor became a driven man, driven to gain his father's respect and love.

Because his goals were all basically external, there was no need to cultivate an inner world. Relationships were not important; winning was. Spiritual health was not significant; physical strength was. Rest was not necessary; available time for more work was. And the accumulation of knowledge and wisdom was not a matter of value; sales technique and product innovation were.

He claimed that it was all part of his desire to provide for his family. Slowly we began to discover together that he was really trying to gain his father's affirmation and acceptance. He wanted to hear his father finally say, "Son, you're not a bum; I was entirely wrong."

What made this matter even stranger was that the unpleasant father had been dead for several years. Yet the son, now in midlife, continued to work to gain that approval. What had started as an objective became a habit of living he could not break.

WHY ARE PEOPLE DRIVEN?

Why do so many people appear to be driven? My friend is an extreme example of one reason. He typifies those who grew up in *environments where "well done" was never heard.* When such acceptance and affirmation is lacking, it is by no means unusual for the respect-starved person to conclude that more work, greater accumulation of symbols of success, or worldly praise will finally convince the significant person who has withheld approval to finally say, "Son (daughter), you are not a bum after all. I'm terribly proud to be your father."

Many people in leadership positions share this sort of background and this sort of insecurity. Some leaders appear to be highly benevolent people, doing good things, and are praised for dedicated, selfless actions; the fact may be that they are pushed toward the hope of gaining the acceptance and approval of just one significant person in their past. And if they cannot gain that, then they develop an insatiable appetite for applause, wealth, or power from other sources in an attempt to compensate for the loss. Rarely, however, is satisfaction reached. This is because their pursuit is in the public world; the private world is left empty and wanting. And that is where the real ache lies.

Another source of drivenness *is an early experience of serious deprivation or shame.* In his book *Creative Suffering* (New York: Harper & Row, 1983), Paul Tournier points out that an enormous number of world political leaders over the past several centuries have been orphans. Having grown up in a context of personal loss in terms of intimate parental love and emotional closeness, they may have sought a compensatory experience in the embrace of the crowds. Behind their great drive for power may be the simple need for love. Rather than meeting this need through the ordering of the private world within, they have chosen to pursue it on the external level.

Driven people can also come from backgrounds in which

there has been a sense of great shame or embarrassment. In his remarkably candid *The Man Who Could Do No Wrong* (Lincoln, Va.: Chosen Books, 1981), pastor Charles Blair describes his own childhood during the Depression days in Oklahoma. With pain he recalls his daily task of hauling the free government-issue milk from the local firehouse to home. As he carried the milk pail down the street, he had to endure what he felt was raw scorn from boys his own age. Out of the agony of such moments came the resolve that the day would come when he would never again carry a symbolic milk pail, which signified a feeling of worthlessness.

Blair tells the story of an unforgettable walk home from school in the company of a girl about whom he had strong feelings. Suddenly a boy with a shiny new bicycle came up beside them and offered the girl a ride. Without hesitation she hopped onto the back fender, leaving Blair behind as she and the other boy rode off together. The humiliation of that moment caused Blair to quietly resolve that someday *he* would have the equivalent of a shiny bicycle, that *he* would have the wherewithal to make impressions that would command the attentions and loyalties of others.

And those resolves burned their way into his life. They became a source of the drive that subsequently, by his own account, betrayed him. He would later need to own the most attractive automobile, lead the most beautiful and largest church, and wear the most stylish of men's fashions. These things would prove that he had made it out of the Oklahoma Depression. He was not worthless; he was not poor. He could prove it. Look!

Charles Blair was running from something, and that meant that he had to run toward something. Although his drive was clothed in all sorts of impressive spiritual motives, and although his ministry was remarkably effective, down at the center were unresolved hurts of the past. Because these hurts remained a point of disorder in his private world, they came back to haunt him. They affected his choices and values and blinded him to what was really happening at a crucial moment of his life. The result? Serious disaster. Failure, embarrassment, and public humiliation.

But it must be added that he rebounded. That alone suggests hope for the driven man. Charles Blair the *driven* man of earlier years, running from shame, is now a *called* man, and he deserves the admiration of his friends. I consider his book to be one of the most significant I have ever read. It ought to be required reading for any man or woman who is in leadership.

Finally, *some people are simply raised in an environment where drivenness is a way of life.* In a book called *Wealth Addiction*, Philip Slater details the backgrounds of several living billionaires. In almost every account there is indication that as children these billionaires made the accumulation of things and the conquest of people their amusement. There was little if any play for the purpose of pure fun or exercise. They only knew how to win, how to accumulate. It was what they saw their parents doing, and they assumed that it was the only way to live. Thus the drive to grow rich and powerful began in the earliest days.

To such people an ordered private world has little meaning. The only thing worth giving attention to is the public world, where things can be measured, admired, and used.

Of course, driven people come out of many other backgrounds, and these are but a few samples. But one thing is sure in all cases: driven people will never enjoy the tranquility of an ordered private world. Their prime targets are all external, material, and measurable. Nothing else seems real; nothing else makes much sense. And it all must be held onto, as it was with Saul, who found that power was more important than the integrity of a friendship with David.

Let us be sure we understand that when we speak of driven people, we are not merely thinking of a highly competitive business person or a professional athlete. We are considering something much more pervasive than "workaholism." Any of us can look within and suddenly discover that *drivenness is our way of life.* We can be driven toward a superior Christian reputation, toward a desire for some dramatic spiritual experience, or toward a form of leadership that is really more a quest for domination of people than servanthood. A homemaker can be a driven person; so can a student. A driven person can be any of us.

HOPE FOR THE DRIVEN PERSON

Can the driven person be changed? Most certainly. It begins when such a person faces up to the fact that he is operating according to drives and not calls. That discovery is usually made in the blinding, searching light of an encounter with Christ. As the twelve disciples discovered, an audience with Jesus over a period of time exposes all the roots and expressions of drivenness.

To deal with drivenness, one must begin to ruthlessly appraise one's own motives and values just as Peter was forced to do in his periodic confrontations with Jesus. The person seeking relief from drivenness will find it wise to listen to mentors and critics who speak Christ's words to us today.

He may have some humbling acts of renunciation, some disciplined gestures of surrender of things—things that are not necessarily bad, but that have been important for all the wrong reasons.

Perhaps the driven person will have to grant forgiveness to some of those who in the past never offered the proper kind of affection and affirmation. And all of that may just be the beginning.

Paul the apostle in his pre-Christian days was driven. As a driven man, he studied, he joined, he attained, he defended, and he was applauded. The pace at which he was operating shortly before his conversion was almost manic. He was driven toward some illusive goal, and, later, when he could look back at that life-style with all of its compulsions, he would say, "It was all worthless."

Paul was driven until Christ called him. One gets the feeling that when Paul fell to his knees before the Lord while on the road to Damascus, there was an explosion of relief within his private world. What a change from the drivenness that had pushed him toward Damascus in an attempt to stamp out Christianity to that dramatic moment when, in complete submission, he asked Jesus Christ, "What shall I do, Lord?" A driven man was converted into a called one.

I could have wished this for the man who came to talk with me about his wife's demand that he leave their house. Time after time we talked about his insatiable drive to win, to earn, to impress. There were a few occasions when I thought he was catching the message, when I allowed myself to be convinced we were making progress. I actually believed that he was going to move the center of his life from the public aspect of his world to the private side.

I could almost see him kneeling before Christ offering up his drivenness, being washed clean of all the old terribly painful memories of a father who had flung a sense of "bumness" into his private world. How much I wanted my friend, the successful bum, to see himself a disciple called by Christ, and not one driven to achieve in order to prove something.

But it never happened. And eventually we lost contact. The last I heard, his drivenness cost him everything: family, marriage, business. For it drove him right to his grave.

Memo to the Disorganized:

If my private world is in order, it will be because I see myself as Christ's steward and not as master of my purpose, my role, and my identity.

5

Living as
a Called Person

In his book *A Casket of Cameos*, F. W. Boreham reflects on
the faith of Harriet Beecher Stowe's Uncle Tom. The old slave
had been wrenched from his old Kentucky home and put upon
a steamship headed for unknown places. It was a terrible moment of crisis, and, Boreham observes, "Uncle Tom's faith was
staggered. It really seemed to him that, in leaving Aunt Chloe
and the children and his old companions, he was leaving God!"

Falling asleep, the slave had a dream. "He dreamed that he
was back again, and that little Eva was reading to him from
the Bible as of old. He could hear her voice: 'When thou pass-
est through the waters, I will be with thee; for I am the Lord
thy God, the Holy One of Israel, Thy Saviour.'" Boreham continues:

> A little later, poor Tom was writhing under the cruel lash of his
> new owner. "But," says Mrs. Stowe, *"The blows fell only upon the
> outer man, and not, as before, on the heart.* Tom stood sub-
> missive; and yet Legree could not hide from himself the fact that
> his power over his victim had gone. As Tom disappeared in his
> cabin, and Legree wheeled his horse suddenly round, there
> passed through the tyrant's mind one of those vivid flashes that
> often send the lightning of conscience across the dark and wicked
> soul. He understood full well that it was God who was standing
> between him and Tom, and he blasphemed Him!" (Italics added)[1]

1. Frank W. Boreham, *A Casket of Cameos* (1924: reprint, Valley Forge,
   Pa.: Judson, 1950), p. 266.

THE CALLED PERSON

It is this quality of certitude for which we seek when we compare *driven* persons and *called* persons. Driven people are confident they have that quality as they forge ahead. But often, at the moment when it is least expected, hostile events conspire, and there can be collapse. Called people have strength from within, perseverance and power that are impervious to the blows from without.

Called men and women can come from the strangest places and carry the most unique qualifications. They may be the unnoticed, the unappreciated, the unsophisticated. Look again at the men Christ picked: few if any of them would have been candidates for high positions in organized religion or big business. It is not that they were unusually awkward. It is just that they were among the ordinary. But Christ called them, and that made all the difference.

Rather than living according to drivenness, some are drawn toward the beckoning hand of the calling Father. Such calls are usually heard within an ordered private world.

JOHN—A PICTURE OF A CALLED MAN

John the Baptizer is a powerful example of a called man. He had the audacity to tell fellow Jews that they ought to quit justifying themselves on the basis of their sense of superior racial identity and face up to their need for spiritual and moral repentance. Baptism, he said, would testify to the genuineness of their contrition. No wonder no one was ever neutral about John. He never minced his words. He was a man one loved or hated; one of the latter type finally took off his head. But not until he finished his work.

John, the called man, is a remarkable contrast to Saul, the driven man. John seems to have had from the very beginning a vivid sense of destiny, the result of a heavenly assignment that came from deep within himself. One sees the contrast between Saul and John most vividly when their personal identities and their sense of vocational security are under attack. Saul, the driven man, you will remember, reacted violently, lashing out against his perceived enemies when he became convinced that the preservation of his power and the survival of his position relied solely upon himself.

But John is another story. Watch him when news comes that his popularity may be on the verge of serious decline. To be just a bit dramatic, let me suggest that John is facing the loss of his job. The account I have in mind opens after John has introduced Christ to the multitudes and they have begun to transfer their affections to this "Lamb of God" (John 1:36). It is brought to John's attention that the crowds, even some of his own disciples, are turning to Jesus, listening to His teaching and being baptized by His disciples. One gets the feeling that those who brought the news to John concerning the decline of his ratings may have hoped that they would get the chance to see John react just a bit negatively. But they didn't; he let them down.

> A man can receive nothing, unless it has been given him from heaven. You yourselves bear me witness, that I said, "I am not the Christ," but "I have been sent before Him." He who has the bride is the bridegroom; but the friend of the bridegroom, who stands and hears him, rejoices greatly at the bridegroom's voice. And so this joy of mine has been made full. He must increase, but I must decrease (John 3:27–30).

CALLED PEOPLE UNDERSTAND STEWARDSHIP

Notice John's concept of life by stewardship. That is to say that his interviewers built their question on the assumption that the crowds once *belonged* to John, that he had earned them with his charisma. And if that were true, then John was losing something: his prophetic stardom.

But that was not John's perspective at all. He never owned anything, much less the crowds. John thought like a steward, and that is the quality of a called person. The task of a steward is simply to properly manage something for the owner until the owner comes to take it back. John knew that the crowd leaving him for Christ was never his in the first place. God had placed them under his care for a period of time and now had taken them back. With John that was apparently just fine.

How different this is from the driven Saul, who assumed that he owned his throne in Israel and could do anything with it that he wished. When one owns something, it has to be held onto, it has to be protected. But John did not think of things that way. So when Christ came to command the crowds, John was only too glad to give them back.

John's view of stewardship presents us with an important contemporary principle. For his crowds may be our careers, our assets, our natural and spiritual gifts, our health. Are these things owned, or merely managed in the name of the One who gave them? Driven people consider them owned; called people do not. When driven people lose those things, it is a major crisis. When called people lose them, nothing has changed. The private world remains the same, perhaps even stronger.

CALLED PEOPLE KNOW EXACTLY WHO THEY ARE

A second quality of calledness is seen in John's awareness of his own identity. You will remember, he said to them, that I've told you often who I am not: namely, the Christ. Knowing who he was not was the beginning of knowing who he was. And John had no illusions as to his personal identity. That had already been established in his inner world.

By contrast, those whose private worlds are in disarray tend to get their identities confused. They can have an increasing inability to separate role from person. What they *do* is indistinguishable from what they *are*. That is why people who have wielded great power find it very difficult to give it up, and will often fight to the death to retain it. It is why retirement is difficult for many men and women. And it helps to explain why a mother may suffer depression when her last child has left the home.

We need to ponder this matter of identity carefully, for it happens to be a very contemporary subject. John could easily have taken advantage of the crowd's gullibility during the early days when he was popular. Or he could have been seduced by their applause. The fact that the masses were switching their loyalty from the priests of Jerusalem to him could have supercharged him with arrogance and ambition. It would have been rather simple to nod yes to questions as to whether or not he was the Messiah.

You can almost hear a man of lesser integrity than John in a moment of temptation saying, "Well, I hadn't thought about it quite like you're saying it, but perhaps you're right, there is something Messiah-like about me. Why don't we just assume that I am the Christ and see what happens?"

If that had been John, he probably could have pulled off the hoax for a short while. But the genuine John would not even try. His inner sphere was too well ordered for him not to have seen through the terrible implications of a misplaced identity.

If there was a moment when the crowd's praise became thunderous, the voice of God from within John was even louder. And that voice spoke more convincingly because John had first ordered his inner world out on the desert.

Don't underestimate the significance of this principle. Today in our media-oriented world many good and talented leaders face the constant temptation to begin believing the text of their own publicity releases. And if they do, a messianic fantasy gradually infects their personalities and leadership styles. Forgetting who they are not, they begin to distort who they are. What has happened? They have become too busy to take time in the desert to get their private worlds in order. The needs of the organization become too overwhelming; the praise of followers becomes too enchanting. Thus, in the furious style of public living, God's calling voice is drowned out.

CALLED PEOPLE POSSESS AN UNWAVERING SENSE OF PURPOSE

A third look at John's remarkable response to his interviewers will reveal that the prophet from the desert also understood the purpose of his activity as forerunner to Christ. And this is another dimension of calledness. To those who questioned him regarding his feelings about the growing popularity of the Man from Nazareth, he likened his purpose to that of the best man at a wedding: "He who has the bride is the bridegroom; but the friend [that's John] of the bridegroom, who stands and hears him, rejoices greatly because of the bridegroom's voice" (John 3:29). The purpose of the best man is simply to stand with the groom, to make sure that all attention is riveted upon him. The best man would be a fool if in the middle of the wedding processional he suddenly turned to the wedding guests and began to sing a song or engage in a humorous monologue. The best man has fulfilled his purpose most admirably when he draws no attention to himself but focuses all attention upon the bride and groom.

And that is what John did. If Jesus Christ was the groom, to use John's metaphor, then the Baptizer was committed to being best man *and nothing else*. That was the purpose that flowed from his call, and he had no desire to aspire to anything beyond. Thus to see the crowd headed toward Christ was all the affirmation John needed; his purpose had been fulfilled. But only called people like this man can relax under such circumstances.

CALLED PEOPLE UNDERSTAND UNSWERVING COMMITMENT

Finally, John, as a called man, also understood the meaning of commitment. "He must increase, but I must decrease" (John 3:30), he said to those who had queried him about his attitude. No driven person could ever say what John said, because driven people have to keep gaining more and more attention, more and more power, more and more material assets. The seductions of the public life would have led to a competitive posture, but the original call to commitment from within spoke louder. What John had started out to accomplish—the introduction of Christ as the Lamb of God—had been accomplished. Having made the connection, John was satisfied and ready to withdraw.

It is these kinds of qualities—John's sense of stewardship, his awareness of his identity, his perspective about his role, and his unswerving commitment—that mark a called person. And they are the characteristics of a person who builds first in the interior or private world so that out of it will flow fountains of life.

How totally different were the lives of Saul the king and John the Baptizer. The one sought to defend a golden cage, and lost; the other was pleased with a place on the desert and a chance to serve, and won.

PEACE AND JOY

There are all sorts of special qualities in John's life worth admiring. There is a *peacefulness* about him which is not tied to the security of a career. I often spend time with men and women whose careers have suddenly been washed out for various reasons, and they become "basket cases." These circumstances reveal that their lives may have been built upon a career base rather than upon the firmness and stability of a private world where God speaks.

John reveals a kind of *joy*, which ought not to be confused with the modern-day version of happiness—a state of feelings dependent upon everything turning out all right. When others thought that John might be worried about ending up as a failure, they discovered that he actually was quite satisfied, in spite of the fact that his audiences were leaving him. Some folk in John's generation might not have thought so, but John had such an assurance because his evaluations were based first on his private world, where real values can be fully formed in concert with God.

John is in fact a called man. He illustrates what Stowe meant when she wrote that Simon Legree's blows fell only upon Uncle Tom's outer man, but not upon his heart. Something stood between John and the public evidence that he may have been a failure. It was the unquestioned reality of God's call, which John had heard in that private world of his. And that voice was louder than any other sound. It came from a quiet place of order.

BECOMING CALLED

As one looks with admiration at John the Baptizer, the obvious question is how he got that way. What was the source of this determination, this stamina, this unswerving ability to look at events in a totally different way than others did? A look at John's background will help us examine the structure and substance of his inner life.

If there is one thing that begins to explain John, it has to be the kind of parents he had, who shaped him in his earliest days. It is clear from Scripture that Zacharias and Elizabeth were godly people with extraordinary sensitivity to John's call. It had been revealed to them through various angelic visions. And they in turn from the earliest days began to pump that destiny into John's soul. We have little indication of John's family life after he was born, but we do know that his parents were marked with an extraordinary depth of integrity, godliness, and perseverance.

John's parents must have died when he was still a very young man. How he handled the loss we do not know. But when the Scripture next highlights John, he is living alone in the desert, separate from the society to which he would later speak as a prophet.

> In the fifteenth year of the reign of Tiberius Caesar, when Pontius Pilate was governor of Judea, and Herod was tetrarch of Galilee, and his brother Philip was tetrarch of the region of Ituraea and Trachonitis, and Lysanias was tetrarch of Abilene, in the high priesthood of Annas and Caiaphas, the word of God came to John, the son of Zacharias, in the wilderness. And he came into all the district around the Jordan, preaching a baptism of repentance for the forgiveness of sins (Luke 3:1–3).

These words contain a challenging insight. Caesar was in Rome doing whatever important things caesars do. Annas and Caiaphas were in the Jerusalem Temple maintaining organized religion. And various other political personalities were going and coming in public places participating in seemingly newsworthy events. Their worlds were the impressive public worlds of power, notoriety, and human connection.

But *the word of God came to John*, an insignificant man in the most insignificant of places: a desert. Why John? And why a desert?

I am reminded of Herbert Butterfield's words, which have marked me deeply:

> Both in history and in life it is a phenomenon by no means rare to meet with comparatively unlettered people who seem to have struck profound spiritual depths . . . while there are many highly educated people of whom one feels that they are performing

clever antics with their minds to cover a gaping hollowness that lies within.[2]

Why John? Basically because God called John, and he responded. The call demanded submission to God's ways, God's methods, and God's criteria for success. And John was willing to accept those terms no matter what the cost to him in pain or loneliness.

Why a desert? Perhaps because in deserts people can hear and brood upon things not easily heard or thought about in busy cities, where people are usually busy, surrounded by noise, and steeped in self-importance. Sometimes in cities the shrillness of the public life is so great that the whispering voice of God cannot be heard. And sometimes in cities, people are too proud to listen to God amidst all of their steel and concrete skyscrapers, their colorful theaters, or their incredible temples.

God drew John into the desert where He could speak to him. And when He got him there He began to stamp impressions onto John's inner world that gave the son of Zacharias a totally different perspective on his times. There in the desert he gained a new view of religion, of right and wrong, of God's purposes for history. And there he developed a special sensitivity and courage that would prepare him for his most extraordinary task: introducing his generation to the Christ. His private world was under construction—in the desert.

The word of God came to John in the desert. Such a strange place for God to speak. What can one learn in deserts? I am inclined to forsake deserts, to detour around them whenever possible. To me, deserts mean pain, isolation, and suffering. And no one cares for any of that. Deserts are hard places in which to live, physically or spiritually. But the fact is unavoidable: the greatest lessons are potentially learned in deserts if one, in the midst of struggle, listens for God's call.

In deserts, one learns about *dryness*, because deserts are dry. John would learn not only to cope with the dryness of the

2. Herbert Butterfield, *Christianity and History* (New York: Charles Scribner's Sons, 1949), p. 115.

desert, but it doubtless taught him to appreciate the aridity of
the spirits of the people to whom he'd speak at the Jordan.

On the desert a person learns *dependence* upon God. Life in
the wilderness, as the Hebrews had found out centuries before, cannot be sustained without the benevolence of a merciful God. Only a person who has suffered desert-like hardship
knows what it is like to totally cast himself upon God because
there is nothing else left.

There is a slightly brighter side to deserts, however. Wildernesses provide a place where one is free to think, to plan,
to prepare. And then at an appointed time, like John, he
comes charging out of the dry land with a message, something
to say that will expose hypocrisy and superficiality. Issues are
addressed that cut through to the bottomless depths of the
human spirit. And an age of people is introduced to the Christ
of God.

On the desert a person can be called. As John stood up first
to his critics and then to the furiously defensive Herod, whose
immoral life the prophet rebuked, he began to reveal that special quality of calledness. You can see it in his serenity in the
midst of his prophetic performance. Something special within
was operating, providing him with an independent base of
judgment and wisdom. Few could withstand his message.

What was the makeup of that private world that was formed
on the desert? Frankly, the biblical writers do not give us
much of an answer. We are simply treated to the evidence of
an ordered inner life. John is a prototype of the product we are
looking for. In a public world where all seems chaotic and disordered, he moves with assurance and certitude.

Have Saul, John, and my friend the "successful bum" taught
us anything? I think their message is plain. Look inside, they
say. What makes you tick? Why are you doing all of that?
What do you hope to gain as a result? And what would be your
reaction if it was all taken away?

I look inside my private world and discover that almost
every day I have to wrestle with whether I will be a Saul or a
John. Living in a competitive world where achievement is almost everything, I would find it easy to join Saul, to be driven
to hold on, to protect, to dominate. And I might even find

myself doing those sorts of things while telling myself that I was doing God's work. But the stress of doing so can become too great.

Then there are days when I might be like John. Having listened to God's call, I can know my mission. It may demand courage and discipline, of course, but now the results are in the hands of the Caller. Whether I increase or decrease is His concern, not mine. To order my life according to the expectations of myself and others; and to value myself according to the opinions of others; these can play havoc with my inner world. But to operate on the basis of God's call is to enjoy a great deal of order within.

Sector Two

Memo to the Disorganized:

If my private world is in order, it will be because I have made a daily determination to see time as God's gift and worthy of careful investment.

6

Has Anyone Seen
My Time?
I've Misplaced It!

I had just finished a lecture to a group of pastors in which I mentioned a number of books I'd recently read. When the talk was finished, a young pastor asked, "Where have you found the time to read all of those books? When I entered the pastorate, I was sure I was going to be able to do that kind of reading too. But I haven't read anything for weeks now. I'm too busy!"

We talked for a short while about the discipline of reading, and the conversation began to branch out into other aspects of his personal life. He shared his guilt about his spiritual exercises; they were almost non-existent. He admitted that it had been a long time since he had spent anything approaching quality time with his wife. He bemoaned the fact that his sermons were usually substandard by his own evaluation. And at the conclusion of our conversation, he conceded that his failure even to read a book was merely the hint of an even bigger struggle. "Frankly," he said, "I'm totally disorganized. I'm not getting anything of consequence done."

I am very sympathetic with this young man and his admission. There was a time in my own life when I could have said the same thing. And I don't think either one of us would have found ourselves alone if our colleagues at that lecture had been honest. The world is full of disorganized people who have lost control of their time.

William Barclay, commenting upon the undisciplined life of Samuel Taylor Coleridge, writes:

> Coleridge is the supreme tragedy of indiscipline. Never did so great a mind produce so little. He left Cambridge University to join the army; he left the army because he could not rub down a horse; he returned to Oxford and left without a degree. He began a paper called *The Watchman* which lived for ten numbers and then died. It has been said of him: "he lost himself in visions of work to be done, that always remained to be done. Coleridge had every poetic gift but one—the gift of sustained and concentrated effort." In his head and in his mind he had all kinds of books, as he said, himself, "completed save for transcription. I am on the even," he says, "of sending to the press two octavo volumes." But the books were never composed outside Coleridge's mind, because he would not face the discipline of sitting down to write them out. No one ever reached any eminence, and no one having reached it ever maintained it, without discipline.[1]

Coleridge was living proof that a man or woman may be multi-talented, possess enormous intelligence and remarkable communicative gifts, and yet end up squandering it all because of an inability to seize control of time. His futile pursuits in the literary world are matched by some whose vocation is in the home, in the church, or at the office.

None of us, I am sure, wants to come to the end of his life and look back with regrets on things that could have been accomplished but were not, as happened to Coleridge. But to prevent that from happening, it is necessary to understand how we can command the time God has given to us.

SYMPTOMS OF DISORGANIZATION

The first step we may have to take is that of a ruthless self-appraisal about our habits of time use. Are we actually disorganized or not? Let us consider the traits of a disorganized life. Some of these symptoms may seem a bit ridiculous, even petty. But they are usually part of a larger picture that all fits together. Let me suggest a handful of sample symptoms.

1. William Barclay, *The Gospel of Matthew* (Philadelphia: Westminster, 1975), p. 280.

When I am slipping into disorganization, for example, I know it because *my desk takes on a cluttered appearance.* The same thing happens to the top of my bedroom dresser. In fact almost every horizontal surface in the path of my daily travel becomes littered with papers, memos to which I have not responded, and pieces of tasks that are unfinished. I can see some spouse saying, "Here, read this; he's been in your office lately." But my desk can be another's kitchen counter, work bench or basement workroom. The same principle applies.

The symptoms of disorganization tend to show themselves in *the condition of my car.* It becomes dirty inside and out. I lose track of its maintenance schedule, and I find that I am pressing deadlines for things like changing snow tires and getting the annual safety sticker.

When disorganization takes over, *I become aware of a diminution in my self-esteem.* I feel the slightest tinge of paranoia, a low-level fear that people are going to discover they are not getting their money's worth out of my labor, that they are going to come to the conclusion that I am not half the man they thought I was.

I know I'm disorganized when *there are a series of forgotten appointments, telephone messages to which I have failed to respond, and deadlines which I have begun to miss.* The day becomes filled with broken commitments and lame excuses. (I must be careful to say, incidentally, that I am not thinking of times when events beyond my control have conspired to derail even the best intentions. All of us have those kinds of days, even the most organized of us.)

If I am disorganized, *I tend to invest my energies in unproductive tasks.* I actually find myself doing small and boring things just to get something accomplished. There is a tendency toward daydreaming, an avoidance of decisions that have to be made, and procrastination. Disorganization begins to affect every part of my will to work steadily and excellently.

Disorganized people feel poor about their work. What they manage to finish they do not like. They find it very hard to accept the compliments of others. In the secrecy of their hearts they know that they have turned in a second-best job.

I have more than once driven home from Sunday morning worship services where I have preached in this sort of mood. And as I drove, I found myself pounding the steering wheel in frustration because I knew that I could have preached better if I had used my time during the week more effectively in study and preparation.

Disorganized Christians rarely enjoy intimacy with God. They certainly have intentions of pursuing that camaraderie, but it never quite gets established. No one has to tell them that time must be set aside for the purpose of Bible study and reflection, for intercession, for worship. They know all of that. They simply are not doing it. They excuse themselves, saying there is no time, but within their private worlds they know it is more a matter of organization and personal will than anything else.

If I am in a state of disorganization, *the quality of my personal relationships usually reveals it.* The days pass without a significant conversation with my son or daughter. My wife and I will be in contact, but our conversations may be shallow, devoid of self-revelation, and unaffirming. I may become irritable, resenting any attempt on her part to call to my attention things I have left undone or people I appear to have let down.

The fact of the matter is that when we are disorganized in our control of time, *we just don't like ourselves, our jobs, or much else about our worlds.* And it is difficult to break the destructive pattern that settles in.

This terrible habit-pattern of disorganization must be broken, or our private worlds will fall quickly into total disorder. We must resolve to seize control of our time.

Psychologists can suggest many reasons for people's being disorganized, and it is helpful to think some of these through. There is a large body of helpful literature available on the subject of time management and organization. But beneath the gimmicks and tricks of organization are some fundamental principles that have to be seriously considered by any person seeking an ordering of the private world. Putting these principles into practice will be a challenge for some men and women who have ignored the importance of controlling their time.

BUDGETING TIME

The central principle of all personal organization of time is simple: *time must be budgeted!*

Most of us learned this about money a long time ago. When we discovered that we rarely had enough money to do all the things we wanted to do with it, we found it prudent to sit down and think through our financial priorities.

With money, the priorities were obvious. Since my wife and I are committed to God's plan of stewardship, our first financial priority has always been our tithe and offerings. Then the fixed expenditures, food, house, utilities, books (both of us insist that books are a fixed expenditure), and so on have been set aside in amounts that we have learned to anticipate.

Only after we have budgeted these amounts of money for the necessities have we ventured into the discretionary side of the budget, namely those things that are more wants than needs. Here we may be talking about a meal out at a favorite restaurant, an appliance that makes life a bit easier, or a particularly attractive winter coat.

When men and women do not understand the difference between the fixed and the discretionary aspects of their financial lives, they usually end up in debt, which is the financial version of disorganization.

When money is limited, one budgets. And when time is in limited supply, the same principle holds. The disorganized person must have a budgeting perspective. And that means determining the difference between the fixed—what one *must* do—and the discretionary—what one would *like* to do.

These were the items I raised when my young pastor friend came to talk about why he felt so unproductive. He was surprised when I told him that we were talking about one of my own daily battles.

"Gordon," he said, "you don't convey the impression that time is ever out of your control."

I protested, "I sometimes wonder if I've ever got any of it under control." All of those symptoms of the disorganized life were at one time or another *my* symptoms, but I had made a decision (actually on more than one occasion) that I was not going to live that way for one more minute than I had to.

THE LORD OF TIME

My young pastor friend was obviously hoping I would share with him a few of the insights that have challenged me to order my private world in the area of time use. If he thought I had a bag of answers that would make it easy, he was to be disappointed. As our conversation continued, I suggested that he take a hard look at one Person who never seems to have wasted a moment.

When I look into the Bible, I am deeply impressed with the practical lessons on organization that one can learn from the life and work of Jesus Christ. All four gospel writers present to us a picture of Jesus under constant pressure, as He was pursued by friend and enemy alike. Every word of His was monitored, every action was analyzed, every gesture was commented upon. Essentially, Jesus had no private life to speak of.

I have tried to imagine our Lord in today's world. Would He take long distance phone calls? Would He fly rather than walk? Would He be interested in direct mail campaigns? How would He handle the huge number of relationships that modern technology has made it possible for us to maintain? How would He fit into a time where a word spoken can be flashed around the world in seconds to become headlines for the next morning's paper?

Although His world was on a much smaller scale, it would appear that He lived with very much the same sort of intrusions and demands with which we are familiar. But one never gets the feeling when studying the life of Christ that He ever hurried, that He ever had to play "catch up ball," or that He was ever taken by surprise. Not only was He adept at handling His public time without an appointments secretary, He managed adequate amounts of time alone for the purpose of prayer and meditation, and for being with the few He had gathered around Him for the purpose of discipleship. Again, all this was made possible because He had brought His time under control.

It is worth taking time to ask how our Lord's command of time is demonstrated. What caused Him to be such an organized person?

The first thing that impresses me is that *He clearly under-stood His mission.* He had a key task to perform, and He measured His use of time against that sense of mission.

This is quite apparent during His final walk toward Jerusalem, where He would be crucified. As Jesus approached Jericho, Luke writes (chapter 18), His ears picked up the shrill voice of a blind man and He stopped, much to the consternation of both His friends and critics. They were irritated that Jesus did not appreciate that Jerusalem was still six or seven hours away, and that they would like to get there to achieve *their* purpose, the celebration of Passover.

And indeed they had a point—*if* the purpose of Christ was merely to reach Jerusalem in time for a religious celebration. But, as we soon learn, that was not Jesus' prime mission. Touching broken people like the blind man was a more significant matter, important enough for Jesus to invest His time.

Not long after the first encounter, Jesus stopped once again, this time under the branch of a tree to call down Zacchaeus, a well-known tax collector. It was the Lord's idea that the two get together for a conversation at Zacchaeus's house. Once again the crowd surrounding Jesus was incensed, first because the trip to Jerusalem was again interrupted, and second because of Zacchaeus's reputation.

From where they were standing, it appeared that Jesus was misusing His time. From where Jesus was standing, however, the time was well spent, *for it fit the criteria of His mission.*

Luke records the words of Jesus about this very fact: "The Son of Man has come to seek and save that which was lost" (Luke 19:10). The disciples had a difficult time understanding this, and Jesus had to constantly confront them with the specific facts of His mission. Until they perceived that mission, they would never understand how and with what criteria He organized His time.

A second insight into Jesus' personal organization of time is that *He understood His own limits.* When Jesus came to earth as the incarnate Son of God, He set aside certain of His rights as the Prince of Heaven and accepted, for a time, certain human limitations in order to fully identify with us. He shared our limitations but coped with them effectively—just as we must.

We dare not minimize the fact that Jesus sought time in solitude with the heavenly Father before every important decision and action during His public ministry.

There are thirty years of virtual silence before Jesus went public with His mission. Only when we are permitted audience with Christ in eternity will we fully understand the importance of those three decades. At best, we can now conclude that they were a significant time of preparation. It is impressive to realize that there were thirty years of relative obscurity and privacy in preparation for three years of important activity.

We should not be surprised, then, that Moses spent forty years in the desert before confronting Pharaoh. Paul spent an extensive amount of time in the desert listening to God before assuming apostolic duties. And the experience of these men was not exceptional.

Just before Jesus assumed public ministry, He spent forty days in the wilderness communing with the Father. Don't forget the night spent in prayer before the choosing of the twelve. There was an early morning vigil on the mountainside the day after a busy time in Capernaum. And of course there was withdrawal to the Mount of Transfiguration to prepare for the final trek to Jerusalem. Finally, there was Gethsemane.

Jesus knew His limits well. Strange as it may seem, He knew what we conveniently forget: *that time must be properly budgeted for the gathering of inner strength and resolve in order to compensate for one's weaknesses when spiritual warfare begins.* Such private moments were a fixed item on Jesus' time budget because He knew His limits. And it was very hard even for those closest to Him to fully appreciate this.

I think Jesus included a third important element in His philosophy of time budgeting, for He *set time aside for the training of the twelve.* With a world of millions to reach, Jesus budgeted the majority of His time to be with just a few simple men.

Prime time was invested in taking them through the Scriptures and sharing His heavenly insights. Key moments were spent sharing ministry with individuals and permitting them to watch every action and hear every word. Special days were set aside to explain to them the deeper meanings of His talks to the crowds. And valuable hours were seized in order to debrief them when they returned from assignments, to rebuke them when they failed, and to affirm them when they succeeded.

We might have been tempted to ask more than once why Jesus was spending so much valuable time with a group of simple-minded men when He could have taught men who could have intellectually appreciated His theological expertise. But Jesus was aware of where true importance lies, where the priorities are. And where your priorities are, there your time will be.

For reasons like these, Jesus was never to be caught short on time. Because He knew His sense of mission, because He was spiritually sharpened by moments alone with the Father, and because He knew who the men were that would perpetuate His mission long after He ascended into heaven, it was never difficult for Him to say a firm NO to invitations and demands which might have looked good or acceptable to us.

There came a time in my own life when my study of Jesus made me deeply desire this capacity. I wanted to make sound decisions about the budgeting of my time, and I wanted to be free of that frantic pitch of daily life in which one is always playing catch-up. Was it possible? Not the way I was going!

The young pastor who had come up to me at the end of my lecture remained very interested. I suggested that we get together on another day. Perhaps there would be some practical things I could share with him. But I would have to be brutally honest with him. I learned most of them the hard way.

Memo to the Disorganized:

If my private world is in order, it is because I have begun to seal the "time leaks" and allocate my productive hours in the light of my capabilities, my limits, and my priorities.

7
Recapturing My Time

The young pastor and I were to resume our conversation some days later. In the interim I began gathering thoughts about what I had learned over the past few years that had helped me begin getting my own life together in this area. What had I learned through the experience of failure, and what had I learned in talking with others in the same way that this young man was coming to talk with me?

The more I looked at the lessons learned, the more I realized how important it is to gain control of time as early in life as possible. Putting them down on paper, I discovered that there were only a few basic principles. But until those were mastered, the time issue would always be big and potentially discouraging. What I found myself writing down in preparation for my next conversation was something I came to call "MacDonald's Laws of Unseized Time." Here is what I collected.

MacDonald's Laws of Unseized Time

LAW #1: UNSEIZED TIME FLOWS TOWARD MY WEAKNESSES

Because I had not adequately defined a sense of mission in the early days of my work, and because I had not been ruthless enough with my weaknesses, I found that I normally invested inordinately large amounts of time doing things I was not good at, while the tasks I should have been able to do with excellence and effectiveness were preempted.

I know many Christian leaders who will candidly admit that they spend up to 80 percent of their time doing things at which they are second-best. For example, my strongest gift is in the areas of preaching and teaching. While I am a reasonably good administrator, that is certainly not the best arrow in my pastoral quiver.

So why did I spend almost 75 percent of my available time trying to administrate and relatively little time studying and preparing to preach good sermons when I was younger? Because unseized time will flow in the direction of one's relative weakness. Since I knew I could preach an acceptable sermon with a minimum of preparation, I was actually doing less than my best in the pulpit. That is what happens when one does not evaluate this matter and do something drastic about it.

I finally did something drastic. I had the aid of a few sensitive laymen who cared enough to help me face what was happening and show me how I might be wasting my potential. With their help I made a decision to delegate the administration of our congregation's ministry to a competent administrative pastor. It was not easy at first because I still wanted to have a word on every decision, to express an opinion on every subject. I had to back off and leave that in his hands. But it worked! And when I was able to fully trust our administrative pastor (which I found easy to do), I was able to redirect a great amount of energy into things that, God willing, I am most likely to do well.

I can almost hear someone say, "That's fine if the money is available to hire someone to fill in my weaknesses." And perhaps in some cases the only help these comments may offer is to make us realize *why* we are frustrated when time seems to escape us. But I must add that it may be more possible than we realize to find creative ways to share tasks with others. First, we must sit ourselves down and consider: who is best at doing what? This applies in the home, in the office, in the church.

LAW #2: UNSEIZED TIME COMES UNDER THE INFLUENCE
        OF DOMINANT PEOPLE IN MY WORLD

A famous "spiritual law" states that "God loves you and has a plan for your life." Men and women who do not have control of their time discover that the same can be said about dominating people.

Because they have not set up their own time budgets, people succumbing to this law find that others enter their worlds and force agendas and priorities upon them. As a young pastor I discovered that because my time was not fully organized, I was at the mercy of anyone who had a notion to visit, took me to coffee, or wanted my attendance at a committee meeting. Since my calendar was disorganized, how could I say no? Especially when, as a young man, I was eager to please people.

Not only was I deprived of my best time due to this lack of organization, but my family was often cheated out of precious hours that I should have given them. And so it continued: strong people in my world controlled my time better than I did because I had not taken the initiative to command the time before they got to me.

LAW #3: UNSEIZED TIME SURRENDERS TO THE DEMANDS
        OF ALL EMERGENCIES

Charles Hummel in a small and classic booklet says it best: we are governed by the tyranny of the urgent. Those of us with any sort of responsibility for leadership in vocation, in the home, or in our faith will find ourselves continually surrounded by events that cry out for immediate attention.

One recent summer, when our associate pastor and I were both on vacation, our minister of Christian education took a phone call from a church member who wanted me to preside at the funeral of a distant relative of his. When told that I was away for the month, he asked for my associate and was disappointed to discover that he was also gone. He was offered the services of one of the other pastors on the staff, but he refused, saying, "No, I won't go any lower than number two."

His thinking was the sort that creates urgent situations for leaders. Everyone would like the attention of the number-one person. Every committee and board would like the number-one person to attend their meetings, even if they do not always wish to hear his opinions. Most people in any sort of trouble would like the immediate response of the number-one leader.

One Saturday afternoon the phone rang in our home, and when I answered, the woman's voice at the other end of the line sounded quite upset. "I've got to see you right away," she said. When I learned her name, I quickly realized that I had never met this person before and that she had rarely ever visited our church.

"What is the reason that we have to visit right now?" I asked. It was an important question, one of several I've learned through experience to ask. Had this been many years ago when I was young, I would have responded immediately to her sense of emergency and arranged to meet her in ten minutes at my office, even if I had previously hoped to be with the family or involved with study.

"My marriage is breaking up," she responded.

I then asked, "When did you become aware that it was going to break up?"

She answered, "Last Tuesday."

I asked another question. "How long do you think the process of breaking up has been going on?" Her next comment was unforgettable.

"Oh, it's been coming for five years."

I managed to muffle my real reaction and said, "Since you've seen this coming for almost five years, and since you knew it was going to happen since last Tuesday, why is it important to visit with me right at this moment? I need to know that."

She answered, "Oh, I had some free time this afternoon and just thought it might be a good time to get together with you."

Law number three would usually mean that I would have given in to her desire to see me immediately. But by this point in my life, most of my time was accounted for; so I said, "I can understand why you think you have a serious problem. Now I'm going to be very candid with you. I have to preach three times tomorrow morning, and frankly my mind is preoccupied with that responsibility. Since you've been living with this situation for several years now, and since you've had several days to think about your situation, I'm going to propose that you call me on Monday morning when we can arrange a time where my mind is in much better shape. I want to be able to give you the utmost in concentration. But that's probably not possible this afternoon. How does that sound?"

She thought it was a terrific idea and could see why I would suggest that sort of plan. Both of us hung up reasonably happy. She, knowing she would eventually get to talk to me; me, because I had reserved my time for the matter that was most important on that Saturday afternoon. A seemingly urgent thing had not broken through the time budget. Not everything that cries the loudest is the most urgent thing.

In his spiritual autobiography, *While It Is Yet Day*, Elton Trueblood writes:

> A public man, though he is necessarily available at many times, must learn to hide. If he is always available, he is not worth enough when he is available. I once wrote a chapter in the Cincinnati Union Station, but that was itself a form of hiding because nobody knew who the man with the writing pad was. Consequently nobody approached me during five wonderful hours until the departure of the next train to Richmond. *We must use the time which we have because even at best there is never enough.*[1] (Italics added)

LAW #4: UNSEIZED TIME GETS INVESTED IN THINGS THAT
      GAIN PUBLIC ACCLAMATION

In other words, we are more likely to give our unbudgeted time to events that will bring the most immediate and greatest praise.

When my wife and I were first married, we found that we could attract a lot of invitations to banquets and meetings of various sorts if we were willing to sing solos and duets. It was nice to receive the warm applause and gain the popularity. But the performance of music was not our call or our priority. Preaching and pastoral care were. Unfortunately, young

1. Elton Trueblood, *While It Is Day* (New York: Harper & Row, 1974), p. 67.

preachers were not in great demand, and the temptation was to do exactly what made people want us.

We had to make a critical decision. Would we involve our time in doing what people most liked for us to do? Or would we buckle down and give our attention to what was most important: learning the ways of preaching and counseling. Fortunately, we chose to avoid the seduction of the former and embrace the latter. It paid off.

We have had to make choices like that throughout our married life. And more than once I have made the wrong choice. There was a time when it seemed successful to fly across the country to speak at a banquet. But it was a poor use of time. The old comment "A sermon is something I'd go across the country to preach but not across the street to hear" is too close to the truth to be comfortable. It once seemed glamourous to be at the head table of some politician's prayer breakfast or to be interviewed on a Christian radio program, but it may not have been a high priority use of time.

Thus, the laws of unseized time come back to haunt the disorganized person again and again, until he decides to gain the initiative before everyone and every event does it for him.

How Time Is Recaptured

In gathering material for the upcoming conversation with the young pastor, I looked back on my own experience, trying to identify the principles that, when implemented, brought some order into my private world. And when I thought hard about the process that I had come through, I found that I was able to come up with three ways of successfully laying siege on time.

I MUST KNOW MY RHYTHMS OF MAXIMUM EFFECTIVENESS

A careful study of my work habits has revealed to me an important insight. There are various tasks I accomplish best at certain times and under certain conditions.

For example, I do not study effectively for my Sunday preaching during the early days of the week. Two hours of study on Monday are relatively worthless, while one hour on Thursday or Friday is almost priceless. I simply concentrate better. On the other hand, I am at my best with people in the early days of a week when the tension of anticipated preaching has not yet grabbed my mind. I tend to diminish in effectiveness with people later in the week when I become preoccupied with Sunday's pulpit experience.

I can fine-tune that observation even further. What study time I do take is best taken early in the morning, when I have reasonable amounts of unbroken solitude. And "people time" for me is best taken in the afternoon, when I feel reflective and insightful.

Learning about my rhythms has taught me to reserve study time for the last half of the week and to plan time with people and committees as much as possible in the first part of the week. In this way, my time budget reflects and uses the rhythms of my life.

I have also taken notice of the fact that I am a morning person. I can rise early and be quite alert if I have gone to bed at a reasonable hour the night before. So it is important to me to maintain a fairly standard bedtime. We enforced that principle with our children when they were young. I don't know why it never dawned upon us that a standard bedtime as much as possible was probably a wise thing for us as adults. And when I finally saw this, I tried to go to bed at the same time each night.

After reading an article by a specialist on the subject of sleep, I began to experiment to find out how much sleep I needed. The writer suggested that one can determine his sleep requirements by setting his alarm for a certain hour and rising at that time for three mornings in a row. Then the alarm should be set ten minutes earlier for the next three days. By so continuing in three-day increments, setting the alarm back ten minutes in each period, one will finally come to a natural fatigue point, where throughout the following day he does not feel properly rested. I tried it, found I could rise much earlier than I had thought, and it added almost two full hours—valuable hours—onto my day.

So there are weekly rhythms, daily rhythms, and annual rhythms. I found that there were certain months of the year when I was apt to face abnormal emotional fatigue, times when part of me wanted to run from people and from responsibility. I had to face up to that.

On the other hand, I saw that there were times in the year when I had to be relatively stronger as a Christian leader because many people around me were living with too much fatigue and pressure. The months of February and March are times like that, when all of us in New England fight the effects of a long winter and tend toward irritability and a critical spirit. I have learned to prepare myself to be an extra special encouragement to others during those times. And when spring comes and people feel revitalized, then I can enjoy my own private time of letdown. Knowing those things were likely to happen was a great help to me. I could plan for them.

I have learned that the summer months are a fine time for extra reading and for spiritually preparing myself for the coming year. But during January through March, for reasons I have just mentioned, I plan to be with people much of the time, because the counseling schedule is likely to jump dramatically. All of my books have been written in the summer months; there is no way they could have been done in winter.

Knowing my rhythms, I am not surprised when I feel inwardly empty after a period of heavy speaking and teaching. I cannot live day after day above the emotional line without coming to a moment when I must dip just a bit beneath the line of emotional normalcy to regather strength that has been lost. Thus it is wise not to make important decisions on a Monday after a day of preaching several sermons. And if I have pushed hard day after day during a holiday season, it is wise for me to plan a short letdown period when it is all over.

There was once a time when I had not yet learned to take notice of my personal rhythms. I remember coming to a particular day when everything seemed to suddenly cave in. I had officiated at two very sad funerals in one week; I had had insufficient rest for ten days. During that time I had read an upsetting book and had not maintained my spiritual disciplines at all. My family time had been disordered for several days, and a part of my work was at a point of frustration. So I should not have been surprised when, on a Saturday afternoon in the midst of a small personal crisis, I suddenly began to weep. Tears flowed that I was unable to stop for almost three hours.

Although I was nowhere near a breakdown in the classic sense, I learned from that painful experience how important it is to keep track of pressures and stresses, and how to know when and how I operate best doing certain tasks. I did not want that to happen again, and it hasn't. I was too frightened from that experience ever to allow myself to get so emotionally in debt again. My time had to be better budgeted than that.

I can now appreciate a part of a letter that William Booth, the founder of the Salvation Army, once received from his wife when he was on an extensive trip. She wrote:

> Your Tuesday's notes arrived safe, and I was rejoiced to hear of the continued prosperity of the work, though sorry you were so worn out; I fear the effect of all this excitement and exertion upon your health, and though I would not hinder your usefulness, I would caution you against an injudicious prodigality of your strength.
>
> Remember a long life of steady, consistent, holy labour will produce twice as much fruit as one shortened and destroyed by spasmodic and extravagant exertions; be careful and sparing of your strength when and where exertion is unnecessary.[2]

I MUST HAVE GOOD CRITERIA FOR CHOOSING HOW TO USE MY TIME

Years ago my father wisely shared with me that one of the great tests of human character is found in making critical choices of selection and rejection amidst all of the opportunities that lurk in life's path. "Your challenge," he told me, "will not be in separating out the good from the bad, but in grabbing the *best* out of all the possible good." He was absolutely correct. I did indeed have to learn, sometimes the hard way, that I had to say no to things I really wanted to do in order to say yes to the very best things.

Heeding that counsel has meant saying an occasional no to dinner parties and sporting events on Saturday night so that I could be fresh mentally and physically on Sunday morning. It

2. Harold Begbie, *Life of General William Booth* (New York: Macmillan, 1920), p. 178.

has meant saying no to certain speaking dates when I really wanted to say yes.

Sometimes I find such choices hard to make, simply because I like people to approve of me. When a person learns to say no to good things, he runs the risk of making enemies and gaining critics; and who needs more of those? So I find it hard to say no.

I have discovered that most people whose lives are centered on forms of leadership have the same problem. But if we are to command our time, we will have to bite the bullet and say a firm but courteous no to opportunities that are good but not the best.

Once again that demands, as it did in the ministry of our Lord, a sense of our mission. What are we called to do? What do we do best with our time? What are the necessities without which we cannot get along? Everything else has to be considered negotiable: discretionary, not necessary.

I love the words C. S. Lewis wrote in *Letters to an American Lady* about the importance of these choices:

> Don't be too easily convinced that God really wants you to do all sorts of work you needn't do. Each must do his duty "in that state of life to which God has called him." Remember that a belief in the virtues of doing for doing's sake is characteristically feminine, characteristically American, and characteristically modern: so that *three* veils may divide you from the correct view! There can be intemperance in work just as in drink. What feels like zeal may be only fidgets or even the flattering of one's self importance . . . By doing what "one's station and its duties" does not demand, one can make oneself less fit for the duties it *does* demand and so commit some injustice. Just you give Mary a little chance as well as Martha.[3]

I SEIZE TIME AND COMMAND IT WHEN I BUDGET IT FAR IN ADVANCE

This last principle is the most important; here is where the battle is won or lost.

I have learned the hard way that the principal elements of my time budget have to be in the calendar eight weeks in advance of the date. Eight weeks!

3. C. S. Lewis, *Letters to an American Lady* (Grand Rapids: Eerdmans, 1975), p. 53.

If this is August, then I am already beginning to think through October. And what goes into the calendar? Those non-negotiable aspects of my private world: my spiritual disciplines, my mental disciplines, my Sabbath rest, and of course my commitments to family and special friendships. Then a second tier of priorities will enter the calendar: the schedule of the main work to which I am committed—sermon study, writing, leadership development, and discipling.

As much as possible all of this is placed in the calendar many, many weeks in advance of the target week, because as I get closer to that week I discover that people move in to make demands upon the available time. Some of them will have legitimate demands, and it is to be hoped there will be space for them.

But others will have demands that are not appropriate. They will request an evening that I have scheduled for the family. Or they will want an hour in a morning reserved for study. How much better my private world is when I allow that work to *flow around* the priorities and into available slots than when things are the other way around.

It occurred to me one day that my most important time allocations had something in common. They never screamed out immediately when ignored. I could neglect my spiritual disciplines, for example, and God did not seem to shout loudly about it. I could make it just fine for a while. And when I did not allocate time for the family, Gail and the children were generally understanding and forgiving—often more so than certain church members who demanded instant response and attention. And when I set study aside as a priority, I could get away with it for a while. These things could be ignored for a while without adverse consequences. And that is why they were so often crowded out when I did not budget for them in advance. Other less important issues had a way of wedging them aside week after week. Tragically, if they are neglected too long, when family, rest, and spiritual disciplines are finally noticed it is often too late for adverse consequences to be avoided.

When our son, Mark, was in high school, he was a successful athlete; our teenaged daughter, Kristen, was an actress and musician. Both were in games and performances. It would have been easy to have missed those events had I not penciled the dates into the calendar weeks and weeks in advance. My secretary always kept the game schedules in the office calendar, for example, and knew full well not to expect me to commit to anything that would violate those times.

When someone would ask me to meet with him on the afternoon of a game, I was liable to take out my calendar and stroke my chin thoughtfully saying, "I'm sorry, I'm unable to do it that day; I already have a commitment. How about this as an alternative?" I rarely had a problem. The key was in planning and budgeting, weeks in advance.

What are your non-negotiables? I discover that most of us who complain that we are disorganized simply do not know the answer. As a result, the important functions that will make the supreme difference in our effectiveness miss getting into the calendar until it is too late. The consequence? Disorganization and frustration; the non-essentials crowd into the datebook before the necessities do. And that is painful over the long run.

The other day a man caught up with me and asked if we could have an early morning breakfast on a certain day. "How early?" I asked.

"You're an early riser," he said. "Why not six?"

I looked at my calendar and said, "I'm sorry, I've already got a commitment for that hour; how about seven?" He agreed on seven rather quickly but looked quite surprised that my calendar might reflect plans for that early in the morning.

I did have a commitment for six that morning. In fact it started earlier than that. It was a commitment to God. He was first on the calendar that day where He belongs every day. And it is not the sort of commitment one compromises. Not if one wants to seize time and keep it under control. It is the start of an organized day, an organized life, and an organized private world.

Sector Three

Memo to the Disorganized:

If my private world is in order, it will be because I have determined that every day will be for me a day of growth in knowledge and wisdom.

8

The Better Man Lost

The only gold medals and blue ribbons I have ever won were gained on track and cross country fields. Although I could have been a more successful runner if I had been tougher on myself, those years of competitive running in prep school and college were nevertheless an opportunity for rich learning experiences in terms of the development of self-discipline and character.

Of all those youthful experiences, the greatest lesson came at the Pennsylvania Relays in Philadelphia one spring day. On that occasion, I was the lead-off man for our prep school mile relay team, a very important position. My mission was to gain the lead in the race and, when I had completed my quarter mile leg, hand that advantage on to the second runner on our team.

For me to finish that leg out of first place would mean that our second man would receive the relay baton while back among a cluster of runners. There one risked a loss of stride in the jostling and shoving that often took place, and it could cost precious tenths of a second. That time could be quite valuable if the race was closely contested in the final lap.

Since our team had drawn the number two lane, I was curious to see who had received the "pole," or inside, lane position. It turned out to be a runner from Poly Prep with an impressive record as a sprinter in the 100-yard dash. We had competed against each other on a couple of other occasions at the shorter distance, and he had beaten me rather badly. Could he do the same when the race was 340 yards longer?

It was obvious that he thought so, because he said as much when we shook hands at the starting line. Looking squarely at me he said, "MacDonald, may the best man win; I'll be waiting for you at the finish line."

You might call it a brand of athletic psychological warfare. It partially worked, and for a moment I had to struggle to gain my equilibrium.

The gun went off, and so did the man from Poly Prep. I can remember feeling the sting of the cinders that his spikes shot backward on my shins as he seemed to instantly disappear around the first turn. Meanwhile the remaining seven runners began what looked like a competition for positions number two through eight. Before I had run fifty yards, I began to mentally prepare for finishing in second place, assuming I could make even that happen.

And that is indeed what would have happened—if the race had been shorter. Somewhere around the 300 yard marker, however, affairs abruptly changed. The man from Poly Prep, far out in front, suddenly slowed down from sprint to jog. A second later, as I charged around him now running at my peak stride, I could hear him struggling to breathe. He was barely moving. As athletes put it, he was out of gas. I don't remember in what place he finished, but I do know that I was waiting for him at the finish line, trying hard not to gloat.

I learned a valuable lesson that day at the expense of the man from Poly Prep. Inadvertently, he had taught me that even men and women of great talent and energy have to run the *complete* course before they can claim the victory. To be in front at the first turn is meaningless without the endurance to finish strongly. The race must be run at a steady pace all the way to the finish. And a good runner is even prepared to complete the course with a "kick," an extra burst of speed. Athletic talent is of little consequence unless it is matched to adequate endurance.

THE COST OF MENTAL FLABBINESS

I tell this story because it speaks to another segment of our private lives that must be consistently in the process of organization. The ordering of our private world cannot take place without strong mental endurance and the intellectual growth this endurance produces.

In our pressurized society, people who are out of shape mentally usually fall victim to ideas and systems that are destructive to the human spirit and to human relationships. They are victimized because they have not taught themselves how to think; nor have they set themselves to the life-long pursuit of the growth of the mind. Not having the facility of a strong mind, they grow dependent upon the thoughts and opinions of others Rather than deal with ideas and issues, they reduce themselves to lives full of rules, regulations, and programs.

The 1978 mass suicide in Guyana by members of the Peoples' Temple is a poignant example of where mindlessness can lead. Allowing Jim Jones to do their thinking for them, the membership courted disaster. They emptied their minds and depended upon the functioning of his. And when Jones's mind ceased working correctly, everyone suffered the consequences. A leader had promised people guidance in the midst of a hostile and angry world. He had offered answers and sustenance. And people signed away their right to independent judgment as the price of such security.

People whose minds are not strengthened for endurance are by no means always unintelligent. They simply have never stopped to think that the use of the mind for the purpose of growth is a necessary part of a God-pleasing life-style. It is easy to fall into the trap of allowing the mind to grow flaccid, especially when there are many dominant people all around who would just as soon do our thinking for us.

Such mindlessness can be seen in an unbalanced—and ungodly—family, where one person intimidates all other family members into letting him or her do all the decision-making and opinion-forming. We have many examples of churches where lay people delegate the thinking to a highly dominant pastor. The epistle of 3 John speaks against a man named Diotrephes, a lay leader who, like Jim Jones, had virtually everyone under his control. The Christians simply surrendered thinking to him.

THE DANGER OF BEING A FAST STARTER

As in a race where the naturally talented runner springs from the starting blocks with a blinding burst of speed, there are those who enjoy fast starts in adult life—not because they are great thinkers or mental giants, but rather because of natural abilities and useful connections. They may have had the benefit of growing up in talented families, where the people around them were highly communicative and gifted in dealing with ideas and problem-solving. As a result, they may have acquired considerable self-confidence at an early age.

Such early exposures teach the young person how to lead, how to compete against others, and how to handle himself in difficult situations. The result could be called "pre-mature success." And pre-mature success is often more an obstacle than a help.

The pre-mature succeeder is usually a fast learner, able to acquire expertise with minimum effort. He is usually blessed with good health and abundant energy. He can talk his way into or out of anything, it seems. And he may conclude that he can do just about anything he sets his mind to, because things appear to come easily to him.

How long things can go on this way is anyone's guess. For a lifetime, I suppose, in certain cases. But my observation is that somewhere in his early thirties, indications of possible trouble will begin to show in the life of the naturally talented fast starter. There may be the first hints that the rest of the race in life will have to be run on endurance and discipline and not talent. And, like the runner from Poly Prep, he may start to see that the slower but better conditioned runners are beginning to catch up.

In my counseling I have met many people who are struggling through midlife for this reason. I see a startling number of exhausted, mentally empty people who have stopped growing and are spending their lives in the pursuit of little more than amusement.

I use the word *amusement* because of its literal meaning. It suggests *function without thought* (*a* meaning "without"; *muse*, "to think"). Functioning without thought leads to a feeling of personal disorganization. Who are the people who function without thought? They can easily be folk of whom it was said twenty years before, "He is going places; he can't miss." It can be the preacher who at the age of twenty-one had unusual pulpit powers, the salesman who began his career with a remarkable record of completed deals, the woman who graduated valedictorian of her class. It tends to be those who never realized that the mind must be pushed, filled, stretched, and forced in order to function. Natural talent takes such people only so far and lets them down long before the race is finished.

THE NEED TO DISCIPLINE OUR MINDS

The mind must be *trained* to think, to analyze, to innovate. People fully organized in their private worlds *work* at being thinkers. Their minds are alert and alive, taking on fresh amounts of information every day, regularly producing new discoveries and conclusions. They commit themselves to the daily exercise of the mind.

"No vital Christianity is possible unless at least three aspects of it are developed," writes Elton Trueblood. "These three are the inner life of devotion, the outer life of service, and the *intellectual life of rationality*."[1] the third aspect is the easiest for many evangelicals to ignore, thinking it too worldly and offensive to the gospel. But the dulling of the mind leads to ultimate disorganization of the private world.

I understand pre-mature success because I too discovered in my early thirties that I was coasting on natural talent and not giving adequate attention to the development of my mind. I began to see that unless I did something about it, my mind would not adequately serve me in later years when I wanted

1. Elton Trueblood, *While It Is Day* (New York: Harper & Row, 1974), pp. 97–98.

to be running at peak mental stride, doing and giving my very best.

For me it meant that if I was going to become a more effective preacher, a more sensitive understander of hurting people, and a more useful leader, I would have to take seriously the challenge of sharpening my mental capacities so that I could deal with my public world. Although I was not entirely asleep intellectually, I was not doing the hard disciplined work that would help me to be the innovative and seminal person I thought God wanted me to be.

No wonder I felt the pangs of disorganization when I faced situations where I was not smart enough to understand what was going on. Like someone with a weight too heavy to lift, I found myself more and more trying to hoist ideas and perplexities that I was not mentally strong enough to get off the ground.

Although evangelical Christians have made an outspoken commitment to Christian education, there has not always been a high enough value placed upon the development of the mind. Few of us have fully appreciated the contrast between gatherers of details and rules and skilled handlers of truth. There may be some who know a little about a lot of things, but that does not guarantee that many of us know how to think deeply and insightfully about what we know.

I have watched men and women who have pressed enormous amounts of information about the Bible into their heads. They have learned to speak a rich vocabulary of correct Christian jargon. Their prayers can be so smooth-sounding that all those about them sit in awe. We think them to be spiritual people. But at other times, we begin to see that they are rigid and inflexible, impervious to change and innovation. Their response to any serious challenge to their thought is a burst of anger or accusation.

Like others, I am convinced that Christians ought to be the strongest, broadest, most creative thinkers in the world. It was Paul who said that as Christians we are given the mind of Christ. This provides a potential intellectual breadth that the unregenerate mind does not possess. It offers an eternal, a timeless perspective in which to think. In Christ there is a foundation of truth that ought to make our ideas, our analysis of things, and our innovations among the most powerful of the age. But because there is an essential laziness and internal disorganization in many Christian lives, this is not always the case. We are forfeiting one of the great gifts God provided through Christ.

Missionary-evangelist Stanley Jones writes:

> Swami Shivananda, a famous swami in India, used to tell his disciples: "Kill the mind and then, and then only, can you meditate." The Christian position is "Thou shalt love the Lord thy God with all thy mind"—the intellectual nature; "with all thy heart"—the emotional nature; "with all thy soul"—the willing nature; and "with all thy strength"—the physical nature. The total person is to love him—mind, emotion, will, strength. But the "strength" might mean the strength of all three. Some love him with the strength of the mind and the weakness of the emotion—the intellectualist in religion; some love him with the strength of emotion and the weakness of the mind—the sentimentalist in religion; some love him with the strength of the will and the weakness of emotion—the man of iron who is not very approachable. *But loving God with the strength of the mind, the strength of the emotion, and the strength of the will—that makes the truly Christian and the truly balanced and the truly strong character.* (Italics added)[2]

For many years Admiral Hyman Rickover was the head of the United States Nuclear Navy. His admirers and his critics held strongly opposing views about the stern and demanding admiral. For many years every officer aboard a nuclear submarine was personally interviewed and approved by Rickover. Those who went through those interviews usually came out shaking in fear, anger, or total intimidation. Among them was ex-President Jimmy Carter who, years ago, applied for service under Rickover. This is his account of a Rickover interview:

> I had applied for the nuclear submarine program, and Admiral Rickover was interviewing me for the job. It was the first time I met Admiral Rickover, and we sat in a large room by ourselves for more than two hours, and he let me choose any subjects I wished

2. E. Stanley Jones, *Song of Ascents* (Nashville: Abingdon, 1968), p. 189.

to discuss. Very carefully, I chose those about which I knew most at the time—current events, seamanship, music, literature, naval tactics, electronics, gunnery—and he began to ask me a series of questions of increasing difficulty. In each instance, he soon proved that I knew relatively little about the subject I had chosen.

He always looked right into my eyes, and he never smiled. I was saturated with cold sweat.

Finally, he asked a question and I thought I could redeem myself. He said, "How did you stand in your class at the Naval Academy?" Since I had completed my sophomore year at Georgia Tech before entering Annapolis as a plebe, I had done very well, and I swelled my chest with pride and answered, "Sir, I stood fifty-ninth in a class of 820!" I sat back to wait for the congratulations—which never came. Instead, the question: "Did you do your best?" I started to say, "Yes, sir," but I remembered who this was and recalled several of the many times at the Academy when I could have learned more about our allies, our enemies, weapons, strategy, and so forth. I was just human. I finally gulped and said, "No, sir, I didn't always do my best."

He looked at me for a long time, and then turned his chair around to end the interview. He asked one final question, which I have never been able to forget—or to answer. He said, "Why not?" I sat there for a while, shaken, and then slowly left the room.[3]

That encounter became the thought-starter for Carter's book *Why Not the Best?* And it is a worthwhile story to ponder. Does not the man or woman who claims to walk with Christ owe the Creator excellence in terms of thought?

Thinking is the amazing capacity God has given the human being to discover and observe the stuff of creation, to compare and contrast each of its parts, and when possible, to use them properly so as to reflect the glory of the Creator. Thinkers see old things in new ways; they analyze hypotheses, separating out the true from the false. Thinkers sometimes describe old truths in new words and forms; they help others to see how applications to life can be made. Thinkers make bold decisions, help us see new visions, and overcome obstacles in previously unseen ways.

These are not merely the exercises of the great and the bril-

3. Norman Polmar and Thomas B. Allen, *Rickover: Controversy and Genius* (New York: Simon & Schuster, 1982), p. 267.

liant. They are the tasks of everyone with a healthy mind. As with physical bodies, some of us may be stronger than others, but that does not relieve us of the responsibility of using our bodies or our minds.

It is said that even though he held over a thousand patents, Thomas Edison felt he could only claim one invention—the phonograph—as his original idea. All his other "inventions," he said, were adaptations and improvements upon ideas that other people had left undeveloped.

It would do us good to see ourselves as sponges. Throughout the expanse of creation God has hidden things for humankind to discover, to enjoy, and with which to perceive the nature of the Creator Himself. We should sponge it all up.

> It is the glory of God to conceal a matter,
> But the glory of kings is to search out a matter.
>   (Proverbs 25:2)

The work of the first man and woman was to discover and identify things God had made. Because of their disobedience against God's laws, some of the opportunity for that kind of marvelous work was forfeited. They now had to worry more about surviving in a hostile world than continuing to discover what was in it. The nature of work abruptly changed. I have a conviction that the heavenly life will in some way recover that original form of work.

But the principle and privilege of discovery still prevails in part. Some discoveries come through hard physical labor, such as digging gold out of the side of a hill. Other discoveries are made as we observe the progress of living things in the plant, animal, and human kingdoms. And much of the exploration of creation is done purely within the mind. We dig, as it were, and uncover ideas and truths; then we turn around to express them artistically, worshipfully, and inventively.

Thinking is a great work. It is best done with a mind that has trained and is in shape just as competitive running is done with a body that has trained and is in shape. The best kind of thinking is accomplished when it is done in the context of reverence for God's kingly reign over all creation. It is sad to see great thinking and artistic work accomplished by men and women who have no interest in uncovering knowledge of the Creator. They think and innovate purely for self-aggrandizement or for the development of a human system that assumes it can get along without God.

Some Christians appear to be afraid to think. They mistake the gathering of facts, doctrinal systems, and lists of rules for thinking. They are uneasy when dealing with open-ended questions. And they do not see the significance of wrestling with great ideas if they cannot always come up with easily packaged answers. The consequences are a drift toward mediocrity in personal living and mental activity and a loss of much that God meant for His children to enjoy as they walk through creation discovering His handiwork. Life under such circumstances becomes *amusement,* function without thought.

The unthinking Christian does not realize it, but he is dangerously absorbed into the culture about him. Because his mind is untrained and unfilled, it lacks the ability to produce the hard questions with which the world needs to be challenged. The challenge for the modern Christian in a secular society may be to ask prophetic questions before there is going to be an opportunity to provide Christ-oriented answers.

Sometimes, because of the massive amounts of information bombarding us regularly, the unthinking Christian longs to run in retreat, leaving heavy thinking up to a few elite Christian leaders or theologians.

Harry Blamires, in an insightful book called *The Christian Mind,* asks where there are Christians with minds sharp enough to confront a culture that steadily drifts away from God. He calls for people who think "Christianly" about great moral issues. His fear, which I share, is that we fool ourselves into thinking that we are thinking people when we are not. With a stinging rebuke against the Christian public, he writes:

> Christianity is emasculated of its intellectual relevance. It remains a vehicle of spirituality and moral guidance at the individual level perhaps; at the communal level it is little more than an expression of sentimentalized togetherness.[4]

4. Harry A. Blamires, *The Christian Mind* (Ann Arbor: Servant, 1978).

When the Christian's mind becomes dull, he can fall prey to the propaganda of a non-Christian scheme of things, led by people who have not neglected their thinking powers—and have simply out-thought us.

Just as my coach once taught me to train my body in order to finish the entire race, so I had to learn what others are having to learn: that the mind also has to be trained. The private world of the Christian will be weak, defenseless, and disorganized if serious attention has not been given to this sector of intellectual growth.

The man from Poly Prep was a better runner, but he lost. He lost because 100 yards of talent is not good enough for 440 yards of race.

When I once evaluated the order of the intellectual sector of my private world, I thankfully came to see that a few natural gifts or a few years of education were never going to make me the man God wanted to use in any part of the world where He wanted me to do work. If I was going to endure and become useful to the level of my potential, it would not be because I was talented or degreed, but because I had learned to take the muscles of my mind and work them into shape.

I had to become a thinker. I had to become conversant with the directions that history was taking. I needed to know how to grapple with the great ideas of humankind. And I had to learn how to make independent judgments about what I was seeing. It was time for me to start working—hard. Other runners were catching up, and the race was far from over. I didn't want to be a better man in the first turn and a loser at the finish line because I had talent but no endurance.

Memo to the Disorganized:

If my private world is in order, it will be because I seek to use all I learn in service to others, as Christ did.

9

The Sadness of a
Book Never Read

My wife and I were browsing in an old bookstore one day looking for those special titles among secondhand books that are such a delight when found. Gail found a copy of a biography of Daniel Webster that had been published in the 1840s. It looked interesting, and since we are lovers of biographies, she purchased the book.

The cover of the book appeared worn enough to convey the notion that it had been well read. One could imagine that it had been a prized edition in the library of several generations of a New England family. Perhaps it had been loaned out on a number of occasions and brought enlightenment to a dozen different readers.

Not so! When Gail began to leaf through the old book, she discovered that the printer had failed to properly cut the pages, and many of them could not be opened until one took a blade and cut them apart. The uncut pages were clear evidence that the book had never been read! It looked on the outside as if it had been constantly used. But if it had, it was only in gracing a library shelf, or playing doorstop, or providing height to a small child so that he could sit and reach the table while he ate. The book may have been used, but it certainly had never been read.

The Christian who is not growing intellectually is like a book whose many pages remain unopened and unread. Like the book, he may be of some value, but not nearly as much as if he had chosen to sharpen and develop his mind.

PUTTING YOURSELF IN A GROWTH MODE

When a person sets out to deliberately use his mind for the purpose of growth and development as a person, new order comes into his private world. His mind—an organ largely undeveloped in many people—comes alive with new possibility when he sets himself in what I call a *growth mode*.

There are at least three objectives in developing the intellectual dimension of our private worlds. Let me offer them to you as a scheme for mental development.

OBJECTIVE ONE: THE MIND MUST BE DISCIPLINED TO THINK CHRISTIANLY

I understand this objective because I grew up in a Christian context and had the full advantage of Christian teaching from infancy.

To think Christianly means to look at our world from the perspective that it is made and owned by God, that what we do with creation will have to be accounted for, and that it is important to make choices according to the laws of God. The Bible calls this stewardship. Christian thinking looks at all issues and ideas from the standpoint of what God desires and what might give honor to Him.

A person who has not enjoyed the advantage of a lifelong Christian context is not liable to gain that total perspective easily. If he becomes a follower of Christ at a later age, it will be particularly bothersome to compare his instincts and reactions to those of more mature believers. He will tend to be hard on himself, wondering if he will ever get ahead in matters of faith.

For this kind of person, thinking will be done more by commitment than by Christian instinct. In other words, the newer Christian's reaction to a problem or opportunity is apt to be a non-Christian one, and he will then have to reverse and replace it with a learned Christian response.

The person who thinks Christianly by background probably thinks with all the proper reactions, unless he deliberately chooses to embrace a life of rebellion. But whether or not he will follow up the Christian mental response with Christian action is another matter.

I describe these two styles of thought because I have found it to be helpful to people, especially younger Christians who are struggling with the meaning of spiritual growth. They wonder why they are always just a second behind the older Christians and seem unable to catch up. The key is often in Christian acculturation, which is certainly an advantage and testifies to the importance of the Christian family. This kind of Christian acculturation is becoming less and less frequent as the world around us grows increasingly secular and drifts from a Christian base.

For the new Christian, mental growth will be in part the cultivation of the Christian perspective, the Christian response to life, and the Christian value system in the market place.

The long-term Christian has a struggle of a different sort. Although he may have an instinctive Christian reaction to most situations, his commitment may not be as enthusiastic as the newly converted believer. He simply assumes that Christianized mechanisms will work automatically. And this can be very dangerous over a period of time. Thinking Christianly without a regular renewal of our commitment to Christ leads to a deadness of religion, a boring faith, an ineffective witness to God. And we who have grown up with the gospel of Christ have to be very careful to avoid this.

OBJECTIVE TWO: THE MIND MUST BE TAUGHT TO OBSERVE AND
APPRECIATE THE MESSAGES GOD HAS WRITTEN IN
CREATION

"The heavens are telling of the glory of God" (Psalm 19:1). Everything God made—even human beings—has as its key purpose the reflection of the honor of God.

Unfortunately, the power of sin has tarnished the capacity of some aspects of creation to reflect that honor. In fact, sin first appears to have done its job on humanity; then, through men and women, sin systematically tarnished everything else in creation. But where man has not been able to confuse the issue, the creation continues to shout out its message: God the Creator be praised!

The growing mind, filled with the love of Christ, searches creation for these messages. Because of our spiritual and natural gifts, each of us is able to see and hear them in particular areas more than in others. And we are enabled to take this creation material and identify it, shape it, reconfigure it, or in other ways use it so that God is further glorified. The carpenter works with wood; the physician listens to the body; the musician shapes sounds; the executive manages people; the educator trains youth; the researcher analyzes, innovates, and implements with the elements of the universe.

We develop our minds for these tasks and rejoice as we do them for all that God is revealing to us out of His loving heart.

OBJECTIVE THREE: THE MIND MUST BE TRAINED TO PURSUE
INFORMATION, IDEAS, AND INSIGHTS FOR THE
PURPOSE OF SERVING THE PEOPLE OF MY PUBLIC
WORLD

The development of the mind makes it possible for men and women to be servants to the generation in which they live. I think of the contributions of missionary-physician Paul Brand, who is credited with the development of surgical procedures that have restored the use of limbs to those suffering from Hansen's disease (leprosy). We have all been enriched by the mind of C. S. Lewis in literature or John Perkins in the area of race relations. And there are men and women whose names are not as well known: a young civil engineer who uses his expertise helping build a hydroelectric dam in Ecuador; an accountant who gives precious time to help disadvantaged people restructure themselves financially; a builder who goes into the center city and teaches men and women to rehabilitate and winterize old houses; and a computer operator who gives time to teach immigrant children to read. All of these are using their minds in ministry to others.

We do not develop our intellects merely for our own personal advancement, but we put our thinking power to work for the use of others. I remember this when I push myself in my reading and filing: I am collecting the raw material that will become a sermon of encouragement or insight for others one day. As my mind grows, it may make possible the growth of others.

ORGANIZING YOUR MIND TO MAKE IT GROW

Looking back across the early years of my life, I recall once coming to the startling realization that although I had amassed enormous amounts of information about many things, I had never really pushed myself to be an aggressive thinker. In fact, I am not sure I had ever learned to love learning.

Moving through my educational years, I had tended toward being one of those who played the margins. "Tell me what it takes to pass this course," I said, "and I'll give it to you." With rare exceptions, I adopted that philosophy throughout high school, college, and graduate school. Occasionally I would be confronted by an instructor who saw through that limited view and would push me toward a higher excellence. I never stopped to ask myself why I appreciated those instructors more than the others. It was indeed fun to be stretched, to have something better than the average pulled out of me.

But when I finally left the formal education process behind, there was no one to push or pull me, no one to require excellence except myself. And soon I learned that I would have to accept full responsibility for my own mental growth. That was when I achieved intellectual puberty. For the first time, I became serious about learning how to think and learn on my own.

How does one go about this process of intellectual organization in the private world? Let me list several ways.

WE GROW BY BECOMING LISTENERS

My intellectual organization began when I learned to listen. For someone like me who enjoys talking, listening can be difficult. But if a person is not a listener, he denies his mind a major source of information by which to grow.

Perhaps the first step in becoming a listener is to *learn to ask questions*. I have rarely met a person or been in a situation where there was not something valuable worth learning. On many occasions, I have had to generate listening by first asking questions. That has meant learning how to be a good question-asker. Right questions elicit valuable information for the purposes of growth. I like to ask men and women about their jobs, where they met their spouses, what they have been reading about, what they consider their greatest present challenges, and where they find God most alive in their lives. The answers are always useful.

In the process of becoming a listener, I have come to see that most people are eager to share something of themselves. Many older people rarely have anyone to listen to them, and they are usually wellsprings of insight. Suffering people, people under stress and tension, have much to share with those who can learn to ask the right questions. And in asking we not only learn, but we are also able to encourage and love.

We particularly need to learn to listen to older people and children. They all have stories to tell that enrich the mind and the heart. Children simplify things, often with brutal honesty. Older people bring the perspective of their long years on issues. Suffering people also help us understand what are the truly important matters of life. There is something to learn from all people if we are only willing to sit at their feet and humble ourselves enough to ask the right questions.

A second part of mental growth by listening came when I started to *visit people at their places of labor*, to see what they do, meet the people with whom they work, and so learn something of the particular challenges they face. I pushed myself to gain a new appreciation of the differing sorts of contributions people around me are making to my world. I enjoy asking men and women about their vocations: "Tell me what it takes to do a job like yours with excellence. What are the great challenges a person faces? Where do you confront ethical and moral questions? What is there about this sort of task that brings on fatigue or discouragement? Do you ever ask yourself about the ways God is present in this job?"

A third way of growing through listening comes when we *listen to mentors*. Throughout my life God has surrounded me with a chain of men and women who believed in me, cared for me, and tried to make a contribution to the bringing forth of whatever potential God placed in me. I am grateful that I was taught by my parents to listen to such people, for many of my colleagues tended to slough off the counsel and wisdom of such mentors and so lost valuable information.

Fourth, I can suggest that growth always comes when we

also *listen to our critics*. And that is not an easy thing for any of us to do. Dawson Trotman, the founder of the Navigators, had a good method for handling all criticisms directed at himself. No matter how unfair the criticism might seem to be, he would always take it into his prayer closet and in effect spread it before the Lord. Then he would say, "Lord, please show me the kernel of truth hidden in this criticism."

The truth may certainly be small on occasion, but it is always worth finding and thinking through. I have been grateful to learn of Dawson Trotman's secret. It has saved me countless bad moments when I might have otherwise been tempted to be defensive when criticized. Instead I began to learn to grow at the hands of my critics. I have seldom ever heard a criticism about myself that didn't indeed contain a kernel of useful truth. Some of the kernels have been on the small side, but they were there.

When I mentally list the most important truths on which I have based my own character and personality development, I am astonished to discover that a large majority of them came through painful situations where someone, either out of love or anger, rebuked or criticized me soundly. I carry with me the memory of a time when my missiology professor at Denver Seminary, Dr. Raymond Buker, approached me at the end of a special convocation where I had read a paper on some moral issue that was burning in the hearts of the student generation of that day. I had cut two of his classes that day to prepare the paper, and it had not gone unnoticed.

"Gordon," he said, "the paper you read tonight was a good one, but it wasn't a great one. Would you like to know why?"

I wasn't sure I really wanted to know because I anticipated a bit of humiliation coming my way, but I swallowed hard and told Dr. Buker that I would like to hear his analysis.

"The paper wasn't a great one," he said as he thumped his finger on my chest, "because you sacrificed the routine to write it."

In pain I learned one of the most important lessons I ever needed to learn. Because my time as a Christian leader is generally my own to use as I please, it would be very easy to avoid routine, unspectacular duties and give myself only to the exciting things that come along. But most of life is lived in the routine, and Buker was right: the man or woman who learns to make peace with routine responsibilities and obligations will make the greatest contributions in the long run.

But I would not have learned that lesson and grown from it, at least at that point in my life, if there had not been a man willing to rebuke me and if I had not been willing to listen and learn.

We grow through listening, aggressive listening: asking questions, watching intently what is happening around us, taking note of the good or ill consequences that befall people as a result of their choice making.

WE GROW THROUGH READING

A second way we grow is through reading. In our age of mass media, the younger generation is finding it harder and harder to acquire the discipline of reading, and that may be one of the greatest losses of our time. Nothing substitutes for what can be found when we master books.

Paul gave evidence of his own hunger for reading when he wrote to Timothy asking for parchments and books. Even at that older age, he was anxious to grow. Some of us are not naturally given to reading, and it is hard for us. But to whatever extent we can press ourselves in this direction, we should acquire the habit of reading systematically.

My wife and I are students of biography, and there is hardly a time in our home when the two of us are not making our way through two or three biographical accounts. These books have poured priceless insights into our minds.

Others will be drawn to psychology, theology, history, or good fiction. But all of us need to have at least one good book going at all times, more if possible. When I visit with pastors who are struggling with their own effectiveness, I often ask, "What are you reading lately?" It is almost predictable that if a pastor is struggling with failure in his ministry, he will be unable to name a title or an author that he has been reading in recent days. If he is not reading, the chances are strong that he is not growing. And if he is not growing, then he may rapidly slip into ineffectiveness.

During the hostage crisis in Iran, one woman seemed to stand out from the other fifty or more victims of that terrible ordeal. Katherine Koob became an inspiration to many in the embassy and here in the United States. When she returned to her home and was able to describe what kept her both sane and strong while in such conditions, she readily acknowledged that it was the reading and memorizing she had done throughout her life. In her mind was stored an almost infinite amount of material from which she drew strength and resolve as well as the truth with which to comfort others.

In my own disciplines, I have tried to set aside a minimum of an hour each day for the purpose of reading. I have found that one should never read without a pencil in hand to mark salient passages, and I have developed a simple series of codes that will remind me of impressive thoughts or quotes worth clipping and filing for future use.

As I read, I jot down key thoughts and ideas, which become the grist for sermons or articles. Not infrequently an insight jumps out that can be of value to someone I know. It has often been a form of ministry to make a copy of that particular quote or reference and send it along as a piece of encouragement or instruction.

If an author has been particularly stimulating to my mind and heart, I will attempt to acquire everything he or she has written. And I will take careful note of bibliographies, footnotes, and indexes for material worth checking into myself.

Over the years, I have learned to ask anyone I know to be a student or reader of any kind, "What are you reading?" If the person can suggest a half dozen titles, I am most grateful and put them on a reading list. You can always tell the readers in a group when someone mentions a particularly excellent book. The readers are the ones who immediately take out notebook or reference card and jot down the name and author.

WE GROW THROUGH DISCIPLINED STUDY

A third way to grow mentally is through the discipline of study. The amount of time spent studying will vary for all of us and will have a lot to do with our vocations. Preachers simply have to study if they are going to provide the sort of pulpit "feeding" that they have been mandated to do.

In my earliest years of ministry, when this business of mental growth had not yet become a discipline for me, most of my study was what I now call *defensive study*. By that I mean that I studied frantically simply because I had an upcoming sermon to preach or talk to give. And all my study was centered on the completion of that task.

But later I discovered the importance of something I now call *offensive study*. This is study that has as its objective the gathering of large clusters of information and insight out of which future sermons and talks, books, and articles may grow. In the former kind of study, one is restricted to one chosen subject. In the latter, one is exploring, turning up truth and understanding from scores of sources. Both forms of study, offensive and defensive, are necessary in my life.

We grow when we pursue the discipline of offensive study. This is done through reading, taking occasional courses that stretch our minds, taking on challenges that force us to learn new things, and exploring various disciplines for the sheer joy of learning more about God's world.

I have found that summer is an ideal time for great offensive study; winter is not. Each year I set aside certain books and projects with which I wish to acquaint myself, and when the summer months provide extra space, I get busy. It is to be hoped that by the end of the summer I will be ready to move into the heavier months of the year with considerable amounts of raw material in my notebooks for sermons and Bible studies throughout the coming year.

As I mentioned earlier in this book, my study time is best accomplished in the early morning hours. But I am able to achieve it only because I have budgeted space for it in the calendar far in advance of the date. If I cheat on the time, I almost always end up regretting it. It is a date that ought never to be broken.

I have a supportive wife who protects and encourages my study time, and that is part of her growth as well. In our early years of marriage and ministry she had to learn the importance of offensive and defensive study just as I had to. As a young wife, when she saw me reading a book or sitting at my desk, she didn't hesitate to interrupt me. After all, it was easy to surmise, what is a thirty-second interruption for a question or a quick break to take out the garbage?

But Gail came to see that study is hard work for me and that interruptions often shatter mental momentum. With that realization, she not only became a protector of my time but a creator of it, skillfully admonishing me if she caught me wasting any of it or procrastinating on my commitments. None of my books would ever have been written if she had not determined with me that my writing was the will of God and that I would need her support as well as her prodding.

Some months ago I led a seminar for pastors on the subject of preaching, and discussed the matters of study and preparation. Since a number of spouses were present when I spoke, I said to the group, "Now some of you may be tempted to think that when your husband or wife is reading, they are really expending second-class time. So you are liable to feel free to interrupt them on impulse. What you need to realize is that they are working every bit as much as the carpenter who is in his shop sharpening the blade of a saw. Within reason, you ought not only to avoid interrupting your spouses, you ought to try your best to maximize their privacy if you want them to grow in effectiveness."

A couple of months later, a couple came up to me at another meeting where I was giving some talks. They were hand in hand and both beaming. The young man extended his hand and said, "We've come to thank you for changing our lives."

Since I'm not given to thinking that I can change lives very often, I was curious to know what I had done.

The wife responded, "We were present at your seminar on preaching a few months back, and you told us about the importance of reading and studying as work. You emphasized the guarding of one another's times for that. Remember?"

Yes, I certainly remembered.

"I realized," she went on to say, "that I'd never seen my husband's reading and study from that perspective. I promised God that I would do things differently when we got home—"

"—and it's changed my life," the young pastor said. "We're grateful to you."

Studying means developing good filing systems to store my information so that it is never wasted. It means making sacrifices to acquire a good library of reference books. But most of all, it means determination and discipline. And the result is always growth.

One more comment about the importance of studying for all of us. I have talked primarily about pastors because that is my world, and because study is so important to pastors. But I am speaking in principle to all Christians, to all men and women. I have realized the importance not only of my wife's making it possible for me to study but of my making it possible for her to study. This is a mutual discipline to which we encourage one another—both of us should be engaging in growth of the mind.

I want to make clear that this means that *we who are husbands need to ask whether or not we are creating and guarding time for our wives to read and study.* In the process of marriage counseling, we talk to many couples whose problem is uneven intellectual growth. After ten or fifteen years of marital relationship, one is growing while the other is not. Frankly, we most often encounter the problem of the wife's continuing to maintain intellectual momentum into her forties while the husband prefers sitting in front of the television set. But the problem can work both ways.

You can recognize students of every age primarily because they tend to be notetakers. Many years ago Gail and I adopted a special size notebook paper and bought dozens of looseleaf binders. All of our notes go into those books under special topical codes. We go virtually nowhere without paper so that we are ready to record the thoughts of someone who might come across our path and have something significant to say. One never knows when he will turn up a book or come upon an experience worth recording for future reference.

The Christian who wants to grow will always take notes

when sermons are being preached or Bible classes are being taught. It is one practical way of asserting faith that God is going to give the listener something that will be useful in the future in the service of others. Good notetaking is one way to store the information and insights that are constantly coming at us, and therefore to take advantage of all the possible growth that is available to us.

The Old Testament scribe Ezra believed in the growth of the mind. "And Ezra set himself to study the law of the Lord, to do it, and to teach its statutes in all of Israel." The order of this description of personal growth in a man's private world is worth noting: he studied; he did what he learned; he shared what was worthwhile. Ezra was a professional student of sorts, putting in far more time than any of us will ever do. But he set a great precedent. And because his mind and spirit were full, God tapped Ezra for the gigantic task of leading a large task force of men across the wilderness to rebuild Jerusalem.

If you were to come to our home today and take that old Webster biography off the shelf, you would discover that we have slit open every page so that we could read the story of that great American's life. The book still looks terribly worn, but now it is worn for the right reason: it has finally been read!

Like the book when we found it, many people show the outer marks of the wear and tear of life. But inside large areas of their private world remain unopened. They are disorganized within because they have never stretched and conditioned their minds to handle the information and challenges of the age. They have not taken advantage of all that God has placed here for us to discover, enjoy, and use.

But when we take seriously the growth and development of our minds, a beautiful thing happens. We come to know God more fully, and we are infinitely more useful in the service of others, for in just the way that creation was originally designed, we—our sharpened minds—begin to reflect the glory of God also.

What a beautiful thing to see: a human being in God's world with a sharpened mind, having opened every page with insight and truth.

Sector Four

Memo to the Disorganized:

If my private world is in order, it will be because I regularly choose to enlarge the spiritual center of my life.

10
Order in the Garden

Howard Rutledge, a United States Air Force pilot, was shot down over North Viet Nam during the early stages of the war. He spent several miserable years in the hands of his captors before being released at the war's conclusion.

In his book *In the Presence of Mine Enemies*, he reflects upon the resources from which he drew in those arduous days when life seemed so intolerable.

> During those longer periods of enforced reflection it became so much easier to separate the important from the trivial, the worthwhile from the waste. For example, in the past, I usually worked or played hard on Sundays and had no time for church. For years Phyllis [his wife] had encouraged me to join the family at church. She never nagged or scolded—she just kept hoping. But I was too busy, too preoccupied, to spend one or two short hours a week thinking about the really important things.
>
> Now the sights and sounds and smells of death were all around me. My hunger for spiritual food soon outdid my hunger for a steak. Now I wanted to know about that part of me that will never die. Now I wanted to talk about God and Christ and the church. But in Heartbreak [the name POWs gave their prison camp] solitary confinement, there was no pastor, no Sunday-School teacher, no Bible, no hymnbook, no community of believers to guide and sustain me. *I had completely neglected the spiritual dimension of my life. It took prison to show me how empty life is without God.* (Italics added)[1]

1. Howard Rutledge and Phyllis Rutledge with Mel White and Lyla White, *In the Presence of Mine Enemies* (Old Tappan, N.Y.: Fleming Revell, 1973), p. 34.

It took the pressure of a POW camp to show Rutledge that there was a center to his private world that he had been neglecting virtually all of his life. I like to refer to this center as a person's spirit; others call it the soul. You can't physiologically locate the spiritual center of a person's private world, but it is there. It is eternal, and it is the point at which we most intimately commune with our heavenly Father. The spirit can never lose its eternal nature, but it can exist in a state of such disorganization that almost no communion with God is possible. That usually leads to a general chaos in other parts of one's private world.

The Christian is theologically convinced of the existence of the soul. But many Christians struggle with the quality of life within that center. At least that is the impression I get when I listen for very long to those who are willing to talk about the meaning of private spiritual activity. Many men and women are painfully dissatisfied with their level of contact with God. "I just don't feel like I get through to Him very often" is a typical comment.

A disorganized spirit often means lack of inner serenity. For some, what should be tranquility is in fact only numbness or emptiness. Some suffer from restlessness, a feeling that they never quite measure up to the expectations they think God has for them. A common concern is the inability to maintain spiritual momentum, to have reasonably consistent attitudes and desires. "I start out my week with great intentions," a young person comments, "but by Wednesday morning, I've lost interest. I just can't sustain a spiritual life that is satisfying. So I get to the point where I'm tired of trying."

THE QUICK FIX

A look at the great saints of Scripture sometimes makes us envious. We reflect upon the burning bush experience of Moses, Isaiah's vision in the Temple, and the confrontation Paul had on the road to Damascus.

We are tempted to say, "If I could have had an experience like any of those, I'd be spiritually fixed for life." We think our spirituality might be enhanced by some dramatic moment that would indelibly burn itself upon our consciousness. Having been so impressed by such a spectacular touch with God, we would never be tempted to doubt the matter again.

That is one reason many of us are tempted to reach out for a sort of "quick fix" that makes God seem real and more intimate. Some feel deeply enriched if they are caused to feel terribly guilty by a preacher who angrily thunders forth with accusations and denunciations. Others quest after emotional experiences that lift them out of themselves into ecstatic levels. There are those who immerse themselves in endless rounds of Bible teaching and study, making the search for pure doctrine a way of finding satisfactory intimacy with God. Still others pursue spirituality through busyness in the church. Usually our choice of these or other ways of filling the seemingly empty spirit is based upon our psychological temperament—what most effectively touches us for the moment and makes us feel at peace.

But the fact is that the average person—like you and me—is not likely to have a great biblical confrontation; nor would we be satisfied by the dramatic experiences that happen to others. If we are ever to develop a spiritual life that gives contentment, it will be because we approach spiritual living as a discipline, much as the athlete trains his body for competition.

One thing is certain. If we do not choose to take on that discipline, there will come a day—as it came for Howard Rutledge—when we will regret that we had not undertaken the challenge.

CULTIVATING THE GARDEN

How shall we describe this center, this inner spiritual territory where encounters are almost too sacred for words? Beyond the theological definitions, we are left with not much more than a collection of metaphors.

David of the Psalms was thinking in metaphors when he imagined his inner spirit to be like a pasture where God, the shepherd, led him as a lamb. In his metaphor, there were calm waters, green pastures, and tables loaded with food to be eaten in safety. This was a place, David said, where the soul was restored.

The eighteenth-century Christian poet William Cowper used the metaphor of a quiet pool:

> A life all turbulence and noise may seem
> To him that leads it wise and to be praised,
> But wisdom is a pearl with most success
> Sought in still waters.
>
> (from *The Task*, book 3)

For me the appropriate metaphor for the inner spiritual center is a garden, a place of potential peace and tranquility. This garden is a place where the Spirit of God comes to make self-disclosure, to share wisdom, to give affirmation or rebuke, to provide encouragement, and to give direction and guidance. When this garden is in proper order, it is a quiet place, and there is an absence of busyness, of defiling noise, of confusion.

The inner garden is a delicate place, and if not properly maintained it will be quickly overrun by intrusive undergrowth. God does not often walk in disordered gardens. And that is why inner gardens that are ignored are said to be empty.

That is exactly what Howard Rutledge was struggling with when the pressure was at its highest in "Heartbreak" prison. Total isolation, frequent beatings, and deteriorating health had made his world a hostile place. What resources did he have to draw upon that would sustain him? According to his own admission he'd squandered opportunities earlier in life to store up strength and resolve in his inner garden. "I was too busy, too preoccupied," he says, "to spend one or two short hours a week thinking about the really important things." Nevertheless, what little he had from his childhood, he seized and developed. Suddenly, God was a very real and very important part of his existence.

Bringing order to the spiritual dimension of our private worlds is spiritual gardening. It is the careful cultivation of spiritual ground. The gardener turns up soil, pulls out unwanted growth, plans the use of the ground, plants seeds, waters and nourishes, and enjoys the harvests that result. All of this is what many have called spiritual discipline.

I love the words of Brother Lawrence, a reflective Christian of many centuries ago who used the metaphor of a chapel:

> It is not needful always to be in church to be with God. We make a chapel of our heart, to which we can from time to time withdraw to have gentle, humble, loving communion with Him. Everyone is able to have these familiar conversations with God. Some more, some less—He knows our capabilities. *Let us make a start. Perhaps He only waits for us to make one whole-hearted resolve.* Courage! We have but a short time to live. (Italics added)[2]

Let us begin soon, Brother Lawrence coaxes us; time is short! The discipline of the spirit must begin *now*.

PRIVILEGES WE CAN LOSE

Unless we make that start, we lose out on a number of privileges that God designed in order to make us fully alive. For example, *we will never learn to enjoy the eternal and infinite perspective on reality* that we were created to have. Our powers of judgment will be substantially curtailed.

David shows us a bit of the eternal perspective when he writes of the "kings of the earth" launching movements and systems by which they think to replace God (Psalm 2:2). David would have been intimidated by these kings and movements had he not had the perspective of an eternal and sovereign God, whom he pictures as sitting in the heavens laughing over all these futile machinations. The result? David was not given to fear, as some might have been if their eternal perspective was lacking.

If the spiritual center of our private world goes undisciplined, a second privilege we will lack will be *a vital, life-giving friendship with Christ*. Again, David was very much aware of the loss of this kind of contact with his God when he sinned with Bathsheba. He could stand it just so long, and then he went racing to God with a cry of confession and a plea

2. Brother Lawrence, *The Practice of the Presence of God*, trans. E. M. Blaiklock (Nashville: Thomas Nelson, 1982).

for restoration. That intimacy simply meant too much to him.

A third privilege undisciplined spirits will lose is *the fear of accountability to God*. There will be a growing forgetfulness that all we are and have comes from His good hand, and we will fall into the rut of assuming it is all ours. This happened to Uzziah, king of Judah, who had had a great relationship with God and then let it lapse (2 Chronicles 26). The result was a growth in pride that led to an embarrassing downfall. He began a hero; he ended the fool. The difference was the growing chaos and disorder in his inner garden.

Letting the spiritual center fall into disrepair means, fourth, that we lose *the awareness of our real size in comparison to the Creator*. And conversely, we forget our *specialness and value before Him as His sons and daughters*. Forgetting these things, we make the mistakes of the Prodigal Son and end up making a series of disastrous judgments that have painful consequences.

Finally, a neglected, disordered spiritual center usually means that we have little *reserve or resolve for crisis moments* such as failure, humiliation, suffering, the death of a loved one, or loneliness. This was Rutledge's desperate situation. How unlike Paul in the Roman jail: everyone had left him, for good or bad reasons; but he was sure he was not alone. And where did such assurance come from? It came from years of spiritual discipline, of inner gardening that produced a place where he and God could meet alone regardless of the hostility of the public world about him.

WHAT WILL IT TAKE?

When the inner garden is under cultivation and God's Spirit is present, harvests are regular events. The fruits? Things like courage, hope, love, endurance, joy, and lots of peace. Unusual capacities for self-control, the ability to discern evil and to ferret out truth are also reaped. As the writer of the Proverbs put it:

> For wisdom will enter your heart,
> And knowledge will be pleasant to your soul;

Discretion will guard you,
Understanding will watch over you,
To deliver you from the way of evil,
From the man who speaks perverse things.

(Proverbs 2:10)

Richard Foster quotes a favorite author of mine, Thomas Kelly:

> We feel honestly the pull of many obligations and try to fulfill them all. And we are unhappy, uneasy, strained, oppressed, and fearful we shall be shallow. . . . We have hints that there is a way of life vastly richer and deeper than all this hurried existence, a life of unhurried serenity and peace and power. If only we could slip over into that Center! . . . We have seen and known some people who have found this deep Center of living, where the fretful calls of life are integrated, where No as well as Yes can be said with confidence.[3]

Kelly says it well; if only we could slip over into that Center!

Down through the centuries the Christian mystics were the ones who took spiritual discipline most seriously. They studied it, practiced it, and occasionally carried the disciplines to unhealthy and dangerous extremes. But they believed that there had to be regular experiences of withdrawal from routines and relationships to seek God in an inner garden. They were quick to tell us that church services and religious celebrations were far from adequate. A man or a woman had to develop a chapel, still waters, or a garden in the private world, they said. There was no alternative.

Jesus certainly pursued the discipline of His spirit. We know that David did. And so did Moses, the apostles, and Paul, who wrote of his own routines:

> I run in such a way, as not without aim; I box in such a way, as not beating the air; but I buffet my body and make it my slave, lest possibly, after I have preached to others, I myself should be disqualified (1 Corinthians 9:26–27).

3. Cited in Richard Foster, *Freedom of Simplicity* (New York: Harper & Row, 1981), p. 78.

Have we cheapened this spiritual discipline, this cultivation of the inner garden? Today Christians talk about the importance of "quiet time," a daily devotional often reduced to a system or method that is swift and streamlined. We boil it down to seven minutes or thirty minutes, depending on how much time we have available. We use Bible study guides, devotional guides, devotional booklets, and carefully organized prayer lists. All of which is nice—better, I suppose, than nothing—but not nearly as effective as what the mystics had in mind.

A major Christian magazine called me not long ago to ask if I would spend a day with an outstanding Christian leader from another country who was visiting our city of Boston. They wanted me to lead him through an in-depth interview about himself, so that readers could gain insight into him as a person. I called on him to request permission for the conversation.

"And what shall we talk about?" he asked me.

"I thought we'd talk about your life as a preacher, a writer, and a scholar," I said. "Perhaps we could get into your views of family life, friendships, and your spiritual disciplines—"

"My spiritual disciplines?" he broke in.

"Yes," I came back. "A lot of people would love to know something of the ways in which you've pursued a personal walk with God."

I'll never forget his response.

"That part of my life is far too private to share with anyone."

I still think that many of us who are younger men and women in ministry would have profited from this older man's insights; nevertheless, I heard what he was trying to say. This part of his private world was just that: strictly private. It had been developed in secrecy, and it would stay that way. He and God would share it together—and alone. It would not be reduced to a system.

What will it take to force us into disciplined cultivation of the inner garden of our private worlds? Will it require an experience of severe suffering? That is what history seems to say over and over again: those under pressure seek God, because there is nothing else. Those smothered in "blessings" tend to drift with the current. And that is why I question the word *blessing* sometimes. Surely something is not a blessing if it seduces us away from inward spiritual cultivation.

Can the importance of the inward center ever be appreciated until we have come close to death, defeat, or humiliation? But the command and the precedents come to us over and over again, in the Scriptures and through the history of the great saints. He who orders his inner spiritual world will make a place for God to visit and speak. And when that voice is heard, it will be unlike anything else ever spoken. That is what Howard Rutledge discovered. But it took a prisoner of war experience to force him to find it out.

Brother Lawrence says, "Let us make a start." Thomas Kelly admonishes: "Slip over into that Center!" Christ calls, "Come learn of Me." How does this discipline of the spirit happen?

Memo to the Disorganized:

If my private world is in order, it will be because I am unafraid to be alone and quiet before Christ.

11

No Outer Props Necessary

When E. Stanley Jones, Methodist missionary to India, was an aged man, he had a debilitating stroke that left him immobile and virtually speechless. But not faithless. "I need no outer props to hold up my faith," he wrote, "for my faith holds me." But he sadly saw that his was not the experience of everyone around him.

> I was talking to a bishop who had retired. He was frustrated. When he was no longer in the limelight of the bishopric, he was frustrated and told me so. He wanted to know the secret of victorious living. I told him it was in self-surrender. *The difference was in giving up the innermost self to Jesus.* The difference was in the texture of the things that held him. When the outer strands were broken by retirement, the inner strands were not enough to hold him. Apparently he had a case of "limelight-itis" instead of a case of surrender to Jesus. *Fortunately, with me, surrender to Jesus was the primary thing, and when the outer strands were cut by this stroke, my life didn't shake.* (Italics added)[1]

Jones understood what Thomas Kelly is saying when he calls for us to slip over into the center. Who of us would not like to have Jones's perspective and endurance? But how many of us are destined, due to neglect of our inner garden, to fall

1. E. Stanley Jones, *The Divine Yes* (Nashville: Abingdon, 1975), p. 63.

into the trap the bishop set for himself? How do we cultivate the inner garden of our private worlds?

Because this book is not primarily a treatment of spiritual disciplines, I cannot survey all the ways the saints have found to strengthen the inner spirit. Instead, I have selected four spiritual exercises of fundamental importance, exercises that I find many Christians neglecting. They are: the pursuit of *solitude and silence;* regular *listening to God;* the experience of *reflection and meditation;* and *prayer as worship and intercession.*

SILENCE AND SOLITUDE

The desert fathers of centuries ago, Henri Nouwen tells us, understood the importance of a silent environment for the cultivation of the spirit when they called out to one another, *"Fuge, terche, et quisset"*—silence, solitude, and inner peace.

Few of us can fully appreciate the terrible conspiracy of noise there is about us, noise that denies us the silence and solitude we need for this cultivation of the inner garden. It would not be hard to believe that the archenemy of God has conspired to surround us at every conceivable point in our lives with the interfering noises of civilization that, when left unmuffled, usually drown out the voice of God. He who walks with God will tell you plainly, God does not ordinarily shout to make Himself heard. As Elijah discovered, God tends to whisper in the garden.

Recently I visited a missionary center in Latin America where workmen were constructing a sound studio for a radio station. They were taking careful measures to soundproof the rooms so that no noise from the city streets could mar the broadcasts and recordings that would emanate from that place. We must learn to soundproof the heart against the intruding noises of the public world in order to hear what God has to say. I love the words of Mother Teresa of Calcutta:

We need to find God, and he cannot be found in noise and restlessness. *God is the friend of silence.* See how nature—trees, flowers, grass—grow in silence; see the stars, the moon and sun, how they move in silence . . . the more we receive in silent prayer, the more we can give in our active life. *We need silence to be able to touch souls.* The essential thing is not what we say, but what God says to us and through us. All our words will be useless unless they come from within—words which do not give the light of Christ increase the darkness. (Italics added)[2]

Our worlds are filled with the noise of endless music, chatter, and busy schedules. In many homes there is a stereo in almost every room, in every car, in each office, in the elevator. Now I see that even when I dial a friend at his office I am offered music over the phone until he comes to answer my call. With the intrusion of so much noise, when can we withdraw and monitor the still, small voice of God?

We are so accustomed to noise that we grow restless without it. Worshipers in a congregation find it difficult to sit in quietness for more than a minute or two; we assume that something has gone wrong and someone has forgotten his part. Most of us would find it difficult to go even an hour without saying anything or hearing a word from someone.

The struggle can be the same in the experience of *solitude*. Not only are we often bothered by silence, but few of us are comfortable with times of aloneness. But there must be times of rhythmic withdrawal. There must be those moments when we break from routines, from other relationships, from the demands of the outer world to meet Him in the garden. It cannot be done in large meetings and spectacular celebrations.

Nouwen quotes Thomas Merton, a student of those strange mystics of the early Christian centuries who sometimes pursued solitude to an extreme. What he says about them is instructive. Why did they seek solitude?

They knew that they were helpless to do any good for others as long as they floundered about in the wreckage [of humanity]. But once they got a foothold on solid ground, things were different. Then they had not only the power but even the obligation to pull the whole world to safety after them.[3]

2. Malcolm Muggeridge, *Something Beautiful for God* (Garden City, N.Y.: Image, 1977), p. 48.
3. Henri J. M. Nouwen, *The Way of the Heart* (New York: Seabury, 1981), p. 39.

It is interesting that God's angel used silence to curb the impossibility thinking of aged Zacharias when he found that he and his wife were to become the parents of John the Baptizer. If Zacharias could not accept the word of God as it had come to him, then his tongue would be stilled for several months, and he could think about it. On the other hand, when Elizabeth, his wife, realized what was happening, she withdrew, the Scripture says, partially because that was the custom of pregnant women but also, I believe, because she needed to meditate upon the strange and mysterious things that were happening.

Then there was Mary, who, when she learned of her role in the birth of our Lord, did not blurt out all of God's plans, but chose silence. "Mary treasured up all these things, pondering them in her heart" (Luke 2:19). Christ's coming was heralded not only by singing and praise from angels but also by silence from human partners who needed solitude in order to think through and appreciate the wonder.

Wayne Oates tells us,

> Silence is not native to my world. Silence, more than likely, is a stranger to your world, too. If you and I ever have silence in our noisy hearts, we are going to have to grow it. . . . You can nurture silence in your noisy heart if you value it, cherish it, and are eager to nourish it.[4]

Silence and solitude have not come easily to me at all. I once equated them with laziness, inaction, and unproductivity. The minute I was alone, my mind exploded with a list of things I should do: phone calls to make, papers I should be filing, books unread, sermons unprepared, and people I ought to see.

The slightest noise outside my study door was a massive intrusion to concentration. It seemed as if my hearing became supersensitive, and I could overhear conversations at the other end of our house. My curiosity strained to hear what was being said. Because my study is near our laundry room, it

4. Wayne E. Oates, *Nurturing Silence in a Noisy Heart* (Garden City, N.Y.: Doubleday, 1979), p. 3.

never seemed to fail that the moment I got into spiritual activity the washing machine would decide the load inside was unbalanced, and its foghorn-like buzzer would go off, insisting that I, since everyone else was upstairs, should come and readjust the wash.

But concentrating even when there was silence became desperately difficult. I learned that I had to warm up, to accept the fact that for about fifteen minutes my mind would do everything it could to resist the solitude. So among the things I did was to start by reading or writing on the subject of my spiritual pursuits. Slowly, it seemed, my conscious mind got the message: we (my mind and I) were going to worship and meditate, and the sooner the mind got in touch with the inner garden on the matter, the better it would be.

I expect that I will fight this battle of solitude and silence for as long as I live. I want to say, however, that as time has gone by, and I have begun to reap the benefits of silent time, there has been a growing hunger for more of it. But still there is that first resistance to be overcome. When one is an activist by nature, withdrawal can be hard work. But it is a necessary labor.

For me that silence and solitude is best found in the early morning hours. So it goes in that spot on my calendar before anyone can suggest other purposes for the time. For others, it may be late in the evening. But anyone wanting to bring order to the spiritual sector of the private world must find the place and the time that fits his personal temperament.

LISTENING TO GOD

It must have been like a cold shower on an early morning for Moses when he came off the mountain after having been with God and found his Hebrew people dancing around a golden calf. For days he had lived in the presence of holiness itself, and a sense of God's glory and righteousness had been burned into his spirit. But now this spectacle! He was heartbroken.

How had it happened? While Moses had been listening to God, his brother Aaron, high priest of all the people, had been listening to the people. The input the two received was decidedly different. When Moses listened, he received God's revelation of the law of righteousness. When Aaron listened, he heard complaints, wishes, and demands. Moses brought with him uncompromised standards of heaven; Aaron caved in to the whims of men. *It was all in the listening.*

The garden of our private worlds is cultivated not only when we draw apart for times of silence and solitude, but also when we begin, in that environment, to deliberately practice the discipline of listening. I have not met many who know how to listen to God. Busy people find it hard to learn how. Most Christians learned at an early age how to talk to God, but they did not learn to listen as well.

We listen every time we open the Scriptures and place ourselves at the feet of the inspired writers who unfold the mysteries of God. We listen, as I shall point out later on, when we sensitize ourselves to the proddings of God's indwelling Holy Spirit. Listening happens when the preacher or teacher of Scripture, empowered by God's Spirit, brings instruction.

All these things are worth discussing (not to mention doing!). But right now I would like to talk about another exercise, one that can form a base for all the other ways of listening.

JOURNAL KEEPING—A WAY TO LISTEN TO GOD

When I studied some of the mystic and contemplative Christians, I found that one practical way to learn to listen to God speak in the garden of my private world was to keep a journal. With a pencil in hand ready to write, I found that there was an expectancy, a readiness to hear anything God might wish to whisper through my reading and reflection.

That discovery came almost twenty years ago, while I was reading a biography. The subject of the book had maintained a lifelong habit of recording his spiritual pilgrimage. I was now benefitting from that discipline, even though he had been writing more for his own benefit than for mine. As he had been tutored by God's Spirit, he had kept careful notes. What a tool that must have been—something to go back to again and again and trace the hand of God upon his life.

I became impressed by the fact that many, many godly men

and women down through the centuries had also kept journals, and I began to wonder if they had not put their fingers upon an aid to spiritual growth. To satisfy my curiosity, I decided to experiment and began keeping one for myself.

At first it was difficult. I felt self-conscious. I was worried that I would lose the journal or that someone might peek inside to see what I'd said. But slowly the self-consciousness began to fade, and I found myself sharing in the journal more and more of the thoughts that flooded my inner spirit. Into the journal went words describing my feelings, my fear and sense of weakness, my hopes, and my discoveries about where Christ was leading me. When I felt empty or defeated, I talked about that too in the journal.

Slowly I began to realize that the journal was helping me come to grips with an enormous part of my inner person that I had never been fully honest about. No longer could fears and struggles remain inside without definition. They were surfaced and confronted. And I became aware, little by little, that God's Holy Spirit was directing many of the thoughts and insights as I wrote. On paper, the Lord and I were carrying on a personal communion. He was helping me, in the words of David, to "search my heart." He was prodding me to put words to my fears, shapes to my doubts. And when I was candid about it, then there would often come out of Scripture or from the meditations of my own heart, the reassurances, the rebukes, and the admonishments that I so badly needed. But this began to happen only when the journal was employed.

Because I found that my prayers often seemed disconnected and that I was not able to concentrate (or even stay awake), I often wondered if I could ever develop a vigorous worship and intercessory life. Again, the journal provided a vehicle for writing prayers when my spoken prayers lacked cohesiveness. Now prayer content became sensible, and I began to enjoy recording my progress as a believer and a follower of Christ.

A key contribution of the journal became its record of not only the good moments, but the bad times as well. When there came times of discouragement, even of despair, I was able to describe my feelings and tell how God's Spirit ultimately ministered to me to strengthen my resolve. These became special passages to look back upon; they helped me celebrate the power of God in the midst of my own weakness.

I am reminded that the Lord once had the Israelites save "three quarts of manna" (Exodus 16:33, TLB) so that they would have a tangible reminder of His constant care. The journal became my "three quarts," for in it I had all the testimony I needed to the faithfulness of God in my life. This remembering process, which a journal provides, is very significant.

Today after twenty years of journal keeping, I have acquired a habit. Hardly a morning passes that I do not open the journal and record the things I hear God saying through my reading, meditation, and daily experience. When the journal opens, so does the ear of my heart. If God is going to speak, I am ready to listen.

When W. E. Sangster was a young pastor in England, he grew increasingly restive about the spiritual climate in the English Methodist church. Brooding upon his own role in future leadership, he turned to his journal to sharpen his thinking. In it he could lay out his innermost thoughts and meditations on paper and perceive what God was laying on his heart. Reading his thoughts several decades later reveals how one man used a journal to bring order to his private world so that he could later be used to press order into his outer world. One day he wrote:

> I feel a commission to work under God for the revival of this branch of His Church—careless of my own reputation; indifferent to the comments of older and jealous men. I am thirty-six. If I am to serve God in this way, I must no longer shrink from the task—but do it.
>
> I have examined my heart for ambition. I am certain it is not there. I hate the criticism I shall evoke and the painful chatter of people. Obscurity, quiet browsing among books, and the service of simple people is my taste—but by the will of God, this is my task. . . .
>
> Bewildered and unbelieving, I heard the voice of God saying to me, "I want to sound the note through you." O God, did ever an

apostle shrink from his task more? I dare not say "No" but, like Jonah, I would fain run away.

God help me. God help me. What is the initial task? To call Methodism back to its real work.[5]

Sangster's words offer a beautiful example of a man listening to God in his private world through the use of a journal. He put his dreams on paper in order to separate destructive ambition from genuine call. He searched for hints that his thoughts were not those of his heavenly Father. He wrestled with self-doubt. Isn't it interesting that, as he perceived the divine whisper, he transformed into print the still, small voice of his Lord?

HOW TO JOURNAL

When I have spoken in public on "journaling," I have found that many people are intensely interested and have many questions. Their initial curiosity tends to center on technique more than anything else. What does your journal look like? How often do you write in it? What sort of things do you include? Isn't it really just a diary? Do you let your wife read your journal? Although I am by no means an expert journal keeper, I endeavor to answer as best I can.

My own journals are spiral bound notebooks, which I purchase at an office supply store. They are rather unimpressive in appearance. I can complete one of these notebooks in about three months. The virtue of their smaller size lies not only in portability but in the fact that, should one ever be lost, I would not have misplaced a year or more of writing.

I write in my journal almost every day, but I am not overly disturbed if an occasional day passes without an entry. I have made it a habit to write in the earliest moments of my time of spiritual exercise, and for me that means the first thing in the morning.

And what is in there? An account of things that I accomplished in the preceding day, people I met, things I learned, feelings I experienced, and impressions I believe God wanted me to have.

5. Paul Sangster, *Doctor Sangster* (New York: Epworth, 1962), p. 109.

As I said before, I include prayers if I feel like writing them down, insights that come from reading the Bible and other spiritual literature, and concerns I have about my own personal behavior. I love to record things I am seeing in the lives of members of my family. I anticipate that someday our children will read through some of these journals, and if I can posthumously affirm them for things I see in their growing lives today, it will be a treasure for them.

All of this is part of listening to God. As I write, I am aware that what I am writing may actually be what God wants to tell me. I dare to presume that His Spirit is often operative in the things I am choosing to think about and record. And it becomes important to search my heart to see what conclusions He may be engendering, what matters He wishes to remind me about, what themes He hopes to stamp upon my private world.

On one recent occasion, as I was contemplating an enormous challenge I was facing in my ministry, my journal caught these reflective words:

> Lord, what do I really know about drawing upon your strength? I, with the shallow mind, the weak spirit, the minimal discipline. What is there of me that you could use? I have talents, but others have more and use them better. I have experience, but others have greater and have profited deeper. So what is there?

> Perhaps the answer lies somewhere in [Hudson] Taylor's comment: "God uses men who are weak and feeble enough to lean on him." But, Lord, I worry that while I may be weak enough, will I be smart enough to know from whence comes my help?

> Should you ordain that I do this task, what will sustain me? What of the sleepless nights when I shall be so lonely? The seductions toward applause? The temptation to believe the symbols of leadership? What will keep my judgments clear, my mind sharp, my spirit filled? Now I ask honestly, am I able to receive this cup? What will convince me of the needs of the lost? What will keep me sensitive to the poor? What will make me listen? Pray? Study? Remain simple? O God, nothing but a visitation from Thee.

As I write on consecutive pages of the journal, I also write from the back page toward the front. The back pages hold my list of people and concerns that I have chosen to make a matter of intercessory prayer. At the top of those pages I've written the phrase "Does my prayer list reflect the people and programs to which I am most committed?"

Then, continuing to work from the back pages toward the center of the journal, I often put in excerpts from my current reading that particularly impress me. Often, I will take time to simply read through many of these brief paragraphs. They may be prayers, reflective comments from the writings of people like St. Thomas, A. W. Tozer, and Amy Carmichael, or portions of Scripture.

When the daily record beginning at the front of the journal meets the daily reflections coming from the rear, I simply close the volume out and begin a new one. It has become one more scrapbook portraying my spiritual journey, with its struggles and its learning experiences. And the pile of spiritual scrapbooks continues to grow. Should our house ever begin to burn, and assuming all the family is properly evacuated, I think these journals would be the first things I would try to grab and take out the door with me.

Does my wife read my journals? I suppose she has occasionally sneaked a look. But frankly my handwriting is poor, and I do employ a sort of shorthand; so I suspect that she would have her hands full trying to decipher anything that I might have said. Our relationship is quite intimate enough, however, that there is little in there that would surprise her.

To those who are concerned about a potential lack of privacy in such matters, I suggest that they simply find a place where the journal could be locked up and kept from those you would rather not have see inside. If confidentiality is important, you should be able to find a way to maintain it. Worry about privacy is not an adequate reason for not attempting a journal.

Journal keeping becomes a habit for most people if they will stick with it for the better part of a year. Most people quit too quickly, never achieving the habit pattern, and that is unfortunate.

My journal accompanies me on trips. It helps me to maintain a record of those I have met, so that when I return again to places where I have visited, I can simply review my previous visit in the journal and pick up relationships where they may have been suspended due to distance.

This discussion of journal keeping has led me to talk of its benefits as regards interpersonal relationships. These benefits are certainly great. But the main value of a journal is as a tool for listening to the quiet Voice that comes out of the garden of the private world. Journal keeping serves as a wonderful tool for withdrawing and communing with the Father. When I write, it is as if I am in direct conversation with Him. And there is that sense that in the words that you are led to write, God's Spirit is mysteriously active, and communion at the deepest level is happening.

My mind goes back to Howard Rutledge in his prison camp. Every voice was a hostile one; every noise introduced the possibility of something about to go wrong. In such an ugly place, was there a friendly voice, a lovely sound to be heard anywhere? Yes, if you have trained your ears to hear in the inner garden. There the greatest of all sounds may be heard: those belonging to Him who seeks our companionship and growth. In the words of an old and very sentimental hymn:

> He speaks, and the sound of his voice
> Is so sweet the birds hush their singing.
>   (C. Austin Miles, "In the Garden")

Memo to the Disorganized:

If my private world is in order, it will be because I absorb
the words of Christ into my attitudes and actions.

12

Everything Has to Be Entered

E. Stanley Jones was not always the sort of person who could say, on a painful deathbed, "The innermost strands are the strongest. I need no outer props to hold up my faith, for my faith holds me." In the early days of his ministry there had come a temporary sinkhole collapse. For more than a year he had languished in both spiritual and physical ineffectiveness. "The spiritual sag brought on a physical sag," he wrote. "The outer collapse took place because the inner experience could not sustain it. I had made it a life motto that I would not preach what I was not experiencing, so the outer and the inner came together in collapse."[1]

The discipline of the spirit—what I have called the cultivation of the inner garden—depends upon the willingness of men and women of Christ to seek solitude and silence and to listen for the whisper of God.

But the things that we hear in solitude and silence must be internalized. I am writing this book with the technical assistance of a computer and a word processing program. When I first became acquainted with my computer, I had to learn the function of the "enter" key. The teaching manual instructed me that I could type anything I wanted on the screen in front of me. But until I touched the "enter" key, the com-

---

1. E. Stanley Jones, *Song of Ascents* (Nashville: Abingdon, 1968), p. 104.

puter would not "hear" or respond to a single word I had typed. All of my words, no matter how impressive, would just sit on the screen's surface until I entered them onto the heart (the "memory") of the computer.

I also have the ability to hear things *but not necessarily enter them.* What sits in my mind does not necessarily penetrate my heart.

Salvation Army evangelist Commissioner Samuel Logan Brengle, speaking of his spiritual disciplines, wrote:

> I do a lot of listening. Prayer, you know, is not meant to be a monologue, but a dialogue. It is a communion, a friendly talk. While the Lord communicates with me mainly through His Word, he gives me a great deal of comfort in a direct manner. By "comfort" I do not mean cuddling or coddling, but *assurance*—assurance of His presence with me and His pleasure in my service. It is like the comfort given by a military commander to his soldier or envoy whom he sends on a difficult mission: "You go, put on your armor, I'm watching you, and I'll send you all the reinforcements you need as they are needed." I have to be comforted that way a great deal. I don't just assume that God is near me and pleased with me; I must have a fresh witness daily.[2]

The Bible tells of another Samuel, a young boy interning in the Tabernacle under the discipleship of Eli, the high priest. In the night Samuel heard a voice calling his name. Running to Eli's bed, he assumed that he was being summoned for some task. But Eli had not called, and Samuel returned to his room. But the call came again and again. It was Eli who put things together and suggested how Samuel could respond the next time. "When you hear the voice again, Samuel, respond with these words: 'Speak, Lord, for your servant hears! In others words, Samuel, push the "enter" key.

Samuel did, and God spoke. The words of God penetrated his heart and changed his destiny.

We strengthen the innermost strands, as Jones put it, by making sure that God's words are entering the garden of our private worlds. Our first step in spiritual discipline is finding solitude and silence; the second step is learning to listen to

2. Clarence W. Hall, *Samuel Logan Brengle: Portrait of a Prophet* (Chicago: Salvation Army Supply & Purchasing Dept., 1933), p. 185.

God. The third step, the pushing of the "enter" key, is done through *reflection and meditation.*

Some Christians are uneasy and negative about the mention of such words. They think such practices can open a door to activity that is too undirected and that can lead to misguided conclusions. They conjure up images of people sitting in lotus positions and engaging in trancelike activities.

But the Bible is full of reflective or meditative passages and calls us to open our private worlds to them. Among the most popular are those passages out of the Psalms where the writer fixes his mind upon certain aspects of God's being and consistent care for His children.

The psalmist looked through all sorts of meditative lenses. For example, he saw God as a shepherd, as a commanding general, as a director of spiritual exercise.

The act of meditation is like tuning the spirit to heavenly frequencies. One takes a portion of Scripture and simply allows it to enter into the deepest recesses of self. There are often several different results: cleansing, reassurance, the desire to praise and give thanksgiving. Sometimes meditation on something of God's nature or His actions opens the mind to new guidance or a new awareness of something the Lord may be trying to say to us.

In his book of prayers John Baillie reveals a meditational mood when he prays:

Almighty God, in this quiet hour I seek communion with thee. From the fret and fever of the day's business, from the world's discordant noises, from the praise and blame of men, from the confused thoughts and vain imaginations of my own heart, I would now turn aside and seek the quietness of thy presence. All day long have I toiled and striven; but now in the stillness of heart and the clear light of thine eternity, I would ponder the pattern my life is weaving.[3]

Meditation of course can be done only when we have chosen an environment where there will be adequate amounts of time, silence, and privacy. One does not get much meditation

3. John Baillie, *A Diary of Private Prayer* (New York: Charles Scribner's Sons, 1949), p. 27.

done on a bus or when driving in traffic—although I have
heard people claim that was their time for the spiritual discipline.

Many of us will discover that it takes preparatory time in
order to meditate. You may have had the experience of coming
in from heavy exercise still breathing very hard. You know
that it is virtually impossible to sit down for several minutes
and be still. There is too much gasping and the catching of
breath for quiet sitting. The same is true in reflection. We
often enter the chamber to meet with God while we are still
emotionally out of breath. It is hard at first to concentrate our
thoughts and to bring them into the presence of the Lord. We
have to quietly relax for a short season while the mind ac-
customs itself to spiritual activity in the "garden" environment. Thus, it will take time—time some people are reluctant
to give.

Christians have always considered the Bible to be the central revelation of our faith and worthy of meditation. Let me
add that reading the great classics of Christian literature is a
must for spiritual growth. Down through the centuries there
have been men and women who have recorded their insights
and exercises for us to read. And although these books do not
carry the authoritative power of the Bible itself, they nevertheless contain an enormous amount of spiritual food.

Reflection and meditation demand a certain amount of
imagination. We read the first psalm, for example, and picture
a tree planted by a river. What is true about that tremendous
tree to which the writer likens the man or woman who walks
after God? In Psalm 19 we let our minds sweep across the
universe and imagine the celestial bodies and their incredible
message. When we read the passages describing Jesus' ministry, our reflecting minds place ourselves right into the story:
we see the Savior heal, hear Him teach, and respond to His
directives. In meditation we latch onto phrases from the
prophets, perhaps memorizing small portions, and we allow
the words to trickle down over the structures of our inner
being as we repeat them over and over again. From such exercises come new and wonderful conclusions. The word of God is
entering our private worlds. And because we have fixed our

attention upon His word, we can be sure the Holy Spirit will guide our meditations.

C. S. Lewis, writing to an American friend, speaks of reflective exercises:

> We all go through periods of dryness in our prayers, don't we? I doubt . . . whether they are necessarily a bad symptom. I sometimes suspect that what we *feel* to be our best prayers are really our worst; that what we are enjoying is the satisfaction of apparent success, as in executing a dance or reciting a poem. Do our prayers sometimes go wrong because we insist on trying to talk to God when He wants to talk with us. Joy tells me that once, years ago, she was haunted one morning by a feeling that God wanted something of her, a persistent pressure like the nag of a neglected duty. And till mid-morning she kept on wondering what it was. But the moment she stopped worrying, the answer came through as plain as a spoken voice. It was "I don't want you to *do* anything. I want to *give* you something"; and immediately her heart was peace and delight. St. Augustine says, "God gives where He finds empty hands." A man whose hands are full of parcels can't receive a gift. Perhaps these parcels are not always sins or earthly cares, but sometimes our own fussy attempts to worship Him in *our* way. Incidentally, what most often interrupts my own prayers is not great distractions but tiny ones—things one will have to do or avoid in the course of the next hour.[4]

Here is a good example of the exercise of reflection and meditation. God speaks; we listen, and the message is entered within the heart. The need for outer props is lessened; the inner garden is further cultivated. The man or woman of spiritual discipline is growing strong in the private world.

4. C. S. Lewis, *Letters to an American Lady* (Grand Rapids: Eerdmans, 1975), p. 73.

Memo to the Disorganized:

If my private world is in order, it will be because I have begun to pursue the discipline of seeing events and people through the eyes of Christ so that my prayers reflect my desire to be in alignment with His purposes and promises for them.

13

Seeing Through Heaven's Eyes

In an insightful little book on contemplative faith written more than sixty years ago, a European Christian by the name of Bridget Herman wrote:

> When we read the lives of the saints, we are struck by a certain large leisure which went hand in hand with a remarkable effectiveness. They were never hurried; they did comparatively few things, and these not necessarily striking or important; and they troubled very little about their influence. Yet they always seemed to hit the mark; every bit of their life told; their simplest actions had a distinction, an exquisiteness which suggested the artist. The reason is not far to seek. Their sainthood lay in their habit of referring the smallest actions to God. They lived in God; they acted from a pure motive of love towards God. They were as free from self-regard as from slavery to the good opinion of others. God saw and God rewarded: what else needed they? They possessed God and possessed themselves in God. Hence the inalienable dignity of these meek, quiet figures that seem to produce such marvelous effects with such humble materials.[1]

The fourth way we can enhance communion with God in the garden of our private worlds is through *prayer as worship and intercession*. This is what Bridget Herman says characterized

---

1. E. Herman, *Creative Prayer* (Cincinnati: Forward Movement, n.d.), p. 16.

the saints. "Their sainthood lay in their habit of referring the smallest actions to God."

"Let inward prayer be your last act before you fall asleep and the first act when you awake," Thomas Kelly wrote. "And in time you will find as did Brother Lawrence, that 'those who have the gale of the Holy Spirit go forward even in sleep.'"[2]

Most of us have never experienced this. Daily, disciplined prayer is one of the most difficult exercises Christians undertake.

Married men will often admit, for example, that praying with their wives is a very difficult thing. Why? They really don't have an answer. Sometimes pastors in a moment of self-revelation will reveal that the integrity of their prayer life is usually an embarrassment to them. And they also are hard pressed to explain it.

My impression after visiting with many Christians is that worship and intercession rank at the top of any list of spiritual struggles. No one would deny that prayer is important; but few believe their prayer life to be adequately developing. And this is a major reason the inner gardens of so many private worlds are in a state of disorder. It is why most of us would have a hard time saying, like E. Stanley Jones, "No outer props are necessary."

WHY WE HAVE TROUBLE PRAYING

Why do so many people have struggles when it comes to prayer? Let me suggest three possible reasons.

WORSHIP AND INTERCESSION SEEM TO BE UNNATURAL ACTS

Men and women were originally created to desire communion with God. But the effects of sin have dulled most of that original human desire. Sin turned a natural activity into an unnatural function.

My suspicion is that when sin affected man so deeply, it touched his spiritual dimensions most severely of all, while leaving the original physical appetites and desires virtually

2. Thomas R. Kelly, *A Testament of Devotion* (New York: Harper & Row, 1941), p. 39.

undiminished. Our instinctive preoccupations with food, sexual pleasure, and security are probably close to their original levels. It may be helpful to speculate that man in his sinless nature once probably had as great, if not greater, desire for communion with the Creator as he has for the satisfaction of the natural and very real appetites and instincts that we live with today. But the spiritual hunger, once undoubtedly powerful, has been terribly dulled by the power of sin. Thus, worship and intercession have become difficult challenges.

As a result, praying in any meaningful way militates against virtually everything within our natural selves and is foreign to what our culture teaches us as a way of life.

And that is the heart of the trouble. Few people realize how brainwashed each of us is. Messages bombard our private worlds everyday, telling us that anything of a spiritual nature is really a waste of time. From our earliest years we are subtly taught that the only way to achieve anything is through action. But prayer seems to be a form of inaction. To the person with a disordered private world, it does not seem to accomplish anything.

Until we believe that prayer is indeed a real and highly significant activity, that it does in fact reach beyond space and time to the God who is actually there, we will never acquire the habits of worship and intercession. In order to gain these habits, we must make a conscious effort to overcome the part of us that thinks that praying is not a natural part of life.

WORSHIP AND INTERCESSION ARE TACIT ADMISSIONS OF WEAKNESS

A second reason people find it difficult to enter into worship and intercession is that these acts are by nature admissions of personal weakness. In the acts of prayer, something within the inner garden acknowledges that we are utterly dependent upon the One to whom we address our words.

Now we can *say* that we are weak people, and we can *say* that we depend upon God for all of our sustenance; but the fact is that something deep within us is not willing to *recognize* it. There is something deep within that vigorously denies our dependence.

I have often been fascinated with the reluctance of many

Christian men to pray with their wives, or to feel free to take prayer leadership in a mixed group. It is not unusual for a Christian wife to complain, "My husband never prays with me, and I can't understand it."

The answer may lie in the fact that men have been taught in our culture never to reveal weakness or to engage in any activity that may show it. Prayer in its most authentic form acknowledges that we are weak and dependent upon our God Something in the male knows this and unconsciously fights having to identify with the fact of dependence.

On the other hand, it is my observation that most women, at least until recently, have never had to struggle to face their own weaknesses; and that may be one reason that, as a group, they feel more at ease in prayer than men.

A person shows significant spiritual growth when he finds it possible to admit that he needs a relationship with God in order to be the human being he was created to be. There is an enormous sense of liberation in that realization.

Brother Lawrence wrote:

> We must examine with care what are the virtues of which we stand most in need, what are those which are most difficult to win, the sins to which we most often fall, and the most frequent and inevitable occasions of our falling. We must turn to God in complete confidence in the hour of battle, abide strongly in the presence of his divine majesty, worship him humbly, and set before him our woes and our weaknesses. And thus we shall find in him all virtues though we may lack them all.[3]

Brother Lawrence seemed never to have any problems facing up to his weaknesses, and that is one reason his prayer life was so alive.

PRAYER SOMETIMES SEEMS TO BE UNRELATED TO ACTUAL RESULT

A third reason prayer comes hard to us is the fact that it seems frequently unrelated to actual results. Lest you think I am guilty of denying a substantial teaching of Scripture, hear me carefully. I do in fact believe that God answers prayer. But

Brother Lawrence, *The Practice of the Presence of God*, trans. E. M. Blaiklock (Nashville: Thomas Nelson, 1982), p. 70.

most of us have had enough experience to realize that His answers do not always come in forms or on schedules that we
would have designed.

As a very young pastor, I used to confess my confusion
about this matter of personal prayer to my wife. "Sometimes
it seems as if, on those weeks when I pray very little, my
sermons come out very powerful. And on those weeks when I
feel that I've really done my prayer work, I seem to preach my
worst. Now you tell me," I'd challenge her, "what does God
expect me to do when He doesn't seem to give me, pound for
pound, the blessings that match my prayer investment?"

Like others, I have prayed for healings, for miracles, for
guidance, and for assistance. Frankly, there were times I was
sure God would answer me because I had mustered strong
feelings of faith. But many of those times nothing happened—
or if it did, it was entirely unlike what I had anticipated.

We live in a society that is reasonably organized. Put a letter in the box, and it usually ends up where you want it to go.
Order an item from a catalog, and it usually comes to you in
the right size, color, and model. Ask someone to provide you a
service, and it is reasonable to expect that it will work out
that way. In other words, we are used to results in response to
our arrangements. That is why prayer can be discouraging for
some of us. How can we predict the result? We are tempted to
abandon prayer as a viable exercise and to try getting the
results ourselves.

But the fact is that my prayer life cannot be directly tied to
the results I expect or demand. I have had many opportunities by now to see that the things I want God to do in
response to my prayers can be unhealthy for me. I have begun
to see that *worship and intercession are far more the business
of aligning myself with God's purposes than asking Him to
align with mine.*

Henri Nouwen says it best when he writes:

Prayer is a radical conversion of all our mental processes because
in prayer we move away from ourselves, our worries, preoccupation, and self-gratification—and direct all that we recognize as

ours to God in the simple trust that through his love all will be made new.[4]

When our Lord came to the garden on the night of His crucifixion, His prayer just before His capture centered on affirming His oneness with the Father's purposes. This is mature praying.

Many times I have gone to prayer with results in mind. I wanted to gain control over the people and events I was praying about by dictating to the Father my views on how things should come out. When I do this, I am looking at people and events through an earthly lens and not a heavenly one. I am praying as though I know better than God what is best for the outcome.

Thomas Kelly suggests that a more proper kind of prayer is, "Lord, be thou my will." Perhaps among the purest prayers we can pray is simply to ask, "Father, may I see earth through heaven's eyes."

Again Kelly writes:

The life that intends to be wholly obedient, wholly submissive, wholly listening, is astonishing in its completeness. Its joys are ravishing, its peace profound, its humility the deepest, its power world shaking, its love enveloping, its simplicity that of a trusting child.[5]

It was this kind of thinking that helped me overcome the obstacles to worship and intercession that have often been quite real to me. Yes, praying is unnatural for the natural man. But Christ has entered life, and what once was unnatural now becomes natural if I ask for the power to make it so. Yes, praying signals weakness and dependence. But that is the truth about me, and I am healthier for coming to grips with it. And yes, the answers to my prayers do not always coincide with my expectations. But the problem is in my expectations—not in the capacities or sensitivities of God.

4. Henri J. M. Nouwen, *Clowning in Rome* (Garden City, N.Y.: Image, 1979), p. 73.
5. Kelly, p. 54.

Having encountered these obstacles, how do we develop the discipline of worship and intercession in the garden?

VISITING WITH GOD

The practical side of worship and intercession has to do with *time*—when to pray; *posture*—how to pray; and *content*—what to include during visits with the Father.

All of us will find different parts of the day best for our spiritual disciplines. I am a morning person; but one of my closest friends tells me that he finds the evening hours best. Whereas I begin the day in prayer, he ends it that way. Neither of us has airtight arguments for his choice; I think it is a matter of individual rhythms. Daniel of Babylon solved the problem by being a morning and an evening person—and a noontime person too.

When I come to the morning hour, I find it virtually impossible to enter into worship or intercession the moment I come to my private place of solitude. Remember the out-of-breath principle? Praying with a fully active mind fresh from a host of conversations and decisions is difficult, if not impossible. To pray meaningfully, the mind has to be slowed down to a reflective pace.

In order to make this happen, I often begin by reading or writing in my journal. This sort of thing will slowly convince my mind that I am really serious about spiritual exercise, and so it is less liable to rebel when I turn toward prayer.

Is there a prime posture for prayer? Probably not, although some would like to make us think so. In the biblical cultures, people were most likely to stand while they prayed. However the very word *prayer* from the Old Testament means to prostrate oneself, and that may mean at times full length upon the floor.

Friends of A. W. Tozer, a great man of prayer in our time, tell me that he had a pair of coveralls in the closet in his study. When he came to the moments of prayer in his day, he put them on and stretched out upon the hard floor. The coveralls, of course, prevented him from getting his dress clothes dirty. The Muslim posture for prayer is worth trying. This is done by kneeling and then leaning forward until one's forehead is touching the floor. I have found that when I am tired, the Muslim posture helps me to be mentally and spiritually alert.

Sometimes I pray while pacing back and forth in my study; on other occasions I am content simply to sit. The point is that prayer can be carried on in all different postures—and perhaps it is best to assume all of them from one time to another.

Serious intercessors keep prayer lists. Although I am not implying that I call myself a serious intercessor, I do keep one, and it is—as I have said—in the rear of my journal. There I can review my chief concerns as I pray. It's the only way I know of making sure that those for whom God has given me a burden are responsibly lifted up as an expression of my love and caring.

THE CONTENT OF PRAYER

What should we pray about? Take a look at an excerpt from the prayers of Samuel Logan Brengle, an evangelist of the Salvation Army at the beginning of our century:

> Keep me, O Lord, from waxing mentally and spiritually dull and stupid. Help me to keep the physical, mental, and spiritual fibre of the athlete, of the man who denies himself daily and takes up his cross and follows Thee. Give me good success in my work, but hide pride from me. Save me from the self-complacency that so frequently accompanies success and prosperity. Save me from the spirit of sloth, of self-indulgence, as physical infirmities and decay creep upon me.[6]

No wonder Brengle was effective. He knew how and what to pray for. There was nothing held back, even in a short piece of intercession like this one. Having recorded this prayer, Brengle's biographer adds: "Thus praying daily and hourly, the prophet kept his passion hot and his eye single, even as he came down the decline."

6. C. W. Hall, *Samuel Logan Brengle: Portrait of a Prophet* (Chicago: Salvation Army Supply & Purchasing Dept., 1933), p. 237.

ADORATION

In our spiritual disciplines when we visit with the Father in the inner garden, adoration ought to be the first item on the worship agenda.

. How can we worship in prayer? By first reflecting upon who God is and thanking Him for the things He has revealed about Himself. To worship in prayer is to allow our spirits to feast upon what God has revealed concerning His acts in the distant and recent past, and what He has told us about Himself. Slowly, as we review these things in a spirit of thanksgiving and recognition, we can sense our spirits beginning to expand, to take in the broader reality of God's presence and being. Slowly our consciousness is able to accept the fact that the universe about us is not closed or limited, but is in fact as expansive as the Creator meant for it to be. As we enter into worship we remind ourselves of how great He is.

CONFESSION

In the light of God's majesty, we are called to an honesty about ourselves: what we are by contrast. This is the second aspect of prayer: confession. Spiritual discipline calls for a regular acknowledgement of our true nature and the specific acts and attitudes of the recent past that have not been pleasurable to God as He has sought our fellowship and our obedience.

"God be merciful to me a sinner" is an abbreviated version of the prayer of confession. We need the daily humbling experience of being broken before God as we face up to our imperfection, our propensity to seek evil ways. What has startled me as a Christian has been the constant awareness of new levels of sin that I had not spotted within myself before.

Some years ago, when Gail and I bought the old abandoned New Hampshire farm we now call Peace Ledge, we found the site where we wished to build our country home strewn with rocks and boulders. It was going to take a lot of hard work to clear it all out so there could be grass and plants. The whole family went to work on the clearing process. The first phase of the clearing project was easy. The big boulders went fast. And when they were gone, we began to see that there were a lot of smaller rocks that had to go too. And so we cleared the area again. But when we had cleared the site of the boulders and rocks, we noticed all of the stones and pebbles we had not seen before. This was much harder, more tedious work. But we stuck to it, and there came a day when the soil was ready for planting grass.

Our private lives are much like that field was. When I first began to follow Christ seriously, He pointed out many major behavior and attitude patterns that, like boulders, had to be removed. And as the years went by, many of those great big boulders did indeed get removed. But when they began to disappear, I discovered a whole new layer of action and attitude in my life that I had not previously seen. But Christ saw them and rebuked them one by one. The removal process began again. Then I reached that point in my Christian life where Christ and I were dealing with stones and pebbles. They are too numerous to imagine, and as far as I can see, for the rest of my days on earth I will be working with the many stones and pebbles in my life. Every day at spiritual discipline time, there is likely to be a new stab at the clearing process.

But I must not leave this story without noting something else. Every spring at Peace Ledge, after the frost is out of the ground, we find that new stones and boulders appear around our country home. They have been beneath the surface of the ground, working their way up. And at their appointed times, one by one, they show up. Some of them are very frustrating to deal with because they look small until we try to remove them. And only then do we discover that there is more to those boulders than meets the eye.

My sinfulness is exactly the same. It consists of stones, pebbles, and boulders that come to the surface one by one. And the man or woman who ignores the daily experience of confession in spiritual discipline will soon be overwhelmed by them. I understand why the apostle Paul at an advanced age would call himself the "chief of sinners." Even while in jail facing the end of his life, he was still removing pebbles and boulders.

I smile at young believers who tell me that they are discouraged because of all the sin they see in their lives. The fact that they can at least see and feel repelled by that sin shows they are actually growing. There are too many people claiming to be followers of Christ who lost sight of their own sinfulness years ago. If they attend worship on Sunday, they leave without ever having had the experience of brokenness and repentance before God that indicates true worship. This leads to substandard Christianity.

E. Stanley Jones writes of the importance of confession in our spiritual disciplines:

> I know that there are certain mental and emotional and moral and spiritual attitudes that are anti-health: anger, resentments, fear, worry, desire to dominate, self-preoccupation, guilts, sexual impurity, jealousy, a lack of creative activity, inferiorities, a lack of love. These are the twelve apostles of ill health. *So in prayer I've learned to surrender these things to Jesus Christ as they appear.* I once asked Dr. Kagawa: "What is prayer?" And he answered: "Prayer is self-surrender." I agree. It is primarily self-surrender, blanket surrender, day by day. It is all we know and all we don't know. "All we don't know" covers the unfolding future and involves problems as they arise. So in prayer if any of these twelve things arise, and they do arise, for no one is free from the suggestion of any one of them, I've learned how to deal with them: not to fight them, but to surrender them to Jesus Christ, and say, "Now, Lord, you have this."[7]

THE MINISTRY OF INTERCESSION

The great prayer warriors all seem to agree: that intercession can begin only after we have fully worshiped. Having put ourselves in touch with the living God, we are prepared to pray with what Thomas Kelly called "the eyes of Heaven."

Old Commissioner Brengle was a man of prayer. His biographer writes:

> At prayer, he was a study in communion. It was his habit, except for those periods when he was too ill, to get out of bed between four and five o'clock in the morning and devote at least a full hour before breakfast to communion with his Lord. Dr. Hayes, whose book, "The Heights of Christian Devotion" carries these dedicatory words: "To Commissioner Samuel Logan Brengle, A Man of Prayer," gives us this glimpse:

7. E. Stanley Jones, *Song of Ascents* (Nashville: Abingdon, 1968), p. 337.

"When Brengle has been a guest in my home, I often have found him on his knees with his open Bible on the bed or chair before him, reading his Bible through in that way and saying that the attitude helped him to turn all he read into personal petition: 'O Lord, help me to do this, or not to do that. Help me to be like this man, or to avoid this error.'"[8]

When worship has been completed, intercession can begin. Intercession usually means prayer on behalf of others. It is the greatest single ministry, in my opinion, that the Christian is privileged to have. And perhaps the most difficult.

Have you ever noticed that most faithful intercessors seem to be older people? Why? One reason may be that they have had to simplify their activities. But also note that older people may have become aware that intercession is much more effective than hours of unprayerful activity. And of course, experience through trial and error has taught them the wisdom of leaning on the reliable strength of God.

I have set out in the last few years to master the ministry of intercession for the sake of ministry to others. The progress is slow. Perhaps it is the greatest challenge of my private world.

The greater the spiritual authority and responsibility a person has, the more important it is that he develop intercessory capacities. That takes time and the sort of discipline many of us find difficult.

I think this is what the apostles, the leaders of the early congregation at Jerusalem, were getting at in Acts 6, when they asked for associates to take on the tasks of ministering to the widows and orphans so that they could "give ourselves to prayer and to the preaching of the Word of God." Note what comes first on the priority list of these busy, busy men. They were starting to miss prayer and were quite nervous about the situation.

Intercession literally means to stand between two parties and plead the case of one to the other. Is there a greater example of intercession than the prayerful work of Moses, who gave himself to frequent strenuous petition on behalf of the wayward people of Israel?

8. C. W. Hall, *Portrait of a Prophet*, p. 185.

For whom do we normally intercede? If married, for our spouses and children, obviously. But, intercession also means widening the circle to take in close friends, those for whom God has made us responsible, the men and women with whom we work, and those in our congregations and neighborhoods whose personal needs are known to us.

My intercessory list includes many Christian leaders and organizations. There are many whom I know and like; but I must confess that I do not have much more than an occasional prayer burden for them. By contrast, there are some whose needs and pressures are very real to me, and I hold them before the Lord in my intercessory exercise every day. They find it of immense encouragement to hear me say, "I pray for you every day." Being responsible for a certain amount of Christian leadership myself, I have learned how supportive it feels to know that there is a handful of people who hold me before the throne of God in intercession every day.

Intercession means that we must take into account the mandate for world evangelization. In order to systematically pray around the world, I have divided up the continents in such a way that I can pray each day for one of them: Sunday, Latin America; Monday, Central America; Tuesday, North America; Wednesday, Europe; Thursday, Africa; Friday, Asia; and Saturday, the nations of the Pacific. In each area I include intercession for the national church, for missionaries with whom I am acquainted, and for the terrible suffering people are facing.

We are encouraged to bring our own petitions or requests before the Lord. Somehow I feel that these ought to come last in our prayer activity, but that is purely an opinion. I am thinking of matters in and about my personal life where it seems best to ask God for wisdom and supply. I have struggled with how much I should ask God for (some say everything) and how much He assumes we will handle ourselves. I don't know that I have a good answer to this. I discover as I grow in my faith that I am constrained to ask less and less for myself and more and more for others. And my personal requests tend to be more and more for resources and abilities that would be more of benefit for others.

The garden within our private world cannot remain uncultivated for long before it becomes infested with the sort of growth that makes it uninviting, both to the indwelling Lord and to us ourselves. When neglected for long, it becomes more like a dump than a garden. And then we have to rely upon external sources of strength and direction to keep moving ahead.

That was the reason for Howard Rutledge's struggle in the North Viet Nam prison camp. By God's grace, he testifies, he made it through. But he never forgot what it is like to face such an ordeal when one's private world of the spirit has been left generally uncultivated.

A well-known Christian personality of our century, Eric Liddell, the Olympic champion runner who was the hero of the movie *Chariots of Fire,* had a remarkably different experience in a prison in North China during World War II. His biographer speaks of the high esteem with which Liddell was held in the Weinsen Camp. And what was the secret of his extraordinary leadership power, his joy, and his integrity in the midst of enormous hardship? The biographer quotes a woman who was in the camp at the time and with her husband knew Liddell well:

> What was his secret? Once I asked him, but I really knew already, for my husband was in his dormitory and shared the secret with him. Every morning about 6 am, with curtains tightly drawn to keep in the shining of our peanut-oil lamp, lest the prowling sentries would think someone was trying to escape, he used to climb out of his top bunk, past the sleeping forms of his dormitory mates. Then, at the small Chinese table, the two men would sit close together with the light just enough to illumine their Bibles and notebooks. Silently they read, prayed, thought about what should be done. *Eric was a man of prayer not only at set times—* though he did not like to miss a prayer meeting or communion service when such could be arranged. *He talked to God all the time, naturally, as one can who enters the "School of Prayer" to learn this way of inner discipline.* He seemed to have no weighty mental problems: his life was grounded in God, in faith, and in trust.[9]

9. Sally Magnusson, *The Flying Scotsman* (New York: Quartet Books, 1981), p. 165.

To bring order to our private worlds is to cultivate the garden as Liddell did. From such exercises, according to the writer of the Proverbs (4:23), comes a heart out of which flows life-giving energy.

At eighty years of age, bed-ridden with a stroke that impaired his speech and paralyzed his writing hand, E. Stanley Jones would ask himself: Can I handle this crisis? His answer: Absolutely. "The innermost strands are the strongest. I need no outer props to hold up my faith."

Sector Five

Memo to the Disorganized:

If my private world is in order, it will be because I have chosen to press Sabbath peace into the rush and routine of my daily life in order to find the rest God prescribed for Himself and all of humanity.

14

Rest Beyond Leisure

William Wilberforce, a committed Christian, was a member of the English Parliament in the early years of the nineteenth century. As a politician he was noted for his vigorous leadership in convincing Parliament to pass a historic bill outlawing slavery in the British Empire. It was no mean feat. In fact, it may have been one of the greatest and most courageous acts of statesmanship in the history of democracy.

It took Wilberforce almost twenty years to construct the coalition of lawmakers that eventually passed the anti-slavery measure. It required detailed documentation of the injustices and cruelties of slavery, persuading lawmakers who did not want to offend the interests of big business, and standing strong against a host of political enemies who would have loved to see Wilberforce fall.

Wilberforce's spiritual strength and moral courage had to be immense. We learn something of the source of that strength and courage from an incident that occurred in 1801, some years before the anti-slavery measure was passed.

Lord Addington had led his party into power, and as the new prime minister he had begun to form a new cabinet. The central issue of the day in England was peace; Napoleon was terrorizing Europe, and the concern was whether or not England could stay out of war. Wilberforce was rumored to be among the candidates for a cabinet post, and because of the peace policy he found himself most anxious to gain the appointment. Garth Lean, one of Wilberforce's more recent biographers, tells the story.

> It did not take long for Wilberforce to become preoccupied with the possibility of the appointment. For days it grabbed at his conscious mind, forcing aside everything else. By his own admission he had "risings of ambition," and it was crippling his soul.[1]

But there was a disciplined check and balance to Wilberforce's life, and in this particular situation that routine became indispensable. As Lean says, "Sunday brought the cure." For there came a regular time in Wilberforce's private world every week when he *rested*.

The Christian politician's journal tells the story best, in its entry at the end of that week of furious fantasizing and temptations to politic for position: "Blessed be to God for the day of rest and religious occupation wherein *earthly things assume their true size. Ambition is stunted*" (italics added).

Wilberforce's check and balance to a busy life was Sabbath; he had come to understand genuine rest. Wilberforce had discovered that the person who establishes a block of time for Sabbath rest on a regular basis is most likely to keep all of life in proper perspective and remain free of burnout and breakdown.

Not everyone in Wilberforce's public world held to that secret; workaholism and frantic busyness occurred in that day as it does today. About William Pitt, for example, Wilberforce wrote: "Poor fellow, he never schools his mind *by a cessation from political ruminations*, the most blinding, hardening and souring of all others." Of two other politicians who both took their own lives, Wilberforce wrote, "With peaceful Sundays, the strings would never have snapped as they did from overtension."

There can be little order in the private world of the human being when there is no appreciation for the meaning and pursuit of genuine rest, a *cessation*, as Wilberforce called it, in

1. Garth Lean, *God's Politician* (London: Darton, Longman & Todd, 1980), p. 89.

the routines of our times. From the beginning of all history, it has been an axiom at the base of healthy living; unfortunately, it is a principle badly misunderstood by those whose lives are driven to achievement and acquisition.

WE NEED REST

I get the feeling we are a tired generation. Evidence of that fatigue abounds in a multitude of articles about health problems related to overwork and exhaustion. *Workaholism* is a modern word. No matter how hard we are willing to work in our competitive world, there always seems to be someone willing to put in a few more hours than we are.

What is strange about our general fatigue as a people is the fact that we are such a leisure-oriented society. We actually have what is called a leisure industry, and it is among the most profitable in our economy. Whole companies, organizations, and retail chain stores are committed to providing the goods with which people can pursue fun and good times.

We probably have more time for leisure than we ever had before. The five-day workweek is, after all, a relatively new innovation in history; we have moved away from the farm, where there was always more work to do; we can leave work behind if we want and head for leisure. So why is there so much exhaustion and fatigue today? Is it real? Imagined? Or is the contemporary form of exhaustion evidence that we no longer understand genuine rest, which is different from the pursuit of leisure?

There is a biblical view of rest that needs to be uncovered and examined. In fact, the Bible reveals God Himself to be the first "rester." "On the seventh day, He rested. . . ." An even more enlightening comment is made by Moses in Exodus 31:17: "In six days the Lord made heaven and earth, but on the seventh day, He ceased from labor, and was refreshed." The literal translation suggests the phrase "He refreshed Himself."

Does God indeed need to rest? Of course not! But did God choose to rest? Yes. Why? Because God subjected creation to a rhythm of rest and work that He revealed by observing the rhythm Himself, as a precedent for everyone else. In this way, He showed us a key to order in our private worlds.

This rest was not meant to be a luxury, but rather a *necessity* for those who want to have growth and maturity. Since we have not understood that rest is a necessity, we have perverted its meaning, substituting for the rest that God first demonstrated things called leisure or amusement. These do not bring any order at all to the private world. Leisure and amusement may be enjoyable, but they are to the private world of the individual like cotton candy to the digestive system. They provide a momentary lift, but they will not last.

I am not by any means critical of the pursuit of fun-filled moments, diversion, laughter, or recreation. I am proposing that these alone will not restore the soul in the way that we crave. Although they may provide a sort of momentary rest for the body, they will not satisfy the deep need for rest within the private world.

Years ago there was a famous ad campaign for a liniment, which promised that the product would penetrate deeply into sore muscles, bringing relief from aches and pains. Sabbath rest penetrates to the deepest levels of fatigue in the inner, private world. This fatigue is rarely touched by any of the modern amusements.

THE MEANING OF SABBATH REST

CLOSING THE LOOP

When God rested, He looked upon His work, enjoyed its completed appearance, and then reflected upon its meaning. "And God saw that it was good." This shows us the first of the three principles of genuine rest. God gave His work meaning and acknowledged its completion. In so doing, He taught us that there is a necessary exercise of appreciation and dedication for our routines.

High-tech systems planners like to use the phrase "closing the loop" to describe the completion of a phase in an electrical circuit. They also use the phrase when they want to say that a task has been completed or that every person in a project has been informed or consulted.

So you could say that on the seventh day, God closed the loop on His primary creation activity. He closed it by resting and looking back upon it to survey what had been accomplished.

This rest then is, first of all, a time of looking backward, of loop-closing. We gaze upon our work and ask questions like: What does my work mean? For whom did I do this work? How well was the work done? Why did I do this? and What results did I expect, and what did I receive?

To put it another way, the rest God instituted was meant first and foremost to cause us to *interpret* our work, to *press meaning into it*, to *make sure we know to whom it is properly dedicated.*

Brother Lawrence was a cook in a monastery. He learned to press meaning into virtually every action of his day. Note his capacity to see not only meaning but also purpose in his labor:

> I turn my little omelette in the pan for the love of God. When it is finished, if I have nothing to do, I prostrate myself on the ground and worship my God, who gave me this grace to make it, after which I arise happier than a king. When I can do nothing else, it is enough to have picked up a straw for the love of God. People look for ways of learning how to love God. They hope to attain it by I know not how many different practices. They take much trouble to abide in His presence by varied means. Is it not a shorter and more direct way to do everything for the love of God, to make use of all the tasks one's lot in life demands to show him that love, and to maintain his presence within by the communion of our heart with his? There is nothing complicated about it. One has only to turn to it honestly and simply.[2]

I am sure that most of us desire periods of time like that. The average worker has a desperate need to feel that his work means something, has significance, and is appreciated. But, while we crave that assurance, we do not see the importance of taking time to gain it. A busyness, a frantic pace sets in, and we delay our quest for meaning and interpretation; before long, we have learned to get along without it. We lose sight of the question, What's this all for? We become content to allow

2. Brother Lawrence, *The Practice of the Presence of God*, trans. E. M. Blaiklock (Nashville: Thomas Nelson, 1982), p. 85.

the meaning value of our work to be computed merely in the amount on our paychecks. Few people appreciate how dry and barren this leaves our private world.

A man I like very much was recently terminated by his company after twenty-two years of service. The economy had forced an across-the-board cutback, and his job was considered non-essential to the company's survival. He was out!

My friend was convinced that he would be hired by another company in the same field within a matter of days. After all, he told me, he had numerous connections, a profit-making record, and long term service. He was not worried, he said.

But several months passed with no offers. The "connections" dried up; no one responded to his feelers or to his resumés. He was reduced to sitting at home waiting for the phone to ring.

One day, after those many torturous months, he said to me, "This whole thing has forced me to do a lot of hard thinking. I've given myself to this career of mine for years, and look what it's gotten me. What was all this for anyway? Boy, have I gotten my eyes opened up."

Opened up to what? My friend is a fine Christian layman. But his eyes, by his own admission, had been closed to what his career had come to mean to him. What his eyes had opened up to was the fact that he had worked for years without asking what it all meant, what it was all for, and what might be the result. He had never discovered the exercise of reflection in the context of biblical rest.

A rest-less work style produces a restless person. Work that goes on month after month without a genuine pause to inquire of its meaning and purpose may swell the bank account and enhance the professional reputation. But it will drain the private world of vitality and joy. How important it is to regularly close loops on our activity.

RETURNING TO THE ETERNAL TRUTHS

There is a second way biblical rest restores order to the private world. True rest is happening when we pause regularly amidst daily routines to sort out the truths and commitments by which we are living

We are daily the objects of a bombardment of messages competing for our loyalties and labors. We are pushed and pulled in a thousand different directions, asked to make decisions and value judgments, to invest our resources and our time. By what standard of truth do we make these decisions?

God meant for His people to take a day each week in which this question was firmly dealt with. And in fact, He caused them to set aside a series of annual feast days during which major themes of eternal truth and divine action could be recalled and celebrated. You could call it a recalibration of the spirit.

Separating out the truths that are central to life is essential when one remembers that, according to Jeremiah, the heart is deceitful. We are vulnerable at all times to distortions of the truth, to persuasions that the true is really false and the false really true. Remember the words of the hymnwriter:

> Prone to wander, Lord, I feel it;
> Prone to leave the God I love. . .
> (Robert Robinson)

The hymn reflects upon the inexorable inward drift that must be regularly checked by measuring our thoughts and values against the eternal truths that have been revealed through the Scripture and the mighty acts of God.

The Jewish theologian Abraham Joshua Heschel looked at rest in the Sabbath tradition and wrote:

The meaning of the Sabbath is to celebrate time rather than space. Six days a week, we live under the tyranny of things of space; on the Sabbath we try to become attuned to holiness in time. It is a day on which we are called upon to share what is eternal in time, to turn from the results of creation to the mystery of creation; from the world of creation to the creation of the world.[3]

We need to ask ourselves, Is this happening in my own private world?

---

3. Abraham Heschel, *The Earth Is the Lord's and The Sabbath* (two books published as one, New York: Harper Torchbooks, 1966), p. 10.

The clapboards of our New Hampshire home expand and contract in response to temperature extremes. The result is that some nails work loose and have to be pounded back in to regain a snug hold. This "repounding" is what happens during a genuine rest period, be it in the privacy of that quiet day or in the midst of a congregation while we worship the living God.

One of the great joys of repeating the traditional creeds of the Christian church is that it gives us an opportunity to re-affirm the central truths of God's revelation. As we say, "I believe . . ." we begin to hammer back the nails of our convictions and commitments. And we separate those beliefs out from what we choose not to believe.

The same thing happens when we sing grand old hymns and pray certain prayers. The nails are being pounded back in, and order is being restored to a drifting spirit in our private worlds. Reaffirmations occur on that special rest day, if we take time in private for reading, meditating, and reflecting.

My wife shares with me an entry in her journal on this very subject:

> A glorious Lord's Day. Have been reading at length about the Sabbath. Feel more and more strongly that I've not fully utilized God's command to rest.
>
> It's not a rule that restricts but it is a rule that liberates. For He made me to need rest. And physically and mentally we are freed to better performance if we live within His "design specifications." And it is a day of reminding us who God is. Every seventh day I need to come back to the fixed Center.
>
> Don Stephenson remarked today that for him and others Sunday is just that—a day to come back to the straight edge and be encouraged to go back to the "mire."

I would propose that we need to ask hard questions, both of ourselves and of our churches, concerning whether or not the sort of rest that reaffirms truth is actually happening. It is possible for Christians and their churches to become so busy carrying on programs—for whatever good purpose—that the worship-rest necessary to the private world never happens.

Thus, rest is not only a looking back at the meaning of my work and the path I have so recently walked in my life; but is also a refreshing of my belief and commitment to Christ. It is a fine tuning of my inner navigational instruments so that I can make my way through the world for another week.

DEFINING OUR MISSION

If the first two meanings centered on what was past and present, this one centers on the future. When we rest in the biblical sense, we affirm our intentions to pursue a Christ-centered tomorrow. We ponder where we are headed in the coming week, month or year. We define our intentions and make our dedications.

General George Patton demanded that his men know and be able to articulate exactly what the current mission was. "What is your mission?" he would frequently ask. The definition of the mission was the most important piece of information a soldier could carry into combat. Based on that knowledge, he could make his decisions and implement the plan. That is exactly what happens when I pursue biblical rest. I take a hard look at my mission. And it has taught me to make a small pause even in my spiritual disciplines each morning to ask the question, What is my mission today? Not to regularly ask this question is to leave yourself open to mistakes of judgment and direction.

Jesus often withdrew to seek solitude. While others were lulled to the rest of sleep, Jesus was drawn to the rest of gaining strength and direction for His next phase of mission. No wonder He met every encounter with a fresh burst of wisdom. No wonder He had ample courage not to fight back, not to defend Himself. His spirit was always rested, His private world ordered. Without this kind of rest our private world will always be strained and disordered.

CHOOSING TO REST

One of the noted vicars of the Church of England was Charles Simeon, of Holy Trinity Church in Cambridge. For more than fifty years he preached from its pulpit, and the people crowded the sanctuary, standing in the aisles to hear him.

Simeon was a fellow at Kings College, and he lived in apartments that overlooked the courtyard in the college complex. His second-floor dwellings provided him an exclusive opening out to the roof where he would often walk, one of his physical forms of rest, while he talked with God. That rooftop became known as Simeon's walk.

A busy and brilliant man, Simeon was in touch with students at the colleges in Cambridge, with a large congregation, and with church and missionary leaders around the world. He wrote (in longhand) literally thousands of letters, edited fifty books of his own sermons, and served as one of the founders of several major missionary organizations. But he never ceased to find time for the rest that his private world demanded.

A sample of his private exercises can be found in this entry to his journal, recorded by Hugh Hopkins, a Simeon biographer.

> I spent this day as I have for these 43 last years, as a day of humiliation; having increased need of such season every year I live.

Hopkins writes:

> Self-humiliation for Charles Simeon consisted not of belittling the gifts that God had given him or pretending that he was a man of no account, or exaggerating the sins of which he was very conscious. He went about it by consciously bringing himself into the presence of God, dwelling thoughtfully on his majesty and glory, magnifying the mercy of his forgiveness and the wonder of his love. These were the things that humbled him—not so much his own sinfulness but God's incredible love.[4]

Simeon enjoyed a lifelong effectiveness under enormous strain. I have no doubt that a large part of his secret of endurance was his deliberate and disciplined pursuit of Sabbath rest.

4. Hugh Evan Hopkins, *Charles Simeon of Cambridge* (Grand Rapids: Eerdmans, 1977), pp. 155–56.

For the Jew, the Sabbath was first of all a day. A day set aside in obedience to God. The law forbade work of any kind, allowing only the sort of observances such as we have already reviewed. Christians have little idea of how special the Sabbath was to pious Jews. We would do well to listen and hear what they think. An Israeli tourist brochure tells us that one rabbi wrote of Sabbath:

> Make the Sabbath an eternal monument of the knowledge and sanctification of God, both in the center of your busy public life and in the peaceful retreat of your domestic hearth. For six days cultivate the earth and rule it. . . . But the seventh is the Sabbath of the Lord thy God. . . . Let [a man] therefore realize that the Creator of old is the living God of today, [that He] watches every man and every human effort, to see how man uses or abuses the world loaned to him and the forces bestowed upon him, and that He is the sole architect to Whom every man has to render an account of his week's labors.

What is important behind these statements is the Jewish awareness of a unique pace to Sabbath. Routines are to stop; labor is to cease. Even the homemaker in the pious Jewish family is to refrain from cooking or menial tasks. Food is prepared before Sabbath begins so that she also can enjoy the fruit of the special rest day. This is a far cry from the incredible, filled up, pressurized day many evangelical Christians tend to make of their "day of rest."

Sabbath is first of all a day. In our Christian tradition we have chosen to make that day not the seventh, as the Jew does, but the first day of the week, in recognition of the resurrection of Christ. But having made that choice, what have we done with our day—this time that God gave as a special gift?

A layman with whom I worship every week said to me after one particularly long Sunday of church activity, "I'm sure glad that there is only one rest day per week, I'd burn out if we had to go through two 'days of rest' like this every seven days."

His humor conveys a serious charge against many Christian leaders and churches who have turned Sunday into a day of unrest, perhaps for some the most tension-filled day of the week.

But Sabbath is more than just a day. It is a principle of rest along the lines of the three dimensions I have already mentioned. And what might happen should we choose the peace of Sabbath rest rather than the fun of secular leisure?

First, Sabbath rest means worship with the Christian family. In proper worship we will have a chance to exercise all three aspects that lead to the rest of our private worlds: looking backward, upward, and ahead. Such worship is non-negotiable to the person committed to walking with God.

I am moved by the words of Luke who describes the Sabbath discipline of Jesus: "And He came *to Nazareth, where He had been brought up; and as was His custom, He entered the synagogue on the Sabbath*" (Luke 4:16, italics added). One never sees Christ slipping away from the public worship of the Father.

But, second, Sabbath means a deliberate acceptance of personal rest and tranquility within the individual life. Sabbath means a rest that brings peace into the private world. As Christ pressed stillness into a storm, order into a being of a demon-possessed maniac, health into a desperately sick woman, and life into a dead friend, so He seeks to press peace into the harried private world of the man or woman who has been in the marketplace all week. But there is a condition. We must accept this peace as a gift and take the time to receive it.

As a pastor, I have long felt that Sunday was anything but Sabbath rest for my wife and me. It was many years into my Christian adulthood before I realized that I had been robbing myself of a necessary form of restoration. The fact was that I needed some sort of Sabbath for my own private world, and I wasn't getting it. When I looked at my Sundays, it seemed impossible to think that I would ever enjoy Sabbath's rejuvenating gift. How could I preach three Sunday morning sermons and a frequent evening sermon, as well as be available throughout the day to the people of my congregation, and expect to be restored? Rarely did a Sunday end without Gail and me being on the verge of exhaustion. Day of rest indeed!

What to do? A few years ago, the Grace Chapel congregation was gracious enough to give me a four-month sabbatical leave. Rather than go off to a university to study, I chose to go to New Hampshire, where we built Peace Ledge. The outstanding experience of those four months was the silence and peace we discovered on Sundays.

Although I enjoyed the construction of Peace Ledge immensely, I promised myself that I would do no work on the Lord's Day. Thus, when Sunday came, we spent a few early morning hours reading, thinking, and praying. And then we went to a local church where we could worship. We did not know many of the people, but we tried to throw ourselves into the worship and draw from the prayers, the hymns, and the sermon food for our spirits. We made it a time of affirming our convictions, thanking God for blessings, and committing ourselves to the coming week in which we would try to reflect the honor of the Lord.

Our Sunday afternoons during the four months were quiet hours for walks in the woods, deep conversation, and a searching process as we evaluated our spiritual disciplines and Christian progress. It was a marvelously restful Sabbath experience for us; I had never known what it could be like before that time.

We were hooked on Sabbaths when we returned from our sabbatical. But suddenly it was back to sermons, and counseling, and programming. Business as usual on Sunday. We felt robbed! And so it was that we decided *our* Sabbath would be another day of the week. We were not going to miss God's gift! On Sundays, we would try to help others enjoy their Sabbaths. But for us the peace normally reserved for that day would have to happen at some other time. And that was fine.

Sabbath for Gail and me became Thursday. To the extent that we could achieve it, we budgeted that day of the week for rest in our private worlds. It meant total withdrawal from our congregation whenever possible, even laying aside the routines of our home if we could. We learned that if we were going to be useful to those associated with us in ministry, to our children, and to the congregation, we would have to jealously guard this opportunity for spiritual restoration.

There is no legalism here—rather a freedom to accept a gift. Frankly, I think some have destroyed the joy of Sabbath, as did the Pharisees, by surrounding it with prescriptive laws and precedents. That is not our Sabbath. Our Sabbath was made for us, given to us by God. Its purpose is worship and restoration, and whatever it takes to make that happen, we will do.

It is important to say that we probably could not have pursued Sabbath rest as easily when our children were young and needed more constant attention. And it is also important to say, as Gail often observes, that we do our people a favor by withdrawing from them for rest. For when we return, we have something to offer that God probably could not have given us in any other atmosphere.

Obviously, every Thursday could not be budgeted for Sabbath. But, we discovered that if we made a regular attempt at such a discipline, the results were tremendous. Our private worlds were indeed substantially reordered. The most astounding discovery was that I felt not only rested but able to use the times of other days in a far more effective fashion.

What had happened, much to my amazement, was that by bringing this restful order to my private world through proper Sabbath observance, I was able to impact my public world in the days that followed with much greater wisdom and judgment.

I believe that Sabbath rest may mean a day a week. But it can happen at any time, in large and small doses, when we choose to set aside an hour or more for the pursuit of intimacy with God. All of us need a "Simeon's walk."

But let me be quick to underscore that this rest, which is Sabbathlike, ought to be a fixed allocation in the budgeting of our time. We do not rest because our work is done; we rest because God commanded it and created us to have a need for it.

That is important to think about, because our current view of rest and leisure denies that principle. Most of us think of resting as something we do *after* our work is done. But Sabbath is not something that happens after. It may in fact be something that is pursued *before*. If we assume that this rest comes only after work is complete, many of us are in trouble, for we have jobs where the work is never finished. And that in part is why some of us rarely rest; never finishing our work, we do not think to take the time for Sabbath peace and restoration.

I had to learn to pursue Sabbath rest without a sense of guilt. I had to realize that there was nothing wrong with laying aside other work for the purpose of enjoying God's gift of special time. Thus, Sabbaths have gone into our calendars with regularity. They are planned weeks in advance, along with other priorities. And when someone has proposed a supper, a ball game, or a committee meeting on a day set aside for the reordering of our private worlds, my wife and I have simply said, "Sorry, we have a commitment on that day. It's Sabbath for us."

It was this sort of discipline that enabled William Wilberforce to overcome the consuming thrust of ambition that had crippled his private world for so many days. Having reached the day of rest, he slipped back into that center where God was in full control. He saw things in their true size, "ambition is stunted," he wrote.

One wonders what would have happened if Wilberforce had not had that Sabbath check and balance to face his ambitious nature. Would he have been deterred from his call to lead England away from slavery? Probably. You have to believe that in taking Sabbath, he was able to detect a deviation from his original sense of purpose and, just in time, regain the right course. Because he got back on track, the great landmark achievement of abolition was his to claim.

The world and the church need genuinely *rested* Christians: Christians who are regularly refreshed by true Sabbath rest, not just leisure or time off. When a godly rest is achieved, you will see just how tough and resilient Christians can actually be.

Memo to the Disorganized:

If my private world is in order, it will be because I have made a deliberate decision to begin the "ordering" process . . . Now!

Epilogue:
The Spinning Wheel

One of the celebrated heroes of our century has been Mohandas Gandhi, the Indian leader who sparked the flame of independence for his country. Those who have read his biographies or who have seen his story so brilliantly told upon the screen are often impressed with the tranquil spirit that "India's George Washington" displayed.

Serenity? We see Gandhi among the most poverty-ridden people of Indian cities, where death and disease are rampant. He touches them, offers a word of hope, provides a gentle smile. But a day later the same man is found in palaces and government buildings, where he negotiates with the most clever men of his age. And the question arises: how did he manage to span the gap between the two extremes of people and circumstances?

How could Gandhi maintain his private sense of order, his appropriate humility, and his base wisdom and judgment? How did he avoid losing his own identity and spirit of conviction as he moved between those enormous extremes? Where did the emotional and spiritual force come from?

Perhaps the beginning of an answer to those questions lies in Gandhi's fascination with the simple spinning wheel. The wheel seems to have always been at the center of his life. Gandhi appears to have often returned from public exposure to his humble dwellings where he would, in Indian fashion, sit upon the floor and engage in the simple act of spinning the wool from which his clothes were made.

What was he trying to do? Was this merely part of a plan to project a certain image? Was it purely a political attempt to identify with the masses, whose loyalty he held in his grasp? I would suggest that it was much, much more.

Gandhi's spinning wheel was his center of gravity in life. It was the great leveler in his human experience. When he returned from the great public moments in his life, the spinning-wheel experience restored him to his proper sense of proportion, so that he was not falsely swelled with pride due to the cheers of the people. When he withdrew from the moments of encounter with kings and government leaders, he was not tempted to think of himself in some inflated fashion when he moved to the work of the wheel.

The spinning wheel was always a reminder to Gandhi of who he was and what the practical things in life were all about. In engaging in this regular exercise, he was resisting all the forces of his public world that tried to distort who he knew himself to be.

Gandhi was by no means a Christian, but what he was doing at the wheel is an indispensable lesson for any healthy Christian. For he shows us what every man or woman who wants to move in a public world without being pressed into its mold needs to do. We, too, need the spinning-wheel experience—the ordering of our private worlds so that they are constantly restructured in strength and vitality.

As Thomas Kelly says, "We are trying to be several selves at once, without all our selves being organized by a single, mastering Life within us." Again he says, "Life is meant to be lived from a Center, a divine Center. Each one of us can live such a life of amazing power and peace and serenity, of integration and confidence and simplified multiplicity, on one condition—that is, *if we really want to.*"

And that is the condition with which we must finally deal. Do we really want order within our private worlds? Again, *do we want it?*

If it is true that actions speak louder than words, it would appear that the average Christian does not really seek an ordered private world as a top priority. It would seem that we prefer to find our human effectiveness through busyness, frantic programming, material accumulation, and rushing to various conferences, seminars, film series, and special speakers.

In short, we try to bring order to the inner world by beginning with activity in the outer one. This is exactly the opposite of what the Bible teaches us, what the great saints have shown us, and what our dismal spiritual experiences regularly prove to us.

Somewhere John Wesley is quoted as saying of life in his public world, "Though I am always in haste, I am never in a hurry, because I never undertake more work than I can go through with calmness of spirit."

One of my close associates in ministry, Bob Ludwig, is a stargazer. Occasionally he spends an evening in the countryside, where he can turn his telescope on the darkened sky. But he must leave the city in order to escape all the interfering light. Once he has left all of that behind, the picture of the sky becomes much clearer.

How do we escape such interference in order to gaze into the inner space of our private world? That question remains dangerously unanswered in too many lives. Men and women who command the leadership of large organizations and churches too often are unable to answer the question for themselves. Simple people, busy earning a living and trying to keep up with the Joneses, are wrestling with the question. It yields no easy answer—only a simple one. We escape into the space of the inner world only when we determine that it is an activity more important than anything else we do.

Although I have always believed in the priority of ordering my inner world, it has only begun to become a reality for me as I have advanced toward the middle years of my life. And now that I have grown increasingly aware of my limits, my weaknesses, and even the advance of the years toward the day when my own life shall end, I find it more possible to look within and cultivate the spinning-wheel experience, so that inner strength and spiritual vitality can become a resource.

It is at that center that we begin to see Jesus Christ in all

His majesty. There He is more than what is contained in some doctrinal statement about Him. He is more than the mushy words of some contemporary song. At the center, He commands attention as the risen Lord of life; and we are compelled to follow after Him and draw from the strength of His character and compassion.

At the center, we are appropriately awed by the splendor and majesty of God as heavenly Father. There is solemn but joyful worship; there are confession and breaking. And there is forgiveness, restoration, and assurance.

Finally, at the center, we are filled by the power and strength of God as Holy Spirit. There is a resurgence of confidence and expectancy. We receive insight and wisdom; faith that removes mountains is generated, and a love for others, even for the unlovable, begins to grow.

When we come from an experience at the spinning wheel, where all is returned to proper proportion and value, the public world can be managed and properly touched. Relationships with family and friends, with business associates, neighbors, and even enemies take on a new and healthier perspective. It becomes possible to forgive, to serve, to not seek vengeance, to be generous.

Our work will be affected by exercise at the center. Work will be given new meaning and a higher standard of excellence. Integrity and honesty will become important items of pursuit. Fear will be lost, and compassion will be gained.

Coming from the spinning-wheel experience, we are less apt to be seduced by the false promises and seductions of those out to capture the soul.

All of this and much more goes into motion when the private world is ordered first—*before* the Christian walks in the public world.

Not to do that is to invite the sinkhole syndrome. And history abounds with examples of people who own that consequence.

Today our public worlds demand a few good people who can walk among the masses and negotiate with the powerful, but never change, never capitulate, never compromise.

And how will they manage that? By pursuing the spinning-wheel experience: the retreat into the silent center where time can be ordered by priorities, where the mind can be tuned to discover God's creation, the spirit can be sharpened, and where there is the quietness of Sabbath rest. This is the private world, and when given proper attention, it comes to order.

RENEWING YOUR SPIRITUAL PASSION

Acknowledgements

Scripture quotations marked RSV are from the Revised Standard Version of the Bible, copyrighted 1946, 1952, © 1971, 1973. Scripture quotations marked TEV are from the *Good News Bible*—Old Testament: Copyright © American Bible Society 1976: New Testament: Copyright © American Bible Society 1966, 1971, 1976. Used by permission.

Scripture quotations marked TLB are taken from *The Living Bible*, copyright 1971 by Tyndale House Publishers, Wheaton, IL. Used by permission.

Scripture quotations marked NIV are taken from the HOLY BIBLE: NEW INTERNATIONAL VERSION. Copyright © 1973, 1978, 1984 by the International Bible Society. Used by permission of Zondervan Bible Publishers.

Contents

Preface

The Dark-Road
Times

Within the kaleidoscope of my distorted childhood memories is the image of a dusty, deserted road in rural Canada. As I recall it, there were no signs indicating direction or distance to go, and the route itself was not marked on my father's map.

The hour was late, and my family and I had been traveling that road for an entire day. We were lost, tired, and not a little irritable with one another. Those were not the days of frequently seen motels, and the few (very few) collections of cabins along the way displayed NO VACANCY signs to fend away further inquiries.

Why not turn back? We had simply traveled too far to do so. Besides, the road had to go somewhere. But why keep going? That was the purpose of the trip: to get somewhere. Surely there would be a place ahead where we could find food and rest. So we pushed ahead. The world was not flat; we would not drop off an edge, although my childish perspective contemplated the possibility. We had to be going somewhere. But where?

The trip had begun with such excitement, an adventuresome spirit about going new places. Most vacation trips begin that way. The car had been packed with care, maps marked, a picnic basket prepared. But now all that zeal had dissipated. I guess we began to wonder why we'd ever left home.

I have often recalled the feelings and frustration of that late-night, dark-road experience whenever my life seemed to

187

momentarily turn into a mindless or spiritless journey crammed with events (not experiences) and contacts (not relationships). In such confounding periods my sense is that one feels like my family did that night in Canada. Where is all of this going? What does it mean? And how will I know when the destination has been reached? Why has this exciting trip suddenly turned into a wearisome journey? When will I find tranquillity again?

To claim that such questions do not occur to a Christian is to be unrealistic and, I might add, unhelpful. For most of us such questions come and come often, and for those few who deny it, I will offer them the benefit of the doubt.

I think Simon Peter was in the middle of one of those darkroad times when he said to his friends, "I am going fishing," and they said, "We're going with you." My bet is that Peter was on the edge of exhaustion—physical, spiritual, and psychic. Too many new and stressful things had been happening to the premier disciple: Judas' surprising betrayal of the Lord, Peter's shocking three-time denial of association with Christ, the subsequent trial, the crucifixion, and the resurrection appearances.

The inner personal world of Peter could absorb just so much, and although we could reason that he should have been ready to take it all in and respond with ease, he wasn't. In a kind of numbness he withdrew to the only thing he really knew how to do with certainty: making money catching fish. Perhaps familiarity would restore whatever it was that was lost deep within.

Using Peter's approach, my family would have turned back on that lonely road—back to something familiar where we could get our bearings again, back to a point where we could gain some degree of control over the hours, the energies, and the direction.

Peter's personal struggle with a sort of weariness did not go on indefinitely. With manly gestures and words, Jesus Christ did a beautiful thing for the exhausted, unproductive fisherman.

What were the gestures? He built a fire, cooked a breakfast, and invited Peter to join him.

What were the words? The ones Christ chose siphoned off the pain of guilt, the embarrassment of failure, and the confusion of mixed motives and goals. Then He repainted the big picture of the original call to servanthood so that Peter was able to function again. What was the result? He restored Peter's spiritual passion. And that's what needs to happen to all of us with regularity.

For some time I have sensed that many people claiming a Christian commitment are careening down an unmarked road of life, a road something like the one in my childhood experience. We believe that the road is going somewhere, but we're not sure where that somewhere is or how we will be certain when we've reached the destination. In transit we move at a dangerous kind of top speed, because we think that that will quicken the time of arrival. And with every mile we may grow increasingly frustrated and tired.

Occasionally we hear of fellow travelers on that same road who crash, and we wonder why they were not smart enough to keep in the lane. Others simply seem to disappear as if they had driven off on a side road and found another direction. But the majority keep pressing on ahead unable to turn back but unsure of what's ahead. And the further they go, the more weary they become.

This weariness is a far cry from the excitement that usually marks the beginning of a trip. What happens? What goes wrong?

Renewing Your Spiritual Passion is meant to take a look at the journey we are on as Christians. A traveler for many years, I've looked into my own experiences and those of others to determine what it is that often adds fatigue and weariness to the trip. I've wanted to catalog some of the issues that slowly drain off the zeal and threaten to leave us with a loss of heart.

I've chosen the word *passion* when others might have used words like *power, zeal, enthusiasm,* or maybe even *joy.* All of these words, and many others like them, speak to the sort of inner force that God promised and that many testify to having received.

Who of us does not crave the passion or the power to be godly people? to give witness to our faith? to serve and give selflessly? to own control of our drives and dispositions? But for many it is easier to talk about passion than to find it or, having found it, to maintain it.

A friend of mine once had a serious struggle with cancer. I asked her one day if her pastor brought help to her when he came to visit her in the hospital. "I'd rather he not come," she said, "because when he visits, he tells me how I ought to feel rather than ask how I actually do feel."

Not only was her comment a lesson to me about how to treat suffering people, but it also reminded me of my own attitude when others have come along with a view of spiritual passion or energy that I was supposed to embrace *because* it had worked for them. As a young man I must have tried a dozen techniques that people said were sure to guarantee a measure of passion that would transport me above the ordinary and ineffective. In each case I eagerly embraced whatever it was that I was supposed to do or say. But the results, if any, were short-lived, and what I discovered was that there are no shortcuts, no gimmicks, no easy ways to cultivate an intimacy with God and attain the resulting passion that should carry one through life's journey.

Then slowly it dawned on me that I and scores of others were paying a terrible price for this search for some magical breakthrough. We were trying harder, working longer, breathing heavier, and getting wearier. And it was an unpleasant journey when it shouldn't have been. Other words that describe such a trip are *sour, stale, bored,* and *numb.* We would never have admitted it, but we were tired of God, of faith, and of faith's people. Now, how could a call to abundant living turn into such dullness of spirit? That we should tire of Him was not God's fault. Rather this weariness calls into question the system of spirituality many of us have been taught.

Although the Scriptures frequently describe some tremendous breakthrough in the spiritual performance of a prophet or apostolic personality, I'd like to suggest that the action is not really there. What we have not stopped to think about is the many long hours and days between the major moments of performance. For example, we know barely a handful of the special moments in the life of the apostle Paul. What we need to ask is how did the man live in the times not recorded in the Scriptures. His attitudes and actions at such times probably have more to tell us about normal spiritual life than the great moments of which Luke wrote.

I want to confess that I have struggled more with the writing of this book than with any I have ever written. First, I found it hard to deal on paper with my own failings and frustrations. But I felt that I had to because whenever I have allowed some personal transparency or vulnerability, I have connected with scores of other people who were thankful to discover that they were not alone. Second, I'm embarrassed with the simple and the "un-novel" nature of my thoughts. Third, I struggle every day (let me repeat: every day!) to put these principles in which I believe to work in my own experience. How I wish I could write from a richer, deeper, more experienced heart!

What compels me to write about the renewal of spiritual passion? I write because I sense out there in the real world of Western Christians that there is a growing weariness of spirit. We have tried the gimmicks, the programs, the promises of a thousand and one "gurus" of the faith. Here and there one view or another seems to catch on. But for many, the journey is a boresome task, and like my family on the dark road, we can't turn back, but we're almost too tired to go on.

Renewing Your Spiritual Passion is disarmingly simple. I merely want to ask the question, what are the things that tire us out and drain us of our desire to be people of God? Let's name the issues and face them squarely for what they are. Then let's ask, how did men and women of spiritual antiquity face these same agents of weariness? Did they have insights we've ignored? And finally, what difference would it make if we followed their advice? My guess is that we would find some ways not only to restore spiritual passion but also to maintain some of the passion we still have.

At least that's the way it seems to me.

Gordon MacDonald
Canterbury, New Hampshire
Madison, Wisconsin

1

It's Got to Glow in You All the Time

He was the first professional athlete I had ever known personally. And in his prime as a football player he was an all-pro pass defender, the best in his business. Like many other people, I was drawn to him, to the force within him that made him a winner, a man with the courage to put his body on the line against an opponent before 75,000 people.

On a Monday, six days before his team would play against the Dallas Cowboys, the two of us were having lunch together. The upcoming game was the subject of our conversation. "How will you prepare yourself for the Cowboy pass offense?" I asked him. "What will your schedule be this week?"

"Well the mornings will all be practice at the stadium," he answered. "And then I'll go home to my den and load the projector [these were the days before VCR's] with game films, and I'll study the Cowboy receivers until I know all of them better than their wives do. I'll check every movement they make when they come out of the huddles to see if they reveal what sort of play it's going to be, what pattern they're going to run, or whether or not they're going to stay back and block."

"What about your evenings?" I asked.

"Oh, I'll keep watching those films straight through until midnight every night."

"Ten hours a day? All week? Nothing else?" I was incredulous.

"Easily," he responded. "Hey, I want to beat those men. I want to hit them so hard if they come into my zone that when they're lying on the ground, they'll look up to the sky with glassy eyes and pray that there won't have to be another play in the game. I want to totally dominate their spirits."

That's passion speaking! Extreme, powerful passion! That's one brand of passion, but there are other brands. The kind I've described may even repel some of us because we could never be so intense and because we do not feel comfortable around people with such intensity. And that's OK.

I only know that when I saw my friend's passion to win a football game (the score and winner of which I cannot even remember), I was inwardly embarrassed to realize that there was no part of my life where I could say I was paying a similar price: not in my family life, not in my work, not in the pursuit of my faith.

Why? I asked myself.

I was bothered that I had no adequate answer.

It certainly is mysterious, this word *passion*. It is hard to measure and difficult to pin down. But you know when you have it, and you are quite aware when you don't. One feels passion; it seizes you! Passion stimulates human performance: superior or excellent performance, strange or bizarre performance, compassionate or sacrificial performance.

We identify passion with romance, revolution, extraordinary achievement, and violence. We use it to explain actions we don't understand. All we know is that it appears to be a force within people that moves them beyond ordinary human activities. Some would suggest that almost all the great literature, drama, and music feature the tale of passion in all its grand forms.

Passion in me seems to be selective. I would like to think I'm passionate when it comes to hugging my wife. I think I've sensed a bit of passion when I have been speaking to a crowd of people on certain subjects that grip my imagination or my sense of outrage. I can get passionate about something I'm writing, and once this fascinating force gains control, I can sit at the keyboard of my computer utterly oblivious of the passing hours as I play with words and phrases to make my point.

On the other hand I'm not inclined, like some, to act out of passionate anger. That is not a virtue, understand; it is merely a segment of my natural temperament. Then, too, I find it difficult to commit to a plethora of causes and movements as a few of my acquaintances do. For me even a passionate expression of belief comes hard. Perhaps that is why I'm uncomfortable with Simon Peter (who is passionate no matter what the issue) and sympathetic to Thomas (the doubter? or merely the cautious one?) when I ponder the temperaments of the disciples of our Lord.

It's hard for me to remember when passion first became an issue for me. I think it was sometime in my college years. I have a recollection of sitting as a graduate student in a seminar room at the University of Colorado. About the table were a dozen men and women, all, like myself, in hot pursuit of a doctorate degree in history. On the table were stacks of books, index cards containing bibliographical notes, and pads upon which we jotted notes from the discussion. The topic was the economic impact of the changes in tobacco prices in the Virginia Colony of the seventeenth century. That afternoon there were differing opinions.

The conversation grew hotter and hotter as various students offered their interpretations of the matter at hand. People raced through books or cards, looking for the one piece of evidence that would substantiate their view of the situation. Voice decibels were raised; hands forcefully gestured; gasps of disgust became frequent as disagreement gained momentum. Everyone was intensely involved, except me.

I drifted away from the vigorous exchanges and began to listen from another perspective, one that did not search for the right interpretation to the problem of Virginia's colonial economy. I'm sure I'd seen passion before, but this was the first time I'd actually attempted to analyze it.

These students really cared about this subject. And I didn't! They appeared prepared to come close to physical blows to defend their opinion. I wasn't! Was this the sort of internal energy that it took to gain a research doctorate? Was this what some meant when they talked about passionate commitment?

I had to conclude that I didn't have passion. At least not for the destabilizing effect of changing tobacco prices. And when I left the room that day, I never went back. It was pointless, I concluded, to commit to an all-consuming goal for which I had no passion.

That was the day I learned that the people in our world who rise to the top of business, sports, academia, science, and politics usually do it because they are fueled by passion. It could be a passion for power, notoriety, or raw achievement. But whatever the motive, a brand of passion is called into action. When I saw the passion of my friend the football player who was preparing for the Dallas Cowboys, I recalled the energy I'd seen in that graduate seminar room at the University of Colorado.

Another athlete, Bart Starr, former quarterback of the world champion Green Bay Packers, talked about one of the most passionate men ever associated with professional football, Vincent Lombardi:

> I wasn't mentally tough before I met Coach Lombardi. I hadn't reached the point where I refused to accept second best. I was too nice at times. I don't believe that nice guys necessarily finish last. I think what Leo Durocher really meant is that nice guys don't finish first. To win, you have to have a certain amount of mental toughness. Coach Lombardi gave me that. *He taught me that you must have a flaming desire to win. It's got to dominate all your waking hours. It can't ever wane. It's got to glow in you all the time* (Kramer, *Lombardi*, p. 86, emphasis mine).

"It's got to glow in you," Starr says. What glows? Passion, the flaming desire. And it glows "all the time." That's a big order, probably an impossibility. But even in his exaggeration, Bart Starr is telling us something of the curious stuff within people who want to be a part of the extraordinary in this world, the folk who change things, make statements, move people, do great things for God.

The prize fighter refers to passion as a killer instinct, the way of the hungry boxer. The businessperson thinks of passion when speaking of an eye for the top. The academic might call it the unvarnished quest for truth. The soldier speaks of gung-ho, and the artist of a kind of mystical perfection.

I think my mother was operating from passion when she did not hesitate to get up in the middle of the night and tend to me when I was a sick child. Passion excited her "mother's

ear," and it became sensitive, it seemed, to the slightest
change in my breathing or to my most feeble call from two
rooms away.

With such terms and performance patterns, people are
telling us what passion means in one form or another.

Passion—the kind that causes some to excel beyond anyone
else—dulls one's sense of fatigue, pain, and the need for
pleasure or even well-being. Passion leads some to pay incredible prices to reach a goal of some sort.

Paul spoke from a wellspring of passion when he wrote:
"But one thing I do, forgetting what lies behind and strain-
ing forward to what lies ahead, I press on toward the goal for
the prize of the upward call of God in Christ Jesus" (Phil.
3:13–14 RSV).

A passion is necessary in the performance of Christian
faith. When Athanasius, the early church father, was told by
his judge that the whole world was against him, Athanasius
responded passionately, "Then is Athanasius against the
whole world." And Luther had to be operating from internal
passion when he stood before the intimidating power of the
papal legates from Rome and said, "Here I stand; I can do
nothing else." And Jim Elliot was clearly in the grip of a
passion when he and his missionary team set their tiny plane
down in a jungle area renowned for murderous Aucas.

Some of us experience another form of passion when we
first make a decision to cross a decision line and commit to
Jesus Christ. Most of us have seen the new believer who—
like the healed man in the temple of Jerusalem—leaps for
joy and cares little about what anyone thinks because he is
so excited about a new life. So strong is that initial passion
that it is almost embarrassing to those who have had more
experience in matters of faith, who have a larger perspective.

"He'll quiet down," they say, because they know. Or at
least they think they know that the initial surge of energy
cannot last forever and that it will one day be diminished by
a more realistic view of things.

But true Christian maturity does not preclude passion.
Perhaps a more experienced style of faith may appear to be
controlled or channeled a bit as when engineers redirect a
peaking flood. And that may be important to remember,
because we tend to conclude that a mature faith does not give

way to explosions of joy or to commitments to objectives that defy the rational mind.

Years after the conversation with my friend the football player, I sat at another lunch with still another friend, who matched my age. We had shared similar life and faith styles. Our backgrounds had caused us to know the Bible well, to make fellowship with Christians an important element of life, and to make doing Christian things a priority. But as we talked, I could tell that my friend bordered on boredom as he told about certain activities in his church, and I decided to penetrate the cloud cover of religious jargon.

"Where are you at these days with God," I asked, using the same, casual tone of voice I would have used to ask about the Dow Jones averages.

"Where am I at with God?" he repeated the question as he looked off at a 45-degree angle from me. There was at least a 30-second pause, and I decided to wait it out. "Do you really want to know?" he finally asked.

"Yeah, I'm your friend, and I'm interested," I responded.

"I'm not anywhere," he said, "and I haven't been anywhere for a long time. When it comes to my Christian life, I'm going through the motions." I made a mental note to ponder his meaning. His comment suggested that there was a sector in his world called the Christian life and that there were other sectors that were some other sort of life.

"Gordon, there was a time in my younger years when it all seemed to grab my imagination, Christ and faith, I mean. I really wanted to make my Christian commitment the absolute center of everything. But I've lost it, and so now I perform more out of habit than anything else."

"What drives you to keep on with the habits?" I probed.

"I suppose only the fact that I'm getting to the point in life where it's too late to change. My family life is all centered on Christian activities, and I don't want to hurt my wife or the kids. And besides, life has been good to me. Why upset the routines that have gotten me this far? So I just keep chugging along."

I had heard this sort of observation before. In fact, I've heard it in discussions with pastors, with missionaries, with lay leaders in churches, with the common man who always seems to be in the midst of things whenever church groups are together.

What's missing? Probably passion! And why is it missing? Usually people don't know. They suddenly become aware, if they have the courage to evaluate inwardly (not many do), that there is no longer an energy to their faith experience. Or they realize that their energy has been reallocated toward the pursuit of a career position or toward a hobby or recreational effort or toward some activity that appears more daring, more pleasurable, or more personally affirming.

And once they get involved with alternatives to spiritual passion, Chrisitan activity becomes dull and boring. They are either beset by guilt or numbed to spiritual sensitivities.

The opposite, of course, is the person who has found a way to maintain such a passion. One is impressed with the words of Willard Hotchkiss, a pioneer missionary who served in Africa who, looking back over a long life of service, wrote:

> I have dwelt forty years practically alone in Africa. I have been 39 times stricken with the fever, three times attacked by lions, and several times by rhinoceri; but let me say to you, I would gladly go through the whole thing again, if I could have the joy of again bringing that word "Savior" and flashing it into the darkness that envelopes another tribe in Central Africa (Hefley and Hefley, *By Their Blood*, p. 340).

Now that's passion! It easily matches that of my friend the pass defender. But it's another brand of passion that probably wouldn't impress my lunch companion either. "You know, that's one of the problems that has always bugged me," he said. "People keep quoting someone else—who usually lives far, far away or who lived in another generation—and say in effect, 'Why can't you be like him?' You know what effect it has on me? I just get more and more miserable when I'm asked to live up to someone else. I'm not them, and they're not me. I used to feel guilty and try to conjure up some feelings when I was challenged like that, and sometimes I could actually do it for a while. Then I gave up. So when those sorts of conversations start, I just turn off."

As a young person I remember many drives along the western banks of New York's Hudson River. Some miles north of the city was an anchorage where dozens of World War II liberty ships were tied side by side. They floated lifelessly, silently, in—as they say—mothballs.

I remember those ships that once sailed the wartime

oceans filled with the fuel, the munitions, the supplies that would launch an army toward the heart of the Axis empire. I used to ponder the hostile action they had seen, the drama that must have taken place as they faced the enemy submarines and aircraft. It had been an era of bravery and valor, of action and productivity.

But now, here on the Hudson, the holds were empty, the decks stripped of their guns and armor. The engines were silent; the crews were scattered. The ships were like floating tombs.

Was that the case of the man who sat with me at lunch and had the courage to describe a real-life situation? I suspect it was.

Can the ships be reclaimed? Brought back to productivity? Of course. Unfortunately—and here the parable begins to disintegrate—some of them will become so useless that they will be towed to sea and sunk, if not torn apart for the scrap heap.

What would it take for my friend to renew the spiritual passion of an earlier time? Could he return to a point in the spiritual formation of his life where he could begin a growth track again? Could he resurrect some sense of affection for God and God's activities?

My friend is not an evil man intent upon destroying the world around him. In fact he is a very good man: a loving husband and father, a loyal contributor to his business, a basic asset to his community. He's a very normal man who'd like to go beyond his present limits, but isn't; and doesn't see how it could ever be different or better.

How might he renew that spiritual passion of earlier days? Perhaps it would be good, first of all, if he understood the many and varied ways that such passion is diminished to the point of nonexistence.

Then it might be helpful if he thought through the simple disciplines that aerate the inner spirit from which this kind of passion flows. It's possible, just possible, that spiritual passion could be restored. And if it could be restored for him, why could it not for millions of others who call themselves Christians but sense deep within that what they are into is more habit than passion.

Masculine drives within me cause me to admire the football player who wants to win so badly that he'll pay the price.

But the more I think about it, I admire an even deeper quality about him. Even though a few people might think he's committed to something quite senseless, at least in contrast to the larger issues of life, he is a person committed to something. He knows the feeling of being lifted above ordinary limitations. He understands what it is like to be singularly focused. He appreciates the meaning of risk for something he perceives as larger than himself.

Something in me admires that. Something inside me wants to know it is possible to generate that kind of passion and, if my spiritual passion ever gets dissipated, to know it is possible to renew it. Something prods me to think that the drive that generates that kind of passion can generate a spiritual passion that can lift me to an extraordinary service for God and His people, a passion that does more than win games. It could be an energy that changes things in my little world.

2

Doing More and Enjoying It Less

I'm not sure I understand it, but I have this feeling that an increasing amount of conversational time between friends is spent on the subject of weariness, overcommitment, the perceived need to drop out.

You see someone you know, and you ask a simple question: "What's going on in your world these days?"

You may get an all too common answer: "I've got to cut down! I'm into too many things."

Or you ask someone how he or she is feeling and you're liable to hear the response, "I think I'm on the edge of burnout . . . or something."

You comment on how busy the last few weeks seem to have been, and someone agrees and begins to philosophize: "Tell me, do you ever ask yourself why we're doing all of this anyway?"

Or, being sensitive to someone who appears to have been working too hard, you remark, "You look like you're bushed tonight," and you hear, "I'm absolutely exhausted. I've never been so shot. I'll never get so overinvolved again."

Why on the one Sunday in five years when a New England snowstorm forced us to close down our church was it universally recognized by the congregation as the most wonderful Lord's day they had ever had? What was being said?

"I couldn't believe it," someone commented about the day. "I had an entire twenty-four hours with my family; no schedule, nothing to do, just being quiet. It was marvelous." I remember hearing that observation and wondering why we needed an "act of God" to force us into doing what we all badly wanted to do: enjoy with those whom we love an interlude in the schedule away from all the routine busyness. Strange! These were not spiritual rebels speaking. These were substantial, faithful people.

An old cigarette ad sums up these reactions quite well: "smoking more and enjoying it less." That is exactly what appears to be happening today among many people who have honestly tried to think and act toward the goal of making a contribution to their worlds—their churches, their communities, and other organizations.

We're talking about people with a vision to be useful. They are living according to the principle of responsibility, the belief that they have a contribution to make, that their generation ought to be just a little bit better because of who they are and what they are able to do. They see their abilities and energies as something they must share with others or with the organization of which they are a part. But the more willing they are to get involved, the more opportunities, sometimes even demands, seem to come their way.

What is the possible result? Increasing fatigue, exhaustion, weariness, loss of passion. Not necessarily of the body but of the spirit within. Sometimes you can almost see an erosion of the original excitement and joy begin to set in. And finally, if nothing is done to bring the process of busyness under discipline, the inner weariness begins to show in the quality of outer activity. Suddenly there is a surprising sloppiness and undependability in the work. Irritations with people lead to conflicts. There may be physical sickness, a bitter spirit, and, finally, a crisis moment when one simply quits.

More and more we see people who were in the center of things one year suddenly drift away to the edge of things the next year and then quietly disappear to a more private life. Talk with them, and you discover that they came to a point where they lost their zeal to keep going. "I found myself chasing my tail around the proverbial barn," one woman said to me. "I was tired of being tired all the time."

From Mrs. Lettie Cowman's wonderful book, *Springs in*

the Valley (pp. 196–97), comes this interesting tale from African colonial history:

> In the deep jungles of Africa, a traveler was making a long trek. Coolies had been engaged from a tribe to carry the loads. The first day they marched rapidly and went far. The traveler had high hopes of a speedy journey. But the second morning these jungle tribesmen refused to move. For some strange reason they just sat and rested. On inquiry as to the reason for this strange behavior, the traveler was informed that they had gone too fast the first day, and that *they were now waiting for their souls to catch up with their bodies.*

Then Mrs. Cowman concludes with this penetrating exhortation:

> This whirling rushing life which so many of us live does for us what that first march did for those poor jungle tribesmen. The difference: *they knew* what they needed to restore life's balance; too often *we do not.*

It is incredible to realize that Lettie Cowman wrote these words almost fifty years ago.

The way we get consumed by a schedule of activities suddenly out of control is alarming. It reminds one of the old Uncle Remus story of the tar baby. Hit the figure of tar with one fist, and your hand is stuck. So you hit it with the other in order to get unstuck, and you know what happens. Now you are in real trouble. Kick it with a free foot, and things get increasingly complicated. Use the last free limb, and the tar baby has got you. Sometimes I think modern schedules are like tar babies.

The analogy is a real one to me. I can easily recall the many times when I have accumulated a list of commitments and obligations (all perfectly good) that have made me feel as constrained as if I'd hit and kicked that tar baby.

The list had grown usually because the things asked of me were good things: challenging, needs-oriented things I believed God had equipped and gifted me to do. But at other times? I probably said yes and made the list grow because I wanted people to like me, because I didn't have the courage to say no, because I didn't want to be left out or because there was a stream of guilt (false guilt perhaps) that drowned out the voice of inner wisdom.

And what is the result when the list gets larger than life? It is weariness, the feeling of being trapped, the desire to run. This sort of thing is being expressed when one friend says to another, "You know, I used to enjoy doing this, but it isn't fun anymore."

The good news of modern busyness is the amazing outburst of opportunities to exercise our capacities and skills, our gifts and visions. The bad news is the increasing amount of fatigue and frustration in the spirit, the sense of a personal performance for God that is not spontaneous but rather too automatic, a joyless merry-go-round of activity that never seems to stop.

For those in the salaried Christian ministry, life usually revolves around a never-ending workcycle that is hard to interrupt without a sense of dis-ease about things still undone. Anyone who has given themselves to the leading, caring, or developing of people knows that there is always one more thing that could be done better and more completely.

For the layperson who seeks a faithful life for God in the church and in the marketplace, it would seem as if there is a relentless barrage of good things in which to be involved over and above the responsibilities for which one gets paid. "I do have a living to make and a family to support, you know," a layman said to me once when I had suggested one more thing he could do in the church.

Funny! It was as if that hadn't occurred to me. But the fact is if you do a few things well in any voluntary organization like the church, it will suddenly seem as if interesting folk come out of the wall with potential additions to the agenda or schedule. Doing one thing seems to lead to another. One is never sure when enough is enough.

In the religious world we are all confronted with a whirl of programs, conferences, seminars, and retreats inside and outside the church. The competition for our time and energy grows more fierce with each year and every bright person who has a new idea about something for us to learn or master. (I saw one seminar brochure recently with a money-back guarantee on the registration form: "If you don't agree that this is the most valuable seminar you've attended this year . . .")

How has this happened? It's the result of lots of good things happening to us—innovation, visionary people, techniques and methods borrowed from every sector of modern life.

Weariness comes not only in the things there are to do but also from the incredible amount of experience and information coming at us. I think one can actually grow tired from the constant onrush of spiritual stimulation. Words and more words, sensation and excitement!

Christian media—radio and TV, the publishing empires, and the authors of direct mail—have all romanced us with an avalanche of causes and concerns asking for our money, our time and effort, and our loyalty. Using the most persuasive marketing techniques, the most attractive people, and the most heart-gripping stories, they claw at our emotions and our minds. They invite us to telethons, tours to the Holy Land, cruises in the Caribbean, banquets and retreats. It's not all bad. In fact, it can all be exciting—at first. But, like an addiction, we must experience more and more of it lest it grow weak and lose its ability to stimulate our passion. And it does have a wearying effect.

Most of us have forgotten the era in which the local Christian congregation had a very few basic programs aside from worship on Sunday morning. The modern program explosion has raised our expectations as well as our frustrations. Most of us would feel that we had been cheated or that our church was not keeping up with the times if there were not something going on every day and evening of the week to meet the expanded sense of human need and desire to be doing everything. But of course those busy programs need personnel both to run them and to participate in them. And you know who that is.

An associate of mine is fond of comparing situations in which one is overwhelmed by good things to do and learn to taking a drink from a fire hydrant. A little bit of water from a gentle fountain can go a long way, he says. But put your mouth in front of a flowing hydrant, and things can get dangerous. What could have brought refreshment can also bring injury.

I am one who is convinced that the relentless flow of information, religious stimulation, and opportunity coming at us is indeed like a hydrant under high pressure, and that it is having a subtle effect upon our inner spirits, or as I have called it in other places, our private worlds. If I am correct, we can expect at least two things to happen almost at once.

First, as our eyes are drawn more and more to the events and data of the public world (even the Christian public world, if you please), the private world, the heart, becomes increasingly starved for attention and inner maintenance. More time for activity means less time for devotion. Doing more *for* God may mean less time *with* God. Talking becomes an effective substitute for meditating or listening. After all, something says to us, doing all these noble things isn't all bad. No, it may be good; but it may not always be best.

Second, and happening simultaneously, the busyness of our lifestyles is expending what passion we already have. In other words there is *output but no input!* And then there comes the inevitable moment when we become aware—like my friend of the last chapter—that we are going through motions, responding to habits. But the busyness is passionless. We are doing more and enjoying it less.

Let me propose that we need to understand what is happening to us as modern, Western Christians. Why are we telling one another with increasing repetition that we're tired and burned out? What is this frantic lifestyle doing to us? Shouldn't we occasionally cry *Stop!* and ask if this is the way Christ meant for us to live?

"But wasn't Christ always busy? Didn't He live a fairly pressurized life?" someone asks. "I don't see Jesus taking an evening off, playing miniature golf, scheduling four-week vacations. And when did Paul play? And where do you get any biblical basis for putting limits on the things we should be into? I don't see that as helpful to us when we are trying to get people to be more committed to the Christian mission."

"You may have a good point until you think again about Jesus' lifestyle in the biblical context, not in twentieth-century terms," I respond. "For example, when He went from town to town with His disciples, He moved on foot (or in a boat). There were long hours of quietness in the country-side on those walks. It wasn't the frantic jetting around—breakfast in Jerusalem, lunch in Damascus, and supper in Antioch." As J. B. Phillips put it:

It is refreshing and salutary, to study the poise and quietness of Christ. His task and responsibility might well have driven a man out of his mind. But He was never in a hurry, never impressed by numbers, never a slave of the clock. He was acting, He said, as He observed God to act—never in a hurry (Phillips, *Your God Is Too Small*, p. 56).

And that is important to remember. The fact is that the pace of life in Jesus' time was automatically governed not by inner discipline but by practical obstacles we have overcome by high-speed transportation, telephone, and organizational technique. But those obstacles guaranteed a more serene schedule.

If there were spaces in our calendars created by a slow-paced life, then we would not need to talk about artificial means of recreation, quietness, and renewal. We would know something of genuine tiredness at the end of an honest day's labor. We would not be talking about exhaustion of spirit, the loss of spiritual passion. We would not be checking calendars looking for just one evening when we could spend time getting our minds and hearts back into order again.

My Grandfather MacDonald traveled to Eastern Europe almost every year in the 1920s and 30s to preach and visit missionaries. After the war he resumed his annual schedule. And when he visited the continent, he would travel by steamship. When he arrived in France, he was refreshed by the several days of sailing when he had had the time to relax, read, study, and prepare sermons. The obstacle of the ocean and the slowness of the ship guaranteed the opportunity for the gathering, or the restoration, of his spiritual passion. And when he disembarked, he landed running!

It's different today in my generation. I would think nothing of flying to Europe and trying to engage in ministry within an hour of my arrival. And, most likely, my hosts would keep me as busy as possible since they would want to use every minute of my availability to justify the cost of the plane ticket. And I wonder why I fall into the weariness created by jet lag.

I suspect that Christ knew nothing of jet lag. Neither did my grandfather. Jesus was also not victimized by jangling telephones, filled mailboxes, international consultations, and Sunday school picnics.

Think with me a bit about weariness. It is not the honest tiredness of the body we will all feel at the end of a good working day. Rather it is the weariness of a tired spirit, the state of passionlessness where serving the Lord has become a tasteless experience, where the power and the delight of being a man or woman of God is missing. Where does that kind of spiritual dullness come from? And what are the consequences? And what, if anything, can we do to handle it when it comes or even avoid it so it won't come?

We will discover—when we stop and think—that our sense of weariness is a tricky subject. For example, we can be genuinely tired from busyness and pressure and not actually know it because what we are doing is so exciting and challenging that we lose ourselves in the sheer joy of it and refuse to hear the signals of fatigue. And, for a while, our bodies and minds will cooperate with us and permit us the extra exertion. That's life fueled by spiritual passion.

On other occasions we can think that we are tired, but we actually have much more energy in reserve than our bodies or minds will admit. But the task in which we are engaged is not attractive, and we may be afraid of failure. Now the body and mind protest, and they may signal exhaustion, a false kind. Why, for example, do I automatically grow drowsy the minute I try to pray? Why is it that I might feel an absence of energy the moment my wife suggests doing a task that will benefit a needy person?

Funny, these feelings of weariness. They are hard to depend upon, unless you figure them out.

When I was an athlete on the track and cross-country course, my teammates and I thought about this sort of thing. We studied weariness, its origins and effects. We learned to discriminate between *feelings* of fatigue and *genuine* fatigue. This was important because the challenge in running is as much mental conditioning as it is physical conditioning and development of brute strength. Most of the tiredness I experienced at the midpoint of a competitive run was in the mind, not in the legs. It was helpful to know that. There is a passion of sorts in running, and you can't win a big race without it. The passion is cultivated and has to be maintained. Fatigue is the enemy of the runner's passion, and fatigue is the result when the passion is gone.

Therefore, I learned to analyze my weariness in the midst of competition and to pose the question, *Where is this fatigue I feel coming from?* More than once I had to ask myself in the third mile of a five-mile run, *Why do I want to stop running right now, quit this race—even the team—and go home to a comfortable bed like any other sane person? Are these signals I'm getting from my body real or false?*

These are not unlike the sorts of questions a man or woman in Christian responsibility ought to ask. *What is it that I feel? And where are the feelings coming from? Are they real? What are they telling me?*

Study the life of Christ, and you will discover that He was never on the verge of passionlessness. He obviously understood how one gets into that kind of situation. It is no accident that before and after heavy periods of activity He went apart and stored up, or replenished, the inner energy or passion necessary to carry out His mission. And, again, it is no accident that He never seems to have engaged in activity that was beyond His reasonable limits. He was pulled or guided by a mission—"to seek and to save the lost" (Luke 19:10 RSV)—, but He also seemed to have had an inner governor that effectively checked any urge to do more than was wise and prudent.

It occurs to me that Christ would have been comfortable with the words of John Wesley, "Though I am always in haste, I am never in a hurry because I never undertake more work than I can go through with calmness of spirit."

Calmness of spirit is the necessary condition for a well-ordered life. How might such a calmness be ours? There are of course lots of answers to that question. But I'm convinced that the first answers come in understanding something about the origins of weariness. Let me trace these origins for you in the next chapters.

3
It's All Over!

Let's return to the world of running. Those who compete in the Boston Marathon are well acquainted with Heartbreak Hill, a slow and long, tortuous climb through the streets of Newton, Massachusettes, about two-thirds of the way into the twenty-six-mile race. It is at old Heartbreak that the best runners break from the pack and prove their superiority.

Smart competitors mentally plan for Heartbreak Hill. They know what the mind will tell them at that point in the run, and they stride through the first seventeen miles with that fact in mind. What they have done is to reserve a kind of mental energy, a passion you could say, because they know where the inner battle will be. That's what I mean, in part, when I say that runners study the issue of fatigue.

The Boston runners taught me something about spiritual passion. A wise person, I saw, knows how to look ahead and spot the places where fatigue, the loss of spiritual passion, is likely to happen and why. That person knows, therefore, how to gather the necessary energy or passion ahead of time, how to parcel it out during the most challenging periods, and *how to renew that inner force later on.*

Jesus, greeting His disciples back from their two-by-two mission said, "Let's get away from the crowds for a while and rest" (Mark 6:31 TLB). He knew what kind of shape they'd be in. And so He arranged that boat trip to the countryside where they could be alone. When they got there, they were met by 5,000 people; it was hardly a place to recover one's passion. But the record would seem to suggest that He engaged the crowds while the disciples took most of the day off. You could say they were renewing their spiritual passion.

Interesting it is, however, that even when Jesus called upon them to aid Him in feeding the crowd, they were disinterested and discouraged about the possibilities. They had just returned from a missionary-like experience where they were able to report remarkable happenings that were obviously miraculous, and they could not handle one more simple challenge. "Send the crowd away" (Luke 9:12 RSV), was their only response. Is there an indication here of their loss of inner energy, their fatigued condition?

Yesterday's spiritual passion cannot be today's inner energy. Passion quickly dissipates; it must be renewed. Like the manna God gave the Israelites in the desert, spiritual passion spoils quickly. As Moses and his people had to collect manna daily, so must we restore spiritual passion regularly. We would be wise to know how it so quickly disappears and what we can do when that happens.

As I once learned to study fatigue and loss of courage in the pursuit of athletic excellence, so I have learned to study fatigue and loss of courage in the pursuit of Christian commitment.

It has been helpful to me, first of all, to realize that there are *conditions* of life that affect spiritual passion, conditions like the advisories the weather people put out for sailors, stockmen, and travelers when the elements are turning hostile. So there are conditions when you and I can expect trouble ahead.

Some of these conditions are predictable; others are not. But I have lived long enough now to categorize them for myself, and in the majority of cases I am now capable of looking at events and situations around me and—like the runner at Heartbreak Hill—saying to myself, "No wonder I feel this way; look at what's going on."

When a young pastor, I had a dream to visit the people of my congregation at their places of work. They regularly saw me at my worksite when I was at *my* best; why should I not see them at the point of labor where they were at their best? I strongly believed in this process and began to carry it out.

I visited managers at their offices. I rode with salesmen on

212 Renewing Your Spiritual Passion

their routes. I saw people in manufacturing plants, labs, and stores. The word got around that I was serious about visiting such places.

"Come out to my job," a construction steelworker said to me. And I enthusiastically responded, "Only if you'll take me right up to the top of the building where you work."

"I'll do it," he said.

Three days later I found myself hard-hatted and ascending a ladder (straight up) to the fourth story of a steel skeletal structure. By the second story I was terrified, a surprise since I'd not known that heights could be a problem for me. But the "man" in me was not going to admit to fear. By the third floor I was holding on to each rung of the ladder with extreme care. When I reached the top of the ladder, my friend was standing ten feet away on a steel beam that *seemed* no wider than a clothesline.

"Come out here," he said grinning at my discomfort. And I inched myself along the beam like a first-time horse-back rider. That day I lost my passion for visiting *every* man and woman at their jobs and trying to pretend that I could go wherever they went. I discovered conditions where one's inner resolve disappears and may never return. It took me some time before I was ready to say again, "I'll go anywhere you're doing your thing."

The boxer Sugar Ray Leonard, who retired after an eye injury, attempted a comeback and was knocked flat in the sixth round by a lesser opponent. The newspapers printed a photo of him sitting bewildered on the canvas. "What were you thinking at that moment?" a reporter asked.

"I was saying to myself, *It's all over*," he answered. It was a dramatic picture symbolizing a condition where the passion to come back suddenly disappeared.

SEVEN CONDITIONS THAT THREATEN SPIRITUAL PASSION

When I ponder the varieties of conditions that threaten our passion to know and serve our God, I come up with seven different ones. They are helpful to know and describe because I then can spot the times they are most likely to occur and know how I should perform when they do. Let's start with one of the most obvious of the passion-threatening conditions.

1. THE DRAINED CONDITION

Thankfully, I have never experienced the state of drunkenness in my life, but I do understand hangovers. And so does everyone who has ever engaged in substantial spiritual leadership.

Hangovers—of the type I am describing—often happen on a Monday morning for a preacher or for others at the conclusion of any sustained period of time when there has been a lavish expenditure of inner resources. This is not a religious phenomenon by any means. Any person who is heavily involved with people in highly stressful encounters of problem solving, conflict, or sales will understand what it means to be drained.

As I have already emphasized, the supply of the energy, or passion, within the inner spirit is not inexhaustible; it can and will be depleted.

Young men and women tend *not* to know that. They surmise that the brute strength of their physical energy level can carry them on indefinitely. It can work for a while. But not forever! One day, having ignored this possibility, they awake to the extreme inner stress of exhaustion of spirit. It is a terribly confusing experience.

No description of the drained condition, which I call the hangover, can improve upon the account of the prophet Elijah. When Elijah hit bottom in his own spirit and fled to the wilderness, he determined that death would be preferable to the way he felt. How did the man get that way?

The desert depression was preceded by the Mount Carmel triumph. Elijah had been on the mountain three days earlier, engaged in a remarkable confrontation with the pagan priests of Baal who had been religiously captivating the people of Israel.

The sitting king and queen of the day Ahab and Jezebel were to blame for the ascendancy of the Baal priests, and, as a result, God had judged the land with a "no-rain" edict for three years.

Now the showdown had begun. Elijah had challenged the priests to a duel of sorts, and he had scored a spectacular victory by the end of the day. An altar had been erected on the mountaintop. Two bulls were prepared for sacrifice: one for the Baal folk, one for Elijah. A vast crowd of countrymen had gathered to watch. Reputations were at stake. Elijah was very much alone; the priests had an army of supporters.

"You call on the name of your god and I will call on the name of the Lord; and the God who answers by fire, he is God" (1 Kings 18:24 RSV). It was a fairly straightforward process. Take your best shot, go first, shout loud. And they had.

All morning there had been the absurd scene of sincere, grown men dancing, screaming, cutting themselves in order to gain the attention of their god. And nothing had worked! ". . . they raved on . . . but there was no voice; no one answered, no one heeded" (1 Kings 18:29 RSV).

Finally, it was Elijah's turn. He repaired the long-ignored altar of the Lord, set wood and the prepared animal in place, and then—just to add drama to the situation—drenched the entire piece with water. Finally he prayed, "Let it be known . . . that thou art God in Israel, and that I am thy servant, and that I have done all these things at thy word. Answer me, O Lord . . ." (1 Kings 18:36–37 RSV).

Talk about passion! One man against a spiritually depraved nation, a powerful king and queen, and several hundred priests who by their numbers alone had to be intimidating. I've always considered this one of the great moments in biblical history.

God answered the prayer—with force! Fire flew from heaven; the sacrifice was consumed, and the flippant nation of Israel burst into applause—for the moment. It was an exceptional display of heaven's power in collusion with a faithful man who was angry and passionate about the spiritual corruption in his world.

But a few days later, there was this inevitable hangover. It is difficult to describe what the encounter on the mountain top must have taken out of Elijah. All we have is the record of his foul mood there in the desert. Having descended from the mountain, Elijah had received death threats from the queen, Jezebel, who was not a little embarrassed over the humiliation handed to her team of Baal priests. Her best response for the moment could only come in the form of empty words: We're coming after you.

Then he was afraid, and he arose and went for his life and . . . he himself went a day's journey into the wilderness . . . and he asked that he might die, saying, "It is enough; now, O LORD, take away my life . . ." (1 Kings 19:3-4 RSV).

One might wonder why the man didn't send a message back to the palace, saying "Stick and stones may break my bones, but names will never hurt me." But Elijah was, by this time, wearied enough that he believed the queen's words and, having lost perspective, he fled the country to the desert. Was this the same man who performed on Mount Carmel? Yes, *and he was drained!* Even if it is at Elijah's expense, we should take great comfort and warning from his misery.

Take a hard look at Elijah under the broom tree, asking God that he might die. "It is enough; now, O LORD, take away my life; for I am no better than my fathers" (1 Kings 19:4 RSV). More than anything else, Elijah needed some sleep and some good food, and it was provided. "Arise and eat," an angel told him when he awoke, "else the journey will be too great for you" (1 Kings 19:7 RSV). And although that was not the end of the story, it put the prophet into something of a better mental condition to get on with the restoration of his spiritual passion.

Again, Elijah was simply drained. He had given out everything on the mountain top; nothing was left. Who is there that hasn't had the same experience?

Pastors or Christian workers whose peak days are Sundays awaken on Mondays wondering why they feel so empty. Some of my former partners in ministry used to have a private scheme of measurement by which we gauged our spiritual condition on Monday mornings. Seizing the old phrase "I feel as if a truck ran over me," we often asked one another, "But how many trucks?" Using a scale of one to ten, we considered a one-truck Sunday to be unusually mild while a ten-truck Sunday described the ultimate debacle that might create the need for a week's vacation.

All of us with leadership responsibility, however, will have our version of a pastor's Monday morning. The simple explanation? You can't do work of a spiritual nature without energy going out of you. Jesus felt it acutely when a sick woman reached out and touched the bottom of His robe. "Someone . . . touched me," he said, "for I felt healing power go out from me" (Luke 8:46 TLB).

Individuals in a drained condition feel caught up in a sea of feelings that often runs counter to all the facts. There are strong senses of self-doubt and negativism. The mind seeks out all the possible minor (and major) errors that might have been made in the past hours, and then it amplifies them until all positive contributions are mentally blotted out. Drained people become supercritical of self and, of course, of others. They are convinced they have made fools of themselves, that nothing done or said will be remembered or implemented.

When men and women are drained, they often generate moods that lead to their wanting to quit the tasks they've wanted to do the most. Like Elijah, they are convinced that their usefulness is over, that they are powerless to go any further.

General William Booth, founder of the Salvation Army, came to the point of feeling drained more than once. Once in such a condition, lonely and exhausted while on an extensive traveling itinerary, he was ready to throw his ministry over. Writing to his wife, Catherine, he said:

> I wonder whether I could not get something to do in London of some kind, some secretaryship or something respectable that would keep us going. I know how difficult things are to obtain without friends or influence, as I am fixed. But we must hope against hope, I suppose. (Begbie, *The Life of General Wm. Booth*, p. 422).

Pondering those words—and knowing exactly how the general felt—I realize that most people, then and now, visualized Booth as indestructible, resolved and committed no matter what, a giant of a man of God who could do anything his spirit and passion determined had to be done. Yet here, behind the scenes where no one can see, is the picture of an empty man who, like the boxer knocked flat on the canvas, seems to be saying, "It's all over."

To those of us who have ever worked with university students, the name of Howard Guinness is a special one. More than fifty years ago, Guinness, a young medical doctor, interrupted his career to tour the countries of the British Commonwealth, speaking to student groups and starting Christian student works in scores of colleges and universities. It was an exhausting routine, and Guinness was often drained. He described one moment:

Toward the end of the itinerary I was so tired that when I arrived back in Auckland [New Zealand] and was giving my report of the tour to a public meeting I had to stop and sit down without finishing. If I had said another word I would have found myself in tears. The nervous batteries had completely run down (Guinness, *Journey Among Students*, p. 71).

These drained moments can often be a time in which one feels a terrible sense of loneliness. Those of us who have traveled, giving talks or lectures, can attest to the sense of isolation in a hotel room after one has given out everything to a crowd of people for a day.

Some men will candidly share that in this lonely condition they are mysteriously drawn to sensual entertainment. Why? Simply, they are so drained of spiritual passion that they are open to anything that hints it might be able to renew the emptiness caused by giving out so much.

Knowing the drained condition so well myself, I long ago began to spot those times when I was most likely to face such an emotional and spiritual hangover. I knew of course that Monday was most likely to be a day like that, and I learned to spot periods of time on the calendar when there would be a heavy exhaustion of inner resources because of people contact, traveling, and intense problem solving.

It became important to schedule periods before and after when I could renew myself. And I learned to record the Elijah-like feelings in a journal or share them with my wife so that I could be more objective. And usually it works, but, of course, not always.

The *drained condition*—we ought not to be surprised when it hits us with force.

The runner at Heartbreak Hill in Newton isn't surprised. He knows from experience and from the descriptions of others that he will feel exhausted and ready to quit as he plods along. But if he can make it through what he calls the physical and psychic wall, there will be better moments. If he doesn't quit now, there will be glory ahead. And he doesn't quit because he knows what weariness is all about and where it comes from. The passion to finish the course and to win remains.

4

Running on Empty

I have a childhood memory of my father habitually (or so it seemed to me) driving his car with the gas tank gauge always signaling EMPTY. Was it a subconscious game he played, a sort of gambling process that he secretly enjoyed?

"Dad, you're running on empty," we would say.

"I know," he would respond, "but when the needle gets to that point there's always a gallon or two left in the tank."

Perhaps my father was simply out of gas money and didn't want to admit it. I never found out. I just remember that there were too many worrisome journeys through places like the Holland Tunnel (in New York at rush hour) with the gas gauge silently screaming *the tank is dried out!* He never seemed perturbed by this.

Spiritually speaking, many followers of Christ run on empty most of the time and wonder why there seems to be no natural energy or passion to engage in spiritual life or work. And that highlights another condition of life in which spiritual passion is likely to be missing.

2. THE DRIED-OUT CONDITION

The second condition of weariness can be described by the phrase *dried out*. If the one who is drained has reached that state by exhausting resources, one who is *dried out* has reached that state by not taking anything into the inner chambers of life for quite some time. The two conditions are often closely associated.

The unfilled spiritual tank is an invitation to disaster, and many of us have known that awful moment when, like a car out of gas, we seem to cough and sputter and pull over to the shoulder, out of service, not able to go any farther.

We have all seen the car out of gas in a long tunnel or on a narrow bridge at rush hour. Thousands of people are potentially affected in the clogged-up mess that follows. And it can happen in spiritual life also. One empty spiritual tank can affect a score of other people. It's happened more than once.

Like many others, I am no stranger to the dried-out condition. This condition is often a danger for the multi-gifted person, one who has many differing gifts and capacities and who can appear to go for long periods, as they say, winging it.

Those with natural talents, like musicians, are quite vulnerable here. They can mistake the applause of the admiring crowds for God's blessing. Thinking that their ability to raise the emotions of people in an artistic setting is the same as being a tool in the hand of God, they begin to abandon any sense of need for spiritual passion or energy and move ahead on their own instincts. More often, what power they appear to have is sheer theatrics, not spiritual passion. Often the system seems to work for a long time, and then—disaster.

Some people are good with words, able to put concepts and stories together with ease. The words form into testimonies, Bible studies, sermons. Again, the crowd's response dulls the speakers into thinking that they are God's servants and that a schedule that leaves no time for the refueling of spiritual energy is justified by the apparent results—again, disaster.

How can one describe the dried-out condition? It is action without heart, oratory without power, doctrine without love. People who are dried out within can often be, for a while, the hardest workers. But they can also become the harshest critics and the most negative teammates.

Inside they experience a rising of turbulence—confused goals and motives and inconsistent, unexplainable patterns of personal performance.

W. E. Sangster describes the realities in his world when he concludes that he is spiritually dried out (P. Sangster, *Doctor Sangster*, p. 90):

I am a minister of God, and yet my private life is a failure in these ways:

a. I am irritable and easily put out.

b. I am impatient with my wife and children.

c. I am deceitful in that I often express private annoyance when a caller is announced and simulate pleasure when I actually greet them.

d. From an examination of my heart, I conclude that most of my study has been crudely ambitious: that I wanted degrees more than knowledge and praise rather than equipment for service.

e. Even in my preaching I fear that I am more often wondering what the people think of *me*, than what they think about my Lord and His word.

f. I have long felt in a vague way, that something was hindering the effectiveness of my ministry and I must conclude that the "something" is my failure in living the truly Christian life.

g. I am driven in pain to conclude that the girl who has lived as a maid in my house for more than three years has not felt drawn to the Christian life because of me.

h. I find slight envies in my heart at the greater success of other young ministers. I seem to match myself with them in thought and am vaguely jealous when they attract more notice than I do.

Again, people saw Sangster—as they would have seen General Booth—as a giant. But he alone knew when he was operating from a full heart or an empty one.

Is this not the condition of David when he faced the great dual temptation of adultery and murder? It is a dramatic example, but one can't read the story without realizing that the man was in the wrong place, doing wrong things when he got into personal trouble.

David should have been with his armies, doing what God had purposed him to do. He would have been stretched and pressed by circumstances, forced to seek spiritual guidance and direction. But he wasn't there! Rather, he was at home in a state of undeserved relaxation, with nothing to do and his spiritual disciplines laid aside.

What was the result? He was left with no passion to identify and stand against temptation, no passion to make him hungry for the guidance of God, no passion to produce a hunger to be strong, honorable, and effective as a man of God.

Dried out, David made a series of bad choices, and when he reached the bottom line of performance, he destroyed a number of lives. (One has the mental image of traffic stalled in a tunnel at rush hour because one person entered with an empty tank.) What's worse, it took David a year before he realized the full import of what he'd done.

When Nathan the prophet paid a visit to David, he had to resort to a parable to gain David's attention. Usually, parables are for people whose inner spirits are locked up, impervious to the Holy Spirit of God. It's clear that David was in rough shape spiritually when Nathan came to call. He was in no mood for getting right to the point. So, the parable, and it worked. David was (as they say) "had," shocked into the realization of his performance over the last year.

It must have been a terrible moment of self-realization as David came to grips with his own inconsistencies and hypocrisies. How, he must have wondered, could he have gotten himself into this sort of situation? Weren't the warnings abundant enough? How, after years of intimacy with God, could he have permitted himself to become so empty and resistant? I suspect David asked himself questions of that sort for the rest of his life.

I have known what it is to be dried out. On some occasions I have shared with younger men and women a bitter experience in my late twenties when I encountered the dried-out condition with force.

One Saturday morning I sat in our kitchen obviously rattled and withdrawn, and my wife, Gail, was trying to discern what it was that was bothering me. Suddenly, she asked one question too many, and I broke into weeping. Even now, I remember the next two hours vividly because it seemed as if I would never be able to stop the flow of tears.

Gail handled the situation with grace and strength. She permitted me to exhaust myself of tears and then began to quietly quiz me about the events that had led up to this strange experience.

For the previous two weeks I had minimized my sleep because of busyness; thus I was physically exhausted. I had allowed my schedule to become so packed that I had ignored any times of personal worship; thus I was spiritually empty.

In what seemed to be a remarkable coincidence, I had presided at two funerals of indigent men who had died on the city streets and whose lives and deaths seemed to me to be so terribly meaningless. The experiences had profoundly affected me. Additionally, I had been reading a then well-known author who was launching an attack on matters of personal belief important to me, and I was not responding well to his logic.

On that Saturday morning I was a dried-out man. My resources were nonexistent. Years and accumulated experience later, I would know better than to get backed into such a corner. But I didn't know that then. It was a difficult way to learn an important lesson about being empty.

I can't help but wonder how many good men and women have utterly failed in a public sense because they began to operate on the treadmill of Christian leadership from a spiritually dehydrated condition. This dried-out, empty condition explains the passionlessness of many Christians more than anything else.

3. THE DISTORTED CONDITION

Earl Palmer began one of his great books by providing a transcript of a radio commercial in the early 1940s:

> According to a recent nationwide survey, more doctors smoke Camels than any other cigarette. Three leading independent research organizations asked this question of 113,597 doctors: "What cigarette do you smoke, Doctor?" The brand named most was Camel. Now you probably enjoy rich full flavor and cool mildness in a cigarette just as much as doctors do, and that's why if you're not a Camel smoker now, try a Camel on your T-zone, (that's T for taste and T for throat), your true proving ground for any cigarette. See if Camel's rich flavor of superbly blended choice tobaccos isn't extra delightful to your taste. See if Camel's cool mildness isn't in harmony with your throat. See if you too don't say, "Camels suit my T-zone to a tee" (Palmer, *Alive From the Center*, p. 14).

I was drawn to the commercial, first, because I remember it as a child, but, second, because I was impressed with how persuasive it must have been to people listening in those days. After all, these are doctors, experts, saying these things. If they smoke, why not me? Thousands of cases of cancer are the result of the so-called experts endorsing a product.

Spiritual passion is constantly under attack by the distortions of truth that pervade our times. We pass through a world in which there are, I am told, more than two thousand persuasion messages pressed at us each day. They come to us, for example, in advertising, direct human encounters, signs all about us (STOP HERE; NO FOOD OR DRINK ALLOWED; KEEP OFF GRASS), and endorsements by impressive people.

The mind filters out the large majority of these messages much like an executive secretary might sort the junk or the reroutable out of the boss's mail. We don't realize that some part of us is saying no all the time because the process is so automatic. What we are left with is a small set of decisions in response to a large number of messages—the supposedly major decisions that cannot be left up to our subconscious secretaries.

But even that small set of decisions is huge, and the decisions and choices we must make are wearisome. A newly returning missionary who had been in the two-thirds world[1] where one is fortunate to find any food at all in the stores told my wife of the shock of visiting an American supermarket upon her arrival back home.

"I was astonished to see the numbers of choices one had to make just walking the aisles of the market. Take the potato chip section. When I left the United States, there was one basic kind of potato chip. Now there are seventeen or more kinds: salted or unsalted, ribbed or unribbed, nacho, onion, barbecue, taco, sour cream and onion, and so on. Think of all the time and effort that has to be expended just to make these incredible numbers of choices between things in abundance."

Even though we are not aware of the relentless barrage of messages coming at us, the combined force of them is still doing a job on us. They quietly sandblast the soul, the seat of conviction and value, threatening our ability to make and implement priority decisions.

---

[1] This area has been called the third world for years. But more recently, internationals have been referring to the third world as the two-thirds world since the population and geography of the "third" world actually comprises two-thirds of the people and land mass.

I cannot help but think of the Older Testament[2] character Lot as a man whose inner life became distorted by the realities about him. Always living off his uncle Abraham as a parasite, Lot had little inner defense when it came time to make a major decision regarding his destiny.

The shared business of Abraham and Lot reached a point where it seemed best to split the assets and move in different directions. The supply of resources was inadequate for the flocks and herds they'd built up, and tension was increasing between their staffs. It's conceivable that the two of them had lost the sense of enjoyment in working together.

The magnanimous Abraham did not put the process of a division of assets and lands to negotiation. Rather he gave Lot the first choice to go in whatever direction he wanted. And Lot was only too willing to seize the advantage.

But he made his choice from a distorted perspective. "And Lot lifted up his eyes and saw . . ." (Genesis 13:10 RSV). Messages poured into his mind, suggesting that he should grab the green grass and the lush valleys to the south while they were available and as long as Abraham was "stupid" enough to give him a first shot at the property. And he listened to his eyes.

Malcolm Muggeridge is fond of quoting William Blake's poem (emphasis mine):

> This life's dim windows of the soul
> Distort the heavens from pole to pole
> And lead you to believe a lie
> When you see *with*, not *through*, the eye

Lot looked *with* his eyes and saw the beauty of Sodom. He did not look from an inner spirit of values and convictions that would have permitted him to see moral rot and filth.

What was not included in the headlines of the messages he received from the eyes was more or less in the fine print, only to be read later. The green valleys also included Sodom and Gomorrah and the lifestyle that would ultimately cost Lot his family, his dignity, and any sense of credibility he'd ever enjoyed.

But another kind of distortion—not from the Sodoms of

[2] My choice of using *Older* is quite deliberate. Christians do the OT an injustice when they refer to it as merely *Old*.

this world, but from the Jerusalems—may be observed. I would be suggesting nothing novel if I observed that the person who walks in Christian leadership is always in danger of a distortion of the spirit by negative outside influences that come from our world. But I might startle some if I were to suggest that distortion can come even from within the Christian community.

It has been my experience that one of the greatest enemies of my own inner well-being, my own spiritual passion, is the vast number of good experiences and opportunities available to me.

I have frequently found myself in the state of what I describe as oversensation. As one grows older, it is possible to be involved in so many interesting and exciting things that adrenaline becomes something of an addictive drug. Life becomes a peak-to-peak hopping of wonderful experiences, each a bit emotionally higher than the last until there comes a time when the peaks can't get any higher or more frequent.

The inner being is fed on thrills and excitements. It is a rather spiritually-deficient diet that leaves one exhausted and weary.

Does not all of this simply enforce the importance of maintaining an independent base of judgment about the messages coming our way? Whether the signals come from a world whose motives and methods are predominantly evil or from a world whose methods and motives appear to be biblically oriented, the danger may be the same. It is weariness, loss of spiritual passion: a dried-out tank that offers no energy to get where one has to go tomorrow.

I have memories of anxieties when my father headed across the George Washington Bridge with the needle on E. But the worse memories are those times when I suddenly felt needed by someone and sensed that within me there was nothing to give. My tank was empty. There was no passion from which to operate.

5

Further Threats to Spiritual Passion

On our first visit to Africa, my wife and I visited a tiny, up-country village in the Ivory Coast called Sepikaha where we met Chloe, a blind evangelist. That day the man had walked several dozen miles from his own village to get to Sepikaha where he preached regularly to a small group of Christians. We watched him in action, breathless with admiration for his courage to preach in a town where the religion of Islam was militantly practiced.

A few months after we had met Chloe, he was attacked and severely beaten by those who resisted his presence in Sepikaha. His blindness gave him no opportunity for defense. Yet when he had recovered from his wounds, he went back.

I have often pondered over the extent of the spiritual passion which repeatedly drove that man to walk those miles to villages like Sepikaha, preach to people he could not see, and keep on doing it after he came within an inch of losing his life. The beating had not destroyed his passion.

Paul knew those sorts of moments only too well. And there are indications that his own passion may have been threatened at one time or another.

A weariness is expressed in his words to the Corinthians, "We do not want you to be ignorant of the affliction we experienced in Asia; for we were so utterly, unbearably

226

crushed that we despaired of life itself. Why, we felt that we had received the sentence of death" (2 Cor. 1:8–9 RSV). I call this the devastated condition.

4. THE DEVASTATED CONDITION

The devastated condition is the fatigue that originates with people and events vigorously opposed to what one stands for. I hear Paul saying that there was a time when the opposition almost got to him, that the beatings, the imprisonments, the incidents of ridicule and outright persecution began to wear him down. I hear the old apostle hinting that there was at least one time when he was so tired of it all that he wished he were dead.

We cannot afford to take this Pauline self-disclosure lightly. All too often we have been provided models of the great saints that suggest they never grew tired or disheartened. Here is one of many occasions when Paul was consummately weary, weary enough to want to run from everything, even into the arms of death.

The Greek scholar R. C. H. Lenski pointed out that the word *affliction*, as Paul used it, describes a sense of pressure so intense "that we became weighted down exceedingly beyond ability so that we got to despair even of living on" (Lenski, *Interpretation*, p. 826).

Weariness sets in with conditions such as these. One can go for just so long in the face of outright opposition from people and events, and then there is a slow crumbling of resolve or resistance.

Paul was not specific about the events, and no one really knows why. Perhaps he didn't feel it necessary to be graphic, but he did want the Corinthians to know that he had passed through a numbing experience of inner pain. A lesser person than Paul would have caved in. That Paul did not is a testimony to his ability to renew his spiritual passion.

We do ourselves a serious disservice if we do not face up to Paul's feeling of devastation. We have wrongly read the heroes of faith if we assume that they never had Pauline moments of despair, if we suspect that our moments of hurt and heartsickness are unique and merely an indication of our spiritual immaturity.

David had such a terrible moment in his relationship with his son, Absalom. To a considerable extent he had himself to

blame when Absalom "stole the hearts of the men of Israel"
(2 Sam. 15:6 RSV) and created conditions under which David
had to leave his beloved city of Jerusalem. The writer of
2 Samuel told the sad story of David's evacuation from his
home, his throne, his palace near the worship center of Israel, and then from the city he'd built. To compound the
insult, David was attacked, stoned, and cursed by an outraged distant relative of the late Saul, David's predecessor
on the throne. Which hurt worse—the stones or the verbal
indignities—is hard to tell. But the journey to a safe place out
in the eastern deserts must have been a devastating experience.

When the trip came to a conclusion in the eastern wilderness, the writer said, "The King and all his men were worn
out when they reached the Jordan, and there they rested"
(2 Sam. 16:14 TEV).

It is the story of devastation, a man stripped of everything
by his enemies. He is the epitome of weariness. How will he
act in this terrible situation?

People pass through these sorts of situations all the time.
Some fall apart; others gather strength and discover passion
within that they never knew possible.

Wayne Alderson, known for his great Value of the Person
movement, faced a devastating moment in his career as a
steel executive. R. C. Sproul tells the story in his book
Stronger Than Steel.

Alderson had stepped into a volatile labor situation at
Pittron Steel and had initiated a process of labor relations
that was unprecedented. Within a short time, the working
conditions at Pittron began to change, morale increased, and
so did worker productivity. Alderson had begun to prove
that you can treat employees with dignity and respect and,
as a result, produce a working environment in which everyone wins.

Ironically, Alderson's contribution became his own downfall. Pittron became an attractive acquisition for a larger
company, and before long the Bucyrus-Erie Corporation
consummated a deal to take over Pittron.

Sproul described the dramatic meeting between Alderson,
who was manager of the acquired company, and the man
who was chairman of the acquiring company when Alderson
was informed that his concept of labor relations was incom-

patible with Bucyrus-Erie's policies. He must abandon his relations with labor or get out. The choice was his.

> Wayne's lips began to form an answer. His mouth was open, ready to say "yes," but what came out was "No sir, I will not give it up."

He was fired! Everything he had worked for was suddenly gone.

> Wayne tried to imagine what it would be like to be unemployed. He was now a statistic, a casualty of the corporate wars. But he was not overcome with gloom. His spirits were lifted by the realization that the decision he had been so frightened to make was now behind him. The moment had come and gone; it had seemed almost easy. . . . Wayne was left to face the public's reaction to his firing. Alderson's public image was crumbling. Wayne was crushed with disappointment, but he felt no shame (Sproul, *Stronger Than Steel*, pp. 124-25).

We ought not to be surprised when the devastating moments come, when all outside supports are stripped away. It can be a time when passion is tested and sometimes sucked away. But for the person who knows how to renew and maintain spiritual passion, it can be a moment for great performance.

5. THE DISILLUSIONED CONDITION

Spiritual passion can also be neutralized in disillusionment: the deflation of great dreams.

"My husband's a dreamer," I heard my wife tell some people, "and most of his dreams are very, very expensive." I guess she's right. And being the dreamer that I am, I'm also aware that dreaming costs more than money. It often costs a sense of loss, those extreme moments of disappointment when something you want very, very badly doesn't happen.

You want to see people get behind a program, and they won't. You believe in a sense of direction for an organization, and the people won't provide the support for both good and bad reasons. You invest great personal energy in individuals in whom you see potential, and they fail at a key moment.

Disillusionment is such a painful experience for many of us. We are tempted to withdraw, to pledge that we shall never again dream.

The moments of dream deflation leave large marks upon the soul. It would not take me long to list most of the occasions when I thought I had given birth to a great idea only to have it torn apart by those who were more interested in status quo, or proper procedures, or politics, or their own positions of security or recognition. Of course there were not a few moments when my dreams were just plain ridiculous, and someone had to tell me so.

But, nevertheless, each time a dream is deflated for whatever reason, it hurts badly. In my younger years the reaction was often emotional, and the usual temptation was to stop dreaming altogether. Spiritual passion dissolved, and for a while there was no fight left within.

Is Moses a picture of disillusionment when, at the age of forty, he became aware of the oppressed condition of his people in Egypt and began to dream about their liberation? One day he saw an Egyptian fighting with a Hebrew. In a moment of outrage he stepped into the fracas like a would-be hero, killed the Egyptian, and buried him. The fledgling dream assumed reality.

Did Moses assume that the intervention would make him a hero with his people? If he did, the next day when he attempted to conciliate two Hebrews locked in conflict and they utterly rejected him, he must have been shocked. "Then Moses was afraid" (Exod. 2:14 TEV). In outright fear and disillusionment, having made himself so vulnerable and having taken such a risk, Moses fled town for the desert.

The biblical text is sparing in its description. We are left to fill in the blanks with our imagination, and that is not hard to do. I think of Moses' feelings as he journeyed into unknown territory in the heaviness of the hour. Such dreams; such disaster.

It took *forty years* for Moses to regain his nerve, to recover any sense of passion. The text is usually interpreted to suggest that God had to wait forty years until Moses was ready to listen to a more proper way to achieve liberation. And perhaps the people themselves had to wait forty more years until they were desperate enough to follow the now-prepared Moses.

But when the man returned to the site of his earlier disillusionment, he was ready to perform—God's way. His passion was generated and channeled. We all know what happened.

Moses helps all of us to understand that spiritual passion can be jeopardized when dreams and visions are dashed.

6. THE DEFEATED CONDITION

There is a weariness that comes from total personal defeat. Perhaps this is the most common of all the varieties of weariness.

Who does not know the taste of failure? One suddenly feels utterly impotent, unable to live up to the set standards of faith. Or promises or commitments have been made, but then broken. Or disciplines and goals have been enthusiastically determined, and then abandoned.

Those in leadership have an obligation to their families, or the church, or the business to live at a higher quality level as models. And then comes the terrible moment of embarrassment when the model falls apart.

Peter is a model for us to consult. He was the great man of words, especially enthusiastic ones. His promise to Jesus to follow and die, if necessary, was an empty one. "I'm ready to go to prison with you and to die with you" (Luke 22:33 TEV). The promise may have been sincere, an expression of his deep affection for the Lord perhaps, but we soon discover that it was an unworkable promise.

Within hours Peter was a failure. And the failure wasn't achieved in a quiet, out-of-the-spotlight place. The promise began to unravel in the garden when Peter couldn't keep awake to pray. His failure snowballed when he stood by the Lord in the garden in the presence of the temple guard and drew a sword, the very thing Jesus had been saying wasn't a response to trouble. And it peaked with his several denials in the court of the high priest. And what made the defeat so humiliating was that the denials were not made in the presence of great and powerful figures, but rather in the company of peasants and servants, young people from whom Peter presumably had nothing to fear.

Luke describes the ultimate moment of failure by commenting that the rooster crowed just as the Lord had predicted and that Jesus—from wherever He was in the court—turned and looked at Peter. Peter must have felt that look like one feels the effect of a laser beam. "And he went out and wept bitterly" (Luke 22:62 RSV).

Passion does not dwell in the heart of the defeated. And

Peter is a most graphic picture of a man who thought he was
moving on passion and wasn't. And when he was defeated,
all he could do was weep intensely and futilely. And for the
next several days, Peter was a passionless man. The defeat
was paralyzing.

7. THE DISHEARTENED CONDITION

Perhaps we can identify one more condition in which passion is squelched. I refer to it as the disheartened condition.
Another good word might be *intimidated*. We fall into the
intimidated, or disheartened, condition when we begin to
gain a view of people, events, or institutions that causes them
to appear to be far more powerful than the God of our faith.
And that's not hard to do.

The disciples illustrate intimidation, of course, when they
were paralyzed by the coming of the temple guard in the
Garden of Gethsemane and fearfully scrambled into the
darkness. The spies sent into the Promised Land were, with
the exception of Joshua and Caleb, intimidated by the power
they saw, and they returned to Moses with reports of out-
sized giants and fortresses and led people to believe that they
had gone about as far as they could go.

There is the fascinating description of Ahaz, an intimidated king of Judah, who lost his grip on God's promise that
his throne was under divine protection. Refusing to relax in
that assurance, he assessed the power of the enemies march-
ing on his capital, and his heart "shook as the trees of the
forest shake before the wind" (Isa. 7:2 RSV).

How much in contrast to him is the posture of Isaiah, the
prophet delegated to bring Judah reassurance. Isaiah had
spiritual passion. Why wasn't Isaiah intimidated? His answer was:

> The LORD spoke thus to me with his strong hand upon me, and
> warned me not to walk in the way of this people, saying: "Do not
> call conspiracy all that this people call conspiracy, and do not
> fear what they fear, nor be in dread. But the LORD of hosts, him
> you shall regard as holy; let him be your fear, and let him be your
> dread" (Isa. 8:11-13 RSV).

I have felt the feelings of intimidation as I have driven
Storrow Drive into Boston. To the left as one drives along the
Charles River are the beautiful buildings of Harvard, and to

the right are the more austere dwelling places of the Harvard Business School.

Further down Storrow Drive, again to the left, is the campus of the Massachusetts Institute of Technology (MIT), many of the buildings roofed with antennas, satellite dishes, and other strange looking objects that suggest to the uninitiated that mysterious things go on there, that people are talking to the stars. Ahead are the buildings of Boston's downtown where many multinational corporations have their headquarters.

It is a temptation to allow all of that to rebalance the mind and spirit, to permit oneself to think that in places such as these offices, labs, and classrooms the real power to change and control history is being generated and discharged.

Spiritual passion can quickly dissipate when one compares these concrete symbols of human power to the abstract gospel of Jesus Christ, and it is tempting to say with the disciple who was disheartened over the inadequacy of the lunch to feed thousands, "But what is this gospel among so many?"

Langdon Gilkey's book *Shantung Compound* illustrates the issue powerfully. During World War II, a couple of thousand Westerners were impressed into concentration-camp-like quarters by the Japanese in North China. *Shantung Compound* is the story of how those people forged a community and shared life.

Gilkey, at the time a young optimistic professor, began his account of the camp's life by expressing awe over the knowledge and capacities of the people at Weihsien. As he participated in the attempts to organize the camp, he became persuaded that

> The real issues of life are surely material and political: how we can eat and keep warm, be clothed and protected from the weather, and organize our common efforts. These matters are resolved by practical experience and by techniques, not by this or that philosophy or religious faith, however convincing an expression of that faith may be to the cool observer of the scene.
>
> It was not that I thought religion wrong; I simply thought it irrelevant. What real function in actual life does it perform under conditions where basic problems are dealt with by techniques and organizational skill? I was quite willing to admit that there are people who are interested in the nature of man and the universe; and that apparently there are others who enjoy religion

and going to church. But, unlike food and sanitation which one must have in order to live, is not religion merely a matter of personal taste, of temperament, essential only if someone wants it but useless if one does not happen to be the type that likes it? Is there any "secular" use for religion; does it have any value for the common life of mankind? (Gilkey, *Shantung Compound*, pp. 73-74)

Gilkey's questions bore into the spirit of the reader. They are intimidating questions, disheartening questions until answered. He is suggesting that the person of faith is wasting time in small, irrelevant things.

Wherever I turned, everything I saw reinforced this view. Of what use to our life were the vocations of teaching philosophy or preaching Christianity. Those of us who had performed these tasks in the outside world now carried our weight of camp work yes—but not in *those* roles. We were useful only insofar as teacher or evangelist became able stoker or competent baker.

Then he went on again:

My feelings found full expression one Sunday when, rushing by the church bent on some errand for the Housing Committee, I heard a familiar hymn ringing out through the open windows. I asked myself irritably, "What for—when there are so many important things to be done?" And shaking my head in disbelieving wonder, I went on about my business (Gilkey, *Shantung Compound*, p. 75).

Not a few of us who have chosen to follow Jesus Christ have listened to arguments like this. At times they have seemed quite persuasive, enough to draw off our spiritual passion and make us feel as if, in reality, we have nothing to offer the real world. The temptation grows to think that the fulcrum of history is not in the gospel of Christ but in the visible power of business, politics, or force.

Gilkey's account of affairs at Weihsien concluded with a strange and fascinating twist. The community, marvelously organized with competent skills and expertise, began to come apart. Graft, corruption, and open strife invaded their community. The talented experts—who were able to devise systems, machines, and organizations to solve practical problems—weren't able to provide an ongoing sense of purpose for life, a moral imperative for people to serve one another and strive for common benefit, a rule of life by which people could maintain dignity and hope.

Gilkey had discovered what was the domain of those who practiced their faith devoutly and practically.

> There was a quality seemingly unique to the missionary group, namely, naturally and without pretense to respond to a need which everyone else recognized only to turn aside. Much of this went unnoticed, but our camp could scarcely have survived as well as it did without it. If there were any evidences of the grace of God observable on the surface of our camp existence, they were to be found here (Gilkey, *Shantung Compound*, p. 192).

As Gilkey became aware that there were deeper issues than expertise and power, so did I constantly learn to remind myself that the beautiful towers of Harvard and the antennas of MIT housed the best the human race can offer history. But it is still the power of Christ's gospel that gives meaning to history and provides an insight, as well as a way, to change the human heart. That assurance renews spiritual passion.

I've outlined seven conditions in which spiritual passion is often threatened. There are many more, and perhaps among the seven there are many overlaps. It is difficult to grow or renew passion when one is living in one or more of these conditions. They create a weariness that saps every positive quality and energy we need to be effective followers of the Lord.

I have found it extremely helpful to deliberate over the existence of these various conditions. It is actually quite possible to predict when any of these conditions is approaching; it is much like the symbols on a weather map that tell me a cold or a warm front is coming through. So I've learned to listen to the advisories and to brace myself. For people in whom the Holy Spirit is working, living without spiritual passion is intolerable. An awareness of the conditions that might make that happen is therefore indispensable.

6

Those Who Bring Joy

Our spiritual passion is affected by the conditions in and around us. But spiritual passion, or energy, is also affected by the people who populate our personal worlds.

Being with people is exhausting. Ask a mother who has spent the day with two small children. Talk to the business-person who has spent the day negotiating budgets with department heads. Or get the opinion of a nurse who has spent the day at the bedside of a dying patient. At the end of a day they are spent, sometimes ready to run.

But they have just been talking, sitting and talking. Why, ask those who work with their hands, is that so tiring? It's tiring because people contribute to, or draw from, our inner energy levels in ways we are not even aware of. They tax our minds and our spirits, and the resulting fatigue can sometimes be worse than that after a day's work on a construction crew.

I can think of certain people in my world whose company invigorates me, and when they leave, I am full of resolve, ideas, and intentions about God, self-improvement, and service to others. I can also think of people in my world whose presence exhausts me. And when they leave, I am ready for a long, long nap.

An old friend of mine used to say of people, "Some folk bring joy wherever they go; others bring joy *when* they go." We need to understand the people of our world and how they play a part in the potential invigoration or weariness of our lives.

Understanding the effect people have upon us will help us

to know where our spiritual energy goes and when we can anticipate that we will need to restore it.

In my earliest years of Christian ministry I was not smart enough to understand fully the dynamics of what was happening, but I was quite aware that the people around me on any given day had a significant effect upon my sense of faith and its vitality. As I've already observed, there were those who constantly caused me to reach for higher plateaus of growth, while there were others who left me, as it were, gasping for air. The former I pursued; the latter I fled.

But fleeing, of course, would not have been ministry. I understood that I had been called as a servant to the broken and the hurting, and somehow I was going to have to adjust to that and pay the necessary price.

But I did begin to discover that anyone in the role of a leader becomes a target for many kinds of people—those who want to use the leader as a point of influence for their particular cause or concern; those who want to be near the leader because they deem him or her to be the top of a social pyramid and, therefore, a guarantor of popularity; and those who gain attention by trying to get prominent people to focus upon their problems.

Naturally, I began to discover that there were other kinds of people in my world—those who would not intrude into my calendar unless invited but who always had a word of encouragement or sound counsel; those who came wanting to learn and ask solid questions; and, of course, those with genuine personal need who came seeking a prayer, a strong arm, a word of grace and hope.

You don't have to be the pastor of a large church or a well-known, successful person to face the onrush of people. Any person in any kind of leadership will discover that people work is a never-ending process. And when this process is not understood or carefully monitored, it can have adverse effects upon one's spiritual passion.

FIVE KINDS OF PEOPLE THAT AFFECT SPIRITUAL PASSION

For me, monitoring means measuring and categorizing. And you can do that even in people work. For example, I came to see that in my world there are five kinds of men and women with whom I must constantly deal. An overage of exposure to any one kind sets up imbalances.

1. THE VERY RESOURCEFUL PEOPLE: THEY IGNITE OUR PASSION

Let's call the first group the VRP's, the very resourceful people who *ignite* our passion. Of course my parents were my first set of VRP's when I was a child. But then others came along, and I have enjoyed a chain of VRP relationships ever since the age of eight.

VRP's are those who are sometimes called mentors, shapers of life. Some might even call them surrogate fathers and mothers. One is never sure when a VRP relationship begins; in most cases it just seems to happen naturally. I think it is a gift from God. The important thing about Christian VRP's is that they *ignite* our passion for faith and Christlike performance.

The first VRP I ever remember was a working associate of my father's. I was drawn to his presence as an eight-year-old boy because it was clear to me even in my childish perspective that he believed in me. I felt strangely adult in his presence, a sense of being accepted and appreciated.

Another VRP relationship came in the form of a married couple who invested themselves in young people of high school age. Their home was always open; their time was ours; they appreciated the perceived seriousness of our romantic or family problems and offered (when asked) possible solutions.

A third VRP was a track coach who set performance standards according to personal excellence. His was a relationship not only of encouragement but also of rebuke. One did not want to displease the coach. It wasn't that he showed anger; you simply became aware that he was less than pleased by what was happening, and one experience of that kind was more than enough. He knew how to persuade an athlete to accept a certain amount of pain in order to reach higher levels of potential, and he knew how to turn athletic performance (winning or losing) into a character-building moment.

Other VRP's included a college parachurch worker, a Presbyterian pastor and his wife, an older single man, a seminary president, and a church history professor. All these—and others, of course—played a unique role in shaping me. They rarely entered into my world that they did not provide a resource, a growth point. And they rarely left my world at the conclusion of an encounter that I did not feel lifted, impelled to greater growth, and more aware of both flaws and possibilities.

The fact that they always make a positive contribution to one's world is an important distinction about VRP's, and it sets them apart from some of the others I will be mentioning. When I engage in the monitoring and evaluation of relationships, I note these people as making a three-plus (+ + +) addition to who we are and what we are doing.

Now the temptation is to want to be with people like this all the time. But that could be as unhealthy in the long run as the decision to remain at home in a child-parent relationship for the rest of one's life. It is certainly a protective way to live, and it helps on the bills, but it would never foster the independent and resourceful spiritual passion we're talking about that makes one a force for faith.

To be with a certain number of VRP's is a necessity. We all need those whom we can look to in a moment of uncertainty. But to be with them all the time would be stifling and, eventually, passionless. Jesus understood this all too well and appreciated the fact that three years with the disciples as their VRP was all they needed.

"It is to your advantage that I go away," He said (John 16:7 RSV). They'd had enough; the in-dwelling Holy Spirit could take over now, He told them.

A highlight in Christian history is the work of the Clapham sect, a group of Christian laypersons who lived in nineteenth-century England and marked their generation through their efforts in government, business, and the arts to bring about social change and order in the name of Christ.

One biographer of William Wilberforce, a Clapham sect member, recorded the observation of a young person who watched the men and women of Clapham in their private lives:

These wise men never endeavored to mold our unformed opinions into any particular mold. Indeed it was needless for them to preach to us. Their lives spoke far more plainly and convincingly than any words. We saw their patience, cheerfulness, generosity, wisdom and activity daily before us, and we knew and felt that all this was only a natural expression of hearts given to the service of God (Lean, *God's Politician*, p. 100).

This is a brilliant description of VRP's and their effect upon those around them. They are the kind who make a supreme contribution from which we ourselves draw. We study their ways and then customize them for ourselves. We lean upon them for direction and approval. We gain energy from their courage and maturity. They are in every sense of the word our resource, and from them we can draw our first senses of passion.

2. THE VERY IMPORTANT PEOPLE: THEY SHARE OUR PASSION

The second kind of person in our worlds is what I have often called the VIP's, the very important people who share our passion. These are my teammates, the men and women with whom I am most closely associated: fellow workers, close friends who share the workload to which we are all called, or those with whom we share a common affection.

Barnabas was VIP to Paul (although for a short while he may have been VRP); so were Silas and Luke. I suspect that Aquila and Priscilla would have to be included. Paul used a beautiful word about VIP's in Philippians, chapter 4 when he used the word *yokefellow* to refer to those who had shared the yoke of ministry together. Yokefellows are the VIP's, and most of us have been fortunate to have known a few of them.

VIP's also make a contribution, what I have called a two-plus (+ +) contribution. Are there problems and conflicts with them? Sooner or later. But minimally so, and not so that one dwells upon such experiences. When we are with VIP's, we are all aware that the challenges we face are bigger than we and that the genius of our relationship is in the fact that the whole is greater than the parts. With VIP's we do not spend large amounts of time trying to get along, or debating over whose philosophy will prevail, or determining who is in charge. We are bound together to get a task done, and get it done we will.

VIP's *share* our passion. Together we stir one another up and goad each other to better and more faithful performances. VIP's keep us looking at the right goals; they are not hoodwinked by excuses and rationalizations. They sense when we are hurting or when we are in need. They delight in our successes and weep with us when we are disappointed.

For some years I have been a student of Charles Simeon, a nineteenth-century Church of England pastor in Cambridge. In his younger years his mentor (his VRP) was Henry Venn. In a letter written to Venn in 1783 Simeon, spoke of a VIP friendship with John Riland who gave him sharp but useful criticism on a sermon he had just preached. This friendship was VIP-ship at its best.

> What a blessing—an inestimable blessing is it to have a faithful friend! Satan is ready enough to point out whatever good we have; but it is only a faithful friend that will screen that from your sight, and show you your deficiencies. Our great apostasy seems to consist primarily in making a god of self; and he is the most valuable friend who will draw us most from self-seeking—self pleasing—and self-dependence, and help us to restore to God the authority we have robbed him of (Carvs, *Memories of the Life of Rev. Charles Simeon*, p. 32).

3. THE VERY TRAINABLE PEOPLE: THEY CATCH OUR PASSION

If VRP's *ignite* our passion and VIP's *share* our passion, a third kind of person *catches* our passion. I call them the VTP's, the very trainable people. They are to us what we were to those whom I've called VRP's.

Now *we* are the ones who ignite passion; *they* catch it! Here, of course, we are looking at biblical relationships such as Paul and his relationship to Timothy, Eli to Samuel, and Elijah to Elisha.

We are watching Mordecai ignite passion in Esther (his niece?) when he challenges her by saying, "who knows whether you have not come to the kingdom for such a time as this?" (Esther 4:14 RSV). Those words more than anything else thrust her into action that eventuated in the saving of thousands of lives.

VTP's make a one-plus (+) contribution to our worlds. They usually give, seldom take. And although VTP's tax our strength, we are usually glad to cooperate because we sense the possibilities in them.

We draw them to our side and open our lives to them. In the very sharing of ourselves we stir our own passion to serve and grow because we see the immediate effect it has upon them.

The further we are along the passage through adulthood the more important it becomes to have about us a small collection of very trainable people. It has often been pointed out that this is exactly what Paul is urging on Timothy when he wrote:

> What you have heard from me [VRP] before many witnesses entrust to faithful men [VTP] who will be able to teach others also [more VTP] (2 Tim. 2:2 RSV).

I am of the conviction that after a person passes the fortieth year of life, the investment in VTP's should become an increasing priority. So that we may provide the possibility of a succeeding generation of leaders and godly men and women.

The VRP's, and VIP's, and the VTP's of our lives generally make a positive contribution to our passion. Having been with them, our goals and objectives are clearer than ever. Our desire to pursue higher levels of maturity and effectiveness will increase. Thank God for them. We couldn't make it without their part in our experience.

But there are some others whose contributions are far more taxing. They tax our spiritual passion, drastically.

7

The Happy and
the Hurting

Two other kinds of people in our worlds have an effect upon our spiritual passion, and they are hard to describe in enthusiastic terms. But they are there and we must know who they are. These people crowd our horizon, seeking personal attention. And when they have gotten what they came for, we are tired people.

4. THE VERY NICE PEOPLE: THEY ENJOY OUR PASSION

I call the fourth group the VNP's, the very nice people who *enjoy* our passion. They come in large numbers, and we love to have them around.

VNP's clap and laugh and build our egos. They make people in public Christian leadership very happy because they fill pews and rooms and programs. En masse they provide substantial amounts of money (each giving a very small part) to fuel organizations sometimes called ministries.

VNP's are wonderful people; they are good people. And we make many fine friendships with VNP's. But the truth of the matter is that the overall contribution of the VNP is imperceptible. In contrast to the three-plus contribution of a VRP, the VNP has to be labeled a zero-plus contributor. They do not add to our passion; nor do they seriously diminish it.

They simply enjoy it. Being around people who exude spiritual energy can be a pleasurable experience if one professes Christianity.

One is reminded of a childhood spoof on various breakfast cereals: they don't snap, crackle, and pop. They don't turn colors; they're not coated with sugar; and they're not shot from guns. What do they do? They simply lie in the bowl and sop up the milk. So is the role of the good old VNP who comes into our world often in large numbers.

Jesus never turned His back upon the VNP's in His world. He saw them as sheep without a shepherd, and He treated them with dignity and possibility. That's important to note, for from the midst of the VNP's there came certain folk who eventually became VTP's (each of the twelve was probably a VNP at first) and perhaps even later VIP's.

It is true, however, that when the crowds of VIP's got too large, the Lord would sharpen the blade of His teaching. He would make it clearer and clearer that there was a dramatic cost to discipleship. It was almost as if He were saying the size of this crowd suggests that you haven't heard me plainly enough or some of you wouldn't be here; so let me give it to you another way. And when He finished restating His message, many would then leave because they finally understood that no one can remain forever in the presence of Christ and be a VNP.

That is exactly what happened in John, chapter 6.

> Many of his disciples, when they heard [his message], said, "This is a hard saying; who can listen to it?" But Jesus, knowing in himself that his disciples murmured at it, said to them . . . "there are some of you that do not believe." For Jesus knew from the first who those were that did not believe, and who it was that would betray him. . . . After this many of his disciples drew back and no longer went about with him. Jesus said to the twelve, "Do you also wish to go away?" Simon Peter answered him, "Lord, to whom shall we go? You have the words of eternal life . . ." (John 6:60-61, 64, 66-68 RSV).

You can see the sorting process going on here. VNP's were welcomed into the presence of Christ, but only for a while. And then they had decisions to make.

My comments are not meant to ridicule the overwhelming

numbers of people who crowd churches and religious gatherings. Rather they are meant to help us understand who the VNP's are and what effect they will have upon those of us who are in leadership and people development.

It is startling to realize that in church life most of our heavy expenditures are for the very nice people. VNP's fill the pews, the parking lots, and the classrooms and sop up the milk. We build and expand all too often for the convenience of the VNP's. VIP's and VTP's would normally accept great inconveniences in order to martial and redirect the material resources of the church into the world beyond: evangelism, mission, Christian service. But, unfortunately, VNP's, the large majority of congregations in the Western, unpersecuted world, prefer facilities, times, and programs built on personal convenience and comfort, and they are usually accommodated because the very magnitude of their numbers convinces leaders that the program is successful. This is disturbing to ponder.

Spiritual energy or passion is profoundly affected by the VNP's. In a sense, sopping up the milk means sopping up the passion. Leaders spend exorbitant amounts of time solving the problems of programming, interpersonal conflict, and enlargement that VNP's create by their presence. Laypeople and pastors who are responsible for the guidance and shepherding of VNP's know that in the best of all circumstances, the task is wearing and draining. Although the VNP's may swell the ego with their applause and conditional loyalty, they exhaust the spirit through their desire to take whatever the leader has to give.

When Gail and I were just beginning our ministry, we felt a desperate need to be liked and accepted by the people we had come to serve. Thus we responded to almost every overture for entertainment that came in our direction. It was a way—although quite a deficient way—of knowing that we were doing a good job, that we could make it in the pastoral lifestyle. We did not yet realize that sometimes people drew near to us because of the roles we were in, not because of the persons we were.

We were immediately courted by various groups who graciously invited us to their formal and informal gatherings. Some met monthly, others weekly. When we came, we were usually the center of attention because in the church social whirl our position as pastor and spouse put us—in human eyes—at the top.

We confused this sort of hospitality with an indication of people's spiritual commitment. And it was only after we had been with the congregation for a time that we began to discover that those who wanted our presence at all of their social activities were not always the people to be counted on when it came time to do the things we had come to the church to accomplish.

In this way we came to discover the existence of the VNP's. They were wonderful to be with, often encouraging with their compliments *and* gifts, but they were not always the team on the serving and the growing edge. It was hard to put distance between us and some of the activities of the VNP's. It had to be done wisely and discretely. They were enjoyable people, fun to be with. But we could not allow them to absorb all of our energy doing good things when the best things had to be done with the VTP's and the VIP's.

That was not an easy lesson to learn. And it still isn't!

5. THE VERY DRAINING PEOPLE: THEY SAP OUR PASSION

A fifth and final group of people have a direct effect upon our spiritual passion. I have often quietly referred to them as the VDP's, the very draining people who *sap* our passion.

I do not wish to write of VDP's unkindly, but they exist in all of our worlds and must be carefully identified. Until we understand who they are and how they touch our lives, we will not fully understand why we experience weariness and passionlessness at times.

Very draining people affect our passion in just the way that their label suggests: they *drain* it. And they do so relentlessly. I am not trying to be uncharitable but merely factual when I suggest that their relationship to the leader is usually on the minus (−) side of the flow of energy.

I know that some will quickly wish to argue that there is a certain kind of energy that develops merely from the joy of serving the hurting and the lonely, and I would not want to argue with that. What I will want to point out, however, is that that sort of joy lasts only so long and then, in most cases, changes to a kind of exhaustion that must be addressed quickly or it will have ill effects.

In my early adult years when I was intent upon becoming the very best Christian leader I could, I responded as fully as I could to every person who crossed my path with any hint of need. Those who needed to visit with me immediately gained my attention. My phone was available for all callers, and I generally permitted them to control the length and pace of the conversation. Before and after any meeting in which I was a participant, I was ready to receive anyone who said I was needed.

I have memories of the man who had some serious personal struggles and found the supper hour a convenient time to call me nearly every evening. One member of a church board, who had a problem with virtually every issue we were facing, had to tell me in detail why he disagreed with each decision and why he had to take a stand against it. And a woman who had stumbled into a bad marriage (fifteen years ago) needed to report in full to me the evidence of that unfortunate relationship every Sunday after church.

Add to these an emotionally struggling young man in desperate need of attention from all authority figures, an adult woman who was always causing conflicts among Christians by her undisciplined tongue, and not a few people who were chronically sick and either needed comfort to deal with their aches and pains or explanations to understand why they were in these difficulties.

I discovered as time went by that every cluster of people (business, school, church) has a percentage of people who have to be labeled VDP's. And when that group is Christian in intention and orientation, its members try hard to care for and serve the VDP's. The good news is that this serving often pays off, and those who were draining actually become useful and trainable.

Then again, one can conceivably be a VDP to one person but not to another. For example, Paul considered John Mark a VDP who could not be trusted for a second missionary journey, but fortunately, Barnabas saw John Mark's potential for a VTP or VIP and didn't agree with Paul's assessment.

I would type Judas Iscariot as a VDP among the disciples. He appears to have been a whiner, a constant critic, a hanger-on who contributed—as far as we can see—very little to the group.

Few people in the New Testament qualify for the VDP medal, probably because this section of the Bible is so centered on action people on the move. The obviously immoral church member at Corinth was a drain on the church's life, and Paul was disturbed that the people did not see that. Euodias and Syntyche were becoming drains upon the Philippian congregation by their inability to resolve their conflict. Paul wanted that conflict solved as soon as possible. He knew pending relational disaster when he saw it.

One does see some examples of VDP's in the Older Testament. There were times when Moses must have been tempted to think of the entire Hebrew nation as a drain on his leadership. Joshua would certainly suggest Achan as a draining person since his sin caused the defeat of the army at Ai. Nehemiah had a number of VDP's during his attempt to rebuild Jerusalem's walls. They were in and out of the camp: critics, slow movers, men with hidden agendas.

When God called Gideon to lead the people out from under the domination of their enemies (Judg. 6), He stripped all potential VDP's away in order to get the task completed. The inner drains were cleaned up in Gideon's own family life when he was commanded to destroy the pagan altars in his father's backyard before proceeding any further.

When Gideon massed his armies (over thirty thousand troops) to face the enemy, the first thing God called upon him to do was cut away those who were fearful and send them home (see Judg. 7:3). I've often wondered how Gideon took it when twenty-two thousand men walked away from that reverse invitation. But when it came time for action, there was no place for the VDP's.

We must not go a step further without recognizing that it is often from the ranks of the draining people that we begin ministry and lift people up to a position of growth and usefulness. So the long-term answer in any cluster of people is not to rid oneself of the draining people but rather to understand three important things about them and the groups of which they are a part.

First, VDP's will be drawn (like mosquitoes to blood) to any healthy group of people, and they will remain until they become self-sustaining or until they are pushed away.

Second, a healthy cluster of people will lose its vitality (its group passion) mysteriously and unpredictably because there are simply too many VDP's to sustain. The life of the group becomes problem- and crisis-oriented, and forward movement toward any kind of objective becomes impossible. Like a ship with dead engines, the crowd is dead in the water.

Third, VDP's who are permitted to relentlessly drain leaders of their passion will ultimately create a climate in which no one will want to serve in leadership capacities. Again and again, we have seen examples of young men and women who were ready to give maximum energy to the pursuit of some objective fade out because they were not protected from the VDP's.

I have great affection for certain brothers and sisters (VIP's) who understood this principle when I was the pastor of a large congregation. At the conclusion of worship services, they would come to my side and engage some of those who desired merely to gain my attention, not to call upon me for important pastoral issues. In private I called them my spiritual body guards. I think that I would not have survived if it hadn't been for them.

I was a number of years into my life as a pastor before I made a startling discovery. It was my calendar that taught me the hard lesson: the VNP's and the VDP's were accounting for the major percentage of my available time.

I was making a serious mistake. Because the *nice* people were so pleasant to be with, and because the *draining* people requested so much time, I had little prime time left over for the *resourceful* people, the *important* people, and the *trainable* people. None of these three made the demands upon me that the other two did. And I, because they made so few protests, left them alone as a rule because I thought I was where I was most needed. An error of great magnitude!

A check on the priorities of our Lord will show that He spent ample time with the *draining* and the *nice* people in His path: the sick, the anguished, the critic, the curious. But they never captured His full schedule. In fact they account for relatively little of it. Rather Christ appears to have maximized His time with the *resourceful*, in His case His heavenly Father. He reserved heavy time for the *important* and the *trainable*, for Him the disciples (the twelve, the seventy, and a few close friends).

That was an important discovery for me because I found

that in giving my time to the VNP's and the VDP's, I was making a long-range error both for them and me. By being instantly available at all times for them, I was inadvertently teaching them an unhealthy dependence upon me as a leader; I was feeding their need to relate only to someone they conceived to be a special leader who, by his attention, provided them with a sense of importance that was neither authentic nor earned.

But even more significantly, by spending my prime time with these two groups, I was expending my own energy in nonrenewable ways. Every minute of that time was a one-way flow of passion (outward), sometimes necessary (as in the case of the woman who touched Jesus' robe) but, in the long run, seriously debilitating.

We grow weary when we do not learn this lesson in time. I have watched many laypeople quit responsibilities, even become embittered over church activity, because no one taught them how to protect themselves from draining people.

I do not want to be misinterpreted in my discussion of the VNP's or the VDP's. They are very much a part of the assembly of believers. And they must be ministered to. But we must understand that they will, by their very nature, make greater and greater demands until the healthy Christian's energy level has been dissipated to the point of exhaustion and weariness.

If we wonder why we are often weary, a look at the distribution of time on the calendar in past weeks may well provide the answer.

Time with the VRP's, the resourceful people of our worlds, will build our passion. Time with the VTP's, the trainable people, will tax us for sure, but it is eventually restorative because these sorts of people pick up our passion and our burden and move with us.

But if our calendars reveal that the predominant part of our time is merely with the nice and the draining, then we must not keep wondering why we lose our vitality. These people take but do not give, and unless we pause and rebalance, the result is often disaster.

Years ago my wife and I became acquainted with a young woman in our community. It soon became apparent to us that she was a problem drinker. The day came when it was necessary for her to face the situation, and the pain of coming to grips with her tendency toward alcoholism was for her and us unforgettable.

She was a classic example of the very draining person. The hours of conversation over the phone and in the home were incalculable. The temptation to write her off was great. More and more people entered the mix of caring for her, and when they were together, it was not unusual for the conversation to center on what to do for her.

We all loved this person very much, and we saw that she had large reservoirs of human potential if she could gain a hold over her addiction.

It took ten years! With the power of Christ, the love of people, and the resources of various organizations, the VDP we had known for so long became a VTP, and then a VIP. Today she is for many a VRP. Whenever I think of turning my back upon a VDP, I think twice because I see what she has become.

Nevertheless, I have learned that VDP's cost energy and passion, and that leaders who permit an imbalance of contact with these, the hurting people of our world, can expect to pay a massive bill in inner exhaustion.

The people around us give and they take. Whenever we are in public, we can expect that a flow of passion will be moving one direction or another: toward us or away from us. It's important to know that.

8
Friendly Fire

The monument to the Vietnam War dead in Washington, D.C., is a sobering site. Go there, and you are liable to come away with intense feelings and not a few tears. The architect seems to have understood the mixed passions surrounding that conflict.

Inscribed on the black granite walls are the names of more than thirty thousand men and women who died for their country. But somehow the honor reflected by the monument seems mixed with a sense of futility over the manner in which the war was conducted and the way it ended. Is the emotion one feels when standing before the monument a response to the bravery and sacrifice of the dead? Or is the emotion one feels a response to the waste of human life, given the tragic conclusion?

When the first U.S. military forces hit the beaches of Vietnam, Americans experienced a passion of sorts; as President Johnson announced the escalated military presence, Americans experienced a sense of optimism. Across America there was a general confidence that what we thought was a mess in Southeast Asia would quickly be cleaned up with a minimum of fuss or human loss. Most Americans—some outstanding exceptions, of course—felt confident of that! How complete was our misjudgment!

A few years and many frustrating battles later, the national confidence was shattered, and our young men and women came home, having neither won nor lost. They had been prepared to face concentrated armies on open fields of warfare, and they had been equipped with modern military weapons. But, unfortunately, there was rarely an open field of battle, and the enemy utilized strategies and weapons our troops had never seen before.

The war featured an almost invisible adversary, always there, yet seemingly impossible to locate in gun sights. A major confrontation between the Americans and the massed brigades of the North Vietnam Army would have been easy to handle; but the "nickel and dime" nighttime jungle skirmishes were almost impossible for the gigantic American military machine.

In those final days America was treated to pictures of surplus helicopters being dumped into the ocean, of a once impregnable embassy overrun with people trying vainly to get out, of the ill-equipped but victorious Viet Cong and their North Vietnamese counterparts occupying the city of Saigon. What had happened?

We simply didn't understand the nature of the battle or the enemy, some say. We didn't know the real cost of battling on the Asian mainland, and, worst of all, we didn't really know why we were there.

The passion with which our troops went was totally dissipated when they came home, and the result was bitterness and years of regret. Where have we seen that futile process before? In many other places, in many other times, with nations and individuals.

Such was the case of Samson, for example, who enjoyed a series of spectacular victories in his day. Brute strength—a gift from God—had carried him from one success to another. He effectively intimidated the enemies of Israel, and as long as Samson was able to perform, the people of Israel slept well at night.

But on another day there was another kind of battle. Unlike the rugged confrontations when Samson had faced large numbers of well-equipped soldiers and had destroyed them with ease, there was Delilah, a new enemy of sorts. Who would have thought that within her embrace lay the seeds of Samson's defeat?

The public life of Samson seemed to be marked with invincibility. But his private life was slowly being eaten away by a relationship that—while obviously special and enjoyable to him—was destructive to his passion to be a servant of God.

Samson certainly was warned; he was given more than one opportunity to face up to his increasingly vulnerable situation. But because Delilah gained an important position in his inner life, he chose to ignore the signals, and he was destroyed. Delilah's house became Samson's Vietnam experience.

The person who sets out to serve God must understand that a kind of guerrilla warfare is going on all around us. All too often the spiritual passion needed to carry on the strong life of a leader is dissipated by surrounding battles, battles we have never taken time to adequately understand. The enemy of the spirit is so well camouflaged he is almost impossible to ferret out, much less destroy.

The maintenance, or the restoration, of our spiritual passion requires us to understand not only the *prevailing conditions* and the *people encounters* in which passion is sapped or destroyed but also the kinds of *spiritual battles* that will deny us the energy we need.

Let me isolate a few sample issues that regularly neutralize those who are in any kind of leadership. They are subtle issues, and they are difficult to identify and root out. They yield only to the exercises of spiritual discipline, to those occasions when we take time to locate the source from which we are taking fire. Frankly, I find some of the issues virtually nameless, and when I find names for them, I am embarrassed to admit even to myself that I can find them within me. *But they are there!*

In discussing these, I want to be clear that this is not even the start of an exhaustive list of all those issues that neutralize spiritual passion. They are actually issues with which I am more personally familiar. The value of listing a few and identifying them merely helps us all to think about the nature of our warfare and what it is doing to us.

FOUR SPIRITS THAT DESTROY SPIRITUAL PASSION

"The ministry would be a great calling if it weren't for people," we used to joke on a day when there had been a flow of people problems. For people are always the greatest struggle for someone in leadership—and, of course, the greatest point of joy.

We discussed together the effects of people upon us in a previous chapter. But what we need to look at now is the nature of relationships among those who are themselves leaders. Here is a special brand of spiritual warfare that often breaks out to our shame.

One of the great literary pieces that came out of the Vietnam War was a book called *Friendly Fire*. It detailed the events surrounding the death of a soldier and the failure of the defense department to account for what had actually happened. Only after the dead soldier's persistent parents demanded disclosure did it become clear that the young man had not lost his life to the enemy but to misdirected artillery fire from American guns. Friendly fire, it was called.

Friendly fire is not unusual among Christian leaders. The wounds incurred in spiritual battle come, unfortunately, all too often from friendly guns. When we fire those guns at our fellow soldiers or receive fire from them, spiritual passion is often destroyed.

I have discovered that there are a number of ways this can happen. It is not an attractive list, and what makes it most painful for me is the realization that my finger has sometimes been on the trigger. Friendly fire comes in the form of several poisoned spirits. The first of those might be called the competitive spirit.

1. THE COMPETITIVE SPIRIT

God has called us to work together. We are surrounded by people who are just as excited about their call to leadership as we are by our call. Who are these people? Either they can become our partners, our confidence builders, or they become our *competitors*. The former help build our spiritual passion; the latter, when we see them as competitors, drain it.

Right here we ponder together a most insidious form of spiritual warfare that has destroyed countless people. Diotrephes, "who likes to put himself first" (3 John 9 RSV), evidently saw the apostle John as a competitor and intercepted all the communications that John had sent to that congregation.

Think of it! The people were denied input from one of the

beloved disciples of the Lord because one man reduced his relationship with John to the level of competition.

Being the American that I am, I grew up in a competitive environment. We men in particular were raised with the notion that everyone around us had to be measured to see who was the best. When we were kids, we compared our muscles, our running speeds, the quality of our baseball mitts, and the privileges our parents extended to us. When we were teenagers, we compared our cars, our social skills, our athletic prowess. And as men (now more and more the women have joined us) we are constantly tempted to match the size of our homes, the prestige and power of our jobs, and, strangely enough, the skills of our children (full circle).

Among Christian leaders the competition often continues. Pastors wrestle with feelings of ill will toward another whose congregation is larger; preachers and authors are tempted to compare another's public acceptance to their own; lay leaders suddenly find themselves looking to see who was, and who was not, invited to address or attend the myriad of seminars and conferences around the world today, and using these announcements as a sort of bell-wether to determine who is in, and who is out, with the public.

When we get absorbed by a sense of competition, we are in danger. Our passion subsides as we spend more and more time jealously looking sideways at the roads others are taking rather than looking ahead at the path God has paved for us.

Henri Nouwen wrote of this sort of thing happening in another kind of world, that of the stage performer:

> Recently an actor told me stories about his professional world which seemed symbolic of much of our contemporary situation. While rehearsing the most moving scenes of love, tenderness and intimate relationships, the actors were so jealous of each other and so full of apprehension about their chances to "make it," that the back stage scene was one of hatred, harshness and mutual suspicion. Those who kissed each other on the stage were tempted to hit each other behind it, and those who portrayed the most profound human emotions of love in the footlights displayed the most trivial and hostile rivalries as soon as the footlights had dimmed (Nouwen, *Reaching Out*, pp. 49-50).

"What about this man?" Peter asked Jesus of one of the other disciples. "What is that to you?" Jesus responded. "Follow me!" (John 21:21,22 RSV).

"Some preach the gospel (in the streets of Rome) out of a sense of competition against me," Paul wrote. But that's OK, he adds. At least the gospel is being preached (see Phil. 1:15-17).

The former is Jesus' way of telling Peter, don't think competitively; the latter is Paul's way of saying, I never worry about the success of others.

In Pearson's biography of Oscar Wilde, a discussion is recorded that centers on "the commonly-held view that the good fortune of one's friends makes one discontented."

> Said Wilde: "The devil was once crossing the Libyan desert, and he came upon a spot where a number of small fiends were tormenting a holy hermit. The sainted man easily shook off their evil suggestions. The devil watched their failure, and then he stepped forward to give them a lesson. 'What you do is too crude,' he said. 'Permit me for one moment.' With that he whispered to the holy man, 'Your brother has just been made Bishop of Alexandria.' A scowl of malignant jealousy at once clouded the serene face of the hermit. 'That,' said the devil to his imps, 'is the sort of thing which I should recommend' " (Pearson, *Oscar Wilde*, pp. 127-28).

I discovered a brutal truth about myself, a rather frightening personal flaw, some years ago when I suddenly realized that I rarely delighted in another person's success. In my insecurity as a young pastor, I felt somehow that anyone else's success was a threat to my own. That's the competitive spirit showing.

Rather than delighting in the success and effectiveness of others, I automatically began to explain it away. "He has connections," I might say of one. "She received a lucky break she didn't deserve," it was possible to observe of another. "They liked his preaching only because he had a few well-placed jokes in the sermon." The list of possible rationalizations goes on. We pray for the church to grow, I found, and then we proceed to explain away the church that grows if it is not ours.

Rarely, I painfully discovered, did I ever say to myself, "that man (or woman) deserves praise for that article because it is indeed an excellent piece of writing, and it's a lot better than I could ever have done." Scarcely did it ever occur to me, in my natural state, to be thrilled over the fact that a brother or a sister in faith had achieved something marvelous for the community of believers. How could I say in my heart that I was committed to the expansion of Christ's kingdom since I failed to rejoice when I heard of others in concert with God's Spirit making it happen?

How did I make this discovery about myself? I suspect it came about because I noted how few peers found it possible to express delight in any sort of success I might be enjoying. It was easy to see the competitive spirit in them; it was dreadful, and I mean utterly humiliating, when I discovered that I was the same sort of person. A painful realization! And my competitive feelings had to be rooted out before I could enjoy the spiritual passion God wanted me to have.

Ralph Turnbull recalled an incident recorded in one of my favorite biographies, *Henry Varley's Life Story*. Varley was a great preacher in England's latter nineteenth century. A neighboring pastor had begun to draw some members of Varley's congregation to his services because of his gift as an expositor of the Scriptures. Henry Varley discovered that deep within him he nurtured a serious resentment toward the other man.

> I shall never forget the sense of guilt and sin that possessed me over that business. I was miserable. Was I practically saying to the Lord Jesus, "Unless the prosperity of thy church and people comes in this neighborhood by me, success had better not come"? Was I really showing inability to rejoice in another worker's service? I felt that it was sin of a very hateful character. I never asked the Lord to take away my life either before or since; but I did then, unless his grace gave me victory over this foul image of jealousy (Turnbull, *A Minister's Obstacles*, p. 39).

2. THE CRITICAL SPIRIT

The competitive spirit was not the only poisoned spirit I found in the recesses of my inner life. A critical spirit that often squelches spiritual passion also lurked inside. It was there, in abundance, and while I despised it in others, I was embarrassed to discover it was also ready and waiting in me. When tired or unguarded, I found it easy to find a flaw in every person in my world. I found something to carp about in the reading of every magazine or in the watching of or listening to a Christian presentation on television or radio.

The tendency to emphasize the negative in every situation, to find the ideological or doctrinal difference, to see the character fault, to major in locating the weakness of the program prevented me from generating the positive energy I needed to get on with my part of the work to which I'd been called.

I have a vivid memory of visiting a major city in another country where I was the guest of missionaries. During the days I was there, I was impressed with two things: first, the relative ineffectiveness of their common work, and, second, the critical appraisal fellow missionaries had for one another. It seemed as if every conversation I had with anyone was marked with criticism of another's philosophy or strategy. So poisoned did the atmosphere seem that I found myself counting the hours until the wheels of my plane would lift off the ground to take me away.

Perhaps it was my problem, but in attempting to minister to them from the Scriptures, as I had come to do, I felt stifled and impotent to offer them anything helpful. It was as if each was separated from the others by invisible walls. Together they sang and prayed; apart they criticized and diminished one another.

The good men and women of that area of the world had all gone there at great personal sacrifice to engage in the expansion of Christ's kingdom through evangelism and church planting. How excited and motivated they must have felt when they first arrived, like the Americans who first hit the beaches in Vietnam.

But now an insipidness characterized their combined energy level. It was friendly fire all over again: more attention riveted upon fellow soldiers than upon the frontline where spiritual warfare was actually taking place. Looking back I realize that what I was experiencing was the *absence* of spiritual passion, in them and then in me, an energy nullified by critical spirit.

3. THE VAIN SPIRIT

A third poisoned spirit that destroys spiritual passion makes its presence known when we harbor an insatiable need to impress people in order to have them prefer or like us. This is an inner need that usually arises from private insecurities. We are driven to weigh every word and action in terms of how it will affect people's feelings about us. The passion to impress others overcomes the passion to advance the interest of Christ.

No leader can skip over this one lightly. It is my observation that most would-be leaders have deep insecurities that make them very sensitive to what the crowd thinks about them.

The need to impress emerges in a score of ways: by the way we insist that proper credit be given to our accomplishments, by the attention we pay to titles and privileges, and by the amount of attention we bring to ourselves in conversations.

"Listen to yourself," my wife, Gail, tells me often as we enter a group of people. "Don't fall into the trap of thinking that you have to tell people everything you know. Let them be heard about things in their world. You've enjoyed enough attention for one day. Besides, I'm impressed with you; that's all you need!"

The more we seek to impress others about ourselves, the more security we will develop built around human adulation. And the less God will feel obligated to provide us with *His* gift of security. The more we strive to live off the applause of others, the less we will hunger for the passion that causes us to seek the approval of the heavenly Father.

The great theologian James Denny once wrote, "No man can bear witness to Christ and to himself at the same time. No man can give the impression that he is clever and that Christ is mighty to save."

4. THE ADVERSARIAL SPIRIT

Our spiritual passion will also be affected by how we handle adversarial relationships. I'm thinking of our critics: those who are friendly and those who are unfriendly. And I'm thinking of those who have opposed or failed us and toward whom we feel vengeful.

The adversarial spirit is a poisoned spirit, and it creates an energy of bitterness that will destroy every ounce of spiritual passion we have.

A. B. Bruce wrote of Alcibiades who had been a disciple of Socrates but then became his enemy. Alcibiades recorded his own feelings of resentment and yet reluctant admiration:

> I experience toward this man alone [Socrates] what no one would believe me capable of, a sense of shame. For I am conscious of an inability to contradict him, and decline to do what he bids me; and when I go away I feel myself overcome by the desire of popular esteem. Therefore I flee from him and avoid him. But when I see him, I am ashamed of my admissions, and often times I would be glad if he ceased to exist among the living; and yet I know well that were that to happen, I should be still more grieved (Bruce, *The Training of the Twelve*, p. 371).

I think I know just a little bit about the meaning of hate. I would have denied it at the time, but looking back, I now know that I sometimes have been guilty for short periods of serious feelings of vengeance toward a person or two who, I felt, wronged me. At least that was my perception. On those occasions I was so overcome with adversarial feelings that I did not stop to think how I may have been wrong. That's a serious error.

One memory that burns deep within is that of a plane flight on which I was headed toward a meeting that would determine a major decision in my ministry. I knew I was in desperate need of a spiritual passion that would provide wisdom and submission to God's purposes. But the passion was missing because I was steeped in resentment toward a colleague.

For days I had tried everything to rid myself of vindictive thoughts toward that person. But, try as I might, I would even wake in the night, thinking of ways to subtly get back at him. I wanted to embarrass him for what he had done, to damage his credibility before his peers. My resentment was beginning to dominate me, and on that plane trip I came to a realization of how bad things really were. I could hardly pray; I could hardly think clearly about the future.

As the plane entered the landing pattern, I found myself crying silently to God for power both to forgive and to experience liberation from my poisoned spirit. Suddenly it was as if an invisible knife cut a hole in my chest, and I literally felt a thick substance oozing from within. Moments later I felt as if I'd been flushed out. I'd lost negative spiritual weight, the kind I needed to lose; I was free. I fairly bounced off that

plane and soon entered a meeting that did in fact change the
entire direction of my life. I have often wondered what would
have happened to me if I'd gone to that meeting with the
excess weight of hate still in my heart. Would I not have been
nailed, fixed to that point in my personal history and not
permitted to move ahead under the leadership of the Spirit
of Christ?

Spiritual passion cannot coexist with resentments. We can
do our best to claim that we are in the right, but the Scriptures are clear. The unforgiving spirit is no home to the
energy that causes Christian growth and effectiveness.

Learning to accept the harsh or gentle criticism of others
who may or may not like us is a heavy discipline also. "There
is a kernel of truth in every critique," I was taught by a
mentor; "Look for it, and you'll be a better man."

Usually, in the past, I wasn't looking; I tended to be too
busy ducking in self-defense. But as the time came when I
could actually cultivate appreciation for criticism, my spiritual passion was enhanced.

Now I am impressed by the fact that virtually everything
of value I have learned has come from the mouths of my
critics: both those who care for me and those who feel ani-
mosity toward me. When we look for the kernel of truth, we
find growth, effectiveness, and room for spiritual passion.

Friendly fire is a serious matter, whether given or received. It usually maims good people and leaves them unfit
for the real battles of life. Is there anything sadder than a
passionate soldier who went off to battle but returned dis-
spirited—wounded by his own people? The passion he took to
the battlefield is missing when he returns. We need to brood
over that picture with serious intention. It suggests why
many of us are living joylessly in our work for God.

9

He Knew I Couldn't Handle It!

An inky and mysterious spiritual world lies within us. An inner space that may be as expansive and unexplored as outer space. And in that strange and awesome abyss there dwell motives and values and responses that are almost impossible to define or predict.

The presence of God may dwell in this space if we are careful to offer it to His control. Neglecting that, however, we unwittingly offer that space to energies that are destructive and treasonous. The biblical writers called this *sin*, and they repeatedly warn of its power.

Weariness results from being constantly ambushed by that power. If we experience fatigue of the spirit from the conditions about us in the outer world, and if we are exhausted by the kinds of people with whom we have contact at certain times, then it is important to speak of this third origin of spiritual tiredness: the spiritual battles that find their inception deep within the human spirit.

Jesus warned:

For from within, out of the heart of man, come evil thoughts, fornication, theft, murder, adultery, coveting, wickedness, deceit, licentiousness, envy, slander, pride, foolishness. All these evil things come from within, and they defile a man (Mark 7:21–23 RSV).

Not a pretty description, but an accurate one. And if we do not take great care to shine a light regularly into that darkness to discover what lurks there, almost surely that spiritual attack will be relentless and debilitating.

Catherine Drinker Bowen has written an excellent biography of Sir Francis Bacon, the seventeenth-century Englishman who knew the heights and depths of honor and disgrace. A gifted man with an appetite for power and wealth, Bacon was driven from within to succeed and to gain prominence in the king's court. By hard work and wit he rose to the position of Lord Chancellor of England. Then at the peak of his career, he was impeached by Parliament for taking bribes while in office. Convicted, he was disbarred and banished from London. Bacon was a whipped, spiritually exhausted man.

Bowen recorded a prayer the deposed Lord Chancellor wrote in which he confessed the squandering of his life. From his words it becomes clear that Bacon realized he had ignored the one place in his world where there was power that could bring him down—the evil that ambushes from within. "So as I may truly say," he wrote, "my soul hath been a stranger in the course of my pilgrimage."

Bacon is telling us that a failure to light up the territory within is to invite a spiritual attack from the one place we can least afford to be vulnerable.

François Fénelon wrote of the importance of keeping light focused upon the inner world lest we become victimized like Bacon. But shining the light within may be a frightening experience, for when we do, there may be an unpleasant surprise.

> As that light increased, we see ourselves to be worse than we thought. We are amazed at our former blindness as we see issuing forth from the depths of our heart a whole swarm of shameful feelings, like filthy reptiles crawling from a hidden cave. We never could have believed that we had harbored such things, and we stand aghast as we watch them gradually appear. But we must neither be amazed nor disheartened. We are not worse than we were; on the contrary, we are not better (Fénelon, *Spiritual Letters to Women*, pp. 21-22).

It is certainly not a flattering picture Fénelon paints of our inner worlds in his seventeenth-century description. But it is imagery that could be helpful when we begin to think of the "reptiles" within that fight the development of spiritual passion and seek to quench its force.

TWO INNER BATTLES THAT WAR AGAINST SPIRITUAL PASSION

We could not list the many battles initiated in the inner world. The best we can do is put the spotlight on a limited few of the issues a person in Christian leadership is likely to face. And we can establish greater vigilance over those things that, if left untouched, emerge at our most vulnerable times and nullify our attempts to develop a spiritual passion.

THE BATTLE OF AMBITION

Take the incredible force of *ambition*, which shows its head at the strangest of times. Ambition is the urge to get ahead, to establish oneself powerfully and securely. It was the key to Lord Bacon's downfall.

Christian leaders are not expected to be ambitious. Somehow we have accepted a system in our community of believers that suggests it is usually proper for laypeople to pursue careers and vocations ambitiously, at least if they do not do it blatantly. There is nothing wrong, we imply, in a person's seeking or changing jobs for advancement and salary increases. As long as one keeps morally upright, relationally committed, and ethically clean, we are not disturbed by the reasonable concern to get ahead.

Now of course we would be shocked if a Christian pastor or missionary applied the same reasoning. No one would appreciate a pastor's telling his deacons or elders, "I am leaving this church because a larger, better-paying church has offered me a position." People in Christian service are simply not permitted to talk, or even think, that way. Or are they?

Ambition is a difficult spiritual enemy to pin down. It covers itself in devious ways. It can sneak in through vocabulary such as "the Lord has led me . . ." or "I have this vision for. . ." or "the door has been opened to. . . ."

Ambition can cloak itself in one's "burdens for . . ." or "concern toward. . . ." It can hide behind the effort to expel or unseat rivals because they hold divergent theologies.

But ambition is most dangerous when it settles into the cracks of the heart and tempts a person to weigh every situation in terms of the possibilities of advancing into positions where there is fame or reward.

A close parallel exists between raw personal ambition and the spiritually-passionate desire to advance the kingdom of Christ. Sometimes it is difficult at first to tell the difference between the two.

Simon the magician appeared in his early days of Christian conversion to be a humbled, repentant believer—until Peter and his colleagues came to town and displayed some remarkable gifts of the Spirit.

> Now when Simon saw that the Spirit was given through the laying on of the apostles' hands, he offered them money, saying, "Give me also this power, that any one on whom I lay my hands may receive the Holy Spirit" (Acts 8:18,19 RSV).

One should have known that the old showman who had dazzled people for years was still likely to have some of his original ambition for the crowd's affection. It had been there all the time just waiting to burst out. Apparently, he'd never shined the light within and found the enemy waiting for the right moment to attack. And when Peter came north to Samaria, the fight was on.

Peter was not particularly diplomatic in his handling of the exposed ambition of Simon: "Your heart is not right before God. Repent therefore of this wickedness of yours . . . that . . . the intent of your heart may be forgiven you" (Acts 8:21,22 RSV).

The intent of the heart is those hidden reptiles of which Fénelon spoke—in this case, the reptiles of ambition. You could say that since Simon had not shined the light into his own inner world, Peter did it for him.

Most of us who have entered Christian service as pastors or laypeople understand ambition. In our youngest years, ambition does its job upon us. We want to get ahead and seize opportunities in which we will be able to prove ourselves and our gifts.

Our service for Christ takes on twisted motives we find it difficult to sort out. We pray that the honor of God will be seen in our efforts, yet we are all too conscious that the approval of the crowd is at least of equal importance.

We claim that we do not wish to get ahead of God's purpose or His programs, yet we find within us a drive to take advantage of every situation to advance our own dreams and persuasions. We hear of openings, and we are tempted to manipulate ourselves into position to be considered. We crave the attention of notables and the invitations of organizations to participate in whatever capacity will provide a higher reputation.

My first congregation was a small group of lovable farmers in Western Kansas. To this day I hold all of them in the highest esteem for their faithfulness and loyalty to God and to one another. The congregation barely totaled forty on most Sunday mornings, and that was cut in half if we were in mud or harvest season. The church sanctuary and the parsonage across the road were seven miles north of the nearest paved road, almost twenty miles from the nearest town, not exactly Main Street, U.S.A.

We were genuinely happy serving that congregation during our seminary days. But my happiness did not disrupt my immature ambition, a hope that one day God would lift me up to "bigger things."

One hot July Sunday afternoon, I was walking across the section road to the church parsonage, pondering the possibility that God might one day do that lifting to bigger things.

Do I dare claim some sort of "section-road" revelation? For it was as if I heard God speak to me aloud in nonreligious terms. Was it a voice within me or without? I don't know. But the message was plain. *Gordon, I will never permit you to play in the big leagues* (the bigger things) *until you have faithfully played in the little leagues.*

God had put the light deep within me and had exposed ambition, my discontent with where I was and what I was doing. It was a moment of confrontation, and I had to pause right there and confess what had been exposed. I made a promise before the day was over that I would live as if I were destined to remain serving that congregation for the rest of my life.

Some would say, perhaps, that I did indeed go on to bigger things as most pastors do. Strangely, today I do not feel as if I do anything that has any greater significance than what I did with those people in the country. In fact there are moments when Gail and I wonder what it would be like to return to the tranquillity of the farmland—ambition reversed!

Spiritual passion and ambition cannot share the same space. Young men and women painfully learn that. Older men and women who have never learned that suffer because they can never be satisfied with what they have.

Ambition is tiring; it overcomes spiritual passion and leaves one tired from the constant mental game playing that starts with "what-if" thoughts and goes on to "if-only" thoughts. A fatigue results from the dissatisfaction with where one is and what one is doing. We wonder why there isn't something better, and in the wondering we forfeit the desire to do well with *what is*.

The Holy Spirit's light shining within to expose ambition is a necessary thing.

THE BATTLE OF PRIDE

Akin to ambition is pride, the inability to handle success. Our Christian world includes men and women in both the pastoral and lay sectors who started into leadership not through the energy of ambition but by sincere commitment to God's purposes. But something happened along the way. Their success became intoxicating.

Uzziah, king of Israel, is a warning signal to us all. "As long as he sought the Lord," we are told, "God made him prosper" (2 Chron. 26:5 RSV). The man hit the top. He was successful in everything he did: the urban renewal of Jerusalem, the reorganization and reequipping of the army, and the invigoration of a sick economy. Nothing could go wrong except that which was deep within the darkness of the king's heart.

"When he was strong he grew proud, to his destruction," (2 Chron. 26:16 RSV) the reader is informed. And from there it was downhill. Uzziah died a leper in disgrace under the judgment of God.

Some years ago I had a conversation I've never forgotten. It was with a man I deeply admired for his skill in Bible teaching. Everyone who came into contact with him was impressed with his abilities. Yet throughout his adult life, he had never had the breakthrough into a larger ministry that some others have coveted. That perplexed me because I was convinced he had many superior gifts in comparison to others who were into the bigger things.

When I asked him whether he had ever resented the fact that greater opportunities had never come his way, his answer impressed me. "I know that God would not permit such things for me. He knows I would be unable to handle them." He was speaking of the temptation to pride. I admired the man for his frankness and for his self-awareness. And I came away, realizing how shackled a person can become if pride is not exposed and brought under control.

We watch the all too frequent crashes of leaders in our Christian community: men and women who are boosted by the public to heights never thought possible before. The applause and the adulation are seductive and blinding. They generate pride in all but the most vigilant, and they effectively squelch spiritual passion, substituting for it the counterfeits of showmanship and charisma.

If we want to be men and women of spiritual passion, pride and ambition will have to be dealt with—harshly and repeatedly. They rarely surrender unconditionally. They hide in the interior jungles of inner space, emerging in the dark hours when no one suspects, when there is no light to expose their existence.

"He knew I couldn't handle it," my friend told me. I love the man for his honesty; I wonder what might have been.

10
It's What's Inside That Counts

A few years ago our country was shocked by a strange airplane accident. A well-known college football coach was flying in a private jet from the Midwest to the East Coast. There is some confusion as to the actual details, but during the flight, it became apparent to the ground controllers that the pilot was not flying according to a filed flight plan. Subsequent efforts to communicate with him failed.

Soon it was clear that both the pilot and his passenger were not conscious because of an oxygen deficiency or some other kind of malfunction. Eventually, the aircraft headed out over the ocean, the plane controlled only by autopilot. When the fuel was exhausted, the jet fell from the air.

Had you and I been standing on the ground looking upward as that small plane flew eastward, we would not have known that anything was wrong inside. Assuming that we could see it in its high flight, I might have been apt to say, "Look at that sleek jet. It sure is flying high and fast."

You might have said, "Can you imagine how important a person has to be in order to be flown around in a plane as expensive as that?"

Our impressions would likely have been quite positive until the plane began its exhausted descent to tragedy. Then we might have reflected on how little we actually knew about what was going on inside.

Although the plane incident was unique in the annals of aviation history, a similar pattern in people's lives is not. In the Christian community there are men and women who, like the jet, appear to be flying high and fast. Every external sign suggests a straight and true course. Only when they run out of some sort of inner fuel and reveal their internal exhaustion do we realize that something was wrong.

Weary people. Action without passion. Words without substance. Perhaps we have touched one of the reasons so many people in our nation today claim faith but feel as if they make so little difference in their worlds.

The passionless life shows itself in the numbers of marriages and family relationships crumbling because the energy to overcome the things that separate and divide is no longer there. In the place of what was once fresh and dynamic is a staleness and boredom, a feeling of being trapped, the occasional desire to run.

Honest Christian men and women respond to the call to faith with a belief they have found what it means to integrate all the sectors of life in the lordship of Christ. But a few years later, they may be tempted to abandon their commitment because the resulting activity does not seem to fill a gaping emptiness still within. They are tired of words, of unfilled promises, of expectations never met.

I am constantly made aware of the relatively small knot of people in most churches and Christian groups who have paid a great price to serve, to hold things together for the benefit of the large numbers (the very nice people, we called them) who merely come and enjoy the fruits of it all. Those few are often tired; they grow restive, trying hard not to complain; and one by one they silently grapple with the appealing prospect of calling it quits and letting someone else do the job. We have done them an injustice if we simply write them off as ones who couldn't finish the race.

I sat with a pastor who is my own age, and we spoke together of the dynamics of midlife. "I've been doing this for eighteen years," he says. "I have always believed that God wanted me to be a pastor. But there are times when I get tired of the words, sick of saying and doing the same old things over and over again while very little changes."

"Is it time to do something different?" I asked.

"I can't; I'm too set in my ways. And I don't have the

slightest idea what I'd do. But what's worse, I don't know how much longer I can keep up the pace doing this."

Is there anything new or different about comments and problems of this sort? Many will say no. It is a matter of recommitment, some will say. A few will suggest the need for a good old-fashioned revival. I have good friends who will sincerely suggest a charismatic experience may be in order.

But I'm prepared to propose that there is indeed something new going on. I believe we are headed toward an epidemic of fatigue and weariness that never has been seen before. And in the first half of this book I've outlined some of the things that contribute to that contemporary exhaustion.

Christians have always worked hard. They have always known honest tiredness, the result of work and servanthood.

But something is different today. The believing community has never been so busy, never had so many voices to listen to, never so many choices to make, never so many ways to respond. That, I believe, explains why we are facing the potential of a wholesale exhaustion of the spirit. To ignore that unique phenomenon is to invite spiritual disaster.

I have spent half a lifetime listening to explanations of how to gain control and capability in spiritual things. On not a few occasions, I went away believing I had finally found the answer in the interpretations of one speaker or another. But my enthusiasm was usually dampened fairly quickly as I descended from the emotional high of the initial experience.

It only takes a few dashed expectations before one is tempted to give up trying. It is not that following the Lord isn't a desirable thing. This is no matter of doubting the basic biblical good news, the gospel of Jesus Christ. Nor is this a trip into theological deviation.

We are overwhelmed by the work of Christ on the cross. We are prepared to affirm that the power that raised Him from the dead is mightier than the power of all the stars combined. We delight to the stories of the early apostles and believers, and in the deepest levels of our hearts, we long for the same fervency and commitment—and of course for the powerful results!

But, for the most part and for most people, the fervency isn't there! And on the few occasions when it is, we fear it will too quickly disappear, and it often does.

Among the things that disappoint me the most is the sense

that many Christians have hoped one too many times something would happen in their lives that would make them vibrant disciples of the Lord. But, with their hopes dashed, they have simply lost interest and made other things their chief target of interest. They are impervious to the promises of one more preacher, one more system, one more experience.

What we may have failed to see in the midst of all of this contemporary religious and irreligious noise are a few simple facts consistent in the lives of holy men and women down through the centuries.

Look inside their lives for secrets, and you will discover a handful of things that defy system and definition. Just a few principles that when followed seem to develop, maintain, or renew spiritual passion.

11

Rack 'Em Up

The last time I remember having any serious amounts of extra time was during my university days. The simple lifestyle of a student meant that it was either work, study, or play. I opted frequently for play, and idle time was often spent with friends in the student union, the basement area where there were scores of pool tables. Leaning over each table were earnest young students, cue sticks in hand, searching for ways to knock one more ball into a corner or side pocket.

I headed for those tables many times to join friends for a game or two. Previous players would have left the table in a disheveled condition. Some balls would be in the pockets; others would be scattered across the table. It would be necessary to gather and realign all of them into a tight, triangular configuration at one end of the table.

To do that, one went to the wall on which hung a form, a simple wooden triangle called a rack. All of the balls were placed inside the form, those with a circle around them, alternating with those of a solid color. The black eight ball was placed in the center. Once the re-collected balls were in proper order, the form was lifted, and the players were ready to begin. "Your turn to break," someone would say, pointing to a partner or an opponent. *Break* was a good description of what happened.

The designated breaker would approach the table and

smack the white cue ball down the length of the table to crash against the balls, sending them in every direction. Instantly the balls were bashed apart! And the rest of the game involved picking them off one by one, sending each in its turn rolling toward a pocket.

Each time I brood upon that process which begins with a perfect triangular configuration of pool balls being systematically smashed apart, I see the typical cycle through which a busy person passes almost daily. In real life, the cycle begins with the forming of a dream and the amassing of spiritual passion. The cycle is further formed with a defined objective, a formal or informal plan of attack, and the matching of suitable capabilities and resources. And the action begins.

But as the hours pass, the fatigue and weariness I have previously described begins to set in. It is as if various environmental conditions, people (especially the VNP's and the VDP's), and spiritual realities, in and out of our control, come at us like cue balls, systematically threatening to bash the pieces of our lives apart. And if one is not paying attention, spiritual passion begins to drain away. We become aware that the dreams at the start, both large and small, are now foggy and illusive at best, dissipated at worst.

I don't mind admitting that this cycle from passion development to near passion dissipation has been a familiar picture in my own world. In the early days of my adult Christian commitment, the experience often demoralized me since no one had effectively communicated that this cycle was common to everyone. As one privileged to offer leadership in a family, in a church, and in various organizations, I know what it is like to reach a point where it is hard to care any longer about a dream or a vision. In such times it is as if the cue balls keep coming at me (internally and externally), and the bits of pieces of my life scatter like the balls on the pool table.

But at that same pool table we all might learn a valuable lesson for those busy moments when weariness begins to take its toll. The learning experience begins when the players reach for the rack to begin a new game. The scattered balls are collected again inside the rack, and the perfect triangular shape is re-formed.

That re-forming process is a picture of the experience that

must happen regularly and systematically within those of us who want to maintain or, if necessary, restore our spiritual passion.

Why have we not fully understood that law of spiritual reality? We too are victims—by choice or by circumstance—of the cue balls in our personal history. Sometimes it is as if some monster took aim at us and cried Break!, and we feel hit from every side. Crushed, split, and propelled in directions we didn't wish to pursue, we frequently come to points where we are sure that we will never feel whole again.

After all of this discussion about weariness and passionlessness, is there anything positive to say? Are there principles and truths that, when properly applied, permit one to put the inner, and even the outer, life back into form in much the same way as we realign the pool balls at the beginning of a game?

I'm not asking about one more gimmick or simple formula like the kind we have been sold by enthusiasts. Nor am I asking for a method that appears to work for people of one temperament but not of another. Personally, my quest for answers moves in the direction of men and women of the past who seem to have found a simple basic secret relevant to all of God's people, regardless of generation or culture.

The early mystics called this exercise the act of *recollection*. Our English word *collect* is compounded with the prefix *re-* to suggest that there is a collection process that must happen over and over again because the breaks come so frequently.

Re-collection: those who have majored in the disciplines of the inner spirit have often seized upon that word as a description of what one does when there is a need for a renewal of spiritual passion. Hearing the word, I think of the act at the pool table. And I see it once again in the quiet but necessary actions of the heart: the recollection of the pieces of my being so that once again my inner self is a reservoir of spiritual passion, the energy that enables me to hear God's voice and to act as His child.

"I used to dislike the term 'to re-collect' as in 'to recollect oneself,' wrote Michael Quoist. "I thought it tired and deformed; it reminded me of angular, grey faces perched above scrawny necks more precarious than the tower of Pisa. But I rediscovered the term and find it quite marvelous now."

Quoist continued:

To recollect yourself is to recover all your scattered energies—those of the mind, the heart and the body. It is to reassemble all the pieces of yourself flung in the four corners of your past or the mists of your future, pieces clinging to the fringes of our desires (Quoist, *With Open Heart*, p. 245).

Most of us have neither time nor place for recollection in this busy life of ours—and thus the exhaustion. Recollection becomes a matter of priority *only* when we have experienced one too many times the tastelessness of a passionless life.

I recall an evening when the phone rang, and I was informed that there had been an auto accident and a man had been killed. Would I come quickly to the home to be with the spouse and children when the news was broken?

"I'm not ready for this," I remember thinking as I drove toward the home. "I'm empty; I have nothing to give." As I reviewed why I felt that way, it was clear that the reason lay in my failure for the past few days to have recollected myself so that when the times for true spiritual passion arose I would be prepared. How I got through the evening I will never know. Perhaps I drew on hidden resources, but I remember resolving that I would not be caught unprepared like that again.

Innumerable volumes have been written about inner realignment or recollection. Some have offered simple solutions; others have offered very complex and mysterious ones.

I would like to highlight three major themes in which I believe the recollective process happens. Each of the three demands a choice on our part: *to take time, to seek relationships, to set priorities.* And in the regularity of doing these things, spiritual passion overcomes weariness and provides the resolve one needs to pursue the kingdom lifestyle.

The three themes revolve around questions such as these:
QUESTION: *In what sort of places can recollection happen?* Are there any "consecratable" spaces in my life where I can form and enlarge my view of God, where I can discover the true size and eternal significance of things? ANSWER: in the *safe places* where I am free from the disruptions and interferences that corrupt the inner spirit.

QUESTION: *At what times might personal recollection happen?* Are there moments in my personal schedule during which I must take a hard look at where I've been and where I am going? ANSWER: in the *still* or *sabbath times* of life.

QUESTION: *Who are the people or what are the relationships that both enforce my recollective experiences and benefit from them?* ANSWER: among those whom I call the *special friends* in my life.

QUESTION: *What happens as a result of the recollection experience?* What can one expect if the safe places, the still times, and the special friends form the core of daily experience? ANSWER: the heart is retuned; heaven's signals are received; *spiritual passion is renewed.*

Break! shout the random, sometimes harsh, events of the day. Not until I have been formed and realigned, not until the parts of my life have been recollected and put into touch with the guiding hand and the whispering voice of the Spirit of God, will I cry, "Take your best shot. I may appear scattered for a moment, but I will always be in form."

12
Safe Places

My wife, Gail, and I were walking through the neighborhood one day, commenting on the appearance and architecture of various homes when I noticed a small but bright poster in one front window. It featured the silhouette of an open hand. The poster was obviously positioned in a prominent place where it could not be missed—even by a child. It was then that I learned that the simple emblem was indeed for a child.

"That poster is a sign of a safe place," Gail told me. It is a signal to a frightened or sick child that here is a home offering protection or assistance. If one only knocks on the door, there will be safety from trouble.

I immediately had a mental flashback to a time in my childhood when a safe place of that kind would have been a welcomed sight. I had accepted responsibility to deliver newspapers for a friend, and it took me into a strange neighborhood. The afternoon weather had suddenly turned cold, and I was poorly dressed to face the temperature change. I had no money to make a phone call to my home, and my parents had no idea where I was. But the papers had to be delivered.

Chilled to the bone, slowed down by the heavy weight of the papers, and confused by poorly written directions and addresses, I remember coming to a point of total frustration.

I needed assistance and had no idea where to get it. I felt absolute helplessness. It would have been a wonderful moment to have seen one of those posters with a hand on it. I needed a safe place, a warm place, a place to pull myself together and revive my flagging spirit.

We need safe places in our worlds. Not merely when we are in trouble but when we need to rest a bit, to regain our measure of spiritual passion and composure for the continuing challenges of the cue balls that constantly come at us.

No biblical character seems to have understood that better than King David of Israel. He was apparently acquainted with trouble and stress from the early years of his life. But he also appears to have coped well, perhaps because he understood the principle of the safe place.

As a young boy, David's father, Jesse, had given David responsibilities for tending the sheep. His objective was to care for and protect the family flock. That meant leading sheep to sites where quiet water, adequate pasture, and protective rest were available. It meant that David was to be guardian of the flock, standing between the sheep and their enemies when necessary. In short, as a shepherd, David was finder and guarantor of the safe places.

Later the boy became a soldier, and danger came not from wild animals or inadequate shelter, but from human enemies. And the matter of safe places took on new meaning.

Who knows what danger David was pondering when he wrote of the safe places and the protection of the shepherd from his childhood.

"The LORD is my shepherd," he wrote. ". . . he makes me lie down in green pastures. He leads me beside still waters; he restores my soul" (Ps. 23:1,2 RSV). Here his perception of God was shaped by the view of a shepherd leading sheep into places of sustenance and safety. The result was the renewal of soul or spiritual passion, the lifting of weariness.

The image of a shepherd is a tender, most stimulating view of the Creator. It is a picture that our hustle-and-bustle view of life does not permit us to adequately contemplate or appreciate. Only those who come to understand the significance of safe places will fully appreciate what David is talking about.

Safe places were important to David when he felt vulnerable because of the consequences of his own sins and errors of judgment.

I am surrounded by many troubles—
   too many to count!
My sins have caught up with me,
   and I can no longer see;
they are more than the hairs of my head,
   and I have lost my courage.
Save me, Lord! Help me now! (Ps. 40:12–13 TEV)

One pictures a man who could have used a window with a hand signaling a safe place.

David also lived with the relentless rivalry created by Saul. Later as king, David would be involved in many battles perpetrated by the annual invasions of Israel's enemies. Then serious family problems would crop up, many the result of his poor judgment as a father.

In all these situations, David knew what it was like to be on the run, seeking places of safety until he could gather strength and restore his fortunes. Read David's reflections about these times, and you will discover that he was looking first for *protection*, second, for strength or *renewal of soul*, and third, for the opportunity to *rebound*. Such excursions often took him to the desert where he could lose his enemies and find God.

A map of David's travels would probably reveal all sorts of localities that he would refer to as the safe places—mountain tops, caves, oases, and forest groves. To each of these places he would flee when under fire, and there he would stop for however long he needed to tend to his weariness.

In a larger sense, God's people have always adhered to a doctrine of safe places. The Garden of Eden was the ultimate safe place. In it there was no confusion, only order. Eden was a place where the glory and splendor of God were seen and appreciated. We are told that the first man and woman communed regularly with God in an intimacy that defies description. One imagines that there was an absence of weariness, both of body and spirit, as we have come to know it.

But Adam and Eve forfeited their right to that Edenic safe place, and before long they found themselves in a world marked with hostility and work of another kind. The labor they now gave to the earth produced only a fraction of the original abundance. Few places were now safe in any sense.

Succeeding generations had to deliberately create safe

places in the form of altars, limited localities where for a short period they could reestablish their relationship with God. At the altar there was a moment of remembrance for special events or experiences. There was the sacrifice with the shedding of blood, reflecting the need for a reconciling action between God and the person. Supposedly one left the site of the altar newly invigorated and possessed of a sense of guidance for the future.

Abraham was a great safe-place builder, and a map of his travels would show altars all over the Promised Land where he encountered God, heard the voice of reassurance, and was provided direction and wisdom for the next set of challenges.

When Moses had lived eighty years, God called him to a safe place in the desert known by us as the burning bush. "Take off your shoes," God said, "for you are standing on holy ground" (Exod. 3:5 TLB). And from that safe place came a word from God that sent Moses off to confront the Pharaoh of Egypt. Later Moses would ascend Mount Sinai, another safe place, and engage in a series of conversations out of which would come the law and other instructions about a new way of life.

Soon the Hebrews had another kind of safe place, the tabernacle, built according to carefully given instructions. The specifications of this safe place reflected all sorts of truths about God and His promises. You apparently couldn't go near it without being reminded of something pertaining to God's covenant with His people. This tabernacle was always located in the center of the community. Everyone knew that it was the place to go when you had personal, spiritual turbulence or a need for reconciliation with God. A priest would be there to receive you or your family. You could always see the hand on the poster in the window.

Before the people crossed into the Promised Land, they came upon another safe place, Gilgal. Three things seemed to have transpired at Gilgal. First, an altar of stones was erected to commemorate what God had done in the miraculous crossing of the Jordan. Joshua then told them the altar would always be a place of remembrance, a reminder of how God brought us over into a new land.

Gilgal was, second, a place of reaffirmation of the special relationship God had with the Hebrews. The men of the nation were circumcised, a physical sign since the days of

Abraham of their positive response to God's call. And third, while in Gilgal Joshua and his people received instructions as to how they were to defeat the city of Jericho in battle. The instructions were a strange, but nevertheless effective, battle plan. Gilgal is a classic safe place—a place of rest, remembrance, reaffirmation, and redirection.

The temple became a safe place many generations later. It was to have been a place of prayer for the nations, Jesus would later say. That was why he was so upset when he saw a safe place changed into a "den of thieves": a noisy and exploitive place, a congested shortcut people could take from one side of the city to the other (see Matt. 21:13). Additionally, the temple had become a marketplace where tired travelers were often swindled in their attempt to exchange foreign money for special offerings and the purchase of animals for sacrifice. A safe place had become the most dangerous of places.

Today the closest thing to a safe place that would pop up into our minds would be the church building where we regularly go to worship. And so it can be.

Henri Nouwen wrote in this vein when he said:

When you look out over the city of Rome, walk in its streets, or ride in its buses, you quickly realize that it is a crowded city full of houses, full of people, full of cars, yes—even full of cats. You see men and women moving quickly in all directions, you hear joyful and angry voices mixed with a great variety of street sounds, you smell many odors—especially cappuccino—and you feel the Italian embrace by which you gain a friend or lose your money. It is a busy, congested city, in which life manifests itself in all its boisterous intensity.

But in the midst of this lively and colorful conglomeration of houses, people and cars, there are the domes of Rome pointing to the places set apart for the Holy One. The churches of Rome are like beautiful frames around empty spaces witnessing to him who is the quiet, still center of all human life. The churches are not useful, not practical, not requiring immediate action or quick response. They are tranquil spaces, strangely empty most of the time. They speak a language different from the world around them. They do not want to be museums. They want to invite us to be silent, to sit or kneel, to listen attentively, and to rest with our whole being.

A city without carefully protected empty spaces where one can sense the silence from which all words grow, and rest in the

stillness from which all actions flow, such a city is in danger of
losing its real character (Nouwen, *Clowning in Rome*, pp. 37–38).

Spiritual passion can be renewed in such places. These
domes of silence, as Nouwen calls them, can be our homes as if
they had a hand in the window inviting us to protection, rest,
and redirection. But, sadly, they often are not those sorts of
places. They could be and should, but often they are not.

What Henri Nouwen describes as a place of silence and
stillness "from which all things grow" is exactly what I mean
when I talk about a safe place. But when the cathedral or the
church fails us, other safe places can be just as useful and
effective.

The consummate safe place is the heavenly one. The evangelist John was permitted to peek through the door in a
vision, we are told in Revelation 4 and 5. Working hard to
record his impressions, he wrote of the heavenly family
about the throne of God.

First, there was activity regarding the being of God:
"Holy, Holy, Holy," they sang in praise to the Mighty One
(Rev. 4:8 RSV). Then, there was reflection on the great acts of
God: "Thou didst create all things" (Rev. 4:11 RSV).

From there the family of God moved to ponder the atoning
work of God in Christ: "Who is worthy to open the scrolls?"
(Rev. 5:2 RSV) is the towering question. Then "I saw a Lamb"
(Rev. 5:6 RSV) John wrote, and he wept as he saw the mystery
of it all. Finally, the people of heaven are seen in their
exaltation of the triumphant work of God, for they had
"made them a kingdom of priests" (Rev. 5:10 TEV). It is a
remarkable display of safe-place action. Perhaps it is meant
to be an ideal picture for the reader of what sorts of things
ought to happen when we enter safe places in our world.

The ancient Christian mystics (and a few modern ones)
thought that safe places of any value could only be erected in
obscure localities. So they built monasteries and hermitages
out in deserts, on mountain tops, or in forests. Hoping to find
that spot where God could be touched and worshiped, they
sometimes abandoned civilization: the noisy city streets, the
cries of enraged people, and the clanging sounds of men and
women at work or play.

But, as Michael Quoist points out, that may not have been a
necessary venture (if even possible) for them or us:

I've always dreamed of solitude, the hermit's life, a cabin in the woods or a tiny chalet on the edge of a mountain. I've always dreamed of deserts and silence. But I've resisted the dream, with the exception of one time when I offered myself the luxury of a retreat with a hermit: four hours by foot, far from any living creature and a hermit happy to see me. We talked a lot.

I understood then that I carry my hermitage around with me and that I don't need to go too far to meet my Lord. I often need to withdraw into my retreat, *if only for a few minutes. Christ waits for me there* (Quoist, *With Open Heart*, p. 155).

Frank Laubach came to understand the need for safe places in his world.[1] In his journal he reflected:

Are you building sacred palaces for yourself? I meant to write "places" to be sure, but I think I shall leave the word "palaces" for that is what any house becomes when it is sacred. The most important discovery of my whole life is that one can take a little rough cabin and transform it into a palace just by flooding it with thoughts of God. When one has spent many months in a little house like this in daily thoughts about God, the very entering of the house, the very sight of it as one approaches, starts associations which set the heart tingling and the mind flowing. I have come to the point where I must have my house, in order to write the best letters or think the richest thoughts.

So in this sense one man after the other builds his own heaven or his hell. It does not matter where one is, one can at once begin to build heaven, by thoughts which one thinks while in that place ... I have learned the secret of heaven building—anywhere (Laubach, *Frank Laubach*, p. 27).

What have these men learned? Safe places can be anywhere. "I don't need to go far," Quoist wrote. And Laubach turned a cabin into a "palace" by filling it with thoughts of God.

Can we transform hostile places into momentary safe places merely by declaring them so? Can a bus seat become a safe place? an automobile stopped in a rush-hour traffic jam? an office between appointments? a sickroom where a mother waits over a suffering child? a sidewalk during a stroll? a lunch counter before a class? Are we not learning that men and women can build altars any place—if not altars in the

[1] Some of us may have a problem with the precision of Dr. Laubach's theology, but remember that he is speaking in mystical terminology as he seeks to express his sense of a safe place.

street, then altars in the heart; if not for an entire day, then for ninety seconds.

People who create safe places with regularity do not have to worry about weariness. Or when it comes, a visit to the safe place dispels it. Those who are constantly weary are those who think they can always move forward with no pauses, that they can always endlessly achieve with no rests at the safe places.

Some time ago Gail and I were driving along a busy freeway. In the car with us was a special friend, a man known to people around the world. He shared the fact that he was very tired and not a little frightened about an upcoming assignment later that day. Additionally, he admitted to great feelings of loneliness because his wife was ill and unable to be with him.

It was rush hour; the car was moving in the start-and-stop rhythm of heavy traffic. From the backseat Gail suddenly said, "Gordon, let's intercede for——right now." The car immediately became a safe place. Jesus was there; we invited His presence. First Gail prayed, and then I—with my eyes open, of course.

Later our friend shared with others the meaning of that moment and its restorative value to him. Rush hour, a car, a busy schedule—but we'd created an instant safe place. We had put a hand in the window.

When we drive across the country, we frequently check the map for upcoming rest stops. Here and there along the line of our route on the map are tiny rectangles. The map key says that these rectangles represent places for fuel, food, and rest. The travelers count the miles until they reach the turn-off marked REST STOP. It is the safe place for road-weary travelers.

The biographical maps of holy men and women are marked with countless rectangles: the places they made safe by meeting Christ there. Or should I say, the places Christ made safe by meeting them there. On such occasions they saw the hand in the window. Their safe places did not need to be beautiful cathedrals; they could be in the public square or even in the waiting area of the coliseum where they awaited a coming encounter with the lions. The roar of the crowd meant danger. But the Spirit of God meant, strangely enough, safety.

13

The Place of Secrets

Sir William Osler is among the most highly esteemed physicians in modern medical history. The classic two-volume biography of Osler abounds with stories depicting not only his genius as a practitioner of medicine but also his unusually compassionate nature.

It is said that one day he entered the pediatric ward of a London hospital and noted with delight the children who were playing at one end of the room. Then his gaze was drawn to one small girl who sat off to one side alone on her bed, a doll in her arms. She was clearly oppressed by feelings of loneliness.

A question about her to the head nurse brought the response that she was ostracized by the other children. Her mother was dead, Osler was told; her father had paid but one visit, bringing at that time the doll, which she now tightly clutched. Apart from that one visit, no one had ever come to see her again. As a result, the other children, concluding that she was unimportant, had treated her with disdain.

Sir William was at his best in moments like that, and he immediately walked to the child's bed. "May I sit down, please?" he asked in a voice loud enough to carry to where the other children were at play. "I can't stay long on this visit, but I have wanted to see you so badly." Those describing the moment say that the girl's eyes became electric with joy.

287

For several minutes the physician conversed with her, now in quiet, almost secretive tones. He inquired about her doll's health and appeared to be carefully listening to its heart with his stethoscope. And then as he rose to leave, his voice lifted again so that everyone heard, "You won't forget our secret, will you? And mind you, don't tell anyone." As Osler left the room, he turned to see the once-ignored youngster now the center of attention of every other child on the ward.

I would like to think that the wise physician created a safe place with the child for a moment, shared a secret or two, and restored her personal passion for life. His attentiveness and intimacy affirmed her specialness in her own eyes and the eyes of others.

The tender encounter between Osler and the child provides for me a parable about a life in intimate touch with God. We are all children at one point or another in our experience. Perhaps we are always children and don't wish to admit it. Sometimes we feel alone; at other times we are weary from our futile attempts to succeed or improve our lot; on yet other occasions our sense is that of complete vulnerability before the critic or the rival. We come to crave the safe place, a refuge where we can restore our strength, gain our bearings, and begin again.

"There is a place of quiet rest," the poet Cleland McAfee wrote, "near to the heart of God. A place where sin cannot molest." It can be a place to meet the One whom Helmut Thielike called *The Waiting Father*. No one can live well without such places; but many try.

Psalm 63 is a poem about safe places. Some believe that the early church sang the words of this psalm at almost every worship service as they gathered in the safe place of congregational meeting, away from the stress of the world.

The psalm was written with the desert in mind, and it is likely that it was written while the writer was in the desert, fleeing from a dangerous enemy. Some believe the author, David, was running from Saul, the increasingly deranged king who saw the young shepherd boy as a rival to his throne. Others, including myself, believe that the psalm was constructed when David was in flight from Jerusalem after his son staged a sudden coup.

If Psalm 63 was written in the second of these two possible

contexts, then I come to an even better appreciation of the words "And the king . . . arrived weary at the Jordan; and there he refreshed himself" (2 Sam. 16:14 RSV). The psalm would give a strong indication of just how David went about refreshing himself.

And how did he do it? He declared the wilderness where he found himself to be a safe place. There the young man on the run entered into a time of personal intimacy with the waiting Father.

"O God, thou art my God, I seek thee, my soul thirsts for thee; my flesh faints for thee, as in a dry and weary land where no water is" (Ps. 63:1 RSV). The writer had looked about and matched the state of his inner being with the environment. My private world is much like the desert; there is thirst and terrible weakness of spirit, the absence of spiritual passion.

Apparently stripped of everything, David turned to the state of his inner being. He could afford to lose the resources of his outer or public world, but he was smart enough to know that he could not go much further if his private world was empty.

Wherever the writer was, he had stopped everything: running, fighting, panicking. He had entered a safe place and called for the Lord's presence. His desert could have been a modern office, a living room, a picnic table. All that counted was that he had announced his intention to meet with his God.

It is fascinating what David did with special imagery. He set his imagination running freely, seizing past experiences in which he had communed with God and renewed his spiritual passion.

FOUR KINDS OF SAFE PLACES THAT RENEW SPIRITUAL PASSION

At least four different experiences came to his mind as he sought to regain the energy of the spirit. And each provides an insight both to what a safe place can actually be and to what sorts of themes one is liable to hear when God whispers secrets in the safe places.

1. THE SANCTUARY

There are no buildings in a wilderness, certainly no temples or churches. And yet it seems clear that David had a craving to enjoy an experience in the sanctuary. All his life he had understood the meaning of sanctuaries: first, as a shepherd when he created fortified places for his sheep, then as a soldier when he learned to seek strongholds or high places. As king in Jerusalem, the sanctuary at the tabernacle became a place for spiritual retreat, a place where he joined the congregation to worship.

But the sanctuary in Jerusalem was far away; it was only a memory. But David had gone there so many times in the past that it became possible to create an imaginary sanctuary in his private world. There in the desert he could walk right into a specially designed sanctuary that offered the possibility of personal renewal. "So I have looked upon thee in the sanctuary, beholding thy power and glory. Because thy steadfast love is better than life, my lips will praise thee" (Ps 63:2-3 RSV).

The significance of these words grows when one remembers that the writer was greatly threatened. Whether you believe that he was on the run from Saul or Absalom, the issue is the same. David had been overwhelmed by a human power greater than he was. How should he cope with this? How did every great man or woman of God in the Bible cope with the issue of momentary defeat or threat? They set their inner beings on the power and glory of God, a power much greater than anything in the world. And when the contrast is made, all things become reduced to true size.

David entered the imagined sanctuary just as he had done in the real one so many times in the past. And the first message that came to him was God's majesty and glory. When he finished this experience of worship, his fear was abated; he was in touch with reality once again.

This experience was Daniel's when he was under the death threats of King Nebuchadnezzar. His prayer revealed his preoccupation: "He changes times and seasons; he removes kings and sets up Kings" (Dan. 2:21 RSV). It was a prayer of reorientation that focuses on true power and true majesty.

The same thing happened with the early church when Peter and John returned fresh from the cease-and-desist threats of the Jerusalem city leadership. What was their prayer in the sanctuary? "Sovereign Lord who didst make the heaven and the earth. . . . look upon their threats" (Acts 4:24,29 RSV).

The weariness that comes from intimidation or defeat, the fatigue that comes from being drained by people who attempt to dominate our world, and the exhaustion that comes from fighting spiritual battles need to be cast in the context of the God of ultimate might and strength. And that is exactly what David did in his safe place. It became a sanctuary for eternal perspectives.

In this sanctuary David not only perceived the greatness of the majesty and power of God, but he was also refreshed with the reassurance of the steadfast love of the Lord: "Because thy steadfast love is better than life, my lips will praise thee" (Ps. 63:3 RSV).

If this psalm came out of the tragedy with Absalom, then David had a right to brood in the desert about the meaning of loyalty, not only from his family but also from his countrymen who had turned him out of power. At one time they had cheered him on in battle; they had applauded his efforts as king. But now many of them had abandoned him for the silver-tongued Absalom who had out-promised David.

What did David have now? Only the reminder, in this sanctuary of the desert, that God's love for him was steadfast. To put it in the words of a later prophet, Jeremiah: "The steadfast love of the LORD never ceases, his mercies never come to an end; they are new every morning; great is thy faithfulness" (Lam. 3:22,23 RSV).

No person in any form of leadership is going to go on forever without certain feelings of betrayal or terrible loneliness. And if leaders put their trust in the applause or loyalty of human beings, a terrible letdown will likely result.

For such people a safe place like David's sanctuary becomes emphatically important. Here things are regularly brought to true size, and here there is a reminder of the loyal love of God. It is God's secret between Himself and the one seeking sanctuary. And it is heard only in the safe place. And having heard the secret over and over again in the safe place, one has never to panic over the loyalty or disloyalty of people who can often make serious errors of judgment and strip the leader of everything. David knew.

2. THE NIGHT ROOM

As David pondered his outer world in the desert, a second kind of safe place came to mind. There too he had met God in the past. It was his place of rest, where he usually slept, the night room in his palace. "As I lie in bed, I remember you; all night long I think of you, because you have always been my help" (Ps. 63:6,7 TEV).

Although his private quarters were geographically back in Jerusalem, David reconstructed them in the desert where he felt the need for surroundings speaking of safety.

Now the theme in the night room, this second kind of safe place, is *the helpfulness of God*, a theme that had been at the root of David's spiritual thinking all his life. When the help-fulness of God was real to him, his spiritual passion was renewed and unlimited. Most of us would have preferred to use such moments to strengthen our bitterness, to erect de-fenses, and to recruit and motivate the people who would help get back what has been lost. Not David. It was a time for safe-place reflection.

David reflected upon the helpfulness of God on the day when he had stood before Saul, discussing the giant Goliath. He had volunteered to take on Goliath, and Saul was ready for any sort of proposed solution, no matter how zany it seemed.

How could David dare to think that he could handle Goli-ath? The young man spoke of his shepherding days, the moments when the flock was attacked by lions and bears. On every occasion David had handled such enemies.

How had he done it? "The LORD who delivered me from the paw of the lion and from the paw of the bear, will deliver me from the hand of this Philistine." He must have been believable because Saul said, "Go, and the LORD be with you" (1 Sam 17:37 RSV).

And the Lord had been with David. History has told the story over and over again: one dead giant. The Lord was with David.

Over and over again in the quietness of the nighttime hours, David had lain upon his bed thinking of times like those. Over and over again in that safe place, he had heard the words of God: *I will be your help*. And now out on the desert he was prepared to create a safe place like his night room in Jerusalem where he could once again hear the same promise.

When our daughter, Kristy, was five years old, the room where she slept was a safe place to her, but only if it was carefully arranged before she fell into sleep. I remember her earnest instructions before I would leave her. Her dolls and stuffed animals had to be lined up against the wall in a carefully prescribed order, each one having its nightly turn to be tucked in with her. The window shade had to be lowered to a set point: no lower, no higher. The top sheet had to be folded over the edge of the blanket. And, finally, the bedroom door had to be left open just far enough so that it admitted the glow of the night light in the hall but not so that the direct light would shine into her eyes as she slept.

The final words as I said goodnight were always, "Daddy, where will you be, and what time are you going to bed?" And after I answered her questions, she would remind me, "Now don't you go to sleep before I'm asleep."

In her childhood, the bedroom would be a safe place if all the routines were properly established. Then she could drift off to sleep comfortably confident that everything was under control and that her mother and dad were nearby to provide protection if it were needed.

I hear David relating to the same thing. He seems to be saying: *In the night hours when I am at rest, I am reminded that "you have always been my help." I know where you are, and I know that you're not asleep.*

In the tidal wave of a day's events and experiences, many of us even though we are busy and preoccupied, stop and create a safe place like David's sleeping room. And for a moment we ponder the reminder that God will be our help. We may even ask of Him, "Where will you be?" and we are apt to hear His whisper that settles the troubled heart and renews lost passion: "I will be with you; I will not fail you or forsake you" (Josh. 1:5 RSV).

3. THE PROTECTIVE WINGS

Not too many living things can be easily seen at first glance in a desert. Only with a studied look will one spot insects, reptiles, rodents, and small, fast-moving animals.

But one will always see the birds—hovering, spiraling about on the air currents, darting occasionally to the ground to pick off quarry. They are free to sing.

Birds understand safe places; that's how they survive. Safe places in the air *above* the danger, in well-placed nests *away* from the danger, and close to protective parents' wings *covered* or *lifted* from the danger.

As David brooded upon safe places, the wings of a bird came to mind.

Those in trouble seek safe places where they can get back their courage, their hope, their desire to return to the battle. In the safe place they will think about the higher power that is greater than the power that now threatens them. They will consider the meaning of love and loyalty that does not wane or turn on them. And they will think about where help might come from.

But sooner or later they are apt to think about protection. And that's where the birds come in. Birds raise the issue of protection, and in protected places one feels free to rejoice, to laugh, to sing.

When was the last time, David might have wondered, when he was free to sing? Perhaps as he asked these questions, David began to recall the many times he had seen parent birds with outstretched wings offering protection to their young. And he was caused to write: "In the shadow of thy wings, I sing for joy" (Ps. 63:7 RSV).

The wings of the parent bird are a theme in Scripture, a theme always speaking of protection and care. Moses, like David, had watched birds in action and used them to remind his people of God's protective concern for them as he made them into his people: "Like an eagle teaching its young to fly, catching them safely on its spreading wings, the LORD kept Israel from falling" (Deut. 32:11 TEV).

Moses had obviously watched the parent eagle push the eaglets out of the nest to force them into flying lessons. But had the tiny eaglet failed to use its wings properly and begin flight, its parent would have swooped under the falling youngster and caught it on outstretched wings. The upper surface of the wing meant protection when falling.

A psalmist seized the theme of the wings of a bird and wrote: "He will cover you with his wings; you will be safe in his care; his faithfulness will protect and defend you" (Ps. 91:4 TEV).

The underside of the parent bird's wings provided protection from enemies on the ground or near the nest. Jesus Himself alluded to the birds when He talked passionately to the people of Jerusalem on the purpose of His redemptive love: "How many times I wanted to put my arms around all your people, just as a hen gathers her chicks under her wings, but you would not let me!" (Matt. 23:37 TEV). The wings spoken of by our Lord appear to speak of warmth, nurture, and rest—protective elements.

David himself had thought of bird's wings on other occasions when he'd written, "In the shadow of your wings I find protection until the raging storms are over" (Ps. 57:1 TEV).

All of these allusions to a safe place come alive when one is caught up in the maelstrom of a day's events where there is a sense of vulnerability and defenselessness.

"There are times when I feel like an unprotected goalie in a hockey game," a friend told me. "More pucks coming at me than I can handle: decisions to make, criticisms to respond to, problems to solve, conflicts to resolve. My stomach knots up, and I find myself breathing hard. Frankly, I just get scared. I'm not supposed to admit that I get scared, but I do nevertheless."

My friend needed a safe place, a covering like the wings of a bird. It was time to close the door, take the phone off the hook, and declare the space a safe place while the protective wings of God brought reassurance to the inner spirit. Regular occasions such as this throughout a day not only prevent weariness but also replace fear with a confidence that permits the song of joy.

4. THE STRONG HANDS

As we've already noted, it is likely that Psalm 63 was written in the context of a humiliating defeat. And, therefore, one of the issues any person in David's position is going to wrestle with is the matter of personal confidence. For in moments like these, any human-oriented confidence is probably gone.

Confidence is a state of mind and heart that permits a person to act with assurance that yesterday's defeat or failure will turn into tomorrow's victory. Real confidence is not merely a psychic energy created on a base of unfounded hopes. It is a sense of a new source of power from beyond ourselves—a power, a passion if you please, which has proved itself before and which is available to us as Christians in unlimited amounts.

We have all seen examples of people trying to build up false confidence: the boxer who makes preposterous claims before his match, the salesperson who deals in exaggerated tales about a product, the loud-mouthed adolescent who feigns bravado to cover up a load of insecurity.

But a defenseless child walking beside his or her father, held by a strong hand, is another story. This is the picture of one who assumes that his strength is an extension of the father's power. The connection of the hands makes the difference between confidence and fear.

"My soul clings to thee," David wrote, "thy right hand upholds me" (Ps. 63:8 RSV). From somewhere the king had imagined one more kind of safe place: the grip of a powerful hand offering transfused inner strength and direction.

I have a special memory of a day with my father on the ski slopes. It was my first time on skis, and I was as awkward and clumsy as any beginner. We rode together on the ski tow to the top of the novice's slope. And when we had positioned ourselves at the brow of the hill, I began to have second thoughts. I could hardly stand up, let alone begin any sort of glide toward the bottom.

But my father had skied the mountains for years; he had confidence, and I had trust. He drew me between his skis so that my two were inside and parallel to his. Then he put his hands on my small shoulders and pressed my body against his. "Relax," he said, "and let me guide us down the hill. You concentrate on feeling the way my body turns and makes us move from one side to the other."

It was hard at first, but I soon learned that his hands could direct me in any direction he wanted me to go. All I had to do was relax in the grasp of his hands. We actually made it to the bottom without falling, a thrilling first run. By the third time down the hill, I could almost anticipate the shift of his weight and the turning of his skis. But what I wasn't aware of at first was that the grip of his hands was becoming lighter and lighter until it was merely the light touch of his fingers.

Suddenly, the grip was no more; my dad was releasing me and permitting me to ski ahead a foot or two, reaching out to steady me only when I began to wobble. "Go ahead, son," he said halfway down the hill. "You're skiing by yourself." And I continued the descent on my own, always on the edge of losing my confidence, but nevertheless just confident enough because I could sense his strong hands just behind should I begin to fall.

Those moments in the grasp of my father's strong hands are among the most precious of my childhood memories. They were there as long as I needed a transfusion of guidance and direction; they dropped away as soon as I had developed enough of my own.

The grasp of the Father's hands was a safe place to David. Like a frightened child devoid of any confidence, he reached out the imagined hands of his soul to the outstretched hand of God. Perhaps he too could visualize such an act because in his childhood he had experienced the touch of Jesse's hand at a dangerous moment. That sense of safety then became larger when he relaxed in God's hands.

Many of us were taught to act confidently even if we didn't feel confident. "Act like a man," a small boy with a bleeding knee is told. It means don't cry; don't admit that your heart is breaking and your knee hurts a lot. "Don't be such a sissy," we have heard more than once. And from words like these we learned that one should pretend that fear isn't real, that hurt shouldn't be acknowledged, that failure is a sign of weakness.

In such unfortunate ways we were denied an appreciation of the safe place. We learned to manufacture a false sense of confidence and bravery. We mastered the outward appearance of happiness even though we were crying within. We developed techniques to conceal our insecurities, techniques such as speaking boastfully, laughing heartily, and taking risks. But often, then and now, younger *or* older, we were and are just heartbroken children who refuse to let anyone decode our real language. What we usually need is the strong hand of a Father—now the heavenly Father—who says to us, "My confidence is yours. Relax, lean on me."

Why can't we stop frequently in a bone-tiring day and declare the place in which we find ourselves a safe place? In that quiet moment or hour we extend our inner spirit as a child does his or her hand, and we meditate on the confidence that comes from the grip of the Holy Spirit. Frequent moments like these reinforce the promise of the Father who said, "I will uphold you with my victorious right hand" (Isa. 41:10 RSV).

In this sense the promise is reminiscent of the voice of my dad on the ski slope: "Go ahead, son." And I do because I am sure that his hands are just behind me when I will once again need a strong grip.

It is in these kinds of safe places that we hear the secrets God whispers to the inner spirit. The desert became a safe place in which Elijah could dispel the weariness of a drained condition. There he heard the still small voice of God as David might have heard it in the night hours in his sleeping room. The shoreline where Jesus cooked an early morning breakfast for the tired disciples became a safe place for the defeated Simon Peter who must have wondered whether he would ever get a second chance.

Where are your safe places and mine? Sir William Osler met a lonely child and established a safe place where she could share a confidence-building secret. Where is it that God can meet us and share His secrets?

I speak of the secrets of His power and glory, the affirmations of His steadfast love, the promises of His willingness to help when we are at wit's end, the offer of parent-like protection, the extension of His strong hand of stability and guidance.

As my life has increased in busyness and responsibility, I have found that the urgency for establishing personal and corporate safe places where these assurances can be renewed has significantly increased. The failure to understand this and act on it leads to the onset of numbing weariness and the loss of spiritual passion.

Thus I have established a safe place in my home where I pursue an encounter with God each morning. For me it is my study; for others it could be a bedroom, a kitchen, or a corner in the basement. It must be a place away from other people and varying interferences as much as possible.

Other versions of the safe place can be realized. Some of us will find them where we work or at other localities within the circumference of our daily journeys.

Occasionally we need to enter the safe places set aside by

the Christian community for all to use. Those of us who have lived in the freer Protestant traditions have not been adequately taught the value of the holy places: sites exclusively reserved for worship and spiritual listening. Hearing only of the dangers of excessive emphasis upon religious architecture, we have denied ourselves the peaceful atmospheres of altars, shrines, and chapels. However legitimate the reasons for concerns about these things, insufficient thought has been given to what takes their place as an alternative.

How important it is to understand that safe places can be those where all the senses are involved in lifting us to heaven and into the presence of the waiting Father. A safe place is a place of silence where the inward ears can hear, a place of beauty where the eyes can take in color, form, and order (the symbols of God's being and actions), and a place of peace where the body can relax as the inward person reaches upward to hear the Spirit speak.

The world constructs its places of amusement, of imprisonment, of violence, and of material consumption. Why should we not be just as diligent in the development of safe places where there is the promise of peace and restoration of spiritual energy?

We must come to see that genius is involved in setting aside on the maps of our lives places reserved only for the restoration of spiritual passion. We do not appreciate how much we lose by trying to renew our passion in spaces used for other things. Whenever possible, sanctuaries should not be treated as public auditoriums. And chapels should be set aside for more than occasional weddings.

Some years ago I spent a couple of weeks among a group of South American Indians to whom the gospel of Christ was a relatively new experience. At first they had chosen to worship in their community hut, the place where all the business and the conversations of the tribe took place.

But one day the missionaries were surprised by the visit of the tribal chief, who was also the pastor. "We are not pleased with worshiping God in the community hut. We think that God should be met in a special hut built only for that purpose."

I think the Indians knew something that many modern American Christians do not understand. In their desperate desire to get the church into the marketplace, some have thought it wise to combine the safe place of corporate worship with utilitarian areas for secular activities. When necessary, this is acceptable. But it is not ideal. It is highly beneficial, although not essential, to have quiet places where the secrets of the Father are shared.

Basil Pennington wrote:

> We in the West are not so sensitively aware of vibrations. Yet they inevitably take their toll on us. A room that has been very full of busy activity or loud, hard music carries its charge long after. It is well to be aware of this when we have a choice of places to meditate (Pennington, *Centering Prayer*, p. 67).

We should urge upon our churches, when necessary, a greater respect for the sanctuary as a safe place so that followers of the Lord are free to come to kneel and bow down when there is a need for the protective wing or the strong hand.

When the congregation I once served as a pastor built a new sanctuary, many of us found ourselves disliking it after our initial experience of worship in it. Why? The acoustics were different; people sat in different places during worship; a strangeness seemed to pervade the atmosphere. The feelings of God's presence were not so strong as they had been in the former place. As a worship leader, I found myself with a sense of emptiness after each Sunday morning.

We wondered what had happened. Had we made a colossal mistake? Then we realized that a sanctuary, a safe place, is only part architecture and structure; the rest comprises memories and experiences with God. Our new safe place needed some time in which to store the memories of the special times when God had met us.

My wife, Gail, uses an old black frying pan when she wants to make the best pancakes. "The secret of this pan," she told me, "is in the buildup of grease from all the times I've used it." The buildup she called it.

Special safe places get better and better because of the buildup. Our new sanctuary needed a buildup of memories: memories of God's comfort when we were grieving, of God's blessing when someone got married, of God's majesty when we had profound experiences of worship, of God's redeeming mercy when various individuals found Christ in conversion, of God's forgiveness when people shook off spiritual coldness and recommitted themselves to following Christ. Then a new auditorium became a sanctuary, a safe place to which we all love to come.

Not only can we create safe places in our homes and in our sanctuaries, but we can occasionally go to other places where spiritual discipline and activity are encouraged.

The retreat movement across the country is advancing with exciting speed because busy people are discovering safe places away from the relentless noises and intrusions of modern society.

Our Roman Catholic friends have known this for centuries. And the good news is that many Protestant churches and organizations are realizing the value of maintaining places where hurting, confused, or spiritually-disoriented men and women can go to find peace and renewal for a short time. But the remedial purposes are not the only ones. Many of us should consider retreats to *avoid* confusion and exhaustion.

Throughout the day, one should not be reluctant to create momentary safe places: at the desk, in the car, on public transportation, in a waiting room. They are not the best of places, but they can work.

These moments of sanctuary become mini-versions of what Abraham did in the countryside when he stopped his traveling and built an altar to his God. "This is a safe place," he declared by constructing the altar. And there God came and spoke to him. So we too build altars in our hearts just as David built in his a sanctuary on the desert.

The first recorded martyr of the Christian church was Stephen. Because he spoke boldly before his fellow Jews, he was dragged beyond the city walls to a place of execution. The rocks began to fall upon his body, and soon he was dying. It is important to note what Stephen did as he lay there feeling the terrible blows of the stones crashing upon him. He created a safe place, and he cried out, "Lord Jesus, receive my spirit." And kneeling down, he cried out, "Lord do not hold this sin against them" (Acts 7:59,60 RSV).

Luke, the writer, continued, "And when he had said this, he fell asleep" (Acts 7:60 RSV). Stephen's declared safe place became a resting place. A map of his life journey will show that ugly spot as a place of violence for his persecutors. But the map will also show it as a safe place for Stephen. If there is such a map of my life, where might it show the safe places I have established? That is a piercing question.

14

The Still Times

The asphalt road on which we drive the last few miles to Peace Ledge, our New Hampshire retreat, is beautiful in the fall. In the early spring, however, the road looks like a disaster area. FROST HEAVES, a sign explains to drivers in late March as the ground begins to thaw on warm days.

Each day the road seems to buckle more and more until it has the properties of an old washboard. Here and there potholes open up where water has seeped in and frozen in the night air. The car tires beat the road surface into chunks, and before long the entire length of Shaker Road is a mess.

It occurred to me one day that while Shaker Road was like that in the early spring, the connecting State Route 106 wasn't. In fact it was as smooth as glass, a pleasure to drive, spring or fall. What made the difference between the two?

The road repair gang gave me the simple explanation one day. When Route 106 had been constructed, the work crew had carefully laid a thick bed of gravel beneath the roadbed that provided the necessary drainage. The roadbed was deep enough that it was untouched by the cold going into the ground or the frost coming out of it.

Not so with the Shaker Road, the men told me. There, the ground had simply been graded and a thick patch of asphalt laid over it. "A quick and dirty job," someone said.

With an inadequate bed, the road was torn up every spring by the moisture underneath that worked into every crack and made the subsurface unreliable. The auto and truck tires did the rest.

How important it is, I thought as I compared the two kinds of roads, to make sure that my public life does not have the marks of a Shaker-Road construction. If I do not give attention to the subsurface, the cracks and strains will quickly show the minute the surface changes or stresses occur.

How important it is for me to give careful attention to the subsurface, my inner spirit, making sure it is strong enough and properly maintained so that it can support the stress of the real world.

That's when I began to think about the *rest* component in my life. For in proper rest I am tending to the subsurface upon which the road of daily living is laid. I say *proper rest* because much of what we call rest today is merely amusement or leisure, a temporary patch over weariness. It has about the same value as the quick hot patches the road crew puts over holes and ridges on Shaker Road. Their job makes for smooth driving for about three days, and then it's back to the washboard again.

The only answer to a "washboardy" road is to tear it up and treat the roadbed to a deep thickness of drainage material. The only answer to an exhausted, passionless life is to check the condition of the subsurface, the inner spirit. That's where Sabbath, the *still time*, comes in.

When I wrote of Sabbath in the book *Ordering Your Private World*, I was impressed with the number of people who sent letters to me, responding with curiosity and fascination on that subject. Often they spoke of their frustration with an enlarging schedule, of events and commitments seemingly out of control, of calendars jammed with good things to do. Did I really believe, many asked, that the Sabbath principle was the answer to the problem or the prevention of exhaustion? Yes, I answered, in many cases; perhaps it is not the entire answer, but it is a major step in the right direction.

As I write this chapter, I am in Brazil where I have been giving a series of talks to missionaries. On this very day, one of the men stopped to talk with me about his fellow workers. "They have so much to do," he said, "and they are absolutely spent. I see them going about from one task to another almost as if they are in a daze. There is a joylessness in what they are doing. I fear that many of them are on the edge of a dreadful burnout."

I asked him when he and his colleagues stopped their work. "They never do, really, " he replied. "We seem to goad each other on actually. You see, it wouldn't be good to be playing or relaxing when another missionary stopped by on business and found us doing something that wasn't serious. I'm afraid we have a way of making one another feel quite small when we catch each other napping. We don't have to say anything; the other knows he's been caught. So if we stop working, we do it on the sly; we don't let anyone know about it. Which means we are ashamed of rest."

Is rest not considered a "serious" thing? I wondered aloud. Do we think of time away from work as a waste, as a second-class hour? That certainly doesn't reflect a biblical view of things.

Sabbath is God's antidote to workaholism. It is the check-mate to men and women who have fallen into the trap of believing that their personal worth is built upon what they do rather than what they are. I like the word *Sabbath*; it falls into the same family of words from which we get *rest* and *peace*. In the larger sense it has the notion of things being in proper order, like the balls racked inside the form on the pool table.

I like to refer to Sabbath as the still time, the special moment in my calendar. If the map of my life should be marked with frequent safe places, the calendar of my life should show sabbaths or still times. These are the moments (or hours) when we say to the noise and turmoil of the schedule just what Jesus said to a storm that seemed to be threatening the life of His disciples: "Peace! Be still!" (Mark 4:39 RSV). Instantly, a raging lake became a safe place in a still time.

SEVEN PRINCIPLES OF STILL TIMES THAT RENEW SPIRITUAL PASSION

Just as I must regularly assume control over places and say, "This is a safe place," so must I wrest away control of my time and say, "This is a still time. Accordingly, I press peace and rest into the calendar."

THE ROLE-MODEL PRINCIPLE

God has taught us the special principle of *still time* in a number of ways. He taught it by modeling it in His own self-revelation.

There is a still time inferred at the conclusion of each of the days of creation. "And God said . . . " refers to the work God gave Himself to do. "And God saw . . . " refers to the still moments at the end of the work in which God stamped value and closure on what he had done. "And God saw that it was good" (Gen. 1:18 RSV).

It would appear that God our Creator never engaged in a succeeding phase of work before He had brought to conclusion the previous phase by a "Sabbathing" moment, a still time in which value was assigned to the creative labor.

Then when the entire week of creation labor was complete, there was a major still time as the entire project was studied and valued.

"A work unexamined by a superior is valueless," a close and admired friend told me as he talked about the practice of responsible management. Who could examine God's work except God? The fact that the Bible records that He appraised His own work and placed value upon it is very significant. Why mention the matter at all? Because it is to be a precedent and an example for us.

THE RHYTHM PRINCIPLE

The writer of Genesis said:

> By the seventh day God had finished the work he had been doing; so on the seventh day he rested from all his work. And God blessed the seventh day and made it holy, because on it he rested from all the work of creating that he had done" (Gen. 2:2,3 NIV).

This remarkable rhythm in the work of God ought not to be taken lightly. Combined with the rhythms of rest we see in almost all of nature, it provides us with a stunning lesson on the importance of true rest—not merely the rest of the body but also the rest of the spirit. The heart, probably the strongest and most resilient of our muscles, is designed to be still between every beat. Most growing things observe a period of dormancy every year. Every cycle is completed by a period of stillness.

It is said of one of the famous composers that he had a rebellious son who used to come in late at night after his father and mother had gone to bed. And before going to his own room, he would go to his father's piano and slowly, as well as loudly, play a simple scale, all but the final note. Then leaving the scale uncompleted, he would retire to his room. Meanwhile the father, hearing the scale minus the final note, would writhe on his bed, his mind unable to relax because the scale was unresolved. Finally, in consternation, he would stumble down the stairs and hit the previously unstruck note. Only then would his mind surrender to sleep once again.

God's labor seems never to be complete until, like the final note on the scale, the concluding still time, a pause that looks backward and pronounces completion and value.

After the creation account of God's own still times, we do not come again to the Sabbath principle until Exodus 16 when the chosen people were well on their way from Egypt toward Mount Sinai. Food had become an issue: how would they eat? where was the sustenance going to come from?

God will provide, Moses informed the people. Every morning you will go out of your tents, and you will find manna, a strange kind of nourishment, on the ground. You can gather just enough for you and your family. Save more than that, and it will spoil on you.

In such a way the God of Israel was teaching his people about a new and healthier concept of work. It is important to remember that they had been slaves for almost four hundred years, their labor always at the behest of someone who owned them and ordered them into action. It is probable that they had had no control over their own time and that they had no conception of how to order their own days now that the yoke of slavery had been overthrown.

God's gifts of food were not to be hoarded and turned into wealth for those who could gather faster than others. And it was no time for one family to go into business gathering for another family, thus perpetuating the slavery all over again. But, the rules pointed toward a time of rest also.

Each morning everyone gathered as much as he needed, and when the sun grew hot, it melted away. On the sixth day, they gathered twice as much—two omers for each person—and the leaders of the community came and reported this to Moses. He said to them, "This is what the LORD commanded: 'Tomorrow is to be a day of rest, a holy Sabbath to the LORD. So bake what you want to bake and boil what you want to boil. Save whatever is left and keep it until morning'" (Exod. 16:21-23 NIV).

Some people learned a few things the hard way. Those who had originally disobeyed Moses and gathered more than they needed during the weekdays had been surprised by maggots in their hoarded food the next morning. But this was not so for food gathered before the Sabbath.

THE REST PRINCIPLE

Now perhaps there was another lesson to learn the hard way. Those who may not have seen the importance of gathering a twofold portion on the day before Sabbath learned on Sabbath morning that they were going to be hungry for a while. Nothing was going to materialize. Previously, they'd not eaten because of spoiled food. Now they could not eat because of their failure to collect food when it was available and because God insisted that work stop on the Sabbath.

In such elementary, but nevertheless effective, ways did the God of Moses teach the people that he meant business about a time of rest. If it seems that He was going about things in an extreme way, it is important to remember that this Sabbath concept was being taught to virtual children, who had not known the meaning of rest or personal discipline for centuries. You have to start somewhere, and this is how God did it. An object lesson whose consequences and rewards were extremely practical.

Thus it would not be a surprise when later Moses would appear before the same people with Ten Commandments, the irreducible minimums of behavior that would become the core principles of their life together before Him. Think of it! *Just ten!* And among the ten was a commandment speaking to the issue of the still time.

Remember the Sabbath day by keeping it holy. Six days you shall labor and do all your work, but the seventh day is a Sabbath to the LORD your God. On it you shall not do any work, neither you, nor your son or daughter, nor your manservant or maidservant, nor your animals, nor the alien within your gates. For in six days the LORD made the heavens and the earth, the sea, and all that is in them, but he rested on the seventh day. Therefore the LORD blessed the Sabbath day and made it holy (Exod. 20:8-11 NIV).

This would be the first of a number of fences God would build into the kingdom lifestyle of the chosen people. The fences, or disciplines, were important, first of all, because they provided marks of distinctiveness for those living in agreement with God's Lordship. In the case of the Sabbath day, a uniqueness of life was being demonstrated, a way to divide time.

I am convinced additionally that the Sabbath was a necessary discipline protecting against what we would later call workaholism, the tendency to use time flagrantly in the building of one's fortune at the expense of a more balanced and spiritually oriented life. This would not be the only place such a discipline would check the tendency toward excessive living.

If the Sabbath was a hedge against workaholism, forcing an interruption to the workweek, the tithe (the giving of the first and the best of a person's productivity) would be a bar against materialism. It is virtually impossible for a person to become an obsessive hoarder of material things when the tithe is built in as a discipline. In those areas most likely to dominate a life to excess—workaholism and materialism—working principles prevent people from destroying themselves by imbalanced living.

The Sabbath, the still time, began as a law. It is my conviction that it would later become a principle of time budgeting. By principle rather than by law, I am suggesting that the Sabbath, become less a legal requirement—one day per week—and more a principle of rest that should be observed by the mature person on many, many occasions, perhaps even several times per day.

My friends in Orthodox Judaism and those whom I know in the Seventh Day Adventist tradition strongly reject this idea, believing the Sabbath can never be seen in any light other than that of a law about a specific span of time, and they have my admiration and respect.

But I am convinced that what begins as law in the life of a child (the first-generation Hebrews) becomes principle in the life of an adult (we who are the inheritors of centuries of teaching and experience). The principle of Sabbath should be an even more healthy perspective than the law of Sabbath if we understand its purpose and commit to observing it with frequency.

THE REMEMBRANCE PRINCIPLE

What were the components of the legal Sabbath that God taught to Israel? First, *remember!* In the Hebrew world it was a dynamic action when one remembered. The effort was that of attempting to fully experience a previous event as if it were happening all over again.

In this case the event is specifically the seventh day of creation when God rested. Thus to remember is to rest from labor as God rested. It is to look back over the work and appraise it as God appraised His work.

To keep the day holy meant that it should be set apart and treated unlike any other parcel of time during the week. This still time was to be absolutely unique from any other time: a different set of activities, a different kind of thinking.

THE RENUNCIATION PRINCIPLE

When Moses first set forth the Sabbath concept as part of the law, an important component of what he was saying had to do with the concept of renunciation, the renunciation of work—not because work is a bad thing, but because if it is not contained, it gets out of control and captures the affections of the worker, causing work to lose its meaning and leaving no time for worship or rest. Moses was telling the people that a good thing must be renounced because a better thing must take precedence for a short while.

The law also indicates how strongly this renunciation was meant to be. The *entire household* had to renounce work. Little would have been accomplished if the house-holder had merely remanded the regular workload to his servants and hirelings. Then he could have enjoyed the fruits of the work without any exertion himself. No! The entire community had to stop and enter into still time.

THE REFRESHMENT PRINCIPLE

In later amplifications on the Sabbath matter, Moses is even more explicit. In Exodus 31, for example, he told the people that the day was not only holy to God but holy *for* them. I hear him telling the people that everyone profits from this sort of rest-rhythm. And for what purposes?

First, it was a sign of the special relationship between the nation and the Lord. But, second, it brings a kind of refreshment. "And God rested and refreshed himself" is the literal wording of verse 17.

How can God be in need of refreshment since he never exhausts Himself? That is hard to answer except to say that if God reveals Himself and refreshes Himself, it is in part because He wants to point out to us the importance of our refreshing ourselves.

And that fact simply isn't going over too well with many Christian people today—either because they struggle to know what genuine rest is or because they have filled their lives with so many things to do that Sabbath rest has been squeezed out and put in the discretionary column. Such action means, of course, that Sabbath rest will rarely be seen, if at all.

The first of the struggles, a knowledge of real rest, is a great one, because leisure and amusement have so completely covered up our concept of genuine rest. Although a certain release and relaxation accompany most forms of leisure and amusement, I think it is safe to say that the real deep-seated exhaustion, that of the spirit, is hardly touched at all.

Modern play is good, of course, for building relationships, for exercising the body, and for stimulating the mind. But this play may not reach down to the lowest layers of our real weariness, where the inner spirit takes the battering of spiritual warfare.

The awareness that we need to give attention to the resting of our spirits is almost nonexistent. What the early saints knew so well about taking time each day in the Sabbath tradition for the recollecting of the spirit has been reduced in modern times to something called the "quiet time," neglected by most and overorganized by many others—neglected because quiet time usually brings so little sense of value; overorganized because it falls victim to those who typically think that everything is best reduced to a method even if it does destroy spontaneity or, ironically, the ability of the Spirit of God to speak to us.

Need I say more about the second struggle, that of simply

crowding Sabbath out of the calendar altogether? As I have often observed, being too busy has been so very easy for many of us, including myself. I am an action person. I prefer motion to stillness, noise to silence, and initiation to passivity. Thus, when instant choices have to be made about what is the best use of any period of time, those of us engaged in busyness are most likely to decide on apparent productive activity rather than on quiet and reflective activity. That kind of thinking is the culture's "gift" to us.

My friend Margaret Jensen in her lovely book about a friend, Lena, tells of a moment when the two spoke of the meaning of rest and our struggle to accept it as part of life. Lena said,

> God rested on the seventh day. He just finished creating everything. If that had been you and me, most likely we would have organized all we did those six days. Sometimes God says, "Sit down, child. Take the weight off your feet and start believing in your heart" (Jensen, *Lena*, p. 64).

I am convinced that every one of us who has chosen to follow after Christ must take this still-time discipline seriously. Not to do it is to violate a principle of life taught to the people of Israel. And not to do it is to strangle our inner spirit to the point of inaction—weariness of the worst kind.

THE RECURRENCE PRINCIPLE

I am also convinced that Sabbath, the recollection of the spirit, is more than just a day in our time. It is a recurring event throughout each of our days. Just as a safe place can be more than a sanctuary, a Sabbath can be more than a day each week. Sabbaths can be short bursts of spiritual recollecting, reminding me of the quick pitstops of the Indianapolis racer when there is a need for fuel, tires, and refreshment. (But of course, I would hope that our Sabbath pauses are not as frantic as the Indianapolis pitstops.)

François Fénelon wrote to a friend in need of spiritual instruction:

> You must learn ... to make good use of chance moments, when waiting for someone, when going from place to place, or when in society where to be a good listener is all that is required; ... at such times it is easy to lift the heart to God, and thereby gain fresh strength for further duties. The less time one has the more

carefully it should be managed. If you wait for free, convenient seasons in which to fulfill real duties, you run the risk of waiting forever; especially in such a life as yours. No, make use of chance moments (Fénelon, *Spiritual Letters to Women*, p. 16).

Busy people like young mothers will be comforted by Fénelon's words because his "short snatches" are all they have for several years when their children are small and weariness from sleepless nights are a regularity. The key, of course, is to snatch something.

Ruth Graham has shared many times that she used to leave books open all over the house so that when a chance offered itself for her to get a moment or two of reading and meditation, she could reach for the nearest ready volume. To "create the Sabbathing moment," even if it is a terribly brief one, is an all-important pursuit whether we're talking about mothers or businesspeople or students. One thought in such a pause can be the big difference in how the next hours are going to be lived, whether they will be in spiritual passion or in drudgery.

God is not desirous of making us feel guilty when extended periods of silence and worship are impossible. He would prefer, I believe, that we be prodded toward Sabbaths by a spiritual homesickness for His renewal presence. There's a great difference between the two motivating forces. If we discover the habit of snatching Sabbath moments, we will be pressing God's presence into the day, something like holes in a piece of Swiss cheese.

So it is that the frost heaves of personal life are confronted and smoothed out. By laying an adequate roadbed in the inner spirit, we can prevent the hostile elements that cause fatigue. And that happens only when Sabbaths find their way into the calendars of our lives: monthly, weekly, daily, hourly.

15

Special Friends

In Joseph Heller's novel *Something Happened*, the fictional narrator, Bob Slocum, describes the nature of human relationships among the people in the company for which he has worked for almost twenty years. It is a bleak description of tired and directionless men and women. The overarching theme lacing those relationships together, Slocum indicates, is fear. Of his peers and subordinates, he says:

> In my department, there are six people who are afraid of me, and one small secretary who is afraid of all of us. I have one other person working for me who is not afraid of anyone, not even me. . . .

> The thought occurs to me often that there must be mail clerks, office boys and girls, stock boys, messengers, and assistants of all kinds and ages who are afraid of everyone in the company (Heller, *Something Happened*, p. 12).

Bob Slocum is even more descriptive of his relationship to his boss, Jack Green.

> Often, I protect and defend [Jack Green] when he is late or forgetful with work of his own, and I frequently give him credit for good work from my department that he does not deserve. But I never tell him I do this; and I never let him know when I hear anything favorable about him. I enjoy seeing Green apprehensive. I'm pleased he distrusts me (it does wonders for my self-esteem), and I do no more than necessary to reassure him.

> And I am the best friend he has here (p. 27).

Slocum describes an exhausting work environment. This is a place where people are drained of productive and creative energy because they spend so much time wondering whether a "teammate" is really a competitor. People get weary in a place like that.

I strongly suspect that many people we know work in similar situations. Perhaps even more people might admit, if asked, that their family lives are marked with this unfortunate kind of interpersonal play. Would yet another group suggest that their church experiences are characterized by similar dynamics?

When you see a cluster of people who drain each other in this fashion, mentally picture a stretched tandem bicycle where three people are supposed to be peddling. Most of us have seen the humorous vignette, usually in cartoon form, in which only the first person peddles strenuously while the second and third become passengers who sit back and enjoy the view. The first never looks around to see what the other two are doing. He assumes that they are working as hard as he is. But they're not, and one is left to do the work of three, spending most of his energy just to keep the bicycle upright and in motion rather than going somewhere. Therefore, weariness sets in, a slow and certain loss of desire to keep on going.

The opposite picture of Joseph Heller's fear-filled office staff is that of Moses on a hilltop in the book of Exodus. He and his people had encountered the hostile Amalek who would not permit them to pass through the land on their way to Mount Sinai. It was the first serious crisis in the life of the chosen people since they had crossed the Red Sea.

Moses won because he operated from relational strength as he faced the battle. His battle plan depended upon relationships, the kind I'll eventually call special friends.

"Choose for us men, and go out and fight with Amalek," he said to Joshua. "Tomorrow I will stand on the top of the hill with the rod of God in my hand" (Exod. 17:9 RSV). So Joshua went with the army of Israel to the valley to face Amalek, and Moses went with his aides, Aaron and Hur, to the mountaintop to hold the rod, symbolizing God's power and authority.

It was an interesting day of ups and downs as one army and then the other prevailed in battle. The Scripture says that whenever Moses held his hands with the rod upward, the armies of Israel began to advance against Amalek. But when he dropped his arms, the battle turned against the Israelites.

"But Moses' hands grew weary," the writer noted. And that was the cue for his aides to move into action. Finding a stone for Moses to sit on, Aaron and Hur stood on each side and held up his arms "so that his hands were steady until the going down of the sun" (v. 12).

Down in the valley, "Joshua mowed down Amalek and his people" (v. 13). Strange circumstances; uncommon strategies. But the underlying message is timeless. A man was surrounded with what I want to call *special friends*, and together *they accomplished what no one of them could have done alone.*

If each of us has a map in our lives showing our safe places and a calendar showing our still times, then we also should have an address book that lists our special friends. Who are they?

Special friends. Moses' address book would have included *Joshua*, the man in the valley coordinating the effort as well as *Aaron* and *Hur*, the men on each side holding Moses' arms heavenward "so that his hands were steady." What weariness would have made impossible if Moses had insisted on performing alone, the help of special friends made triumphant. Clearly a team.

Special friends are part of the economy of spiritual passion, and in most cases an indispensable part. Unlike the very draining and the very nice people of our worlds, special friends are committed to helping one another discover and maintain spiritual passion. Each member of a team of special friends rejoices when another succeeds. Each weeps when another falls. Special friends do not envy when someone wins; nor do they gloat at failure.

In recent years there has been a welcomed revolution in our understanding of Christian relationships. We have a superabundance of books on marriage, family, and the healing of the hurting. And this revolution has affected our consciousness in building strong personal relationships. Perhaps not enough has been written, however, from a proactive perspective on relationships—that is, from a continuing value placed on the team and teamwork. I'm speaking of the way we enter into fellowship with one another in order to enhance and protect each other's potential or vulnerabilities.

A recent novel and movie featured a young U.S. Air Force fighter pilot who struggles against the concept of teamwork. As the story develops, it becomes clear that the pilot's peers in the fighter squadron easily agree that he is the best pilot in the Air Force . . . but, they always add, also the most dangerous. He regularly breaks the basic rules of flying protocol; he flies his planes to the outermost limits of stress; and he ruthlessly competes to win every inter-squadron flying contest.

In spite of the fact that he is the best, no one wants him around. Why? Because others have learned that he cares for no one but himself. He is incapable of being part of a team of special friends.

The story line highlights the struggle of an individualist who will ultimately accomplish nothing if he cannot become a team player. Refusing to obey orders, he abandons a fellow flyer in the midst of a simulated aerial battle and the other pilot is shot down. Unwilling to accept the stress limits of his plane, he crashes himself and his navigator dies in the accident. Only then does the horror of the consequences of his lone-ranger performance begin to settle deep within. By the conclusion of the story, the young man has begun to understand the meaning of special friends who lift one another to even greater personal achievement.

May I emphasize that I am saying special *friends* and not *acquaintances*. For it is the latter that most of us have; not the former. Our busy lives and calendars make little room for special friends. In order to have them, one must invest prime time to cultivate and maintain them, time that might have to be taken from other good goals and objectives.

Most of us would be tempted to think that cultivating special friends is something done over and above our work. I have come to believe that developing special friends is *part* of our work.

The apostle Paul was clearly a man committed to raising up a band of special friends. He knew who they were, and he regularly recognized them for their contribution to his spiritual passion. His friends were a resource upon which he obviously depended and without which he would not have survived.

His address book of special friends would have included Acquilla and Priscilla with whom he occasionally worked and lived (see Acts 18:3), Onesiphorus ("for he oft refreshed me" 2 Tim. 1:16 KJV), Philemon ("I have derived much joy and comfort from your love" Philem. 1:7 RSV), Luke, and a host of others. Paul's friends came in all ages and backgrounds, and he seems to have taken great care to cultivate them.

God "comforted us," he wrote when describing his own numbing weariness, "by the coming of Titus" (2 Cor. 7:6 RSV). On the terribly tiring trip to Rome, there was a moment when the brethren from the church heard that Paul was not far from his destination.

> And the brethren there, when they heard of us, came as far as the Forum of Appius and Three Taverns to meet us. *On seeing them Paul thanked God and took courage.* (Acts 28:15 RSV, emphasis added).

We are reading about a cadre of special friends in motion, and when they came, they brought the possibility of the restoration of Paul's spiritual passion, much of which had probably been drained away in the exhaustion of travel. Quite different, wouldn't you say, from the office climate of Joseph Heller's novel?

Who are the special friends, the teammates in our address books? Our special friends are the men and women for whom the subject of spiritual passion is an important item. I have pondered this question recently with great seriousness. And perhaps the question is an important one which men (*particularly* men) ask in their midlife years.

Recently I had the opportunity to sit for several hours with a group of brilliant and very successful engineers and executives and to talk with them about spiritual and personal disciplines. At no time during the day did the group show greater interest in what I had come to say than when we began to talk about special friends.

"It is not uncommon for middle-life men to discover that they are very lonely," I had said. "If you ask them who their close friends are, most will say, 'I don't think I have any close friends.'"

The group wanted to talk about why that was true for so many of them. Why had they lost the ability to make such friendships? And why did most of them look back at their college days as the last time when there had been that sort of intimacy?

The probable answer? I proposed to them that middle-life men have probably spent so much of their energies establishing themselves as functional successes in their careers that they had not taken the time to think about relational success. Then at the "noon of life," as Carl Jung once called it, they realize they have not attained adequate intimacy with their spouses and children, who are now probably passing into adolescence. What's more, they have lost contact with almost all intimate friends from school days, leaving only their working associates.

As I talked of these things, it became clear that this matter of special friends was a serious issue with these men, and we spent a significant amount of time talking about how to regain the momentum of special-friend building.

What are the component parts of the special friend resource? I am thinking of the kind of teammates we need. Some of us are just old enough to remember the old corner-lot baseball games. Garbage can lids served as bases; lines hastily toed into the ground served as foul-ball indicators. And the teams were divvied up by two captains who threw a bat back and forth to determine who got first choice. The alternative choices of the captains were determined by who could play what position. The important thing, if you were captain, was knowing what kind of teammates you needed to complement your own strengths.

SIX SPECIAL-FRIEND TEAMMATES THAT HELP YOU MAINTAIN SPIRITUAL PASSION

Let's think through the sort of team capable of providing spiritual passion for each of its players. What kind of players and positions are necessary to the objective? There are several positions, if you please, and I doubt that any one person could ever fulfill (or should fulfill) all of these parts. But what is important is that the man or woman wanting to maintain and develop spiritual passion should take an inventory of personal relationships to see if these special-friend teammates are there. For if they are not, we may find ourselves the front rider on the tandem bike, pedaling more weight than our own and wondering why we are not making more headway. Let me list a few special-friend teammates.

1. THE SPONSOR

Students of the life of President Dwight David Eisenhower generally agree that his military career in the U.S. Army was colorless and devoid of recognition until he was transferred to the Panama Canal Zone, where he served for several years under the command of General Fox Connor. A special relationship between the two developed, and Connor became Eisenhower's *sponsor*. The result? Eisenhower suddenly began to show the leadership and organizational qualities that ultimately brought him to the notice of General George Marshall, who appointed him to lead the armies that invaded Europe in World War II. Looking back on that special-friend relationship with Fox Connor, Eisenhower later wrote:

> Life with General Connor was a sort of graduate school in military affairs and the humanities, leavened by a man who was experienced in his knowledge of men and their conduct. I can never adequately express my gratitude to this one gentleman. . . . In a lifetime of association with great and good men, he is the one more or less invisible figure to whom I owe an incalculable debt (Eisenhower, *At Ease*, p. 136)

Those comments suggest why I'd call Fox Connor a sponsor. The sponsor, of course, is another name for mentor or discipler. We have already looked at the role of the sponsor in another context when we thought about VRP's, the very resourceful people who pour energy or passion into us rather than drain it away.

But let's take a second look at this role now in the context of the special-friend team. The sponsor is that Very Resourceful Person (the VRP) who ushers us into opportunity and possibility. He or she is usually close by and can be drawn upon when courage, guidance, or assurance is needed that a path chosen is the right one.

Few examples of the sponsor relationship are better than the one between Mordecai and Esther in the Older Testament. The Jews in Babylon had been threatened by a holocaust through the manipulations of Haman, a close counselor to the king. For a while it appeared as if nothing could be done to set aside the edict the king had signed, apparently in ignorance of its implications (see Esther 3:7–12).

Parallel to these events, the king had brought into his palace a new wife, Esther, chosen as far as we can tell for her remarkable beauty. As was the custom in those days, Esther could come into the presence of the king only when she was invited (see Esther 4:11). To do otherwise was to call down upon herself the sentence of death.

It was Mordecai who was Esther's sponsor. A close relative, he had raised her from childhood. And in the midst of the crisis he sent a message asking if she would approach the king and appeal the matter of Haman's edict and the Jewish predicament. Her first response to her sponsor was negative because of the rules. And Mordecai responded:

> "Think not that in the king's palace you will escape any more than all the other Jews. For if you keep silence at such a time as this, relief and deliverance will rise for the Jews from another quarter, but you and your father's house will perish. And who knows whether you have not come to the kingdom for such a time as this?" (Esther 4:13-14).

With this sort of urging, Esther changed her mind and sprang into action, and it eventuated in the saving of the entire Jewish population in the empire.

But how had it happened? Was it Esther's own passion that did the job? Not by any stretch of the imagination. Alone she would have been paralyzed in inaction. No, the passion came through performance of a sponsor. You could say that Esther had a special friend, one who urged her on, convinced her that this was her responsibility, her opportunity. He literally seems to have pressed courage into her, and he did it merely through a written message.

Such was the extent of Mordecai's influence on the young woman that that was all it took, and she headed for the king's quarters (see Esther 5:1).

What had Mordecai done? He had communicated from a larger perspective outside the palace and interpreted it to Esther: the issue, the danger, the possibility, the heavenly viewpoint. Esther's situation had limited her to seeing only the restrictive customs and the personal dangers. Alone, she didn't have the slightest idea what to do. But Mordecai appreciated the potential of her position, and he called her attention to it. His was the role of the cheerleader: "You can do it!" And she did.

That is the classic role of sponsors or mentors. When they do their job, there is a whole new dimension of reality for the one who is being sponsored. Sponsors help generate spiritual passion and vision. They often convey the sense of possibility. God uses sponsors to move the Esthers into action.

My own feeling is that all of us need sponsors until we are well into midlife. Then perhaps we outgrow the need. We may not draw upon them with great frequency, but it is good to know they are there and we can draw from them in a healthy sense whenever there is a need for an Esther-like decision.

Whenever I have the chance to sit and talk with young men and women about sponsors or mentors I am inevitably asked the same question: "Where can I find a sponsor like the one you describe?" The simple answer I usually give is, "Go out and find one whose lifestyle and performance seem to fulfill what you dream of becoming."

"I have," often comes back the answer. "But when I locate someone like that, I usually find out the person is too busy."

Too busy! I suspect they're right. Contemporary life is so clogged with things to do that the sponsorship relationship is being sacrificed all too often, both by the would-be sponsor and the "sponsoree." Sponsorship takes time, more time than most people involved in programs and highflying activities have to give. The result? The Christian community will probably lose a significant number of potential leaders who needed the kind of strength a special friend, like a sponsor, might have given.

The sponsor is not necessarily a friend. He or she enters our lives for a specific purpose and for a given period of time. There is usually an objective to the relationship: to develop a younger or more inexperienced person into something. Then, even as Christ said to his disciples at the end of almost three years, "It is to your advantage that I go away: (John 16:7 RSV).

"My sponsors tend to be dead people," I've often heard my wife, Gail, say. "I found them in the great biographies where I was able to discover the hidden secrets of great men and women of God. It's not quite the same, but it helped a lot when there were no older, more experienced people who were willing to provide me with the time I needed to grow."

Very few things would be more effective in the raising up of a powerful and passionate people to expand Christ's kingdom than the choice by mature Christians to become special-friend sponsors to younger Christians in need of models and cheerleaders.

A severe price the church is paying today is the choice of older women to return to work in the marketplace after childraising for no reason other than to make more money or to find an extra dosage of "meaning and identity in life."

Granted, some must do this for economic reasons—college tuition is a common reason—but one notes with concern those who have not seen the biblical injunction for the older to disciple or sponsor the younger. Is there a greater contribution to society than the gift of one's self to a younger generation? Young people cry out for sponsors, especially if they come from homes broken with relational sickness.

In my list of special-friend teammates, I would next call attention to the position of the affirmer.

2. THE AFFIRMER

The *affirmer* has to be the second person in our address book of special friends. He or she is the one who moves alongside and inspirits us as we act out our destiny. The affirmer takes up where the sponsor leaves off. The affirmer takes note of what we are doing and what we are becoming and attaches value to it.

Nowhere is the role of the affirmer more beautifully illustrated than in the moments following the baptism of Jesus. The baptism was for sinners, for those in need of public repentance. Because he was sinless Jesus had no need of such baptism, but He chose to do it anyway, both as an example and as an identification with the people for whom He would later die.

Is there any temptation on His part as He leaves the waters to wonder what the heavenly Father thinks of what He has just done? Is there any sensation pointing up the coming agony of the cross that could cause undue fear? Could He be tempted to feel that He has diminished Himself by identifying with the sins of the human race?

If there were temptations to self-doubt, they had to have

been quickly dispelled by the affirmation of the Father who from Heaven said, "Thou art my beloved Son; with thee I am well pleased" (Mark 1:11 RSV). In one simple statement the solidarity of the Father/Son relationship was affirmed, the act which Jesus had gone through was positively acknowledged, and the correctness of His motivation was underscored. His spiritual passion was renewed, if indeed it had at all been diminished.

We must not mistake affirmation for the empty compliments and plaudits that are carelessly tossed about in human relationships. Affirmation is the genuine act of mutual discovery and evaluation. Affirmation is not impulsive, and it is not given with the motive of obtaining a reciprocal favor. Affirmation is one person's assistance to another so that he or she can see the life of God in action and in being.

I have worked in ministry with a number of people who were the product of a tradition that mindlessly ignored affirmation because it robbed glory from God. If that were the case, Paul robbed God of glory when he affirmed the Thessalonian congregation for becoming an example "to all the believers in Macedonia" (1 Thess. 1:7), when he affirmed Philemon for the love he had "toward all the saints" (Philem. 1:5), and when he affirmed Epaphroditus for the faithfulness of his service to Paul at the risk of his own life.

When affirmation is denied—especially among the younger of us—it leaves people struggling, wondering if their contribution is substantial, whether or not it makes a difference. Thus the resulting loss of nerve, of spiritual passion.

Like others, I have experienced both the work of the affirmer and the *de-firmer*. (I have just coined a word.)

The de-firmer works from insensitivity, ignorance, indifference, or (worse yet) plain, pure malice. The de-firmer picks the time when you have finished something that has cost you spiritual, emotional, and physical energy and then questions your motives, the quality of your work, or the results you set out to achieve. Instantly, you are hurt, tempted to quit, angry and wanting to fight back. In expending your passion, you become vulnerable to even the slightest attack (remember Elijah!), and the de-firmer senses that and uses the leverage of the moment to put you down.

We not only have to be able to spot the de-firmer coming at us, but we need to ask ourselves if we too have been guilty of de-firmation on occasions. It is easy to become a de-firmer and not know it until too late.

But there are the affirming experiences also. Recently, I was preparing to preach at a well-known church in the Midwest. I was tired, wishing I was home and wondering how I'd gotten into the responsibility I was facing. You could hardly say I was spiritually impassioned to face that congregation with a word from God.

Then an usher stepped to my side and handed me a note. An anonymous writer reminded me of a recent place where I had given a series of talks and described the difference my talks had made in his life and that of his family. He included in the note a written prayer asking the Spirit of God to anoint me for the coming pulpit experience. Instantly I took on a new quantity of courage and desire. Passion came about as the result of an affirmation. I had no doubt that the notewriter, whose name was not included on the paper, was God's gift to me.

Sponsors and affirmers make great teammates. They're nice to have around, and we wish we had them to draw upon. But while it is good to ask if these people exist in our date books, it may be just as significant to question whether we fill these roles in the date books of others. For we not only need them on our team, but we need to be making it possible to serve on someone else's team.

A few sponsors and affirmers could have changed the climate in Bob Slocum's office. But they were nowhere to be found. The result? A tiring, boresome place where people lost their drive and desire to do their work well. A passionless place. You need a Mordecai in places like that.

16
More Special Friends

There are certain positions on a baseball team that almost no one wants to play. On the corner lot when the teams were chosen for the baseball game, it was clear that no one wanted to play catcher. "Joey, you catch," the captain would say, usually pointing to the little guy on the field.

"Oh come on," Joey would cry out, "I caught last week. Let Smitty do it. He can't catch fly balls anyway." The truth of the matter is that the catcher's job is dangerous. The catcher gets sore knees from crouching, bruises from thrown bats, and aches from collisions with sliding runners at home plate. Being the catcher simply isn't an enviable job.

The team of special friends also has a position that is unpleasant. I call it the position of the rebuker.

3. THE REBUKER

It takes courage to include the *rebuker* on the team. For what he or she says often hurts and leaves bruises on the spirit. *But we may be talking about the most important member among our special friends.* We all need truth-tellers, even if we don't really want them. Pass them up or avoid them, and spiritual passion may be in great jeopardy.

The writers of the book of Proverbs put a great premium on the position of the rebuker: "Open rebuke is better than hidden love! Wounds from a friend are better than kisses from an enemy" (Prov. 27:5,6 TLB).

Truth-telling is in short supply in our world. Our relationships often include those who are willing to speak the truth behind our backs but not in front. The former is destructive; the latter constructive. Conversely, many of us who have been given the responsibility of leadership actually fear the truth because we get used to the feeling of being right, of being the person with the right answers. So it bothers us when someone comes along to tell us that we don't have everything together after all. Thus, the issue of truth-telling is a two-sided problem. Not many people want to *tell* the truth when it's painful, and not a lot of people want to *hear* the truth if it's painful.

Back to Joseph Heller's novel *Something Happened*. Bob Slocum describes a work world where people aren't truthful with one another either.

> People in the company are almost never fired; if they grow inadequate or obsolete ahead of schedule, they are encouraged to retire early or are eased aside into hollow, insignificant, newly created positions with fake functions and no authority, where they are sheepish and unhappy for as long as they remain; nearly always, they must occupy a small and less convenient office, sometimes with another person already in it; or, if they are still young, they are simply encouraged directly (though with courtesy) to find better jobs with other companies and then resign. Even the wide-awake young branch manager with the brilliant future who got drunk and sick one afternoon and threw up into the hotel swimming pool during the company convention in Florida two years ago wasn't fired, although everyone knew he would not be permitted to remain. He knew it, too. Probably nothing was ever said to him. But he knew it. And four weeks after the convention ended, he found a better job with another company and resigned (Heller, *Something Happened*, p. 37).

No one wins in such a world. At first it is thought that people are simply protecting each other, watching out for each other's feelings. But no one grows where truth is absent. No one is pushed *to be* and *to do* the best. And when you look at this deficit from a Christian perspective, it describes a situation where men and women are never going to become all that God has made them to be nor will they gather the spiritual energy or passion to make it happen.

Recently I faced a traumatic week. I had appointments with three people or groups who examined aspects of my life with intense care—my doctor, who gave me my annual physical; my tax man, who carefully studied my financial picture; and the appraisal and review task force of InterVarsity's Board of Trustees, who wanted to investigate my year's performance as president.

Their jobs? To uncover any places where I have been abusing or misusing my body, my assets, or my job. To point out places where I can do better, avoid problems, and perform with greater excellence. You could call them the potential rebukers in my larger circle of special friends. In all three cases, I would have been silly to have avoided the encounters or to have refused to listen to what they had to say to me.

And yet some people do. I have acquaintances who will always avoid a physical, who apparently cut corners in their financial dealings, and who refuse to listen to experienced counselors critique their way of doing their work or developing their spiritual lives.

One rarely grows without a rebuke. One solid and loving rebuke is worth a hundred affirmations. Rebukes are the purifiers which keep spiritual passion clear and forceful.

A significant portion of Paul's letters to Timothy are actually rebuke. Paul was disturbed that the young man he'd been sponsoring was losing his passion to pastorally confront people. There were older men in the church who were spiritually lazy and there were those who were spreading inaccurate teaching. Timothy may have been pulling his punches. But Paul wasn't going to pull his. Preach! Exhort! Don't permit people to back you down. So went Paul's rebukes and admonitions. Presumably, Timothy was galvanized into action when he received the strong words of his sponsor/rebuker.

The rebukes of Jesus to Peter must have been stinging. "You're looking at this from a human point of view and not from God's" (Mark 8:33 TLB), he says at one time. "You will deny me three times" (Mark 14:30 RSV), he said some time later when Peter was long on words and generally short on performance. "Asleep? Couldn't you watch with me even one hour?" (Mark 14:37 TLB), he asked in the garden.

When Peter did indeed deny the Lord in the high priest's court, "the Lord turned and looked at Peter" (Luke 22:61 RSV). In this case a look was as good as a word. Later on the Galilee shoreline around a breakfast fire, Peter again heard the rebuke of Jesus. "What is that to you?" Jesus said when the impulsive disciple began to ask questions about another teammate while Jesus wanted him thinking about his own call (see John 21:22). In effect the Savior was saying, "Mind your own business and follow me."

Rebuke and criticism are two different things, the former a valued gift, the latter somewhat cheaper. But I have been taught even to seize the truth in a criticism that may have been leveled for reasons other than for building me up. "There is a kernel of truth in every criticism," I am told Dawson Trotman used to say to his friends. "Look for it, and when you find it, rejoice in its value."

I find that some younger men and women around me bristle at the hint of any rebuke or criticism. Their self-image is suddenly on the line, and you can feel their instinct rising to fight back like that of a cornered animal. But a great mark has been reached when we accept what seems to be a negative word and absorb it, forcing ourselves to grow in the reception, both examining the truth we hear and choosing not to fight back and hurt the one who played the rebuking position.

Looking back, I realize that rebukes were and still are among my greatest learning moments. They set me free from things that otherwise would have destroyed my spiritual passion. They spotlighted things that were hurting me badly but that I did not understand. So I am thankful to my wife and other special friends who play the position of rebuker on my team of special friends. I understand the proverb that says, "In the end, people appreciate frankness more than flattery" (Prov. 28:23 TLB).

I have often told the story of my special friend, Philip Armstrong, a missionary leader lost in a plane crash in Alaska. We were walking along a Japanese street when I made a derogatory comment about a mutual acquaintance. "Gordon," Armstrong immediately said, "a man of God would not say such a thing about another person." I was exposed and knew it. He was right. The rebuke stung, and I lived with its pain for many days afterward. But I will always be thankful for that rebuke, painful as it was, because I hear those words every time I am about to embarrass myself with a needless comment about another person. That was a rebuke that forced me to grow.

If you enjoy being a rebuker, think again about whether or not you are a special friend. Paul tells the Corinthians that he rebukes them with tears. Christ rebukes at the expense of His life. Jeremiah admits that he is so exhausted from rebuking that he wants to run into the desert and forget the whole thing.

The rebuker plays his or her position at great risk. And we, who at any moment become the rebuked, must be careful to listen intently, thanking the rebuker for truth that was shared at such high cost.

Elsewhere I have spoken of my favorite character in English church history, Charles Simeon. Simeon often struggled with irritability and impatience. It showed one night when he visited at the home of a friend, Mr. Edwards. Edwards later wrote to William Carus, Simeon's first biographer, about an encounter between Simeon and a servant:

> We were sitting at dinner when a servant behind [Simeon] stirred the fire, in a way so *unscientific*, that Mr. S. turned round and hit the man a thump on the back, to stay his proceedings. When he was leaving me, on horseback, after the same visit, my servant had put the wrong bridle upon his horse. He was in a hurry to be gone, and his temper broke out so violently, that I ventured to give him a little humorous castigation.

Then Mr. Edwards became a bit creative in his rebuke as he continues to describe.

> His cloak bag was to follow him by coach; so I feigned a letter in my servant's name, saying, how high his character stood in the kitchen; but that they could not understand, how a gentleman, who preached and prayed so well, should be in such passions about nothing, and wear no *bridle* upon his own tongue. This I signed "John Softly", and deposited it in his cloak bag. The hoax so far succeeded, that at first he scarcely discovered it. . . .

But Charles Simeon was not dumb. He soon realized that the letter from "John Softly" was actually from his special friend, Mr. Edwards, and playing out the charade he penned a return letter addressed to Mr. "John Softly."

> I most cordially thank you, my dear friend, for your kind and seasonable reproof. I feel it to be both just and necessary: and will endeavor with God's help to make a suitable improvement of it. If it do not produce its proper effects, I shall be exceedingly

thankful to have a second edition of it. I trust your "precious balm will not break my head;" but hope it will soften the spirit of your much indebted friend.

[signed] Charles. Proud and Irritable

Later Simeon wrote directly to Mr. Edwards about the incident and said

I have day and night thanked God for you, and prayed for blessings on your head, and watched and prayed against my besetting sins. . . . I hope, my dearest brother, that when you find your soul nigh to God, you will remember one who so greatly needs all the help he can get . . . (Carus, *Memories of the Life of Rev. Charles Simeon*, p. 112).

But let us go on to other players on the team of special friends who renew and help to maintain our spiritual passion.

4. THE INTERCESSOR

If I am to gain spiritual passion from my special friends, among them will be those who play the position of the *intercessor*. Intercessors are those who have accepted the responsibility for holding me up to God in prayer.

Gail and I have enjoyed a number of intercessors in our lives. You can spot them. They carefully ask questions about the issues you're facing, the trips you will soon be taking, the problems you're trying to solve. And you know they have not been merely curious when they follow up a few weeks later to say, "I've been praying every day about ———; what's happening? What's God doing?"

One of the most fascinating (but also frightening) examples of intercession I ever heard about came from the mouth of a Salvation Army officer who was praying over some of the first officers of the Army to leave England for America in 1860. He prayed:

Lord, these ladies are going to America to preach the gospel. If they are fully given up to Thee, be with them and bless them and grant them success. But if they are not faithful, drown'em, Lord; drown'em.

Jesus plays the role of intercessor when he sadly confronts Peter about his proneness to denial: "Simon, Simon, behold, Satan demanded to have you, that he might sift you like wheat, *but I have prayed for you* that your faith may not fail; and when you have turned again, strengthen your brethren" (Luke 22:31,32 RSV, emphasis added).

The entire seventeenth chapter of John is a model of intercessory prayer. "I am praying for them" (John 17:9 RSV), Christ says to the Father. That they might be kept from the evil one (v. 15). That they might be one (v. 21). That they would be where He is (v. 24). He prayed as a special friend. When Jesus ascended to Heaven, He assumed the position of intercessor for the Christian, and He plays that position in our lives even now.

"A Christian fellowship lives and exists by the intercession of its members for one another," writes Dietrich Bonhoeffer, "or it collapses."

> I can no longer condemn or hate a brother for whom I pray, no matter how much trouble he causes me. His face, hitherto may have been strange and intolerable to me, is transformed in intercession into the countenance of a brother for whom Christ died, the face of a forgiven sinner. This is a happy discovery for the Christian who begins to pray for others. There is no dislike, no personal tension, no estrangement that cannot be overcome by intercession as far as our side of it is concerned. Intercessory prayer is the purifying bath into which the individual and the fellowship must enter every day. The struggle we undergo with our brother in intercession may be a hard one, but that struggle has the promise that it will gain its goal. . . . To make intercession means to grant our brother the same right that we have received, namely to stand before Christ and share his mercy (Bonhoeffer, *Life Together*, quoted in Benson and Benson, *Disciplines of the Inner Life*, p. 71).

E. Stanley Jones, the great evangelist, once wrote of a time early in his Christian experience. "For months after my conversion," he wrote, "I was running under cloudless skies. And then suddenly I tripped, almost fell, pulled back this side of the sin, but was shaken and humiliated that I could come that close to sin. I thought I was emancipated and found I wasn't."

Then he goes on to write of the effort of special friends who played the intercessory position:

> I went to the class meeting—I'm grateful that I didn't stay away—went, but my (spiritual) music had gone. I had hung my

harp on a weeping willow tree. As the others spoke of their joys and victories of the week, I sat there with the tears rolling down my cheeks. I was heartbroken. After the others had spoken, John Zink, the class leader, said: "Now, Stanley, tell us what is the matter." I told them I couldn't but would they please pray for me? Like one man they fell to their knees, and they lifted me back to the bosom of God by faith and love. When we got up from our knees, I was reconciled. The universe opened its arms and took me in again. The estrangement was gone. I took my heart from the willow tree and began to sing again. . . . (Jones, *A Song of Ascents*, p. 42).

Who are our intercessors? Anyone in Christian leadership should set a goal for himself to identify and regularly connect with at least three intercessors who will "play" on his or her ministry "team." These intercessors should be capable of generating a constant flow of praise or concern as they pray. Their prayers will provide a protective curtain about the one who is engaged in spiritual warfare. And a major part of the intercessors' prayers would be that our spiritual passion be constantly renewed and that we not grow weary.

5. THE PARTNER

Another player on our team of special friends is the generalist, the roving fielder if you please. That player is the *partner*. The restoration and maintenance of spiritual passion frequently depends upon the process of partnership with one or more who share the load. In fact, I am not sure that most of us can ever reach the full extent of our energies if we are not in partnership with someone else.

Unfortunately, we are in a day when there are not many outstanding examples of partnership, but such partnerships are beautiful to behold. The partnership of the Billy Graham team for more than forty years has been an inspiration to all who have watched from a distance. This group of men heard a call from God early in their adulthood, and they banded together for Billy Graham to pursue the goal of world evangelization. And while the world has celebrated the amazing success of Billy Graham, it has not recognized that, humanly speaking, a share of the credit goes to the men about him who quietly gave him courage, insight, and strength. They chose to martial their energies and pour them into him much like the jump start that is necessary for a weak car battery.

I often wonder how many men and women there are whom God could probably have used more effectively had they been a part of a team that included partners. It is not unusual to hear of gifted men and women who fell short of goals they should have met. What happened? Perhaps they—or those about them—refused to act like partners, choosing rather to pursue their own private goals and aims.

A close friend told me that one draft horse can move two tons of weight. But two draft horses in harness, working together, can move twenty-three tons of weight. That probably is not far from properly illustrating how men and women can work together in a common objective.

For many of us, a spouse is the first-line partner. My wife, Gail, has been a partner in Christian growth and service since the day we married. On many occasions, this has meant that one of us (usually Gail) forsook some privilege or personal desire in order to stand alongside the other and provide the support needed to respond to God's call and direction.

Partners pick up a part of the load and accept responsibility for it. Nothing is too menial or too outrageous if partners believe in one another.

One of the great marital partnerships in Christian service was that of Hudson and Maria Taylor. J. C. Pollock, describing the strength that moved between the Taylors, wrote:

> Hudson would lean hard on her, drawing vigor from her spiritual maturity, her tranquility and faith, her unwaivering affection. She gave him and their work all she had, every ounce of strength, every thought that crossed her intelligent mind, all the force of her love. She allowed him to drain her, and if sometimes his demands were unconsciously selfish, she was no more aware of it than he (Pollock, *Hudson Taylor and Maria*, p. 172).

Dixon Hoste, deeply impressed by the Taylors, was one of the famed Cambridge Seven, a group of young university men who shocked all of England in the late 1800s when they decided to abandon great careers to go overseas as missionaries.

One of the young missionaries, Stanley Smith, invited Hoste to work with him but insisted that he, Smith, would have to be the leader since he had a little more qualification in terms of experience than Hoste.

Hoste, ever the competitor, found this invitation to partnership where he would be the second man a bit hard to take.

I was ruffled in my spirit. Why should I serve under him? We were about the same age, and had come to China together. Granted he was brilliant with the language, could make easy contacts, and in other ways was my superior, this did not seem sufficient reason to me, so I suggested he should write to the Mission at Shanghai for a younger man, as it was their business to make appointments.

But Hoste was a godly man who was open even to inner rebuke, and he remained thoughtful.

Later on thinking over the situation, the Spirit of God probed me, and I was forced to admit that I did not relish the thought of being under my friend. I thought of my "face," what friends would surmise, etc. The difficulty was in my own heart. It was impressed upon me that the unwillingness persisted in would mean my having to part company with the Lord Jesus Christ, who dwells with the humble ones, those who willingly go down. I therefore accepted my friend's suggestion, and we worked happily together for several months . . . (Hoste, *If I Am to Lead*, p. 53).

There are of course the great partnerships in the Scriptures which give us a model of this relationship that maintains or renews spiritual passion. The partnership of Paul and Barnabas is probably the most beautiful of all.

It began with Barnabas's desire to sponsor Paul at Jerusalem when he needed an introduction into the church. It became a partnership when Barnabas later went to Tarsus, Paul's hometown, to find him and invite him to Antioch where a team ministry was needed. The partnership hit its full stride as the men began to travel the world engaging in evangelism and planting churches.

Paul was wise enough to realize that he could never operate well without partners. At almost every point in his ministry he linked up with others called "fellow-soldiers," "brothers," or "yokefellows." When he wrote to Timothy (2 Timothy 4:9ff) he shared information on the movements of all his partners: those whom he had sent out, those who had deserted him, those who were still there. And it is very clear that Paul did not like to be without partners in his life and work.

In Robert Sherwood's remarkable account of the partnership between Harry Hopkins and President Franklin D.

Roosevelt, a conversation between FDR and Wendell Willkie, who had just been defeated by Roosevelt in the 1941
election, is described. Willkie was about to head for wartorn
London, and he had been invited to the White House for a
brief visit with the president before he embarked. Roosevelt
told him that he would appreciate it if Willkie would visit
with Harry Hopkins, whom Willkie would find in London on
another assignment.

Wendell Willkie's immediate reaction was negative since
he and many other Americans disliked Hopkins intensely.
At that point, Sherwood writes, Willkie asked FDR a
"pointed question:"

> Why do you keep Hopkins so close to you? You surely must
> realize that people distrust him and they resent his influence.

> Willkie quoted Roosevelt as replying: "I can understand that you
> wonder why I need that half-man around me." (The "half-man"
> was an allusion to Hopkins' extreme physical frailty.) "But—
> someday you may well be sitting here where I am now as Presi-
> dent of the United States. And when you are, you'll be looking at
> that door over there and knowing that practically everybody who
> walks through it wants something out of you. You'll learn what a
> lonely job this is, and you'll discover the need for somebody like
> Harry Hopkins who asks for nothing except to serve you" (Sher-
> wood, *Roosevelt and Hopkins*, p. 2).

6. THE PASTOR

There is one more player on the team of special friends—the
pastor. This is the tender person, the person who comes alongside in the moment of exhaustion. The pastor—and I'm not
necessarily talking about ordained ministers—is the one who
helps make sense out of life when all has become confusing.

Dr. C. Henry Kempe, a specialist in pediatrics and micro-
biology, once wrote of his experiences in an intensive care unit
in Bellevue Hospital in New York when he was recovering
from a heart attack. It was an extremely difficult period
marked with pain and mental confusion. "I have no memory
whatever of the first two weeks of my stay, but the subsequent
weeks are very clear in my mind. On recollection what stands
out is the exquisite nursing care I received." He goes on:

> I remember that when I first emerged from a haze of pain and
> confusing procedures, each nurse coming on shift in this large

twelve-bed unit would introduce herself by her first name, tell me what day and time it was, and, almost without fail, hold one of my hands in her two hands while looking straight into my eyes. I found this very comforting, because I was aware of having lost not only considerable intellectual ability, but I also was having frightening hallucinatory experiences. *These were immediately wiped out by this personal contact.* The nurses would explain what they called "scary dreams" and thus reassure me about the frequency of hallucinations. They said that everybody who has lost a lot of REM sleep was likely to hallucinate; that it was a routine experience in their patients; that these images invariably went away, and that I was neither stupid nor going crazy. During those days the repeated reassurance about regaining intelligence and sanity was perhaps the most important event of the daily nursing contact (Kempe, *Pharos*).

In a medical metaphor, Kempe has described what a pastor does on our team to help restore and maintain our spiritual passion. The word pastor means shepherd; it describes the function of one who leads, feeds, and protects.

Spiritual passion or energy is usually dissipated in the midst of fear and confusion. That is why we need to have in our circle of special friends the one who senses our restiveness and speaks to it in words and gestures.

While I have been a pastor to many, I have also known the need for a pastor. I can recall a short period of serious personal turbulence in which a pastor came alongside with the tender question, "Are there knots in your life today, Gordon?" And he opened the door to a conversation that led to my gaining a more even perspective on what God might be saying. And then my friend concluded the conversation by laying his hands upon me and praying for my strength and guidance.

Gail and I will always recall the visit of another pastor friend when we thought our young daughter was dying. He brought calmness to the hospital waiting room as he sat with us, not always talking, but always there to be our strength and to understand the nature of our panic.

Our special-friend team needs such a person to whom we can turn in a moment of danger. But when I look about at those in Christian leadership and I ask, "Who is your pastor?" I am impressed with the large number whose answer is, "I really have no pastor, no one to whom I would feel comfortable to turn to."

The apostle Paul was a special-friend pastor to a terrified group of soldiers and sailors in the midst of a Mediterranean storm when he intervened in the midst of their panic:

> I now bid you take heart; for there will be no loss of life among you, but only of the ship. For this very night there stood by me an angel of the God to whom I belong and whom I worship, and he said "Do not be afraid, Paul. . . ." So take heart, men, for I have faith in God that it will be exactly as I have been told (Acts 27:22–25 RSV).

This description of performance by sponsors, affirmers, rebukers, intercessors, partners, and pastors is a long way from the sort of people Bob Slocum talked about in Joseph Heller's novel *Something Happened*. His world was one of extreme exhaustion. But the world of the person with special friends is filled with energy and power. The spiritual passion of that person will be renewed to overflowing.

17

Renewing Your Spiritual Passion

In a wonderful book, *The Table of Inwardness*, Calvin Miller wrote of an antique wooden dynamite box in his home. The box was made in the nineteenth century, Miller said, carefully constructed to withstand shock as its explosive contents were transported from the manufacturer to a place of use.

On the lid were large red and black letters which said DANGER DYNAMITE! "But the last I saw it," Miller wrote, "it was filled with common paraphernalia that could be found in any workroom."

I'm drawn to the irony of Calvin Miller's description of a box designed for dynamite which warns that it contains dynamite but which now stores only "common paraphernalia."

This might be the unfortunate picture of the wearied follower of God who has lost heart, whose spiritual passion is nonexistent. Like the box, a man or woman is created to store spiritual dynamite, the marvelous energy of God. And (here the analogy begins to break down) he or she is created to discharge that dynamite. Furthermore, this person is often thrust into situations where the capacity of that heavenly dynamite is verbally affirmed and historically recounted.

We're talking about a person who gets highly involved in a church or religious organization, who attempts to live congenially in the marketplace and in the neighborhood, who would really like to be noted as *trying* to be a pleasure to God. But something is amiss. Either the dynamite is wet or *it really isn't even there*. It's as good as having common paraphernalia within.

When I set out to write this book, I had a difficult time trying to explain to interested people what I was writing about. "Weariness," I would say in response to their questions concerning the topic. "Well, what do you mean by that?" they would ask.

"I'm concerned about the fact that people are doing more, knowing more, and trying to take on more, but in many cases not really getting any further any faster. The worst case under these circumstances is the specter of some folks who just end up dropping out. They get spiritually tired trying to do and say the right things. But they feel a quiet frustration, and they feel as if they're going nowhere. Somehow we've not helped them; we've only given them more guilt or more things to do. So they're gone!"

"Oh you're talking about stress and burnout," comes back the rejoinder. "We need to hear more about that."

"But I'm not sure I'm talking about stress and burnout," I try to say. "I'm talking about something that's deeper than that, a spiritual sensation that can hardly be described apart from the word 'weary.'" What started as a pilgrimage has degenerated into a rat race. And the rats are winning.

"And the King . . . arrived weary at the Jordan; and there he refreshed himself" went the phrase we contemplated in earlier chapters. What did David feel like when he knew that he'd tried his best, given his all, worked his hardest? What was the spiritual fatigue he sensed as he sat there on the edge of the river washing the grime of hurried travel off of his body? Where could he go from there? What could he do?

That Davidic sensation may be old, but it is not obsolete. I strongly suspect that literally millions of evangelical Christians in this world have dropped out of the visible activities of the family of God because they're tired or weary.

Talk to them and find out how they feel. It is not bitterness about which they speak, not even disillusionment. They simply shrug their shoulders and say, "It didn't work for me.

I haven't abandoned Jesus, but I'm tired of all the activity that people say has to be done in the name of Jesus."

To seize a piece of Calvin Miller's analogy, these people decided one day that having DANGER DYNAMITE written on the surface performance but having little more than religious paraphernalia within was an inadequate way to live. It is a hypocrisy of sorts; a gap in integrity. "I don't like singing songs that quote me as saying or doing something when I know in my heart that I'm not there and—at this rate—never will be," a spiritually discouraged man once told me.

I would like to propose that what these people needed—and didn't find or didn't take the time for—were things like safe places, still times, and special friends. The safe places would have allowed them to find out *who* God is. The still times would have given them a chance to *hear* what God says. The special friends would have made possible the encouragement and correctives for them to *obey* what God asks.

But all too often our safe places are too noisy. Our still times are clogged with busyness. And our special friends are little more than acquaintances who don't know or care how to deal with us in this category of life (nor we for them). The result? Weariness, which is to say, loss of spiritual passion, loss of the energy to get on with and produce what Christ called an abundant life.

The secret to spiritual passion, someone may say, is the great enthusiasm spawned in the large and frequent meetings and conferences that Christians can put on better than anyone else. Pack it full with soloists, special speakers, and a thousand seminars. Let us get excited by the numbers of people, the humor and scintillating observations of the teachers, and the new approaches to faith that sharp minds can manufacture.

"No, that's not it," another may argue. "The secret to spiritual passion is the Holy Spirit. I'm surprised you didn't mention that a lot earlier in this book. Just relax and let Him do whatever He wants to do through you. It's worked for me, and I'm positive it will work for you."

"Forget all of that. You've missed it," a third may suggest. "Spiritual passion comes from being exposed to the real world and by seeing the needs of people. Get overseas; go to the ghetto; visit in a mental hospital. You'll get passion quickly!"

Perhaps there is something useful in all of those interpretive answers. Each rests on passages of Scripture that seem to strongly undergird the proffered argument. But the fact is that many Christians, pursuing each line of reasoning, still fall short of the promised results. And no rational explanation seems to help us understand why.

Perhaps we do not adequately visualize what we're searching for when we talk about spiritual passion. We're not positive what actually pleases the God of the Bible when we seek intimacy with Him. And beyond that, we're not entirely confident that we know how He wishes us to act as His children in this broken world.

Is it too dumb a question to ask all over again what might a spiritually passionate person look like? Not all of us can be well-known heroes, speakers, authors, liberators, or organizational heads. Is that what a spiritually passionate person looks like? One might have reason to think so because those roles tend to be the models we hoist up before one another as worthy of emulation.

But there are so many millions of us common, ordinary people, men and women whose lives are routine—making a home for a family, coping as a single, trying to get or keep a job, nursing along a troubled automobile we can't afford to replace, being concerned about retirement, wondering whether or not we're going to amount to anything. What does the spiritually passionate life look like in these contexts?

A somewhat obscure story in the Older Testament might provide a valuable insight. The story appears in 1 Chronicles 11 and recalls a period of time in David's life when, as usual, he found himself in hostile conditions, forced to flee to the desert or wilderness lifestyle to survive.

The enemy this time was the Philistines, a hostile tribe on the southern border of Israel. The Philistines were strong, and their armies were momentarily victorious against David's people. At the time of the story, they held strong positions around Bethlehem, David's original hometown.

Certain men of Israel had drifted into the hills to join David, and from the ranks of what we might call today a guerrilla army came a cadre of what I would like to call special friends, mighty men known for their loyalty and bravery. The word used to describe them was the Hebrew word *hesed* meaning, among other things, "devoted."

You can assume that David was tired of running, tired of living in caves, probably tired in general of being at war. In a quiet moment, David spoke out with some nostalgia. "Oh that some one would give me water to drink from the well of Bethlehem" (1 Chron. 11:17 RSV).

It was clearly not a command that David gave; not even a call for volunteers. *Merely a wish!* And it is important to remember that because of what subsequently happened. Just a wish from the lips of David, but enough of a wish that three of David's mighty men heard it and immediately determined to deliver water as a gift from the Bethlehem well as soon as possible (see 1 Chron. 11:18).

Children have thrilled to the story of the three unnamed men who set out to fight their way through the Philistine lines, draw the brand name water David had been thinking about and, fighting their way back the same way they came, present it to him as an act of intense affection.

So moved was David by this action that he could not drink the water but wisely poured it out on the ground as a drink offering to God. He knew devotion when he saw it, and he appreciated the fact that no human being was worthy of the intense devotion these three men had given to him. The water had to be redesignated as a gift to David's God. A good decision.

I am indebted to my friend Dr. Edwin Clowney for pointing out this passage in an InterVarsity seminar where I was a cospeaker. I was deeply moved as I saw the picture of devotion he painted in his exposition of the passage. In a moment I knew that the three mighty men of David had established a pattern of performance that most describes the man or woman whose spiritual passion is clear and forceful.

THREE POWERFUL TRUTHS THAT PUT THE CHRISTIAN LIFE IN PERSPECTIVE

I saw in the actions of those mighty men a simple but powerful set of truths that put the Christian life in proper perspective. Their action symbolized the way a man or woman with spiritual passion lives.

Let me point out the truths that make this story so useful.

1. INTIMACY MAKES IT POSSIBLE TO HEAR GOD'S WISHES

The fact is that David's wish was most likely uttered quietly, informally. *You had to be in the presence of the commander to have heard it.*

Use your imagination and ask where the others were when this wish was made known. Doing good things, perhaps—pitching tents, shining boots, sharpening weapons, washing laundry, cooking food. All good and necessary activities. But the *best* activity for the moment seems to have been in the presence of the commander in chief, where not only commands could be heard, but also a few wishes.

To be in the presence of the Commander is to be in a *safe place*; and to hear his wishes demands a *still time* when listening is the most important thing. That's intimacy, and it generates passion, a desire to hear and to please. No hearing, no intimacy, no passion.

With my imagination still running, I can see those three mighty men sitting near the commander listening to every word, anxious to know how they can, in fact, please. Theirs is a proactive listening: seeking the wishes of the one to whom they had devoted themselves.

They remind me of one of the unusual traits of my wife, Gail, who has a habit of listening carefully to the wishes of her husband and children. Unlike most of us, she has disciplined herself to write down what she hears. It is simply amazing how every Father's day or every birthday (or any other special day she can manufacture) includes little (or large) gifts that originated in the wistful comments of weeks before. The gifts tell me that she has listened carefully to the serendipitous musings of my heart.

Only in safe places and during still times will one hear the wishes of God—or of anyone else, for that matter. God's wishes are not shouted; often they are hidden behind the commands. Anyone can hear the commandments of God unless he chooses not to. But it takes a sensitive ear to hear the wishes of God, and that only comes—as I've said—in safe places at still times.

The intimacy of the commander's presence is something sought by relatively few people. In a world that offers too many experiences of easily achieved, and therefore cheapened, intimacy, not many people are willing to pay the price demanded to gain the presence of God.

"The incessant and sabbathless pursuit of a man's fortune leaveth out tribute which we owe to God of our time," Sir Francis Bacon wrote as he struggled with the balance in his life of ambition-oriented labor and the need to step back and ask what it all meant and where it was all going.

I have gained great assistance in the development of my own spiritual life as I have thought of the God who has wishes for His people and the world He has created. His commands are there for all to read and see; but His wishes are only for those who set out each day to listen eagerly and carefully.

I am amazed how often the wishes reveal themselves in the intimacy of time with Him: in the quiet moments and still times, in the tragic moments where there is pain and hopelessness, in the opportune moments when an act of potential servanthood presents itself.

When our date books and our personal road maps do not indicate the discipline of safe-place and still-time experiences, we forfeit the chance to monitor the wishes of God. We will have to depend upon what other people tell us, and their interpretations may not be accurate. Our neglect is a serious loss.

That is why I have learned that the time budgeted for safe-place/still-time activity is the most important single event in my daily lifestyle. Ignorance of this need leads to weariness.

2. THE CHOICE TO ACT IS OFTEN TAKEN AT GREAT RISK

The accounts of this exciting story do not include any record of debate among the three men. "Are you crazy?" you can almost hear one of them say. "Do you know where that well is located, how strongly the area is fortified, how many people we'll have to mow down to get there? For water? For one man?"

Perhaps it is significant that the record does not indicate such a scenario. Probably because it didn't happen. The effort of the text is to indicate how devoted, passionate men really think and act. The wish of the general came through like a command to the devoted. The passion generated moved from a listening mode to an action mode.

Convictions generated from a genuine encounter with the living God *create* the passion to act and the strength to carry out the action. What all too often happens, I fear, is that modern Christians try to move on other people's passion: that of an organizational leader, a slick "sales" presentation made by a group that knows marketing and public relations techniques. We respond with genuine excitement, but it is a thin sort of passion easily dissipated or quickly supplanted by the next powerful message.

David's men heard the wish from the lips of their commander. The man or woman who takes the time to hear God speak is apt to have the same reaction: instant motion.

Moses heard the wishes of God at the burning bush. "I have heard the cries of my people. . . . I have seen their pain. . . . I have walked among them. . . . Moses, go and deliver them" (see Exod. 3:7-10). True, Moses was at first reluctant to respond to such a wish. He had lost his passion for heroic action the first time around when he'd killed an Egyptian. (He had probably intended then to be a liberating leader and then belatedly discovered that the Hebrew people weren't ready for heroes.)

But finally Moses responded, and with few exceptions he maintained a force of spiritual passion that carried a whole nation to the edge of the Promised Land (see Exod. 3,4). But how did he keep it all going? By maintaining still times in safe places where he pursued the voice of God, the glory of God, the wishes of God. Busy as he was, he never lacked time to go to the mountain (see Exod. 19, 20).

John the Baptist also heard the wishes of God in the desert; Peter heard them on a rooftop; the apostle Paul on a lonely road. And the men acted. Mary, the mother of the Lord, heard the wishes of God in an appearance from an angel. She was surprised, to be sure, but she made a choice to act.

It is interesting to ponder the amount of action for which common people are responsible simply because of their willingness to listen and their choice to act, even at great risk.

In the biography of General William Booth, founder of the Salvation Army, a poignant moment is described when his son, Bramwell, must tell his father (then 83) that he is going blind from a disease of the eyes.

"You mean that I am blind?"

"Well, General, I fear that we must contemplate that." After a pause the old man said, "I shall never see your face again?"

"No, probably not in this world."

During the next few moments the veteran's hand crept along the counterpane to take hold of his son's, and holding it he said very calmly, "God must know best!" And after another pause, "Bramwell, I have done what I could for God and for the people with my eyes. Now I shall do what I can for God and for the people without my eyes" (Begbie, *The Life of General Wm Booth*, p. 422).

3. A DIVINE ENERGY CREATES THE ULTIMATE PASSION

Throughout the Bible, a mysterious energy of God pulsates, which, when planted within people, makes for formidable accomplishment. We know that energy to be originated by the Holy Spirit, the third person of the God-head.

In the earliest days of biblical history, that energy seemed to come to certain people for special opportunities. And when it came, their passion grew and their performance was extraordinary. Joseph wisely serving as consultant to Egypt's pharaoh (see Gen. 41); David shutting out Goliath (see 1 Sam. 17:50); Gideon leading the charge against overwhelming odds (see Judg. 7, 8); Jeremiah confronting an unusually wicked king (see Jer. 37); Elizabeth providing support for the pregnant Mary (see Luke 1:42-45).

But the hope and expectation of people who sought God was that the passion and energy needed would be available for all people and that it would remain with them during the routine times as well as the unusual times.

I have always been convinced that this passion they sought was the normal life experience of the first man and woman who lived under optimum creation conditions before the fall of humanity. Theirs was the model life of spiritual passion. A daily intimacy with the Creator, the work of discovering the glories of the things created, the ecstasy of the resulting experience. This was a cycle of passion that captured the entire human experience: listening, working, enjoying.

Almost all of that was lost in the acts of disobedience when the first man and woman made a strange and awful choice to deviate from the commands and wishes of their God. Passion lost!

The Christian story is that of restoration. Restoration of intimacy with God and of the passion which comes from renewing our choice to respond to His wishes.

In our somewhat blinded condition, we as human beings have not always been intentional toward the things God wants to give His people. For example, in spite of the fact that Jesus promised His disciples this unusual passion or power, they seem to have remained ignorant as to what it all meant. Almost like a mother who must occasionally press good things upon her children for their good, it would appear that God had to press passion into the apostles. But once they had their passion renewed, they charged into the streets of Jerusalem and began to act in a spirit of bravery and boldness that no one could ever have imagined. Little men become giants!

Down through the centuries, common and somewhat unskilled people have caused remarkable things to happen in their worlds when the passion of God invaded their beings. They took risks, overcame obstacles, and set standards that leave us breathless.

This is the effort of the Spirit of God as He comes to the wearied person. To enliven us, to envision us, to enpower us. And when He does, this is not to say that the primary objective is to make us feel good, or secure, or more successful as is sometimes implied in certain circles. Although some of those things may actually happen, the chief purpose is to enlarge our capacity to join the task of kingdom building: demonstrating in life and in word the splendor of the living Christ and His incredible power to rescue lost people and turn them around to a higher life. "You shall receive power," Christ said, "and you shall be my witnesses" (Acts 1:8 RSV).

I have taken a lot of pages to say a simple thing, something I'm afraid has often gotten buried beneath a host of religious procedures and processes. We have over-complicated our God and His ways of coming to us. We have organized Him, strategized Him, and compartmentalized Him. We have reduced His ways of working with us to cute little formulas, and we have stood off in our own corners critical of others who seek His face in ways that differ from our own temperaments or styles of perception. But it is clear that God longs to renew a spiritual passion within us.

Few rules lead to this renewal, and they appear to be

disarmingly simple. I for one am tired of those who have claimed otherwise.

For the man or woman at the edge of a Jordan, wearied by too many choices and burdened with too many obligations, there is a simple formula: safe places, still times, and special friends.

The combination provides enough room for the faithful God of Jesus Christ to begin to speak to us. Drawn near under such circumstances, we begin to hear Him speak. At first it is a struggle to silence the interfering noises, but God has never made it a problem to approach Him. He does not play games with us, hiding first here and then there until we figure Him out. He is rather straightforward about all of this. *He wants to be heard.* Why have we made it so tough on ourselves?

I have met many passionate people. They come in all ages, from all backgrounds, with all sorts of personal capacities. No two look alike. But you know them when you see them. They are not hurried; they are not shrill; they are not out to impress.

You know them because when you come into their presence, they make you think of Christ. Somehow you feel that you have just understood a little more of what it was like to be in the presence of Jesus.

The energy that pushes them along is not the thunderous noise of a jet, nor the pressure of a Niagara. It's a quiet energy that you sense even if you can't see it.

I suppose what I'm talking about is best seen up at Peace Ledge, our New Hampshire retreat. An enormous rock is in the woods. Rather, *two* rocks. There used to be one, but it is split in two. And it is clear why there is a split.

Long ago (who knows how long?) water seeped into a crevice, froze, and created a deeper split. Then a seed blew into the deepened crack and germinated. From that tiny seed a tree began to grow, and its inexorable development simply pushed the rock apart. Now there are two rocks and a tree right in the middle. That's a quiet passion, quiet, indefatigable, powerful.

That kind of passion quietly splits apart the hardness of hate, greed, and intemperance. It lodges in the crevices of the home, the church, and society. It breaks up things and starts something new. That is the kind of passion we need in this passionless world of ours. And it comes from people who have decided to take the time and to go to the places and establish themselves among the people who can help us hear God speak.

I began this book with a reflection on a childhood memory, a dark Canadian road that my family traveled so long ago. Thinking of those moments, I again remember how tired and frustrated we were: having traveled too far to turn back and yet not knowing whether we had enough fuel or energy to keep moving ahead.

As I replay that night's journey in my mind, I suddenly see a light on the horizon. We drive on, the light getting brighter. And then we are there. The light illuminates a sign: WEARY TRAVELERS WELCOME, VACANCY.

Soon our family is in a small cabin. Our irritabilities are quickly dispelled; we lie down to rest, and soon we are asleep. The weariness of that day that had deflated our enthusiasm for a vacation trip drains away in the nighttime hours. The next morning parents and children will rise again, the prospects and the passion for a continued journey brighter than ever. The night is forgotten.

Holy Father,

In the frenzy of our modern lives at home, in the market place, and in the church, keep before us your invitation to intimacy.

Help us to locate those safe places, where in still times you will speak into our spirits from your Word, by your Spirit, through our special friends. May we learn as a result how to live in pursuit of your wishes.

For all who are weary, empty of spirit, directionless or numb, I pray for the renewal of spiritual passion. The reason? To be a pleasure to you and a light to the world.

AMEN.

Sources

Begbie, Harold. *The Life of General Wm Booth*. New York: MacMillan, 1920.

Benson, Bob, and Michael Benson. *Disciplines of the Inner Life*. Waco, Tex.: Word Books, 1985.

Bonhoeffer, Dietrich. *Life Together*. New York: Harper & Row, 1976.

Bowen, Catherine Drinker. *Francis Bacon: The Temper of a Man*. Boston: Little Brown and Co., 1963.

Bruce, A. B. *The Training of the Twelve*. Grand Rapids: Kregel Publishers, 1979.

Carus, William. *Memories of the Life of Rev. Charles Simeon*. American Edition. New York: Robert Cartier, 1848.

Cowman, Lettie. *Springs in the Valley*. Grand Rapids: Zondervan, 1939.

Eisenhower, D. D. *At Ease: Stories I Tell My Friends*. New York: Doubleday, 1967, quoted in *Harvard Business Review*.

Fénelon, François. *Spiritual Letters to Women*. Grand Rapids: Zondervan, 1984.

Gilkey, Langdon. *Shantung Compound*. New York: Harper & Row, 1966.

Guinness, Howard. *Journey Among Students*. Sydney, Australia: Anglican Information Office, 1978.

Hefley, James, and Marti Hefley. *By Their Blood: Christian Martyrs of the 20th Century*. Milford, Mich.: Mott Media, 1979.

Heller, J. *Something Happened*. New York: Ballantine Books, 1979.

Hoste, D. E. *If I Am to Lead*. Robesonia, Penn.: OMF Books, 1968.

Jensen, Margaret. *Lena*. San Bernardino, Calif.: Heres Life, 1985.

Jones, E. Stanley. *A Song of Ascents: A Spiritual Autobiography*. Nashville: Abingdon Press, 1979.

Kempe, C. Henry. *Pharos*. Winter 1979.

Kramer, Jerry, ed. *Lombardi: Winning Is the Only Thing*. New York: Pocket Books, 1970.

Laubach, Frank. *Frank Laubach: Letters by a Modern Mystic*. Syracuse, N.Y.: New Readers Press, 1979.

Lean, Garth. *God's Politician*. London: Darton, Longman & Todd, 1980.

Lenski, R. C. H. *The Interpretation of St. Paul's First and Second Epistles to the Corinthians*. Minneapolis: Augsburg Publishing House, 1937.

Miller, Calvin. *The Table of Inwardness*. Downers Grove, Ill.: Inter-Varsity Press, 1984.

Nouwen, Henri. *Clowning in Rome*. New York: Doubleday and Co., 1979.

Nouwen, Henri. *Reaching Out*. New York: Doubleday, 1975.

Palmer, Earl. *Alive from the Center*. Waco, Tex.: Word Books, 1982.

Pearson, Hesketh. *Oscar Wilde: His Life and Wit*. New York: Harper & Brothers, 1946.

Pennington, M. Basil. *Centering Prayer: Renewing an Ancient Christian Prayer Form*. New York: Image Books, 1982.

Phillips, J. B. *Your God Is Too Small*. New York: MacMillan, 1961.

Pollock, J. C. *Hudson Taylor and Maria*. New York: McGraw Hill, 1962.

Quoist, Michael. *With Open Heart*. New York: Crossroads, 1983.

Sangster, Paul. *Doctor Sangster*. London: Epworth Press, 1962.

Sherwood, Robert. *Roosevelt and Hopkins*. New York: Universal Library, rev. 1950.

Sproul, R. C. *Stronger Than Steel: The Wayne Alderson Story*. San Francisco: Harper & Row, 1980.

Turnbull, Ralph G. *A Minister's Obstacles*. Westwood, N.J.: Fleming H. Revell Co., 1964.

REBUILDING YOUR BROKEN WORLD

Acknowledgements

Unless otherwise noted, the Bible version used in this publication is the HOLY BIBLE: NEW INTERNATIONAL VERSION. Copyright © 1973, 1978, 1984 by the International Bible Society. Used by permission of Zondervan Bible Publishers.

Scripture quotations marked NKJV are taken from THE NEW KING JAMES VERSION. Copyright © 1979, 1980, 1982, Thomas Nelson, Inc., Publishers.

Verses marked TLB are taken from *The Living Bible*, copyright 1971 by Tyndale House Publishers, Wheaton, IL. Used by permission.

"The Road Not Taken" is copyright 1916, © 1969 by Holt, Rinehart and Winston, Inc. Copyright 1944 by Robert Frost. Reprinted from THE POETRY OF ROBERT FROST edited by Edward Connery Lathem, by permission of Henry Holt and Company, Inc., the estate of Robert Frost, and Jonathan Cape Ltd.

Excerpts of Daniel Golden's June 3, 1984, article on the drowning death of Chris Dilullo reprinted courtesy of The Boston Globe.

Excerpts from SONG OF ASCENTS by E. Stanley Jones. Copyright © 1968 by Abingdon Press. Used by permission.

To Gail
and
the "Angels"
the inner core
of many who have
helped me rebuild
my broken world

Contents

Foreword

As a young pastor, I read a very moving and reassuring sermon by that eloquent Scottish preacher-scholar, Arthur Gossip. After the agonizing death of his wife, he asked himself and his congregation, "When Life Tumbles In, What Then?" When for whatever reasons your personal world goes to pieces, is it possible to do more than simply manage to survive? If the whole structure of your existence is shattered, like a precious vase dropped on a hardwood floor, can those sherds be gathered up and by some recreative miracle be put together again into an object of beauty and usefulness? Once Humpty Dumpty has had his "great fall" are "all the king's horses and all the king's men" incapable of doing anything except lamenting as they consign his fragments into rubble?

That is precisely the problem God deals with in the book of Jeremiah. He issued a directive to his servant: "'Go down to the potter's house, and there I will give you my message.' So I went down to the potter's house, and I saw him working at the wheel. But the pot he was shaping from the clay was marred in his hands. . ." Let me break off the narrative at that point. When the recalcitrant clay resists the moulding hands of the potter, is the marred vessel thrown aside? By no means! Jeremiah's narrative continues: "So the potter formed it into another pot, shaping it as it seemed best to him" (Jer. 18:2-4). God's message to Jeremiah is centuries later God's message to ourselves through Gordon MacDonald, a message of recreative grace that inspires praise, humility and hope.

A few years ago if I had been asked to name ten outstanding leaders in American evangelicalism, I would have unhesitatingly included my friend Gordon MacDonald. I had known him intimately since his childhood. I had followed his development with as much pride as if he had been my own family member, a legitimate pride springing from gratitude to God for the fruitful giftedness of a choice and, I felt and still feel, a chosen servant. As the director of an outstanding campus ministry, a visionary churchman, a best-selling author, a lecturer in constant demand, and a devoted husband and father, he was a spiritual model, a dynamic spokesperson for the Gospel. Then overnight his world tumbled in. His career ground to a screeching halt. He became one more conspicuous casualty in the never-ending battle all of us carry on against evil within and without. But that, I rejoice to add, is not the end to the story. And that is why this book is such an inspiring message of hope.

Exercising what Dietrich Bonhoeffer calls "a certain manly reserve," my friend and brother wisely refuses to satisfy carnal curiosity. Yet with soul-searching candor he uses his own experience in order to help all of us who are his fellow sinners, fellow sufferers, and fellow strugglers.

Though he makes no pretense at being a psychologist, he probes the labyrinth of his own soul and ours too with a penetration reminiscent of Alexander Whyte or Oswald Chambers. He gives us a profoundly insightful analysis of the causes of our sinful wrongdoing, why it is we hypocritically contradict in behavior the norms and ideals to which we sincerely subscribe on a cognitive level. He analyzes as well the external factors that conspire with our own propensities to warp and wreck our lives. But he refuses to minimize in the least our own responsibility for sinful failure.

He does far more, however, than engage in such skillful analysis. He shares the story of a Spirit-guided restorative process, the emotional anguish of confession and repentance by which a broken world can be rebuilt.

Thus this book, born out of indescribable travail, is a message needed by every Christian (and there are really no exceptions) who, only imperfectly sanctified, battles with that unholy trinity of the world, the flesh, and the devil. A powerful testimony to our Lord Jesus as not only Redeemer of sinners but likewise Rebuilder of broken worlds, it is a remarkable twentieth-century testimony to the central New Testament truth that where sin abounds, God's grace superabounds.

Vernon Grounds
Denver Seminary

Introduction

BOTTOM LINE: *"Think of me as a fellow-patient in the same hospital who, having been admitted a little earlier, could give some advice."*

When a much younger man, I had the opportunity to compete as a runner on the track and the cross-country course. Now, it has been decades since I last heard the starter's pistol and sprang away from the line and (with hope) toward the victory tape.

But a love for the sport of running has never left me, even though I am now merely a powerwalker. That's a major reason why I was caught up with the drama of two races I saw in recent years.

The first was a cinematic reenactment of a competition held more than sixty years ago. Eric Liddell, the subject of the film *Chariots of Fire*, was in a pack of runners and breaking for the lead. Suddenly he was thrown off balance, and he crashed heavily to the infield grass. The camera lens zoomed in on him as he lifted his head to see the other athletes pulling away, never looking behind.

The moment on the infield grass only lasted for a second or two, but from my perspective as I watched the film, it seemed as if it lasted for many minutes. Would he get up again? And if he did, could he even finish the race?

He got up! And the man began to run. The movie audience of which I was a part spontaneously cheered as Liddell assumed his famous awkward profile and tore after the now distant pack of competitors. The result? He won, going away.

The other race I often think about happened only a few years ago. Two world-class female athletes were competing in the Los Angeles Olympics. Millions of people around the

363

world were fascinated by their rivalry and were tuned in when they and a host of other runners left their marks. Shoulder to shoulder the two ran together through the first one thousand meters. It was clear they were measuring one another and preparing for the strategic moment when each would try to break for the lead. And then suddenly, so quickly that the slow-motion replay cameras never fully showed what happened, one of them was on the infield grass just as Liddell had been sixty years before.

But this time was different: the runner on the infield grass did not get up. Just like in the movie, the camera zoomed in on a face etched with pain, rage, and instant defeat as the pack of runners pulled away. Could she have gotten up, fought off the pain and the disheartening blow to her psychological edge and reentered the competition? I don't know. Perhaps she does not really know either. To her credit, there came another season when she went back to the track and proved that she was best in her class.

The figures of those two runners lying on the infield grass are drilled deep in my mind. They are visual symbols to me of what happens in the "race of life" when men and women crash either because they have made a terrible choice or set of choices or because they are jostled or upset by what someone else has done.

Those who have fallen to the infield grass in life also have a decision to make that is similar to the one those two runners had to make. Will they get up again? Or will they stay on the grass and pity themselves?

I have a name for men and women in that decision-making situation. I call them the broken-world people, for that is exactly what has happened to them. After years of dreaming, preparing, conditioning, and fighting their way to a particular point, they have (usually by their own initiative) fallen. This "world" they have constructed is suddenly shattered. And the only questions left are versions of the runners' question: Will they get up again? Will they rebuild their broken worlds?

I've come to a high point of sensitivity about broken-world people, for I am a part of those who look back into their personal history and recall with strong regret an act or a series of acts that have resulted in great distress for themselves and many others. And what is worse is the fact that such performances are a terrible offense to God.

What I have called a connection of broken-world people is not a formal or necessarily visible body of men and women. I'm simply highlighting a mass of people who live with a certain kind of suffering. Not the suffering that comes through bereavement, an injustice, a persecution, a painful illness, or poverty. These people suffer from self-inflicted wounds: mistakes, errors, bad choices. Another word might be *misbehavior*. The hardest but most descriptive word for such suffering-inducing actions is *sin*.

When God formed a nation later to be called Israel, one of the first things He dealt with through Moses, their leader, was the matter of behavior. There were ten laws, inviolable, nonnegotiable principles, which were designed to identify human performance that honored God and human performance that dishonored or offended Him and the community. What I call misbehavior, or what the Bible calls sin, flows from those laws and their derivatives.

In the majority of cases, then and now, when sin occurs, there are painful results. They can come directly from the hand of God. That was the case in numerous instances in the Bible: people suddenly struck down in a way that made it clear that the judgment was of divine origin. In other situations, the consequences for misbehavior are facilitated through other people: an enemy's invasion against a misbehaving nation, the justice meted out to a person or family by community leadership, or the pronouncement of consequence upon an errant king or a carnal church by a prophet or an apostle.

Many times, the consequences simply come through the resulting events that flow from misbehavior. God's laws must be obeyed because they come from Him and because, in the scheme of life, they make sense. When they are violated, they usually result in nonsense: people hurting one another, taking from one another, slandering one another, even killing one another. And out of all that flow pain, grief, anger, bitterness, and vengeance.

Misbehavior usually results in bad consequences rather quickly, but some people seem to get away with everything. It's as if they go through life unaware that they are, as we sometimes put it, "getting away with murder." They are unaccountable to anyone or anything as far as we can see.

In Psalm 73, the writer seems confused over this notion that some do get away with murder.

I envied the arrogant
  when I saw the prosperity of the wicked.
They have no struggles;
  their bodies are healthy and strong.
They are free from the burdens common to man;
  they are not plagued by human ills. . . .
From their callous hearts comes iniquity;
  the evil conceits of their minds know no limits.
They scoff, and speak with malice;
  in their arrogance they threaten oppression. . . .
They say, "How can God know?
  Does the Most High have knowledge?" (vv: 3–11).

The psalmist is confused because he doesn't seem to get away with anything. Every misbehavior in his life seems to come under the scrutiny of God, and when he is found out, he pays for it. To him, God's dealings with humankind appear for a moment to be inconsistent, capricious, and maybe (in his finite mind) a bit unfair.

It is true. A study in the Bible of why and how God orchestrates the discipline and punishment of people who misbehave brings inconclusive results. One man murders and goes on to live a full life with God's continuing blessing; another gathers sticks on the Sabbath day and is executed. One king, by his wickedness, brings the judgment of total destruction on his city, but he personally repents and lives to an old age. A soldier hides a cache of war booty under the floor of his tent and is stoned for it.

It all suggests that no one can judge one kind of misbehavior as more serious than another on the basis of the consequences generated. The message? All misbehavior is serious and is sin in God's eyes. And no one knows what consequences are liable to be unleashed when a person steps beyond the bounds of right performance.

None of us would contest the fact that in a large majority of cases there are visible and destructive consequences when people choose sin. On some occasions the consequences result in the total devastation of everything someone has accumulated in the way of reputation, responsibility, or even material security. Integrity, respect, and credibility enter the loss column. Relationships can be dissolved: divorce, severed friendships or working relationships. The right to pursue one's vocation can be denied by professional governing bodies. These are all parts of a personal world that can be shattered into tiny pieces when misbehavior generates its consequences.

When the Chernobyl nuclear power plant in the Soviet Union blew up, not only the managers of the station suffered. Thousands of people who lived in the vicinity lost their homes, and the food supply of millions was affected by the spreading radiation. Just so, the broken-world experience damages not only the misbehaving person; the consequences can threaten scores of innocent people who live with what might be called the fallout. There can be a lot of losses when an ungodly act occurs, and the losses may spread across the network of one's relationships and even endure through several generations.

Of course everyone is a broken-world person in the strictest sense if we believe the Bible's claim that all have sinned or misbehaved. But in this book, I have had to draw an artificial line to identify acts or human performances that have brought about unusual consequences of scandal, major loss, or serious long-term pain. Beyond this, I must leave the definition up to the reader.

I am a broken-world person because a few years ago I betrayed the covenants of my marriage. For the rest of my life I will have to live with the knowledge that I brought deep sorrow to my wife, to my children, and to friends and others who have trusted me for many years.

It is a testimony to the ruggedness of the marriage Gail and I share that our relationship not only survived this damaging body blow but may have taken on extra sinews of strength and vitality in the aftermath as we rebuilt our broken personal worlds. Our rebuilding process began long before the news of my sin and failure was public. It centered on the acts of repentance, forgiveness, grace, and chosen new directions of performance. And it has provided us a costly love that has bonds of steel.

Rebuilding Your Broken World is not an autobiography of misbehavior. It is not a study in self-pity or excuses. *It begins with the premise that individuals who have misbehaved must present themselves before God in openness and acknowledge responsibility and accountability.* NOTHING IN THIS BOOK IS DESIGNED TO MAKE SENSE IF THAT PRINCIPLE IS NOT UNDERSTOOD FIRST.

I don't want to be misunderstood as I write about the sad dynamics of misbehavior. When I talk about some of the circumstances in which a person is more likely to misbehave, I don't want the reader to think I'm blaming the circumstances. But if, as C. S. Lewis says, I can offer a little bit of advice about what goes on in the hospital, then it will be necessary to muse upon the larger context that so often seems to surround the sinful choices people make.

This has been the hardest book I've ever written. It seemed at times as if there were an evil power that resisted any effort to write about restorative grace. And if that indeed was the case, then I must assume that some words here, words of comfort and words of grace, may be useful and gracious for others.

I've written it because I've become conscious of that connection of broken-world people out there. Many of them have written to me; some have called on the telephone if they could find my number; and a few others have visited. My perception is that broken-world people exist in large numbers, and they ask similar questions over and over again. Can my world ever be rebuilt? Do I have any value? Can I be useful again? Is there life after misbehavior?

My answer is yes. That is what grace is all about. A marvelous, forgiving, healing grace says that all things can be new. *And I would like to talk about the grace I have been given by God and by many others.*

As a child, I once knocked over a lamp that was precious to my parents. Its ceramic shaft cracked on one side when it hit the floor. Because I was alone in the room at the time, I was able to place it back on the table and turn the lamp so that the crack was not visible. It remained that way for days, and every morning I would wake up in fear that this was the day the crack would be discovered and I would face a parent's ire.

I froze every time my mother or father went near the lamp. I pictured the reactions in that upcoming moment when the inevitable discovery would occur. The longer the confrontation was delayed, the worse the consequences promised to be in my mind.

Then it came: the day my mother dusted the lamp and found the crack. "Did you do this?" she asked. I could only answer yes and brace myself, telling her what had happened.

But Mother never said a word. She took it to the kitchen, glued the pieces so that they once more fit tightly together, and within a few hours returned the lamp to the table. The crack was always there, but the lamp was rebuilt. And it served its purpose for years.

Broken worlds may always have cracks to remind us of the past; that's reality. But sometimes the grace of God is like the glue my mother used on her lamp. The bonded edges can become stronger than the original surface.

This book includes some of the bottom lines that have become important to me during this rebuilding process. I share them for the broken-world connection out there: the men and women whose cracked lamps have yet to be discovered or who are living in the aftermath of the discovery. I want them to know what I've experienced through the love and affection of lots of godly people: BROKEN WORLDS CAN BE REBUILT.

Perhaps I should have begun this introduction with words that may be fairly familiar to anyone who has been a part of Alcoholics Anonymous. I am Gordon, and I am a broken-world person. The great AA tradition says that anyone who speaks at a meeting of alcoholics will usually begin by saying, "I am G———, and I am an alcoholic. I took my last drink on. . . ." It makes a lot of sense to me that we ought to introduce ourselves in a similar way in the Christian community: "I am Gordon, and I am a sinner." That is our primary affinity when we gather before Jesus. Such a declaration doesn't make us sound very attractive, but then we aren't . . . until we get to the Cross. That's when wonderful things happen, and broken worlds start to be rebuilt.

There are probably few runners who haven't fallen to the infield grass at one time or another. And most of them have their stories of those agonizing moments, stories of the inside battle: to quit the race and head for the locker room or to get up again. This is a book written by one fallen runner in the race who is determined to get off the grass and get back into the race of life.

No one has helped me more in the writing of this book than my faithful partner in twenty-seven years of marriage, Gail. We have discussed every paragraph, prayed over every chapter, and combed the manuscript for any evidence of self-pity or excuse making. What fellowship we have had in its writing! I dearly love and admire her. She is more than a friend.

Beyond Gail is the encouragement of our children, my brother, our parents, the elders and senior pastor of Grace Chapel in Lexington, Massachusetts, and the men to whom, along with Gail, this book is dedicated: THE ANGELS, the incredible team of godly men who long ago surrounded Gail and me and determined that here was one broken world that was going to be rebuilt. Finally, for many years Victor Oliver has been my friend and my publisher. He helped make me an author, and I will never forget that. I owe all of these my life.

Gordon MacDonald
Canterbury, New Hampshire
May 1988

PART I
THE TRAGIC REALITY OF BROKEN WORLDS

1

Broken Worlds

BOTTOM LINE #1: *Broken worlds are not uncommon; they can happen to any of us. And if they do, we may not be able to control the damage. Don't let anyone tell you differently.*

Some people love disaster movies. I do not! But I am aware of such things because I've seen brief portions of a few on late night television when I couldn't sleep. I suspect that they tend to play upon a common fear: the threat of massive destruction of something we normally think to be indestructible. So there are movies about large ocean liners sinking, huge cities disintegrating in earthquakes, and entire nations suddenly being overrun by gigantic insects or prehistoric reptiles.

A science fiction version of this disaster theme features an object from outer space, a gigantic meteor or star, which is discovered as it travels along a collision path toward our planet. If the course of the threatening celestial visitor is not altered, the earth and all of its life-forms will be vaporized. Thus, the mission of the people in the grade-B movie is to find a way to prevent that from happening.

Another version of the disaster theme focuses on a fiendish, gangsterlike character who is bent on holding the world's population hostage to his threat to blow up the earth with a hidden explosive device. Only the villain knows where this megabomb is concealed and how it works. Usually, the movie's hero (or heroes) locates and disarms the weapon just before it can be triggered. A few of these films go a long way, and one is more amused than frightened as the plot unfolds and winds down to its predictable conclusion: everything turns out all right.

But, remember, these are old movies, the kinds that come to pleasant conclusions. I never remember any of them going so far as to permit the meteor or the villain to finish the job and smash the earth to pieces. But then I'm not a movie buff, as they say, and I can't be sure. I suspect that a modern disaster movie might end in a high-tech catastrophe designed to please an audience hungry for bizarre thrills.

As I said, disaster films do nothing for me. But I do see some of them as metaphors of life. They are visual symbols of what happens when our personal worlds are suddenly threatened and subsequently smashed into pieces, broken by the meteoric force of events that crash in upon us from beyond ourselves or broken by bomblike forces that come from deep within ourselves.

Out of these cinematic metaphors I first conceived the phrase *broken world* as an apt way to describe what happens when someone sustains a major blow in life that is either self-inflicted or the result of someone else's unfortunate or treacherous performance. I'm thinking of disasters in the inner spirit, to the mind, to the body, to relationships, to reputation, or to personal usefulness.

We usually use the word *world* to describe the earth and all of its ecosystems. But I have found it a helpful word when referring to the context of a person's being. *World* can convey the notion of a complex personal system of life and relationship, of ownership, of energy, of capability, of feeling, of pain and pleasure, of commitments and choices.

A rough guess would be that over five billion of these individual worlds (or micro-worlds) are alive and scrambling for space on the earth. Over five billion! And like the proportions of a typical iceberg, one-seventh of each personal world (the public world) is visible to others, and six-sevenths of each one (the private world) is invisible to most everyone but God.

The public sector of our worlds extends as far as our senses can take us, perhaps even to the edges of the universe if we can see that far. In this public part we intersect with other human beings and with the stuff of creation. And if we are interested and attentive, we may pick up the voice of God the Creator as He reveals something of Himself in all that He has made.

Then there is the private sector of our worlds. Beneath the surface of our skin, an inner space may be just as expansive in a spiritual dimension as the universe is in a physical dimension. In our private worlds, God, our Creator, is most likely to whisper in the gentle stirrings of conviction, guidance, and the experiences of grace. But also in our private worlds is the grim reality of darker, shadowy forces that we identify with the word *evil or sinfulness*. Not many people like to talk about this dimension of our inner selves, and our very ignorance or neglect of it may portend our vulnerability to brokenness. If God whispers, evil often shouts, and personal worlds break when that shouting gets our attention.

If you're a people-person as I am, you like to know something about the public and private worlds of the people around you. And that's pursued primarily by asking questions. "How is your world today?" I sometimes ask to get someone to share with me how he is feeling. And if I want to go beyond the superficial level of most conversations and find out what motivates or captivates a person, I might begin by inquiring, "What are the top two or three most important themes in your world?"

More than a few people have responded by saying, "No one has ever asked me that before." But questions of that nature usually give individuals an opportunity to range far and wide with answers and observations that fit their current mood and sort out their serious priorities. They may describe how they presently perceive events and circumstances, and in answer to the second question, they may share something that is significant to them but hardly ever gets the attention of others.

If you get into the habit of asking such personal-world-oriented questions, you will soon discover, as I have, that the worlds of people cannot be described only as part public and part private. More than a few of them will be broken, badly broken. Personal worlds are in many cases remarkably fragile, and they can shatter under stress much like an elegant goblet explodes under a barrage of powerful sound waves. I call people who are hurt like that the *broken-world people*.

The television camera zooms in on broken-world people on

virtually every news broadcast. Personal worlds are broken in terrorist activities, in famines, in massive airline or train crashes, or in the horror of physical illnesses such as AIDS. Worlds can be ripped apart by the cruelties of rape, street muggings, wanton murders by drug-crazed or war-stressed gunmen, alcohol-related accidents, or missiles loaded with explosives or nerve gas. The list of ways to break up worlds is endless; the suffering is beyond description. And when such broken-world people survive, they are usually marked by lifelong trauma.

Homes on every city block, in every suburban neighborhood, and in every rural community are overshadowed by broken-world scenes. Family breakups are devastating to those making the decision to terminate the marriage as well as to the children and others in the extended family who must live with the long-term side effects. Firings and layoffs from careers and jobs are as much the fault of politics, economic downturns, and poor management as of incompetency or negligence. Personal worlds are broken without warning when health fails, poor decisions are made, or an accident happens. And one by one we discover that broken worlds do not just happen to someone else; they can happen to us.

Another, more specific kind of broken-world person is the one who makes a terrible choice and deviates from standards set by God, by himself, or by the system in which he lives. More often than not, he reaps the consequence of the choice. His world breaks apart, and maybe the worlds of a few of those around him break up too as they share in the consequence. Such an individual who brings his world to brokenness through personal error, weakness, or failure is my primary concern in this book.

If you are a student of American baseball, you'll remember the name of Ralph Branka, once an exceptional pitcher for the former Brooklyn Dodgers. Some will be aware that he pitched many winning seasons for the Dodgers; but most will only remember, if they're old enough, the autumn afternoon in 1951 when Branka pitched to Bobby Thompson of the New York Giants in the last inning of a National League championship game. The Dodgers were ahead at the time by a score of 5-3, and Branka's assignment was to make sure that Bobby Thompson did nothing to change it. But Thompson did.

Unfortunately for Branka, Thompson hit his pitch far enough into the outfield grandstands to score three runs and win the championship for the Giants. You could say that Ralph Branka's world (or at least part of it) blew up that day with one pitch. He had to stand there on the pitcher's mound and watch the ball fly out of the park while Bobby Thompson jogged around the bases to a triumphant reception at home plate.

Branka was never permitted to forget that moment. From that time forward, people never asked him about his long career as a successful athlete; they wished to hear only about the day he threw one bad pitch. He was nailed to that event.

That's just baseball, an American game, someone says. Hard for those of us who are not professional athletes to take Ralph Branka's personal disaster seriously. But not hard if you're a professional athlete. Then you understand. Pitching was the man's job, the source of his income, the basis of his public reputation. And it all seemed to disintegrate with the crack of a baseball bat.

Ralph Branka's broken-world moment was very public. Most broken-world experiences are less conspicuous, and they may occur over a longer period of time. But anyone's broken-world moment is just as real and just as painful as Branka's must have been. Sudden or gradual, when one's world has been broken, the question of hope usually arises. Is there a tomorrow? Will there be another chance? Is the damage permanent? Do new starts exist? *Can this broken world ever be rebuilt?*

There are some myths about broken worlds. Dangerous myths, I think, because they can disarm us, making us less vigilant on the one hand and less prepared on the other when worlds do break.

BROKEN-WORLD MYTH #1

One myth suggests that *broken worlds are the exception, not the rule.* They are merely anomalies in life, and the less we think about them the better. Broken worlds never happen to good people; only phonies, rebels, and those less than smart really go through broken-world moments. Furthermore, to spend too much time brooding on the possibility of broken-world experiences is to invite the event. It's better to think only happy, positive thoughts.

BROKEN-WORLD MYTH #2

A second myth presumes that a *broken-world experience can never happen to me*. This is a version of the typically human notion that we can live above all the odds, take all the risks, and avoid all the consequences. One senses this myth working when people mourn the death or the misfortune of a good person. "Why her?" they say. "She had everything going for her. Why not some loser, some evil person? Why do these things happen to the best people?"

BROKEN-WORLD MYTH #3

A third myth plays off the second. It is built on the assumption that *if and when my world does break, I can more than handle the results*. This myth is expressed in such "reasoning" as: I'm above the consequences; I have enough energy, resources, influence, and good performance stored up to reduce, if not neutralize, any bad effects; in fact, God owes me something.

We need to refute these myths by espousing some simple principles. If we do not, we are liable to find ourselves caught in some world-breaking ambushes from which we may not escape.

To the first myth (broken worlds are anomalies in life), one must say, *Know history*. To the second myth (it can't or won't happen to me), one must say, *Know thyself*. And to the third (I can handle anything that comes in my direction), one must say, *Know God's laws*.

KNOWING HISTORY

Far more of us live under the presumption of the first myth than we realize. Eschewing the gloom-and-doom prophets and reminding ourselves that the world and great success in general are inherited by those who think positively and act optimistically, we plan our futures and marshal our resources along the lines of what the planner calls "best-case scenarios." We are tempted to leave no room for the possibility of less than "best case."

One of the first jokes of the age of automation describes a planeload of people soon after takeoff. A voice comes on the plane's intercom, "Good afternoon, ladies and gentlemen. Welcome aboard. We are climbing to our planned cruising altitude of 39,000 feet. All of the plane's systems are working perfectly, and we expect to land at our destination on time. This is a fully automated plane. There is no pilot or copilot. Everything is guided and monitored by a computer. We want you to sit back, relax, and enjoy the flight. Nothing can go wrong . . . can go wrong . . . can go wrong. . . ."

For many years I served as a pastor, and one of my responsibilities was to officiate at weddings. There were always two moments as I worked with young bridal couples when I felt a brief bit of despair. One came during the process of premarital counseling. I almost never met a couple who wished to talk about the potential bumps and bruises of merging two lives into a permanent relationship. They were far too anxious to discuss plans for the wedding and the honeymoon.

Rarely was I asked in such conversations, what are the storm warnings for a destructive conflict? Or where are we likely to face temptations and seductions that might cause a drift from our commitments to God or to each other? I can hear someone grimacing, amused that I would seek such grim reality in the midst of youthful joy. Nevertheless, I stick to my original observation that it is not the nature of most of us to ponder the possibility of world-breaking events in our relationships.

A second moment of concern often arose during the ceremony itself as I laid my hands on the kneeling couple and prayed over them. Usually, the pastoral prayer was followed by a solo while the couple remained kneeling. Sometimes I would look down during this solo and note the bride and groom holding hands and snatching glances at each other. And my mind would turn to the morbid statistics that suggested hard times ahead, and I would wonder, "old man" that I was, whether they were ready, whether they had even thought of the potential of broken-world experiences.

The young person doesn't ponder the increased odds of physical or psychic danger when fooling around with alcohol or drugs. The middle-ager is most likely not thinking of the long-range implications of over-eating. Nor is the fast-track executive prone to plan for the day of a company downturn and the resultant firing. Each is liable to assume the best-case-scenario for all of life's events, rarely, if ever, contemplating the likelihood of struggle.

The Bible covers a period of measured history of several thousand years. From the first pages to the last, we are given insight into the noble behavior and the ignoble misbehavior of people from scores of generations, cultures, and classes. We are given family lines to study, intimate (no-holds-barred) biographies to poke into, and analyses of leaders, business people, and military personnel to evaluate. After reading through it all, we will probably be on fairly safe ground when we reach some conclusions about what life brings to human beings then and now in terms of possibility, success, and pain.

One of my conclusions based on the reading I've done is simple: *almost everyone in the Bible had a broken-world experience.* Virtually no one was exempt. In fact, it's tempting to reverse the myth that broken-world experiences are anomalous and suggest that everyone then and now will have a broken-world experience sooner or later. It may not always be the result of one's own performance; it can be just as likely that one has to live with the consequences of someone else's choices.

Furthermore, the Bible seems to suggest through the stories of various men and women that broken-world experiences are usually the turnaround moments ushering people into greater and more powerful performances of character, courage, and achievement. One by one they seem to illustrate exactly what a football coach was trying to express when he said of his team, "We learn almost nothing in victory; but we learn much in defeat."

Moses is connected, educated, and talented, but he amounts to little that means anything to God until his world has been broken and rebuilt, the work commenced in the desert and continued at the site of a burning bush.

Zechariah and Elizabeth, parents of John the Baptizer, seem to play no significant role in God's involvement with His people until they pass through a broken-world experience that drives them to a breaking point through the stress of apparent sterility and/or barrenness. Zechariah's world is further broken when he is struck speechless and forced to live in silence for the extent of Elizabeth's pregnancy. The young man they produced, however, went on to be, in the words of Jesus, the greatest of the prophets.

Saul of Tarsus (later to be St. Paul) is only one more fiery
Jew in his generation until his pompous, religiously structured world is shattered on the road to Damascus, and he
becomes silent and submissive before Christ.

Tell Moses, Zechariah and Elizabeth, and St. Paul that the
broken-world experience is an addendum, an add-on, to life.
Tell them that pressure, failure, and embarrassment are not
part of the course of human development and maturation.
They simply won't agree. They will say that sorrow, pain,
and stress are the "graduate school" of godly character and
capacity if people are willing to enroll. The problem, they
may suggest, is that this school has too many no-shows and
dropouts.

"Are you telling me," a woman asks in a group conversation, "that the things I desire most in terms of being a mature person can be acquired only through some form of
suffering? I don't want to believe that."

I'm not about to offer a quick and easy yes to her question,
but I know in my heart that the vast majority of people down
through history who acquired or achieved the traits of character and endurance that she seeks passed through a broken-
world experience to obtain them. I'm not sure I like it any
more than she does, but when one knows their history, a
startling reality appears. In pain, failure, and brokenness,
God does His finest work in the lives of people.

George Matheson reflected this reality when he wrote:

> There are songs which can only be learned in the valley. No art
> can teach them; no rules of voice can make them perfectly sung.
> Their music is in the heart. They are songs of memory, of per-
> sonal experience. They bring out their burden from the shadow
> of the past; they mount on the wings of yesterday. . . .
>
> The father is training thee for the part the angels cannot sing;
> and the school is sorrow. I have heard many say that He sends
> sorrow to prove thee; may He send sorrow to educate thee, to
> train thee for the choir invisible. (*Streams in the Desert*)

In the 1680s John Bunyan wrote one of the world's great
classics, *Pilgrim's Progress*, while he was in jail (talk about a
broken-world experience), and one safely assumes that this
book would not have been written in any other place. Earlier
in his Christian life, Bunyan passed through a broken world

of another kind—several years of deep, painful searching for a solid relationship with God. It was not that God couldn't be found; rather, it was that Bunyan had a lot of things to work through in his private world.

In his spiritual autobiography, *Grace Abounding*, Bunyan made no attempt to hide the fact that his younger years were characterized by attitudes and performances that can be labeled only as rank evil. And the consequences in his spirit broke his world apart. But Bunyan knew that those broken-world experiences were the foreground for his ultimate commitment to Christ. And he observed this when he wrote:

> I never saw those heights and depths in grace, and love, and mercy, as I saw after this temptation: great sins draw out great grace; and where guilt is most terrible and fierce, there the mercy of God in Christ, when showed to the soul, appears most high and mighty.

Know history! Its startling lesson is that the great qualities of life usually come only when the pain has begun, pain we may bring upon ourselves or pain brought by events and circumstances over which we have no control. When we fight the brokenness, or when we curse it as having no part of our existence, we forfeit the opportunity for quality growth.

KNOWING YOURSELF

The second myth says, *It can't happen to me.* And the challenge ought to be, *Know yourself.* When we utter this myth silently or aloud, we become guilty of a subtle lie.

Simon Peter, to whom I will frequently refer in this book, is a perfect model of this myth holder. On the night of the betrayal of Christ, Simon said, "Lord, I am ready to go with You to prison and to death."

Jesus replied, "I tell you, Peter, before the rooster crows today, you will deny three times that you know Me" (see John 13:31–38).

I have often meditated on this interchange of opinions between Simon Peter and Jesus. Simon simply didn't know himself. Jesus knew Simon better than Simon did. That simple little matter about self-knowledge (or the lack of it) ought to be a cause for major thinking.

How should Jesus have handled Simon that night? Should He have practiced some sort of blind, tell-him-what-he-wants-to-hear affirmation on Simon that night? Should He have said, "Simon, I love your courage, your intention. Keep thinking that way, friend, and you'll make it through just fine"?

Apparently, Jesus didn't think so. He did two things that many of us wouldn't have considered doing. First, He countered Simon's naivete with candor: Simon, you're going to make some major errors tonight; not just once, but several times. How could Simon have missed the pointedness of Jesus' warning? How could he have been so blind to his own weaknesses? His performance record on other stressful occasions was unquestionably poor. Hadn't he learned his lesson yet? No! And it would take a world-breaking experience of major proportions—humiliating, devastating, complete—to develop the kind of character Christ wanted from him.

Second, Jesus let the man fail. He let him pull a sword in the garden after he'd been taught for two years that you don't pull swords when you follow the Lord. He let him run away into the darkness without reminding him of his promise to stand firm. And He let him make a fool of himself as he denied three times an association with Christ, each time more profuse and profane in his denials. Then He let him cry bitterly in the night and sweat out the situation for a while before He restored him. You have to conclude that Jesus thought the broken-world experience was absolutely necessary to the formation of Simon Peter the apostle.

A soccer coach senses that his goalie isn't handling himself well during pregame warm-ups. And since he's not paid to lose games, he sets the goalie on the bench and substitutes another player. But Jesus didn't put Simon Peter on the bench that night. He permitted the broken-world experience because, unlike the coach, Jesus' objective is to build men and women, not simply to win games. And so when the key moments came, Jesus said to Peter and the others, "Rise, let's go forward," and they did: right into a broken world. I doubt if Peter was ever fully caught off guard again due to a lack of self-knowledge.

Almost every personal defeat begins with our failure to

know ourselves, to have a clear view of our capabilities (negative and positive), our propensities, our weak sides. Furthermore, in the larger sense, some of our broken-world experiences result from our failure to estimate the performance capabilities of others. Although Jesus loved every person with whom He came in contact, it is also clearly stated that He "would not entrust himself to them" because "he knew all men" (John 2:24).

This reasoning could lead, of course, to the notion that we should invite pain or defeat, even rejoice in it, if we wish to achieve the character level we seek. And that is a false objective. Rather, we should realize that broken-world experiences are most likely to happen to all of us sooner or later, probably sooner to those who pretend they are infallible or untouchable.

This reasoning could lead to a patent mistrust of others, and that is not the point, either. Jesus wasn't a suspicious person. But He was realistic, and He understood that every man or woman regularly faces moments when failure is a strong possibility. However, He seemed to be less concerned about the failure and more concerned about the ability to learn from the failure and receive the grace that is offered when one is properly humbled.

Oswald Chambers frequently pressed his readers on the matter of self-knowledge. Not always a pleasing or simple exercise, he admitted. But a necessary one. Not to take into account and be prepared for the exposure of our weak sides was to invite a broken-world experience sooner or later.

> Always beware of a friendship, or of a religion, *or of a personal estimate of things* that does not reconcile itself to the fact of sin; that is the way all the disasters in human friendships and in human loves begin, and where the compromises start. Jesus Christ never trusted human nature, but He was never cynical, He trusted absolutely what He could do for human nature. (*The Place of Help*, emphasis mine)

Broken-world experiences happen to almost all of us. We need to major in knowing ourselves to have fairly accurate estimates of where they are likely to happen and to know how we will respond both preventatively and remedially.

Knowing God's Laws

The final myth is, *I can handle anything that comes in my direction*. And its challenge is, *Know God's laws*.

This myth spotlights a foolish optimism. It builds upon the assumption that when the time comes, we can bargain with God, manipulate circumstances and, if necessary, tough it out.

Ask Lot, the nephew of Abraham, about such optimism. If you could, he might relate his calculation of the risks when he moved his family toward the fertile plain of Sodom, toward the attractive city of Sodom itself, toward the society in that city, toward the values and perspectives pervading its marketplace.

Lot had spent a considerable amount of time with his uncle and had thrived spiritually and materially. When he stepped out from Abraham's family umbrella, he obviously took with him a high degree of bravado: the world was his oyster; there were pearls to be found.

But the man lost everything when his world broke. The brotherhood of the community, the respect of his sons-in-law, his material assets, his wife, his good life. Smashed! And there was no damage control throughout the process.

Lot reminds me of a certain Wall Street personality who one day is participating in the purchase and sale of junk bonds, who manages leveraged buyouts of reputable companies, who amasses millions of seemingly easily gained dollars. And then one day we see this same man grimly surrendering to U.S. marshals to begin a five- to ten-year prison term and agreeing with the courts and the government never to work in the financial world again.

Stanley Jones was fond of telling audiences, you can make your own choices; you cannot control the consequences of those choices. Lot learned that principle the hard way.

I know I have also. Too many of us have experienced our own broken-world moments, and even more of us have witnessed the broken worlds of those we love. One major experience teaches us something we usually never forget: the consequences are rarely capable of being controlled. They have an energy of their own, and no one—except God— knows where the effects of a broken world are likely to stop.

Our Lord was never seduced by these three myths. His life patterns strongly declare that He understood that broken-world experiences are a part of life. It's what we do about them that counts. He knew history. And His personal awareness of pain and suffering assure us that He came to our world knowing that He was not exempt from the realities facing every person. He knew Himself and others. And He accepted the consequences of a broken world: the consequences of other people's anger and hatred, the consequences that were poured out upon Him when He took upon Himself the sins of the world. He knew that God the Father had to pour out upon Him the consequences of the evil of humankind. To live genuinely as a Christian means to live on the truthful side of these myths and not be deceived by them.

When Ralph Branka went to the pitcher's mound on that autumn afternoon almost forty years ago, he may have dared to assume that he was only a few pitches away from athletic stardom. Throw hard; bear down; keep your emotion under control. And then that one pitch. And his world broke.

Our planet is rife with the sad stories of men and women who have been hit by something like a meteor or an imbedded explosive device. Yesterday's world so bright and vigorous lies today in pieces. What happened?

Perhaps the myths were too blinding and deceptive. Perhaps one didn't know where the meteor was coming from or where the bomb was planted. Perhaps one didn't know how to mount the proper defenses.

Can a world under threat of breaking be defended? Yes, emphatically yes. Has it been done before? Many times. The precedents abound.

But if my personal world breaks, is there still hope? Can that broken world be rebuilt? Again, the answer is yes. God has put all the pieces in place, and the process for rebuilding has been time-tested and proven authentic.

2

A Broken-World Sampler

BOTTOM LINE #2: *The pain of a broken-world experience is universal; the ancients knew it as well as any of us.*

I have had many enjoyable occasions visiting the personal worlds of people who were at the peak of their success. I've been in the locker room of an acclaimed professional athlete; I've ridden along in a corporate jet with a company CEO; and I've sat at the table with a notable person as everyone stared with admiration at him and then with consternation at me wondering who in the world I was. All in all, those occasions are associated with pleasant memories.

But I've had many more opportunities to enter the personal worlds of people who were in the pit of despair. People hurt and grieved because they were left or cheated or badly defeated in a contest of wills. People grieving over the death of a loved one. People whose life savings were obliterated because of a downturn in a business or market.

I've seen worlds broken because of seemingly random events that offered no satisfactory explanation or answer to the question *why*. I remember standing with a farmer as he watched a vicious hailstorm wipe out an entire season's wheat crop, and as a result his annual income, while his neighbor's field just a few yards across the section road remained untouched. Why? He didn't know, and I certainly didn't. If there was an answer, it lay in the physical interactions of the elements above. And that didn't help much.

But the most common broken world—the primary one I've chosen to write about—is the world that shatters because someone has made a series of bad choices, misbehaved, and now has to live with what he or she has done. No one else to blame; no handy excuses; no injustices to identify.

Sometimes the choices of the broken-world person are premeditated in the darkness of the heart; sometimes the choices seem impulsive and utterly absurd. But the results can be (and usually are) loss of integrity and credibility, humiliation, grief, regret, remorse, fear, and more than a little self-dislike.

And what of those who live with the side effects of broken-world choices? The betrayed spouse? The cheated business partner? The exploited friend? The deceived employer? They often live with a pain they can hardly describe, and they ask hard questions about their rights and their responsibilities. In the final analysis, few broken worlds touch only one life. Like a hand grenade, the effects of one person's terrible choices explode outward to wound many others. For a genuinely sorrowful broken-world person, this unintended wounding of others often brings untold grief

What happens when personal worlds explode, when circumstances get out of control and all hopes and expectations lie in pieces? How do broken-world people feel? What do they think about? And what are their temptations in terms of defending or excusing themselves?

These are hard questions to pin down with adequate answers. We can take only a few sample runs at them and get a general idea of how people in the past acted when their worlds broke because of misbehavior. The Bible abounds with examples of men and women whose worlds crashed from self-inflicted causes, and their responses range within great extremes.

On the dark side of those extremes is the case study of Cain. Jealous of his brother, Cain killed him, denying continually that he was answerable for his attitudes and actions. As far as we know, he never brooded on the warnings that could have helped him avoid the tragedies that occurred. He appears to have ended up living a thoroughly wasted life. Cain represents the rigidity, the hardness of inner being, that can appear when the heat is on and the consequences set in. Cain is not alone when it comes to those who will not accept accountability for their actions.

On the brighter side of the extremes, a woman, Mary Magdalene, came through her broken-world experience permitting the moment to become the beginning of an entirely new life. She was one of numerous New Testament characters who pursued lives of gross immorality and who virtually personified the energy of evil itself. She was obviously living in a kind of human bondage with no hope. No one had to tell her that her way of living was taking her downhill fast, that changes had to be made, or there would be no way back. When Jesus offered the opportunity of liberation to her, she accepted what was given and rebuilt her broken world into something beautiful.

So there is Cain: stiff-necked and unrelenting. And there is Mary: open, unfisted, and ready to submit. All of us have seen samples, perhaps in ourselves as well as in others.

There is nothing to envy in the experience of someone whose world is in the process of breaking up. It is similar to what happens when an airplane is purposely flown into the center of a hurricane for research purposes: tossed and flung about as circumstances and consequences have their way. We are talking of a person who loses much of the control over his life that he has formerly enjoyed.

Initially, the broken-world experience is usually private and very personal. It may include a period of resistance to the truth, shocked disbelief that anything like what has happened could have occurred, and anger at the possible consequences and anyone who might make sure they happen. We call this living in denial. He may attempt to blame others and interpret events so that he is able to see himself in the most charitable light. He may do this to avoid the awful feelings of guilt and self-recrimination. But if this thinking continues, it will lead to nothing good, certainly no hope of a broken world that is capable of being rebuilt.

The more healthy but nevertheless very painful part of this secretive phase occurs when the broken-world person faces facts: a self-realization of what has actually happened and his responsibility for it. There can be times of churning fear and feelings of cheapness, self-dislike, and quiet turmoil when topics too close to his experience are raised in conversation. It can be a time of depression; a period in which there is an overwhelming desire to escape, even hope that somehow life would come to a sudden end in an accident or a physical illness. He may work harder than ever in an attempt to outrun the anguished thoughts or to try to atone—as if he could—for what has happened.

These are the terrible, lonely moments for a broken-world person, and many of us know what they are like. Relief comes only when the individual looks heavenward and treats the matter for what it is: a serious offense against God and His standards. Then, in such an acknowledgment, the initial stages of healing and rebuilding are likely to begin.

This may be the time, a second stage of the broken-world experience, when a man or woman then turns to others who might be willing to forgive and provide the comfort necessary for the rebuilding process to begin. A spouse; close, intimate friends; a pastor or counselor. Ultimately, rebuilding broken worlds can never happen alone. It is a team effort, and it has to be accomplished in concert with those who can give grace and affirm progress.

When we purchase something of value that is fragile or delicate, it comes in a carefully designed box and is packed in various forms of Styrofoam to protect it against all but the most crushing blows. A whole industry is dedicated to such packing and protecting. A broken-world person needs the same kind of protection. That is why Paul called for the Corinthians to forgive and also to comfort a broken-world person in their congregation (2 Cor. 2:7).

Naturally, there are some downside risks when misbehavior and its consequences become known. Perhaps someone who cannot forgive wishes to punish or hurt the broken-world person in return. There is the risk that some relationships will never be restored, that silence and antipathy will be the way of the future. Divorce, lawsuits, periodic acts of vengeance, are some grim possibilities. The broken-world person may not be able to do anything about these unfortunate reactions. Apart from confession, expressions of sorrow, and the pledge to change, it is difficult to see what the individual can offer an offended party that will elicit restoration if the other does not wish to give it.

A possible third stage of the broken-world experience is the one anyone would dread because of the magnitude of its humiliation. And that occurs when news of one's misbehavior reaches a larger public. No matter how one might wish these things would never happen, with public knowledge may come serious damage to one's reputation, the loss of credibility, the requirement to relinquish public responsibilities of leadership, and the loss of some friends who find it expedient to withdraw because they are hurt or feel betrayed. Add to all of that the pain of gossip, of people feeling that they can be perfectly free to discuss and analyze the misbehavior in any forum of their choice.

When my sinful act resulted in a personal broken world, Gail and I chose to wrestle with a significant question that one of our pastoral advisors placed before us. The wording went something like this: *will you concentrate on the pain of this broken-world experience and resist it,* OR *will you permit the pain to become an environment in which God can clearly speak to you about matters He deems of ultimate importance? The choice is yours.*

How often Gail and I have walked the woods around Peace Ledge, our New Hampshire home. Here and there are the junctions of trails and what the township calls "Class-six" roads. Each fork reminds me of Robert Frost's famous poem about choices, "The Road Not Taken," part of which reads:

> Two roads diverged in a yellowed wood,
> And sorry I could not travel both
> And be one traveler, long I stood
> And looked down one as far as I could
> To where it bent in the undergrowth;
>
> Then took the other. . . .

That choice, Frost concluded, "has made all the difference."

We were going to have to make a choice. I was the broken-world person living with self-inflicted wounds. Gail was the victim of a broken-world set of choices. Would we fight the pain of the aftermath of my sin, or would we permit the pain to be part of the rebuilding process?

It wasn't a one-time choice. We made it again and again as time passed. A score of ways could be found to bring back the pain. And each time the choice had to be made again. Would we fight the pain or permit it to be the environment in which God speaks? Usually, we chose the latter. And when for a moment we strayed toward the former, something seemed to happen to soon remind us that there was a better way.

During those dark hours I spent large quantities of time scanning the Scriptures. I looked at familiar, biblical biographies in a whole new light. What startled me more than anything else, however, was one insight regarding the great personalities of the Bible. Almost every one of them had experienced a broken-world moment. As I said in the preceding chapter, I could hardly find an exception. Failures, sufferings, oppositions and oppressions, outright sins of great magnitude, sicknesses, rejections, marital and family catastrophes, and grave moments of spiritual crises.

As I studied the record of these broken worlds, I found comfort. Others had gone through my pain; others had experienced the same feelings I knew; others were at one time or another as undependable as I saw myself to be; others had received great grace and healing as I hoped to receive. And, finally, others had gone on to the greatest moments of their service to God. Permit me for a moment to use my imagination and create some conversations cast in contemporary language that might reflect the broken-world thinking of ancient biblical personalities.

THE BROKEN WORLD OF MOSES

Take, for example, the world of Moses. His world broke into pieces for the first time when he was forty years old.

And what a world it was! As an infant, he'd been marvelously delivered from a pogrom of sorts when the Pharaoh of Egypt decided to slaughter all male Hebrew babies. His mother, determined to protect him, had hidden Moses along the banks of the Nile River, placing him under the care of his older sister. The two of them, baby boy and sister, just happened to be at the right place when an Egyptian princess wandered by and became enchanted with the child she saw in the floating basket. Moses was taken to the palace of the very Pharaoh who was trying to kill him and other Hebrews his age. There he grew up apparently enjoying all the privileges and opportunities of a member of the royal family.

Then in his fortieth year he began to be sensitive to the oppression under which his people, the Hebrews, were living. One day when he saw an Egyptian guard mercilessly beating a Hebrew, he took upon himself the role of liberator and sprang to the defense of the victim, killing the guard.

Give Moses an A for caring, for courage, and for the willingness to risk everything that meant security for him as a human being. Give him a much lower grade for acting without thinking. A swell idea soon exploded in his face.

Within days the Hebrews had made it clear that they weren't interested in his sort of leadership and deliverance. Why, I'm not sure. Fear and cowardice, I suppose. They just weren't interested. Suddenly, Moses was a criminal among his own people and among the royal family with whom he'd grown up. He had no recourse but to run. Talk about a broken world.

That's where my imagination takes over as I ponder the kind of conversation that he and Jethro, his future father-in-law, were likely to have had when they met deep in the desert for the first time.

JETHRO. We don't see many men like you out in these parts. Sure you fit here?

MOSES. Probably not, but then again I guess I don't belong anyplace these days. What causes you to say I don't fit here?

JETHRO. It's obvious. All anyone has to do is listen to you talk, and they'll know you didn't grow up in these parts. You're a city man. You've lived the good life.

MOSES. I *was* a city man, you mean.

JETHRO. What made you leave?

MOSES. I tried being a hero.

JETHRO. A hero?

MOSES. I'd had it up to here with the way the Hebrews were being treated by the system. You must know the situation. And one day I reached my limit. I was headed for an appointment, and I came across an Egyptian foreman beating a Hebrew senseless. The Hebrew was defenseless; I thought he was going to get killed.

JETHRO. So you decided to intervene.

MOSES. Yeah. I didn't even stop to think about what I was doing. I tried to stop this guy, and he pushed me away and started in on the Hebrew again.

JETHRO. And you got mad.

MOSES. I was furious! I jumped the Egyptian from behind and got him down and just started swinging. Before I realized what had happened, I'd hit him too hard and he was dead. There was nothing to do except to bury the guy and hope that no one found out.

JETHRO. Didn't you have enough self-control to . . .

MOSES. No, I didn't. But that wasn't the worst of it.

JETHRO. What do you mean?

MOSES. Well, I thought that maybe the Hebrews who knew what I'd done would realize I was on their side and they'd support me. We could have pulled off an exodus out of Egypt or something. I guess I really thought they'd listen to me.

JETHRO. You mean because you'd defended one of them?

MOSES. Yeah. But you can't believe what happened.

JETHRO. Try me.

MOSES. A day or two later I'm out in the same area, and now I see two Hebrews fighting. So I try to step in and put an end to it. You know, I'm sure they'll recognize me and do exactly what I say.

JETHRO. That's reasonable.

MOSES. Do you know what they did? They turned on me! One of them says, "Who in the world made you lord over us? We know what you did with the Egyptian; you going to kill one of us too? Is that the way you solve everyone's problems?" I couldn't believe it. I was speechless.

JETHRO. What did you do?

MOSES. I panicked and ran. I just ran. Until I got to here. I thought those slaves would pick me up and put me on their shoulders and give me a victory parade. And instead they tell me to bug off.

JETHRO. Are you sure?

MOSES. I'm sure. Before long the Egyptians would have been looking for me, and the Hebrews weren't about to take me on as one of theirs. I knew I wouldn't have a friend in the entire country as soon as the word got out. And it was obvious it would get out.

JETHRO. Are you sure that the Hebrews wouldn't protect you?

MOSES. It couldn't have been clearer. They weren't taking any chances. Their game plan was to save their own hides. No risks. And I was a risk; you can be sure of that.

JETHRO. You must have felt about as low as anyone can feel when you headed out of town.

MOSES. Well, I can tell you one thing: there's no way I'm ever going back in that direction again. No one could ever get me near that palace or those Hebrews again. No way!

For forty years Moses lived with the consequences of a broken personal world. He had had good intentions at the age of forty, but everything had gone wrong. Knowing the rest of the story as we do, we are tempted to exonerate him. After all, he may have made a bad mistake then, but he finished his life strongly with many quality contributions. But if we had lived in Moses' time, our judgment would quite likely have been that Moses was a hot-tempered zealot with an uncontrollable character defect.

When the Bible picks him up again at the age of eighty, we get the feeling that Moses wasn't interested in rebuilding his once broken world. He no longer had a dream for liberating his people. The desert may not have been the most hospitable place in the world, but the man had made it his home. And when God suggested that the world of Moses was to be rebuilt starting back in Egypt, Moses was hardly interested in getting burned again.

What's it like to have your world break up? For Moses, it meant being hunted and chased, losing everything that had meant security for the first forty years, forfeiting his access to power, changing vocations dramatically, and living among people who had little respect, if any, for his former reputation and social position. But that broken world was rebuilt, and the new Moses was a man who presently owns a large piece of history. The people who initially rejected him made him a great hero.

THE BROKEN WORLD OF JONAH

Centuries later another man, now quite famous, saw his world fall apart in a rather unique fashion. If Moses ended up deep in a desert when his world broke, Jonah the prophet ended up deep in the sea, and it's likely that he thought he would never see land again. Again, my imagination attempts to penetrate some of Jonah's more difficult moments, wondering how and what he thinks about.

REPORTER. Mr. Jonah? Sir, I'm from the *Jerusalem Post*.

JONAH. How in the world did you guys find me here?

REPORTER. Little bit of luck, really. We got word that you'd gone overboard in the storm last week, and when the search was called off, we printed your obituary. Then someone up here who saw your picture with the obit called and said that he saw you staying at this inn.

JONAH. So everyone down there thinks I'm dead? Well, I suppose I might as well be dead for all that happened.

REPORTER. That's it. We'd really like to get your story on what happened and how you got here. I mean, this is some distance from Joppa. Someone must have brought you up here.

JONAH. Actually, I came by whale.

REPORTER. Right. Say, could you go into that one a bit?

JONAH. Look, years ago I made a commitment to the God of Israel that I'd live in total obedience to His purposes. That I'd never shrink from saying what He put in my heart. That I'd go anyplace, say anything, and do it at any cost.

REPORTER. OK. So what about the whale?

JONAH. That commitment meant a lot of tough days for me. Being a prophet is not a glamorous life.

REPORTER. How does this connect with the whale?

JONAH. I'm coming to that. You've just got to understand that when God said, "Go to Nineveh," I . . .

REPORTER. You said, "Nineveh"?

JONAH. That was my reaction too. Nineveh? I mean, I haven't made it a habit of questioning God before, but I did then. I protested with energy in me that I didn't know I had.

REPORTER. What were you supposed to do in Nineveh?

JONAH. Preach. What does any prophet of the Lord do?

REPORTER. Preach what?

JONAH. Repentance; offer a promise from God that if the city would repent, God would spare it from judgment.

REPORTER. How does that link up with going overboard in a storm? Could you get to the whale?

JONAH. Frankly, I decided that I wasn't going to Nineveh, that God was going to have to find Himself some other prophet dumb enough to go there. And so you could say I resigned from prophethood.

REPORTER. And the storm?

JONAH. Well, you don't really resign from prophethood exactly. You run, and I ran for Joppa and found the ship that was sailing the farthest the soonest.

REPORTER. And it sailed into a storm.

JONAH. In more ways than one. Those guys thought they had a storm going. I had one far larger inside me.

REPORTER. Inside you?

JONAH. You make a choice, a bad choice, like the one I did, and you suffer for it. I walked around in a daze. I was angry with myself. I was full of self-doubt. I was scared. Here I was leaving everything that was important to me, running to a city I'd never seen before. All I knew was that I was angry with God for the trip He was trying to send me on. And I'd dug in my heels and said no.

REPORTER. Did it work?

JONAH. It worked until the storm hit outside too. I was in such denial that I'd gone to sleep down in the ship after it left port. I found that I could sleep almost around the clock. Apparently even through the early part of that dumb storm. Then the captain woke me up and seemed to think that I somehow knew something about that storm. And if I would help the others on top pray, he'd be very appreciative. Of course he was right; I did know something about the storm.

REPORTER. So what did you know?

JONAH. That the storm outside was merely an extension of the storm inside. So I had them throw me overboard.

REPORTER. They threw you overboard?

JONAH. I made them do it. I felt so cheap and worthless. My sin of rebellion and disobedience was hurting other people. They were about to die in a storm that I had created. If I was devastated, what do you think they were as they watched their world breaking up? I had no recourse but to force them to throw me over. The outside storm cleared up for them immediately.

REPORTER. And for you?

JONAH. You could say that the storm lasted for three more days as God let me live inside a whale and think over whether or not I still wanted to live in rebellion. He just crushed my world; that's what He did. And I had to make a big decision. Would I keep on fighting Him or finally realize that His way was the best?

REPORTER. What did you decide?

JONAH. I'm here, aren't I?

REPORTER. What happens next, Mr. Jonah?

JONAH. You see that road over there? It leads toward Nineveh.

THE BROKEN WORLD OF SIMON PETER

As I've already mentioned one of the saddest descriptions of a broken world is that of Simon Peter. I'm thinking of the moment when Peter heard the rooster crow for the third time and realized that it powerfully underscored his denial of association with Jesus. Of that moment of supreme personal failure, Matthew wrote, "He went outside and wept bitterly" (26:75).

Most scholars agree that Matthew got his description of that moment from Peter himself. One can almost hear the dialogue between them as Matthew sought to recapture the hour when Peter so completely caved in.

MATTHEW. How did you feel when you realized that you had blown it so badly?

SIMON PETER. When I heard that rooster, bells went off inside me. Loud bells! I remembered that Jesus had warned me the night before that this was exactly what was going to happen. But who was listening? I'd been so excited and determined that I was going to be a better soldier than anyone else that I simply didn't listen to a word of what He said.

MATTHEW. So you suddenly saw what He'd been trying to tell you? That you were capable of failure?

SIMON PETER. Saw it? Saw it? I couldn't believe it; I was so shocked at my spinelessness, I was speechless. You think you can handle anything, and then the moment comes and you can't do anything right.

MATTHEW. So what did you do? Did it occur to you to go back and try and set the record straight?

SIMON PETER. No. I wish I would have, but I didn't. I was so devastated, I just made for the door as fast as I could and found the darkest spot I could find where I could be alone.

MATTHEW. So then what happened?

SIMON PETER. I guess I can only tell you that I cried more tears than I'd cried in an entire lifetime.

MATTHEW. Cried? I've known you for almost three years. You're not the crying type.

SIMON PETER. Matthew, I was so torn up inside; so embarrassed; so angry; so confused; so mystified at my own cowardice and stupidity. There was absolutely nothing I could do except cry. Look, I'd made a total jerk out of myself. I mean, in a matter of minutes I had self-destructed. Everything important to me was in shambles. Nothing was left. I could imagine how Jesus felt; I mean, you should have seen how He looked at me. Can you imagine how badly I had let Him down? I was so heartbroken that all I could do was cry.

And that's why Matthew wrote of the moment: "He went outside and wept bitterly." Peter could only blame himself for his dismal performance. In a strange way, his failure should be a comfort to many friends or spouses who have been betrayed by a broken-world person. All too often an insensitive world looks on in the wake of bad consequences and says, "if he or she had been a better spouse," or "if he or she had been a better friend." But who could have been a better friend to Peter than Jesus? And still the fisherman stumbled.

When Moses failed, he disappeared into the desert. When Jonah failed, he put to sea in more ways than one. And when Peter's world fell apart, he ran off into a back alley and subsequently to Galilee where he thought he could get lost back in the fishing business. Who would ever want to hear from him again? It was a reasonable question. The answer is that at least one person wanted to hear from him: Christ. And that was no small thing.

Broken-world moments (or hours) were known by virtually all of those whom we now look upon as saints. It wouldn't be safe to say that such disasters are a part of faith. But it would certainly be accurate to say that they ultimately developed faith. And the men and women who went through them and handled them correctly were the better when the matters were ended.

In the darkest moments of Gail's and my broken world, no modern author offered more consolation and hope than Amy Carmichael, a woman who served as a missionary in India for more than fifty years. Carmichael's last seventeen years of life were broken-world years, for she suffered intensely from a combination of illnesses and the effects of a serious fall. During that time, she hardly ever saw life beyond her bedroom.

Nevertheless, Amy Carmichael's broken world became a pulpit from which, through her writing, she poured faith and hope into tens of thousands of people. And her ministry continues until this day.

Speaking of broken-world moments, she wrote:

The plant called heartsease often grows where we should not expect to find it. And it says, after these sad days have passed you will look back and wonder how you were carried through. It will not always be so hard as it has been of late; for after the darkness cometh light and after tempest cometh calm. And this is no fantasy. It shall be so. (*Gold by Moonlight*)

And so it was for Moses, for Jonah, for Simon Peter, and for countless others.

3
Impenetrable Airspace

BOTTOM LINE #3: *An unguarded strength and an unprepared heart are double weaknesses.*

Military experts say that the Russians have developed and positioned the most effective anti-aircraft system in all the world. Powerful radars probe the air above major Soviet cities, and missiles are poised to bring down enemy aircraft at any altitude. None of the cities is more heavily defended in that system, it is said, than Moscow and its famous Red Square just outside the Kremlin, the seat of the Communist government.

That explains why the world was shocked (and more than a little amused) when a young German piloted a small rented single-engine airplane from Denmark into Soviet territory and buzzed the Kremlin before landing in Red Square. Before he was taken away by the police, he managed to greet some surprised Muscovites who just happened to be in the area at the time. He even signed a few autographs. And when the incident was over, the youthful German was elated; the Russian government was embarrassed; a couple of top generals were abruptly sacked; and the world laughed.

When I read the first accounts of this daring escapade, I smiled with everyone else and mused upon the kind of courage (or foolhardiness) that would make it possible to do something so bold. But almost instantly it occurred to me that a parable of sorts arose out of this bizarre venture.

I thought about a city dumbfounded that its most powerful defenses were thwarted; a city suddenly forced to brood upon its own vulnerability. After all, if an adolescent could land a plane in Red Square without being fired on, what could a dedicated enemy, bent on destruction, accomplish?

As my imagination tuned in on the picture of the plane in Red Square, I also began to see the figures of men like Moses, Jonah, and Simon Peter. Something penetrated their airspace too; something that made it possible for them to make poor choices in a moment when better performance could have been expected. And then I realized that this is what happens to every broken-world person. Personal airspace is violated by temptations from without or by strange stirrings from deep within. And the result is the seedbed of misbehaviors sometimes of the worst possible sort. If that is our own case, we are likely to respond much like the Russians: we can't believe that this can be happening to us. That any of us should be so self-assured as to think that broken-world choices cannot happen to us is a point of maximum danger or double weakness.

I wasn't in Moscow the day the young German made his flight to Red Square so I don't know precisely what happened. But my strong suspicion is that no one in the Russian air defense command was ready for this sort of "invasion." All of their equipment and training was prepared for big, fast-moving, bomb-laden planes. And perhaps it was a nice day, and the people at the radar sets were somewhat relaxed. So when the blip of a tiny airplane was picked up on radar screens here and there along the air route, people reasoned that it was nothing. Nothing worth getting excited about; nothing worth doing anything about.

And then the harmless little aircraft landed just outside the door of the office of the general secretary. Suddenly the matter escalated from a harmless incident to an event of world-shaking significance.

As I already indicated, the Soviets' responses to the failure of their defenses were swift and retributive. General officers were fired; command structures were reorganized; many vituperative speeches were made. Somebody was mad!

When the personal airspace of someone we admire and love is penetrated and there is gross failure, we are usually numbed to the core of our beings. We're liable to pass through a series of reactions as we respond to the bad news, whatever it is: *dismay* and *sorrow*, first; perhaps then *anger* at feeling that our trust has been betrayed; next, a sense of *despair* if we think a good person or effort has been neutralized; and then maybe *fear*, fear that we may be vulnerable to the same failure.

The most important reaction will be the last one, and that, hopefully, is *the perspective and performance of grace.* A great and unique reaction of the Christian toward an individual's broken-world experience is the gracious one: treating someone not as he deserves to be treated but as he needs to be treated in order for his broken world to be rebuilt. Knowing what it is like to receive much grace, I'm deeply aware of its power to heal or redeem when given to a repentant person.

Those first reactions in the chain are human, predictable, and understandable. The act of grace, however, is a supernatural reaction to sinfulness and obviously the superior one in the long run. It is the biblically prescribed reaction, for it sets the scene for the healing and restoration of the one whose world is in pieces. Without grace, broken worlds do not get rebuilt.

Unfortunately, frequent alternatives to grace are gossip and slander. Some people surmise that scandalous news, if it is reasonably true, is fair game for conversation. But the Bible never discriminated between facts and fiction about people when it pointed out that all kinds of gossip and slanderous conversation are, by heavenly standards, wrong.

In her book *A Closer Walk*, Catherine Marshall deals with this matter in a transparent manner:

These further insights have come as I pondered Satan's inroads into my own heart and will:

1. When we rejoice over, or look for, or repeat with relish negative news, then we have placed ourselves on the side of evil.

2. It is possible to take this negative stance so often with regard to situations and persons that this becomes a way of life. Negative thinking is really a weapon of Satan. WE call it "realism"; Christ calls it "not believing the truth."

3. We do not realize how definitely our mind-set—that is, what the mind picks out from all the news to highlight—reveals *whose* side we're really on.

These responses are similar when we are the ones whose worlds have broken up. Until someone has had a broken-world experience, it may be difficult to realize that the chain of responses—dismay, anger, despair, and fear—may be nearly the same for the one who has failed as he or she comes to an awareness of what has been done.

Talk to broken-world persons who have honestly faced up to the realities of the situation, and they will admit that they were unprepared when it happened, disarmed as it did happen, and terribly disillusioned about themselves after it happened. Quite likely they will say, "When I talk about what happened, I almost feel as if I'm speaking about another person. I want to believe that it couldn't be me."

The word *scandal* is often employed for such occasions of optimum failure. It suggests the revelation of an act or actions entirely opposite our convictions and expectations. Because of the nature of human beings, we will always have scandals with us, and—sorry to say—it is always possible that we will be the scandal.

The point then is this: *although we may not like it, we must assume that disasters that break up personal worlds—small/ large, publicized/privatized, self-inflicted/inflicted-upon-us, mega-consequences/minor-consequences—will always be with us, and we must accept them as a tragic part of life.* That means we must comprehend the reasons for and the results of world-breaking moments; we must be prepared so that we can prevent them from happening to us and others; and we must know something about how to restore to fellowship and bring to wholeness those who pass through the experience.

Oswald Chambers urged his readers toward this full-orbed alertness about the power of evil or sin and its capacity to invade personal airspace either from the external world or from deep in the internal or private world. He was more than blunt when he wrote:

> It is *not being reconciled to the fact of sin* that produces all the disasters in life. We talk about noble human nature, self-sacrifice and platonic friendship—all unmitigated nonsense. Unless we recognize the act of sin, there is something that will laugh and spit in the face of every ideal we have. Unless we reconcile ourselves to the fact that there will come a time when the power of darkness will have its own way, and that by God's permission, we will compromise with that power when its hour comes. If we

refuse to take the fact of sin into our calculation, refuse to agree that a base impulse runs through men, that there is such a thing as vice and self-seeking, when our hour of darkness strikes, instead of being acquainted with sin and the grief of it, we will compromise straight away and say there is no use battling against it. (*The Place of Help*, emphasis mine)

The failure to understand this distressing reality often paves the way for those who have been offended or disillusioned by the performance of a broken-world individual to become unredemptive or vindictive persons. It can even include those who secretly revel in the misfortunes of others because they feel superior and look good for the moment. Sometimes it can mean a kind of unfortunate amusement as some scoff at those who momentarily look like fools.

François Fénelon, the great French mystic, wrote:

When the world triumphs over a scandal it shows how little it knows about mankind and virtue. Those who know the depths of human frailty and how even the little good we do is a borrowed thing, though grieved, will be surprised at nothing. Let all men prove themselves mere men—God's truth will not be weakened and the world will show itself as more hateful than ever in having corrupted those who were seeking after virtue. (*Spiritual Letters to Women*)

As I've already observed, in most biblical cases we know more about people's errors and tragedies than about their successes. This is another way of saying that they were, for the most part, rather salty characters. Bold, daring, venturesome to be sure; but well acquainted with what it means to be humiliated and stripped of everything thought to be worthwhile in life.

Like runners who have sustained terrible falls in a race, they sprint toward the finish line with grass stains, dirt smudges, and bruises all over them. For most of them, the fact that they appear in the Bible at all is based on the fact that they ran, fell—usually more than once—got up again, and finished.

I find that rather comforting. It suggests that God communes with and uses people not because they are perfect and antiseptically clean in life but because they have painfully discovered the way of grace. They live as men and women who know they can keep going only because of divine affection and empowerment. Nothing else sustains or strengthens.

The fact that the God of the Bible loves and offers second chances for rebuilding to people who have failed doesn't justify their sin. And we should never fall into the trap of suggesting that the more we fail, the more God will like us and favor our lot in life. Not at all! It is to say, however, that sin and failure is a common event in human history and also that God makes great room in His agenda for those hapless failures who are committed to keep on going. This is a God of the second chance! Consequences? Of course. Restoration and hope? Most definitely. No one need run or hide. His grace calls us out into the open, to a fresh start.

Perhaps we need to reaffirm that Christ called men and women to be godly, not Godlike. Godlikeness is an impossibility; godliness is a description of a particular maturing process that causes people to reflect some of the Creator's personality qualities. There is a significant difference between the two. Each day I can ask the heavenly Father to help me be a godly man. But I will never be Godlike.

When I first read the story of the little plane on Red Square, I applied the parable to my own broken-world experience. I began to see in a clearer light how often our inner space can be invaded from without or from sources deep within us. And when our defenses are inadequate and we are not alert, the results can be as humiliating as the Red Square incident was for the Russian defense ministry.

It was a stunning new reminder that I am actually what the Bible says I have been all along: a sinner. If not in act, then in thought, I have managed to break every one of the Ten Commandments, sometimes in the most subtle ways.

The study of those standards God gave Moses for Israel on Mt. Sinai makes for a frightening but nevertheless illuminating self-measurement. The study suggests that I do not stack up well. No one else seems to, either.

James points out in his New Testament writings what compounds the matter of my culpability as a sinner. If I have broken any of the commandments, I have actually broken them all: "For whoever keeps the whole law and yet stumbles at just one point is guilty of breaking all of it" (James 2:10). Before God, we are all lawbreakers, whether or not our misbehaviors have received special public attention. And

Christians must recognize that as the primary affinity bringing us together before Christ.

But the Scriptures do not focus on the individual actions or attitudes of sin; rather, the focus is on the underlying condition of evil or sinfulness that leaves us all morally and spiritually vulnerable to misbehavior. It is a human tendency, however, to want to spotlight certain misbehaviors that seem worse than others. We do this because they are particularly repugnant to us in our generation or because we perceive that they have greater consequences than others. And when people are exposed or confess guilt in these categories, we refer to them as fallen. But the truth is that we are all fallen people, whether or not we have been guilty of a major misbehavior.

For all the talk in the church about sin and misbehavior, we probably do not take the matter of our vulnerability seriously enough. By unconsciously "grading" certain misbehaviors as more significant than others, we bypass central biblical doctrines: ALL are sinners and stand on equal ground at the Cross; ALL are in need of equal amounts of forgiving and restorative grace; ALL of us are always in danger of the little invaders that enter our airspace and render us to a fallen state; and ALL of us need to learn more about how to defend when the attacks come.

Chambers wrote:

> You hear of one man who has gone safely through battles, and friends tell him it is in answer to prayer; does that mean that the prayers for the men who have gone under have not been answered? We have to remember that the hour of darkness will come in every life. It is not that we are saved from the hour of sorrow, but that we are delivered in it. (*The Place of Help*)

A few years ago I gave a speech at a college commencement. Before the festivities began, a member of that school's board sat with me in the president's office. We'd never met before, and we were asking questions of each other that might help us get better acquainted.

Suddenly, my new friend asked a strange question. I've thought about it many times since then. "If Satan were to blow you out of the water," he asked, "how do you think he would do it?"

"I'm not sure I know," I answered. "All sorts of ways, I suppose; but I know there's one way he wouldn't get me."

"What's that?"

"He'd never get me in the area of my personal relationships. That's one place where I have no doubt that I'm as strong as you can get."

A few years after that conversation my world broke wide open. A chain of seemingly innocent choices became destructive, and it was my fault. Choice by choice by choice, each easier to make, each becoming gradually darker. And then my world broke—in the very area I had predicted I was safe—and my world had to be rebuilt.

In another deeply insightful piece of writing, Oswald Chambers commented on an Older Testament military figure, Joab, whose record of loyalty to David, his commander-in-chief, had been exemplary. One test of his character had come when Absalom, David's son, mounted a rebellion that could have catapulted Joab into greater power. But he resisted the seductiveness of it all and remained faithful. Later the same man, now known for the strength of his loyalty, faced the same moral test but failed. He made a bad choice and joined Adonijah's rebellion against David. Joab's greatest strength became his weakness (see 1 Kings 1:7).

Chambers commented on the tendency of men and women to lose major personal battles not at the points of their weaknesses but, strangely enough, at the points of their perceived strengths. He wrote, "The Bible characters never fell on their weak points but on their strong ones; unguarded strength is double weakness" (*The Place of Help*).

Funny! During my earlier years I'd thought we were most vulnerable at our weakest points, but Chambers said the opposite. I wondered why until I realized from personal experience that where we perceive ourselves to be the strongest is where we're least likely to be prepared for a battle that isn't psychological or emotional. It's spiritual! And when we are unprepared, even our most fortified defenses are in serious jeopardy. Let no person ever say, "I can't be taken." Or as St. Paul wrote, "So, if you think you are standing firm, be careful that you don't fall!" (1 Cor. 10:12).

A tiny airplane buzzes Red Square in the center of Moscow. You don't see tiny planes over the Kremlin very often, I'm told. The airspace is restricted, and the air defense system all the way to Denmark makes a violation of territory impossible. The military is strong and determined; no intruder could ever make it to Red Square. But still that plane circles the area. And then it lands . . . right there next to the Kremlin Wall and Lenin's Tomb. A kid gets out and signs autographs. And the Soviets are humiliated.

And so are the rest of us who have allowed our worlds to be penetrated when we never thought it could be possible.

4

Why Do Worlds
Break Up?

BOTTOM LINE #4: *Personal INSIGHT is not only momentary; it is a healthy way of living. Insight is the first step in rebuilding.*

Among the many stories Jesus told is that of the young man who chose to break with his family and move away. For reasons we do not understand in our culture, he felt within his rights to demand his share of his father's estate. This he apparently turned into cash suitable for traveling and immediately left for another part of the world.

Jesus said nothing about the plans the young man had as he left his father. We only know he wanted to be free from family responsibility, to be independent. And with his father's money, he set out to achieve his goal. We also know nothing about why he picked the city to which he traveled. Perhaps he was drawn by a first-century brand of glitter. Or perhaps he heard of desirable investment or employment opportunities. But when he got there, fun quickly became the primary issue.

It is reasonable to believe that the young man we know as the prodigal son did not plan on, nor did he anticipate, losing his entire nest egg to games and girls. But he did. My imagination suggests that he was the guest of honor at all the parties until his cash flow dried up. Only then did his propped-up personal world collapse. In actuality, it had been breaking up for a long time. It just took certain circumstances to verify the fact.

Once rich (at least in money if not in maturity) and now penniless, the young man had to face a broken-world scenario that included a stint on a pig farm, which would have been just about the worst predicament the Jewish hearers of this story could have imagined. It was Jesus' way of saying: we are talking about a man who has hit bottom.

As the Master unfolded the story, listeners could grasp the consequences of loss, hunger, and humiliation suddenly piling in on the young man and bringing him to a moment of deep personal insight. Jesus described that moment this way: "When [the man] came to himself" (Luke 15:17 NKJV). Only then did he begin to think clearly about what home meant, what personal relationships meant, and—most important—*the implication of the values by which he had lived and the choices he had made.*

Call it the occasion of PERSONAL INSIGHT, the instant of ruthless truth! It's a startling moment. When it's experienced, one will never forget it, especially if one has been avoiding the truth for a while and has gotten out of the habit of facing personal facts. It's an event that almost everyone who has had a broken-world experience would wish had come much earlier so as to avoid the choices that led to terrible consequences. Usually, there are such chances; but the reality is that in those moments, when a different outcome could have been arranged, the person in question, like the prodigal, wasn't watching or listening.

This INSIGHTFUL MOMENT—biblically speaking—is the occasion when individuals see *the truth* for what it is; when they see *themselves* for what they are; and when they see what I would like to call the *environments of choice* for what they make possible.

The first of these, *the truth,* is really God's law, His specification by which life can be lived to produce the maximum amount of personal health and stability. This truth is noncompetitive; it is nonnegotiable; and it is, in the long run, unavoidable. When it is respected and obeyed, everyone wins, and God is honored.

Seeing ourselves for what we really are is another story. Humbling, in fact. In this aspect of insight we human beings quickly discover and affirm that we do not have life all put together; left to ourselves, we are quite liable to drift from what are healthy values and choices and end up dismantling ourselves and the resources God has entrusted to us. History testifies to that. And so does the prodigal.

Being sensitive to the *environments of choice* for what they make possible means realizing that there are times, places, and moods of spirit when we are more likely to make certain choices—good choices *or* bad choices—we might not make on other occasions. For example, it is reasonable to assume that the prodigal would almost certainly have never made the foolish choice of squandering his financial resources if he had elected to remain in his home environment. At home he would have been restrained by the natural accountability he had to loved ones and wiser people who cared for his welfare. Presumably he would have enjoyed the benefit of their counsel and rebuke. But in the environment of a strange place, uncaring people, and unrestrained revelry he formed the choices that lost him everything, including his integrity.

Unfortunately, he came to himself *after* the loss. Naturally one would have wished that the moment of insight had come *before* the accumulated choices. And therein lies the simple answer as to why many personal worlds break up.

I wouldn't be writing this book in quite this way if I hadn't gone through a broken-world experience. Burned into my mind is the occasion when I came to myself, that of personal insight.

You could say that I was in a pigpen mentally and spiritually. I must emphasize that no one around me realized my mental and spiritual location, and I wasn't prepared to reveal it. Rather, I expended great amounts of energy for a brief period of time to mask a torturous inner struggle.

INSIGHT: "he came to himself." I would like to suggest that the moment of insight follows a rather standard order, and men and women who have made poor choices down through the centuries and then come to insight have followed that order almost to the letter.

When I think of this process, I'm reminded of what a person generally goes through in a visit to the dentist because of an aching tooth that has a cavity. A standard process involves locating and probing the extent of the decay, drilling to clean the tooth out, and filling it with a substance that will return it to strength and health.

In coming to oneself, as in the experience of the prodigal, there is first an awareness of mounting circumstances that are more than unpleasant and never anticipated. Call it a massive "ache of the spirit."

For a while, perhaps, the prodigal may have thought that the adversities he faced could be managed and that with a little bit of good fortune, the damages or losses could be repaired or at least concealed. But that wasn't possible for him, and it usually is not for any of us in the long run, though many of us try. Isn't this similar to those days when a tooth hurts, but we keep putting off a visit to the dentist because we hope the pain will go away? Occasionally it does; usually it doesn't.

Then comes the conclusion that one has made a massive error in judgment and choice. Usually a trust has been violated, resources mishandled, or a wrong road of decision making taken. The prodigal in the pigpen now knows this and begins to have remorse that it ever happened. The problem, the ache, must be examined and treated.

But the insightful moment continues. Who is responsible for this choice? Me? Others? Bad timing? And this is often a crossroads in the process of insight. If the prodigal had chosen to blame his performance on others, he might have guaranteed another cycle of brokenness, the second perhaps worse than the first. No, this is one of the moments of supreme inner pain. The prodigal must point the finger at himself and acknowledge that he alone is responsible for his choices.

The drilling is often an anguishing experience. Acknowledging guilt and accountability before God; standing before Him, as it were, offering no excuses and sorrowfully admitting that one has done wrong. It's a very difficult moment, perhaps the hardest of the human condition. The Bible uses the word *repentance* to describe this action.

Repentance is a rather dramatic word. It refers to the act of traveling in one direction and then suddenly changing to go the opposite way. Both John the Baptizer and Jesus used repentance as the centerpoint of their teaching because they were talking to a generation of people whose personal worlds were terribly broken. Yet the people would not face up to the changes necessary to make their worlds come back together again. Stubborn people do not repent very easily, and those people were stubborn.

Repentance is activated, first, in the act of confession: the candid acknowledgment before God, and perhaps to others, that one has sinned and is in need of forgiveness. Both by example and by teaching, the Scriptures place a high priority on confessing, for in so doing, one actually reveals the secrets of the heart. And until the heart is voluntarily opened up, the process of rebuilding a broken world cannot begin.

Our Christian traditions seem to have gone to unfortunate extremes on the matter of confession. The Roman Catholic church has maintained the confessional booth for centuries. But in most places now, the confessional booth appears to be diminished in significance, if not phased out entirely. This is understandable if the encounter between priest and penitent sinner had become incidental and devoid of meaningful restoration, understandable if the act of confession had become an empty obligation, a religious nuisance.

On the other hand, the Protestant penchant for privatizing faith and relegating confession to a singular transaction between that person and God has meant a loss of accountability and a loss of helpful new direction that confession ought to make possible. Anyone can breathe a silent prayer that amounts to little more than a "Sorry, God" and presume to get on with life. How, if things are to be so private and "under the table," is the sinner and the sinned against to know if there has been genuine sorrow and change of heart? All too often this undefined process drifts along as the pursuit of cheap grace.

There needs to be a moment in the life of the Lord's followers where they can clearly acknowledge those things they know to be an offense against God and His church and then hear the words: *you are forgiven in the name of Jesus.*" This need not be the mystical priestly absolution of which Protestants have been afraid for centuries. No, it can be the affirmation from one fellow believer to another that God is faithful to forgive when we are humble enough to confess. How that should actually happen in each of our lives is a question of great importance.

Finally, just as the cavity in a tooth must be filled, so the broken-world person must finally enter into something the Bible calls restoration. Restoration means rebuilding. Some of that one can do for oneself, but the final part must be done by others.

As we will see later on in greater detail, restoration looks to the damage done in a broken-world experience and asks how it can be repaired. Broken relationships must be examined and, if possible, glued back together again. Forgiveness must be requested *and* granted, and that requires people to come together and offer mercy and grace to one another. These are not simple or easy things to give, and sometimes they require time.

But restoration is one of the unique acts of the Christian community. In the final analysis, it cannot be demanded or even earned by the broken-world person; it must be freely given as God once freely gave grace to whoever wished to receive it.

If restoration is genuine, it may provide a rebuilt relationship that is beautiful to behold. I think of this when Gail takes a special glue out of the tool cabinet to join the broken pieces of a cup back together. "This glue is so strong," she says, "that the new joint will be the strongest part of the cup." She has described the possibilities of restoration.

It all began when the young man came to himself: INSIGHT. The logic of insight suggests that we get into trouble when we permit a blindness about the inner world to occur. For it is in the inner world that we handle *God's truth*, we remember *who we really are* with our propensities and weaknesses, and we monitor the *environments of choice*. So if we are not in touch with our private worlds, we are liable to have a broken-world experience.

That's what happened to Israel's King David. He seemed to fight the process of insight all the way, and that is understandable because David seems to have had a problem with insight. Reading David's poems, we note that he frequently talks about the problem of insight, almost as if he's fighting to remind himself that he's stubborn about facing his inner self and that he needs a lot of help in this area.

In one of his most favored psalms, the 139th, David talks about such insight: "You have searched me and known me" (v. 1, NKJV). It isn't clear at first if David likes the fact that there is a God who knows him as well as He says He does. But before the psalm is ended, David is inviting God to a further search. Search my heart (my inner being); search my ways (my outer performance). Let me know if there are errant ways in need of correction.

Like the prodigal son, David had made a series of terrible choices at one time in his life. The most significant bad choice we all know about was his illicit relationship with Bathsheba.

The story might have been different if David had had insight about what was happening in his private world the day he first experienced temptation. What might have changed if he had identified the boredom and laziness that apparently were taking over in his inner being? Would he have been more careful if he had chosen to recognize that he was vulnerable to poor choice making when his key companions and advisors were gone to the battlefield leaving him alone in his palace? If there had been insight, would David have been more on guard and sensitive when lusts and passions from his innermost being attempted to take over and affect his choices?

Since these things did happen, we wish that David had come to his moment of insight soon after he realized he had sinned with another man's wife. But he still didn't! And from all we can surmise, he apparently planned to deliberately cover up his law-breaking performance with Bathsheba and hope that nothing bad would occur.

But something did; she sent him a message informing him that she had become pregnant as a result of their meeting. Her husband, Uriah, was away at battle, and in a short time it would become obvious to everyone who cared to notice that he had been betrayed.

David had to face external consequences. Before that moment the consequences seemed internal and private, relatively simple to handle (albeit painful) if he so chose. The king would have had to deal only with God, Bathsheba and her husband, and perhaps a few others. Now the consequences were soaring out of his control. Others would soon get into the act.

That could have been the time for his moment of personal insight, but it wasn't. David took the wrong fork in the road and chose the cover-up policy again. David invited Uriah home from the battlefield in hopes that he and his wife would spend a few days and nights together. *Surely that would make the consequences go away,* David apparently thought.

But David's cover-up scheme fell apart when Uriah refused to visit his home while on temporary duty at David's palace. "Why should I go home when my comrades are in battle and do not receive the same privilege?" he asked (see 2 Sam. 11:11).

When Uriah intentionally or unintentionally foiled David's cover-up plan (some think that Uriah suspected the plot all along), David had another chance to enter into the further process of insight. But he took the wrong fork again, (deliberately mixing my metaphors) refused the dentist's drill, and arranged a simple plot to make sure that Uriah would be killed on the battlefield.

The perimeter of effects from David's original broken-world choice expanded when he wrote a note to Joab, the commander of the troops on the battlefield, directing that Uriah be assigned to a position of maximum danger. Joab had to know what was going on when he read the unusual request, but instead of confronting David, he complied and participated in the next phase of David's attempt to make the original offense and its consequences go away. Soon Uriah was dead.

With Bathsheba's husband gone and no one asking any questions, David thought that his problems had ended and that his personal world would not break up. He was free to marry Bathsheba, and he did. If you could have entered David's inner space and read his mind for the next few months, you would have probably monitored the thoughts of a man living with a temporary sort of double-mindedness. One part of him was in misery, knowing what he'd done; the other part felt somewhat defiant and clever because of how he'd manipulated people and events to cover his original *indiscretion*. (I use that lighter word for a gross sin because the mind of a person covering up usually likes to diminish the nature of sin at every possible chance.)

A year passed. A year of routine activity. Running the nation; making decisions; writing psalms, although we have to wonder about how many and what kind of quality. A year in which it appeared as if a bad choice was finally history. We can't be sure, but we get the impression that David finally thought he had managed the external consequences to their termination. After all, he had kept people (and God?) from finding out what he'd done. At least it seemed that way.

You enter again into David's mind to learn how a broken-world person thinks. Did the king get to the point that he rationalized the original adulterous meeting? Did he manage his mind so that he justified Uriah's death, perhaps forgetting that the real reason for assigning Uriah a place at the most dangerous part of the battle was not a military decision but a cover-up decision? Did he ever get to the point that he was "uninsightful" enough to thank God for making all the external consequences go away?

Broken-world people can indeed think that way. "Uninsightful" minds that have not "come to themselves" are capable of turning any event toward a favorable interpretation to make themselves look blameless. Human beings are adept at such cover-ups.

Anyone who has studied the mind-set of the Nazi leaders in wartime Germany will remember their effort to justify the killing of the Jews and other enemies under holocaust conditions. They told themselves that this was a difficult but nevertheless heroic act for which generations in the future would thank them. This is how the "uninsightful" mind is capable of thinking.

Back to David. Did his conscience ever bother him during this time? Did he ever replay the events of the previous year like a slow-motion tape in a VCR? How hard did he have to work to keep from "coming to himself"? How much energy did he waste keeping the lid on inner thoughts bursting to be heard?

These might have been the days when he wrote the words:

> When I kept silent,
>   my bones wasted away
>   through my groaning all day long.
> For day and night
>   your hand was heavy upon me;
>   my strength was sapped
>   as in the heat of summer (Ps. 32:3-4).

People whose worlds are beginning to break apart understand that language. They know the discomfort of glancing within and not liking what they see. They know the loneliness of sleepless nights when a carousel projector whirls round and round in the mind playing pictures of the past when choices were made that cannot now be unmade. They visualize an accusing finger pointing at them every time someone raises the subject about which they feel the most guilt.

People like David suddenly realize that they no longer have integrity, that they are not whole or healthy persons. And people like David become increasingly weary of making sure that no one ever discovers the origin of their discomfort.

In David's case it appears that he could or would not make a connection between whatever bad feelings and convictions he had in his inner being and the truth of the past. I reach that conclusion after studying the approach of Nathan the prophet who came to see David about his evil acts of adultery and murder.

Would Nathan have gotten through the door if he had sent a letter to David suggesting a conversation about his sin? I suspect not! Would he have been invited to sit down if he had walked into David's office and said, "I've come to talk with you about a grave offense in your recent past"? Probably not!

Nathan was smart enough to know that David remained in cover-up, impervious to insight. So he entered the back door of David's life by telling him an innocent, though tragic, story. And David was hooked.

> There were two men in a certain town, one rich and the other poor. The rich man had a very large number of sheep and cattle, but the poor man had nothing except one little ewe lamb he had bought. He raised it, and it grew up with him and his children. It shared his food, drank from his cup and even slept in his arms. It was like a daughter to him.
>
> Now a traveler came to the rich man, but the rich man refrained from taking one of his own sheep or cattle to prepare a meal for the traveler who had come to him. Instead, he took the ewe lamb that belonged to the poor man and prepared it for the one who had come to him (2 Sam. 12:1-4).

That was all David needed to hear. Soon he was expressing outrage. I wonder why. Was this the emotion of a man feeling deeply about acts of injustice? Were they the righteous sentiments of a man who was truly indignant about the crime of stealing? Or were these the signals of anger that he really had against himself for what he had done to another "poor man" named Uriah?

We have seen this sort of thing happen many times. Haven't most of us realized that we often become most irritated about characteristics in other people that we really haven't faced in ourselves? On a more public scale, haven't we all seen the occasional public figure who goes to extraordinary lengths to accuse or criticize another and later is exposed as being guilty of a similar offense? What is happening?

Perhaps it's a pattern we are more used to seeing in the life of an alcoholic who has just come off a binge. He swears in his heart that he will never do it again, that the most recent event was really the last time. And for a few days or even weeks, he reinforces his desire to cease and desist from drinking by expressing strong hostility toward all alcohol and drinkers. In so doing he thinks to distance himself from something that has previously victimized him.

But all of the anger he expresses toward someone else is really anger expressed toward himself; it is a subconscious effort at seeking a false kind of cleansing; it is an insufficient attempt to rid himself of his guilt. If he gets mad at the error he has committed, maybe it and its consequences will go away. But they won't.

Nathan picked the moment of David's supreme anger toward a stranger whose sin was infinitesimally smaller than his original sin. He said, "You are the man." And David, like the prodigal, came to himself.

Insight! Its moment has arrived long after it should have.

"I have sinned," David said. And the search for truth, an objective assessment of self, and the matter of restoration begin. Or to put it in its metaphorical setting: the "tooth" was examined, the drilling began, and at the right moment, the filling was accomplished.

No broken world ever begins to be rebuilt until this moment of insight is initiated. And the longer it takes to reach that moment, the more difficult it will be to rebuild a broken world and minimize the consequences.

Perhaps the metaphor of a tooth with a cavity in need of filling is not a pleasant one to most of us. That is why it may be the most apt one for this difficult subject. But I cannot leave the metaphor without remembering the moment when a dentist used the drill on one of my teeth. A rather unpleasant odor arose as the drill probed the cavity of the tooth seeking every bit of decayed material. It was an undesirable event in every way. But necessary!

The moment of insight is not necessarily a pleasant moment. But this book has no value if we do not go deeper into subjects that many people in our day have found distasteful.

And so I wish to take the drill and examine what happens in the moment of insight. If insight in the biblical sense means knowing myself for what I am and then knowing the environments of choice making for what they are, I have an outline for the next couple of chapters.

In my mind I watch the prodigal wend his way from pigsty to home. I think that the story Jesus told that day was a true one, and those in the crowd who heard Him tell it realized that He was rehearsing the experiences of a neighbor. Perhaps the father or the son was there listening. The story is entirely believable. And I ponder what the young man thought about as he headed for the homestead.

Did he think back on the events that led up to his decision to leave home? Did he think through the various moments in his stay in the "far-off" land when he made a chain of seemingly innocent but increasingly dangerous decisions? Did he count the losses he sustained of monies not really his own? And did he consider in his new insight how much he must have hurt his father and anyone else he really loved very much? Of course he did. All of us broken-world people know he thought those thoughts.

5

Life on the Underside

BOTTOM LINE #5: *Almost no one bears a heavier load than the carrier of personal secrets of the past or the present.*

Years ago I had a prolonged experience of lower back pain. After all attempts to live with it failed, I went to see a physician who treats bad backs. I paid him forty-five dollars to tell me to go to bed for fourteen days of rest and not to get up except to take long hot showers. But it wasn't a bad deal because his prescription for my problem worked, and I was soon on my feet again.

The doctor warned me that I would meet a thousand fellow lower-back-pain sufferers who would want to commiserate with my plight. He was concerned, he said, that I not take their homegrown diagnoses and remedies too seriously. "There are some pretty dumb ideas out there," he said. I wasn't sure I knew what he was talking about until I left my bed and the hot showers two weeks later.

The doctor was right; I think I met all one thousand sufferers. It was as if I had been inducted into a society of people whose sole affinity was sore backs. As the man had predicted, every one of them seemed to have an explanation for my discomfort, and each one had a proposal for what I should do about it. Some explanations seemed to make sense; others did indeed seem dumb.

In his most recent book *Recovering the Christian Mind*, Harry Blamires admits to the same experience: "I found I had entered via a slipped disc into a world-wide fellowship in

which the password 'back trouble' would key off reminis-
cences of extraordinary variety and length."

Many years later, I became aware of another more unfortunate society when I experienced a discomfort that was far
more serious: my personal broken world. I call this group the
society of secret carriers.

Like the back-pain sufferers, they had been there all the
time; I just hadn't known how many there were. Some of
them found ways to communicate with me through the mail,
others in conversations when possible, and still others over
the phone if they could get my number. The code words that
almost always introduced a secret carrier began, "I know
exactly what you've been going through . . . "

I had been a pastor for more than twenty-five years, and
during that time I'd probably come into contact with literally tens of thousands of people. Although I was always
aware that congregations were full of men and women who
were living with self-inflicted or other-inflicted wounds, I
never (never, never, never) had any idea of how many more
secret carriers there really were and how deep were their
shame and their pain. I began to learn as I identified this
most sorrowful of all societies.

Recently, I turned over a two-by-six board that had been
lying on the ground behind our home for a long time. I was
startled to discover an enormous city of bugs hiding underneath. It seemed as if there were thousands and thousands of
them dwelling in that dark and damp place. And it was clear
that they did not appreciate my exposure of their life on the
underside of that board.

As I watched them scurry for cover, I thought of what
might be called the underside of the church: those numberless people who walk into sanctuaries all over the world
carrying their secrets behind bright clothing and forced
smiles. They sing the songs, pray the prayers, listen to the
sermons. And all the while the secrets fester within the
private world causing either a constantly broken heart or a
hardened heart. They come in fear of their secrets being
exposed, and they quite likely go in fear that they will have
to live this way for the rest of their lives. Believe me, the
underside of the church is there, listening and watching to
find out whether there is anyone with whom their secret
might be safe if revealed.

Several kinds of people are in this society of secret carriers.

THE CARRIERS OF SECRETS OF THE PAST

The first group of secret carriers living on the underside of the church maintain an active memory of an event or events in the past for which they have consuming regret. They live in the constant fear that their secret will come back to haunt them with consequences that will shatter not only their worlds but the worlds of loved ones and trusted friends.

Their agenda regarding the secret of the past could simply be called BURIAL. In other words, they try to live as if the event(s) never occurred. These secret carriers live in the hope that the past will never penetrate the present. It's a very unpleasant way to live because they can never be sure that someone will not find out what has happened and reveal the secret for them.

The BURIAL scheme is not at all prudent but it often seems to be the only way when one knows his personal world is in trouble. It is usually pursued when one does not feel that there is a place to go and find forgiveness or acceptance, or when one is terrified of hurting those who would be affected if his secret of the past was disclosed. Of course some of these carry their secrets defiantly and conclude that what's done is done.

When I think of these secret carriers, I'm reminded of Edgar Allan Poe's grisly short story, "The Tell-Tale Heart." Poe wrote of a man who had killed another and buried him beneath the floor of his home. Soon afterward he was interrogated by the police. At first he was absolutely confident that he could conceal his secret even from the authorities. So confident that during the questioning, he seated himself in a chair directly over the place of the dead man's burial.

In the enthusiasm of my confidence, I brought chairs into the room, and desired them here to rest from their fatigues, while I myself, in the wild audacity of my perfect triumph, placed my own seat upon the very spot beneath which reposed the corpse of the victim.

The officers were satisfied. My manner had convinced them. I was singularly at ease.

But his coolness evaporated as the conversation went on. Soon he sensed a strange pounding noise in his head. But then he realized that it was coming from beneath the floor where the corpse was located. He was sure that it was the beating of the dead man's heart. He wondered why no one else noticed what he was hearing.

> No doubt I now grew very pale;—but I talked more fluently, and with a heightened voice. Yet the sound increased—and what could I do? . . . I talked more quickly—more vehemently; but the noise steadily increased. I arose and argued about trifles, in a high key and with violent gesticulations, but the noise steadily increased. Why would they not be gone? . . . Oh God! what could I do? I foamed—I raved—I swore! I swung the chair upon which I had been sitting, and grated it upon the boards, but the noise arose over all and continually increased. . . . Was it possible they heard not?

Finally with a shriek the secret carrier confessed:

> "Villains!" I shrieked, "dissemble no more! I admit the deed!—tear up the planks!—here, here!—it is the beating of his hideous heart!"

It is an extreme picture, but it nevertheless faithfully portrays the awesome power of a conscience in revolt. Secret carriers expend tremendous psychic and emotional energy to keep the past from interfering with the present. There is the energy of fear that something from "beneath the plank" may come back to haunt the present. No wonder most secret carriers are not integrated or peaceful people.

SECRET CARRIERS IN THE PRESENT

A second kind of secret carrier lives with hidden matters in the present, covert activities and attitudes that one is consciously attempting to conceal from those in the closer circles of acquaintance. The agenda for this person is COVER-UP.

This present secretive dimension of life might include a destructive habit, a relationship that betrays other covenants, or entrapment in an addiction or an eating disorder. Harder types of present-tense secret carrying to identify are inner attitudes of anger, resentment, or jealousy (there are many others) that can lodge themselves in our private worlds where we think no one can see us as we really are.

Active secret carriers become experts in deception to survive. Large amounts of energy once funneled toward creativity and vital living get siphoned off in the constant planning and implementing of elaborate schemes to cover tracks. The drinker uses vodka to keep from having breath that will tell the story; liquor is squirreled away in obscure places where he or she can sneak an occasional drink. The unfaithful partner creates all sorts of fictional situations to explain blocks of times when he or she has dropped out of sight.

I've known a couple of men who fell into the habit of borrowing money from friends and not paying it back. When pressed for repayment, they would write a check backed by insufficient funds in the bank and then frantically rush about town borrowing more money from others to cover what they had just written. One of those men sometimes drove hundreds of miles between banks each week, moving money back and forth so that checks wouldn't bounce. What a torturous life-style of secret keeping he lived! I understand his is not an uncommon predicament.

When secret attitudes and feelings lie deep within the heart and mind, members of this society will often cover up by exhibiting behavior that appears on the surface to be just the opposite of the truth. Instead of anger that boils within, they may feign calmness and tranquillity; instead of resentment, they may engage in a form of flattery; instead of deep fears and insecurity, they may hold others off through a constant use of humor or talkativeness.

One turns back in the Bible to the story of Achan who disobeyed an explicit order from Joshua (who got it from God) that no one should seize and retain booty from the fallen city of Jericho. But Achan quietly defied the order when he saw things he wanted for himself. He buried the loot under the floor of his tent, where it remained for some time.

Did Achan frequently check the dirt to make sure no one would detect that a hole had been dug there? Did he unconsciously stand over the spot, like a goalie in a hockey game, when visitors came to his home? Did he lie in bed at night and ponder the possibility of digging up the stash and returning it to its original place in the ruins of Jericho? Did he come to a point where he said to himself that having the treasure was no fun anymore?

The startling lesson about Achan's secret was that God would not permit the Hebrew people to advance a step further into the Promised Land until the stolen goods were accounted for. And when he was unmasked, Achan and his family lost everything (see Josh. 7).

He Who Carries Secrets from Himself

A third kind of secret carrier may be the most frightening of all. This person's secrets are so deeply concealed that they have become mysteries to the carrier himself. This takes a bit of explaining.

I'm thinking of the man who lives in what some call denial. This person has permitted the facts of errant behavior or attitude to become so intertwined with life that the conscience has ceased to send out cease-and-desist signals. He hears no tell-tale heart; he no longer imagines that the dirt on the floor of his tent appears freshly dug. He has gone past the point of covering up to others; he has covered up to himself. His agenda is BAU: BUSINESS-AS-USUAL.

A cartoon shows a group of Danish knights sitting around a table in the castle's great room. At the head sits the king who says, "Then it is unanimously resolved that there is nothing rotten in Denmark; things are rotten everywhere else." So might go the thinking of this kind of secret carrier.

When I was a teenager living in Colorado, some of us used to hike to a Rocky Mountain ghost town where an aged woman lived a hermitlike existence. Should anyone go near her shack, she would shout and make threats to drive would-be visitors away. Naturally, we were driven by our curiosity concerning this unusual person and what made her the way she was. On the few occasions that I actually saw her from a distance she was always wearing a black hat.

Memories of that hat came back to me when I heard, years later, that she had been forcibly taken by the local authorities to a hospital. The nurses attempted to remove her clothes in order to bathe her, but her hat had been on her head so long that her hair had grown up through the fabric and colonies of bugs free from disturbance had made nests underneath. To remove the hat and get rid of the bugs, they had to cut away her hair.

The story of that sad, lonely woman reminds me of the secret carrier who lives BAU. His secrets have become secrets even to him. He lives with these destructive performances and attitudes day after day until they simply blend with every other part of his life just as hair grew through the fabric of a hat. He has no notion of how much he hurts others with his actions or his perspective; he cannot be confronted; he rejects the notion that he is the one needing most to be healed. More than likely, he is an angry person who resists any approach by friends or loved ones wanting to get to the core of things.

The ironic thing about this third kind of secret carrier is that his secrets are usually secrets only to him; unlike the situations of the other two kinds, the people around this man usually know more about him and his patterns than he does. He is frequently labeled a fool.

As I've become acquainted with the society of secret carriers, I've seen more than a few of them living BAU. Certain patterns of behavior are consistent over the years, and the results produce long-term pain for loved ones and friends. I know of several men who have established ten- and twenty-year patterns of marital unfaithfulness. Starting and stopping these intermittent relationships of infidelity, they are always one step ahead of those with evidence of their misdeeds. Confronted with the facts, they constantly defend themselves with bland denials. They may even go on the offensive, claiming that they are persecuted and the target of spiritual warfare. They lie to others and to themselves.

It's hard to know where to stop when we think of all the possibilities for living BAU. We are talking of people who possess abrasive and intimidating personality styles, but they will not face what is inside them that causes such hurt for everyone.

Studies suggest that more than half of American mid-life males live with at least one secret in the past of their personal lives, and these men believe its revelation would bring about catastrophic consequences for them and those close to them. If this is true, a lot of people are living unhealthy inner lives today. We need to look hard at the nature of our relationships *to see if we encourage secret carrying by making it difficult for people to come to the truth about themselves.*

The list of possible secrets carried by these three kinds of secretive people is almost infinite. It includes the secrets of people's fears and resentments, their anger, and their memories of devastating experiences in the past. It takes in covert and overt acts of vengeance, outright dishonesty, and sexual promiscuity.

We're thinking of people who permit their life-styles to become increasingly materialistic and try to justify their values and choices on the basis of spiritual terminology. The variations of secret carrying go on and on. We can make a case that one form of it or another touches all of us sooner or later.

Every group of secret carriers is likely to include women who have had secret abortions and who die a little inside every time someone talks about killing or murdering fetuses. There will be men and women who have grown up with the anguish of molestation and abuse in their childhoods. Some people will be struggling with the secrets of substance abuse and other disorders.

As I've already observed, every group includes single and married men and women who live with the bitter memories of indiscretions or infidelities. And every group includes people who are living in serious doubt about their faith, but they feel bound to keep up the outward motions for the sake of a spouse or the children. They and many others are secret carriers; their society is larger than I had ever imagined.

Secret carrying may be a spiritual epidemic. It just might be the common cold of Christian living. Why? Because it is so easy, so natural for all of us. Men and women have tried to carry and live with secrets ever since Adam and Eve tried to hide from God when He sought them in the garden.

"Why are you hiding, Adam?" God asked. He was hiding because he was keeping a secret, and he was ashamed to expose it.

Cover-ups are accomplished in a host of ways in the church. Some do it with the facade of an unusually passionate concern for theological and doctrinal correctness. They keep everyone on the defensive with their accusations and suspicions. Some cover up by being extremely emotionally expressive in their spiritual lives. We find it hard to doubt the sincerity of someone who seems able to weep or rejoice at key moments. Others cover up through a style of never-ending busyness and activism. Who can find fault with some-one who is always serving, always giving, always leading? We've already noted the cover-up of leading by righteous indignation or pointing out the sins and irregularities of others. *All of these categories include individuals who are absolutely sincere and genuine in their pursuits of life and faith*; but people who have secrets to keep can abuse church- and spirit-related endeavors.

The Bible speaks often about secret carrying. It is most likely to come out in verbs like *deceive* or *lie*, or in nouns like *darkness* or *hardness* (as in hardness of heart). And when one studies the great biblical biographies, it's not unusual to see a secretive phase in almost every person's broken-world ex-perience.

But why secrets? The answer has to do with *truth*. We acquire secrets when we do not wish to face or reveal the truth. We do a subtle thing when we play with the truth, but we do it all the time. So much so that few people think seriously about how much the systems in which we live constantly manipulate the truth.

We expect the politician to play with the truth, to tell us what we want to hear. In a recent presidential primary campaign, one candidate seeking his party's nomination was forced out of the process in its earliest stages because, the press said, he was too truthful about his assessment of our national situation and his convictions about what should be done to make corrections. The inference is that we, the pub-lic, are not prepared to hear the truth put so clearly.

We expect advertisers to bend the truth, and the Isuzu people have capitalized on this. They would never lie (the FCC sees to that), but we know that claims are usually exaggerated to the furthermost possible point that legality permits. And thus we become quite cynical about the prom-ises and possibilities of any product. In effect we have made room for the half-lie when we listen to commercials on tele-vision, and we have developed highly sophisticated screening mechanisms in our minds to filter out the mindless and the truthless.

As men and women, we feel at liberty to play with the

truth about ourselves. An entire industry panders to the desires of women to distort the truth about their aging bodies. Men have learned to cover the truth about their real feelings. We learn these capacities at an early age. We are brought up to be skilled liars about some things.

John Gardner noted this spiritual malady when he wrote in *Self-Renewal*:

> Self-knowledge, the beginning of wisdom, is ruled out for most people by the increasingly effective self-deception they practice as they grow older. By middle age, most of us are accomplished fugitives from ourselves. Yet there's a surprising usefulness in learning not to lie to yourself.

Of course all of this happens in the church also. A dangerous margin of mistruth is permitted over and over again in our hymnody if we sing with straight faces the words and phrases we never really intend to carry out. "Take my silver and my gold, not a mite would I withhold," we might sing with all the signs of serious conviction. One Sunday morning Gail and I were standing with the congregation singing the final verse of a five-verse hymn. I suddenly realized that I had sung the entire song, verse by verse, and hadn't contemplated the meaning of one word. And the words were actually frightening in terms of the response they were asking of me. I was glad that the song hadn't carried with it—humanly speaking—the force of a signed contract. But come to think of it. . . .

Have you ever wondered how many people in an audience are actually concentrating on a prayer being prayed? Or (am I losing friends) on a sermon being preached? How many of us have learned appropriate postures and angles of head and neck that indicate involvement but actually mask the secret that we are a hundred miles away solving a computer problem, worrying about a wayward son, or picking the color of a new car?

The day I sang the hymn without recalling any of the words, Gail and I spoke of what had happened all the way home from church. How is it, I asked her, that I can become so used to singing something that the words lose meaning? Perhaps, I reasoned, this is symptomatic of a faith that is cast in revolutionary terms but is usually practiced by people whose best interests are grounded in the status quo.

That helped me to understand a fundamental reason why some churches and groups of Christians struggle for spiritual vitality today. We have too often created an atmosphere for low-level lying in our prayers, in our sermons, in our singing. We actually may encourage the secretive way of life.

This issue of secret carrying and its opposition to the truth is at the very core of broken-world experiences. Personal worlds enter into the first phases of breakup when people consciously or unconsciously decide to compromise the importance of truth, most specifically the truth about themselves. Thus the proposition in the previous chapter: PERSONAL INSIGHT BEGINS WHEN WE SEE THE TRUTH FOR WHAT IT IS.

Alexander Whyte wrote:

> To know myself, and especially as the wise man says, to know the plague of my own heart, is the true and the only key to all other true knowledge: God and man; the Redeemer and the devil; heaven and hell; faith, hope, and charity; unbelief, despair, and malignity, and all things of that kind . . . ; all knowledge will come to the man who knows himself, and to that man alone. (*Bunyan's Characters*)

There are many fraternities and societies in this world. The informal network of lower-back-pain sufferers with their diagnoses and remedies. Others who fellowship around sports, vocations, and causes. And then there is the quiet, desperate society of secret carriers. How great their need for the liberation that begins the process of rebuilding.

6

The Pain of Secret Carrying

BOTTOM LINE #6: *The person who carries a secret has sentenced himself to a dungeon.*

In June 1984, the *Boston Globe* reported the tragic story of the drowning of eight-year-old Chris Dilullo. He had been lost in eight feet of water while on a hunt for golf balls at a local country club.

Chris had been accompanied by three friends who said that when he slipped into the pond, they thought he was playing a trick on them. But the boys were secret carriers.

> They turned the truth into a secret: One of them had pushed Chris in. They didn't realize that by trying to protect each other, they kept a secret that would wreck their own lives, multiplying the tragedy of Chris' death.

It was almost two years before the secret was uncovered when the fifteen-year-old boy who had pushed Chris into the water confessed his guilt to a friend. Soon the police were investigating the incident and charging him with man-slaughter.

> Since the drowning, all three witnesses [to the drowning] have suffered emotional instability, according to their parents, police and their own stories. Their distraught parents say the boys are withdrawn and have nightmares. They are no longer friends.

One of the three "began crying frequently after Chris' death and had to sleep with his mother. . . . Once he cut his head when he ran full-speed into a dumpster." A second, an eighteen-year-old, was fired from a job "because he would stay home from work on days when he felt 'angry and disgusted' about telling a lie to protect a friend." The third boy started "hearing voices and seeing visions and barely talked to his parents." He later entered a hospital for emotionally disturbed children.

Secret carrying is an ancient activity and a modern one. The story of the drowning of Chris Dilullo is simply a dramatic example of what members of the society of secret carriers live with every day. It is more vivid and heart-wrenching because it involves youngsters who were not as adept as many adults at handling their secrets.

King David was a secret carrier. For a year or more he tried to live business-as-usual hoping that the secrets of his recent past would remain in the past.

But when Nathan the prophet confronted David about his BAU agenda, he was able to get the king to dig things up. Psalm 51 was David's subsequent prayer of repentance. It is no accident that David mused on this subject of the truth when he said to God, "Surely you desire truth in the inner parts" (v. 6).

David was dealing most painfully with the fact that he had lost his integrity. Truth on the surface of his life and truth in the inner parts hadn't been connecting. The corrective that had to take place occurred when David stopped lying to God, to himself, and finally to the rest of the world. Whenever God becomes involved as a rebuilder in a person's world, the issue of truth will surge about in the innermost being.

To get the inner and the outer parts together, David had to deal with truth. A friend of mine calls and talks about some painful discoveries he has been making about himself in recent days. He has come to INSIGHT, and in that process he realizes that he has spent a large part of his adult life "changing the furniture," as he puts it, on the surface of his public world. "But while I've been so busy decorating the surface, I've seriously neglected the facts about the ugliness inside. Now I'm looking in, and I've come to realize that until you *name* what is in you and face it, you cannot change anything."

Lodged in the hard disk of my computer is an *integrated system* of programs. It combines computer programs for spread-sheet calculations, word processing, data base formation, communications, and time management. It is called an integrated system because all aspects of the program must fit and be capable of supporting one another with processes and information that will serve me, the user, well.

Each of us is created to be an integrated system of personal and corporate life. The truth by which we live in our public worlds must be the truth by which we live in our private worlds. The gap or the difference between the two will largely determine the state of our personal health.

I've been greatly impressed by the work of Alcoholics Anonymous. And as I've read of the twelve great principles followed by that organization, I cannot escape the fact that this entire process of introducing addictive men and women to the possibility of recovery is based on the notion of the truth and the dissolution of secrets. You cannot adequately aid a secret carrier.

I'm told that it is customary when a person stands to speak in an AA meeting, he introduces himself by first name only and the words, "and I'm an alcoholic." Then he states specifically when and where he had his last drink. There can be no cover-up at an AA meeting. The truth is faced over and over again, and the strengthening fellowship of AA'ers is based on that truth telling.

> After years of drinking, we alcoholics become cognitively impaired. In plain language, we can't think straight. The root of 'intoxicate' is the Latin word toxicum—'poison'. We have systematically poisoned ourselves, damaging the central nervous system.

So said a retired physician who is a recovered alcoholic. Another recovering alcoholic admitted, "I was committing chronic suicide. I was putting a liquid bullet into my brain every night." (*Getting Better*)

One of AA's two founders, Bill Wilson, wrote of the principles that became the original foundation for this remarkable program. Among them are these:

1. We admitted that we were powerless over alcohol—that our lives had become unmanageable.

2. We made a searching and fearless moral inventory of ourselves.

3. We admitted to God, to ourselves, and to another human being
the exact nature of our wrongs. (From *Getting Better*)

As I've pondered this remarkable basis of fellowship in
AA, it has occurred to me that we would be far more genuine
and authentic as brothers and sisters who follow Christ if we
introduced ourselves with a similar phrase, "I'm Gordon,
and I'm a sinner." The church is made up of sinners; there is
no other primary basis for fellowship in the church than
that. And once having affirmed the truth about myself—I
am a sinner—I move to the next affinity point with my fellow
followers of Christ, the Cross.

When I was a secret carrier, I occasionally told people who
were to introduce me as a speaker for a meeting to simply
acknowledge me as Gordon, a sinner. Usually there was
polite laughter; all thought it was a humorous way of expressing humility. Little did they know that it was the truth.
I found it instructive for myself that some people who
thought my suggestion was merely a joke really did not want
to introduce me ever again when they learned I meant what I
said: I was a sinner.

Insight then, as I wish to use the term, is the act of constantly aligning our two worlds, private and public, with the
truth. *Secret carrying*, on the other hand, is the act of stretch-
ing the two worlds further and further apart.

Aaron, brother of Moses and high priest among the Hebrews, was a short-term secret carrier. His specific responsibilities were those of leading in the religious ceremony of
the people. When Moses excused himself to go to the top of
Mt. Sinai for a conference with Jehovah, Aaron picked up
the added responsibility of overall leadership. You might
have assumed that the people were in good hands, but they
weren't.

A score of days passed. Moses was gone longer than anyone
expected, and fear began to trickle through the camp at the
foot of the holy mountain. People speculated on the possibility that Moses was dead, that they no longer had a leader,
and that, in fact, they could not count on a relationship with a
trustworthy deity. In that agitated condition they turned to

Aaron and proposed the creation of other "gods who will go before us" (Exod. 32:1).

It could have been Aaron's grand moment for a display of moral and spiritual courage. But it wasn't. He could have managed the moment by pressing the people for patience and fidelity. But he didn't. Instead, the man caved in to their demands. "Take off the gold earrings that your wives, your sons and your daughters are wearing, and bring them to me," he said (Exod. 32:2).

The people did as Aaron instructed, and before long a calf of gold shaped with a tool (the Scripture is explicit about this; only later do we find out why) was erected in their midst. With that done, Aaron announced a religious festival for the next day. Everyone came, and the Bible describes the event as something akin to a pagan orgy.

At the top of the mountain God was aware of what was going on and angrily expressed Himself to Moses. In a strange but merciful conversation, Moses appears to have taken the role of intercessor and appealed to God's patience and promises, and the situation was momentarily cooled. That was until Moses came down from the mountain and saw for himself what was happening. Then it was his turn to fume.

Storming the camp, Moses destroyed the idol, ground its gold into powder, scattered it in water, and forced the Israelites to drink it. The immediate result was extreme humiliation and embarrassment, not to speak of the loss of lots of gold jewelry. The longer-term forfeit was a powerful judgment unto death for many of those who had acted so uproariously.

But the camera eye of the writer focuses on the conversation between Moses and Aaron. "What did these people do to you, that you led them into such great sin?" Moses asked his brother (Exod. 32:21).

Watch the deception, the distortion of truth, in Aaron's attempt to give an answer that might salvage his dignity.

Do not be angry, my lord. . . . You know how prone these people are to evil. [Deflect accountability by blaming the offense on others.] *They said to me, "Make us gods who will go before us. As for this fellow Moses who brought us up out of Egypt, we don't know what has happened to him."* (Is Aaron hinting that part of the problem might even be Moses' fault for staying away so long?] *So I told them, "Whoever has any gold jewelry, take it off." Then they gave me the gold, and I threw it into the fire, and out came this calf!* [The deceptions grow. Aaron would like Moses to believe that the golden calf was the fault of whatever happened in the fire. Amazing!] (Exod. 32:22–24).

The final sentence makes the reader understand why the earlier part of the account emphasized that the calf was made with a tool. Aaron was lying! The man was simply refusing to deal with truth. He was secret carrying! Perhaps it was part cover-up and part BAU, business-as-usual.

His explanation would be hysterically funny if it wasn't so tragic. Aaron appeared to believe what he was saying to his brother.

What was happening? DECEPTION. Aaron's heart was so twisted that facts made no sense to him whatsoever. Many thousands of years later we look at his ridiculous explanation and laugh. But for Aaron, it was serious business. He was following the track of his darkened heart.

A replay of Aaron's performance prompts three questions. First, why would Aaron so easily betray his brother by yielding to the opinions of the people when they suggested Moses had turned out to be undependable? Second, why would he so quickly betray his brother by directing the creation of the golden calf and the ceremony that heralded its existence? And third, why would Aaron betray his brother by lying about what he'd done when Moses returned from the mountain?

Aaron's performance simply doesn't make sense unless we take into account the biblical theme of deception. The dark side of Aaron's inner being clouded his thinking and his values, and in a clutch moment he led the people into a serious fall.

Jeremiah probably describes the dark side of the human heart as well as any writer in the Scriptures:

> The heart is deceitful above all things
> and beyond cure.
> Who can understand it? (Jer. 17:9).

It isn't a pleasant or an upbeat analysis of the human condition. But a careful reading opens one to a profound reality.

Jeremiah seems to suggest that there is no murkier place in all of the universe than the depths of the human heart. And darkness goes with deceit and lying.

The dark part of Aaron seems to have taken over in the incident. It's likely that he rather enjoyed the attention he received, and it wasn't difficult, therefore, for him to interpret Moses' extended absence as a sign that he wasn't coming back. Furthermore, it was probably easy to give in and supervise the development of the golden calf because it made the people like him all the more. Step by step, the power of deceit from the depths of his heart was taking control. By that time, Aaron was lying to himself. So when the moment of exposure came, it isn't hard to understand why Aaron would twist the truth and attempt to lie to Moses. Having lied to himself, he had no problem lying to Moses.

This is the consistent story of deception. All of us battle it every day. And it is the seedbed of virtually every evil act in the human repertoire. No wonder that one name for the arch enemy of God, Satan, is "slanderer" or "deceiver."

Deception is never more ugly than the moment we reenter the light and realize how we have been living under the influence of a series of inner lies. How could I have believed that? we ask ourselves. How could I have fallen for that line? How could I have ever assumed that what I did in that encounter was OK? How could I have forgotten the potential consequences of such a despicable act?

Why we permit the power of inner deception to gain control is discussed in another part of this book. For now, it is important to point out that this is where a fall of greater or lesser consequence begins. Twisted thinking that encounters questionable opportunities means disaster.

I know what it is like to live with a secret. And having dissolved that secret before God, my loved ones, and the church, I know what it is like to live once again in the light.

But I've never forgotten the loneliness of those secret-carrying days. And they have made me highly sensitive to the scores of people in the society of secret carriers who still walk in that darkness. What energy they expend; what fear they experience; what prisons they make for themselves. But what liberation when the secrets are jettisoned and they walk out of the darkness into the light.

As a policeman put it when the tragedy of Chris Dilullo's death came to light:

> All of them tried to suppress the information, but they couldn't do it. They're just children. They held their secret so long out of fear and guilt, guilt over what had been done and fear of being punished. I couldn't think of a juster outcome than to help those boys overcome those feelings.

7

Implosion

BOTTOM LINE #7: *"The one spiritual disease is thinking that one [is] quite well."* G. K. Chesterton

Fifty thousand people in Boston were recently treated to a spectacular sight: the instant wrecking of a twenty-story skyscraper. It once took two years to construct the building, but it took less than fifteen seconds to topple it.

The job was done by implosion. Hundreds of dynamite charges were attached to the skeletal structure and then set off in a sequence that caused the skyscraper to literally fall in upon itself. It wasn't long before the building lay in a heap of rubble not more than fifty feet high.

Television crews filmed the event with high-speed cameras and then in slow motion played and replayed the event for viewers. Frame by frame we saw every part of the destructive process. The flashes of light when the explosives were detonated, tiny but enlarging cracks in the outside wall, and then a slow-motion plummeting of debris, straight down, followed by a massive cloud of rising dust.

By now you've probably realized that I tend to see a parable or metaphor in almost everything. And this was no exception. For me, the specter of the building's collapse was one more picture of a personal broken world. As the stone blocks toppled downward, I saw a vivid picture of a human life imploding, breaking up, lying in a heap of consequences and sadness.

I saw a strong Samson, for example, making a series of strange, irrational decisions, the consequences of which stripped him of everything that he had formerly achieved and left him in humiliating weakness. A crafty and heroic Gideon whose earlier successes were greatly diminished when he permitted people to build shrines to his accomplishments. And a Solomon in whom God had invested awesome wisdom only to see it slowly dissipate in the king's growing preoccupation with the sensuous life.

In the drama of the imploding building I saw myself and a numberless host of broken-world people who have made terrible choices that may or may not have had anything in common with their previous life-styles. Why do human "implosions" happen regularly? What can we learn from such history?

The experience of INSIGHT in the pigpen where the prodigal son came to himself involved a stunning awareness of the terrible choices he had made, and it also meant that he had to face hard realities about his private world. As he himself admitted, he was no longer worthy to be called his father's son. He had made a deliberate decision to leave the home of his youth, to demand what he had not earned, and to waste it on things he could not really afford. He'd made those choices; no one else made them for him. As he lived among the pigs, there was really only one useful question left: *what had been inside him that had caused this series of choices, and what could he do about it?*

There is really only one adequate answer to such a question, and it is a discomforting one. One word does it all: *evil.* Some may be more accustomed to the word *sin.*

Evil is a distasteful subject to modern people. Not an agenda item on the cocktail circuit to be sure. And in my opinion, evil (or sin) is usually treated with considerable shallowness even among people whose theological convictions affirm its reality. Listening to the judgments and opinions of some who try to analyze and explain the bad choices of others leaves me cold, for I've learned that most of us understand very little about one another. We would do well to think very carefully before we claim to comprehend the reasons why someone has performed in the way he has when implosion happens.

When it comes to talking about the evil of the human

heart, some in our world would probably reflect the opinion of the eighteenth-century Duchess of Buckingham. When she was asked to go to a George Whitefield evangelistic service, she wrote to her hostess, the Countess of Huntingdon:

> It is monstrous to be told, that you have a heart as sinful as common wretches that crawl on the earth. This is highly offensive and insulting; and I cannot but wonder that your Ladyship should relish any sentiments so much at variance with high rank and good breeding. . . . I shall be most happy to accept your kind offer of accompanying me to hear your favorite preacher, and shall wait your arrival. The Duchess of Queensbury insists on my patronizing her on this occasion; consequently she will be an addition to our party. (*George Whitefield*)

Having made her protest concerning her aversion to the subject of sin and evil, the Duchess went to hear Whitefield anyway, if only to be seen in the company of the Countess. But she does represent a large segment of people who find that the best way to deal with evil is simply not to talk about it. Maybe, they seem to assume, it will go away. But it doesn't!

On the other hand, Velma Barfield, a twentieth-century convicted murderer, had an opposite opinion on the evil in the human heart, her own heart to be exact. Some will remember her as the woman who was executed by lethal injection in 1986. Shortly before her life was ended, she wrote:

> I . . . want to make it clear that I am not blaming . . . drugs for my crimes. I am not blaming my troubled childhood or the marriage problems with [my husband] Thomas. Someone said to me, "Velma, you had a lot of pain and hurt and anger and you never found any release for it. You kept pushing it back and it was like a time bomb. It finally went off and exploded." Maybe that's right. I don't know. *I bear the responsibility for the wrongs I have done. I know those things influenced me, but they are my sins and my crimes.* (*Woman on Death Row*, emphasis mine)

The subject of evil has never been new to me. Growing up in a religious context, I heard about sin from my earliest days. But many years later, in my moments of broken-world INSIGHT, I came to a deeper awareness of the topic that seemed to eclipse all earlier knowledge. Previously, by contrast, the matter of evil had been almost academic; now in a broken-world state of my own it was an issue known through anguished experience. Apparently some of us concentrate most carefully on the subject of evil only when we have entered into one kind of pigpen or another.

Oswald Chambers understood this process:

> When God wants to show you what human nature is like apart from Himself, He has to show it (to) you in yourself. If the Spirit of God has given you a vision of what you are apart from the grace of God (and He only does it when His Spirit is at work), you know that there is no criminal who is half so bad in actuality as you know yourself to be in possibility. (*My Utmost for His Highest*)

My insightful moments—does one dare to call them pigpen moments in remembrance of the prodigal?—forced me to look back and replay the history of a series of bad choices and ask the question *why*. Why am I indeed, to use Murray's words, twice (and more) as bad as any criminal?

In pursuit of that uncomfortable question I commenced a journey within myself. What I found was quite mysterious and more than a little distressing. I discovered in my meditations and my readings that the inner space of my life was far *greater* in scope and *evil* in quality than I had ever imagined.

But it made sense to me, nevertheless, that I must vigorously explore my inner space if I was to come to conclusions about why a personal world might implode. The exploration of such space is obviously a lifelong project. I'm not sure a lot of people ever begin the journey.

This is the journey of which David, the born deceiver, spoke:

> Search me, O God, and know my heart [the inner space];
>   test me and know my anxious thoughts.
> See if there is any offensive way in me,
>   and lead me in the way everlasting (Ps. 139:23-24).

Teilhard de Chardin described the beginning of his personal quest into inner space in words like these:

> For the first time in my life perhaps (although I am supposed to meditate every day!), I took the lamps and leaving the zone of every day occupations and relationships where everything seems clear, I went down into my inmost self, to the deep abyss whence

I feel dimly that my power of action emanates. But as I moved further and further away from the conventional certainties by which social life is superficially illuminated, I became aware that I was losing contact with myself. At each step of the descent a new person was disclosed within me of whose name I was no longer sure. And who no longer obeyed me. And when I had to stop my exploration because the path faded from beneath my steps, I found a bottomless abyss at my feet, and out of it came— arising I know not from where—the current which I dare to call my life. (*The Divine Milieu*)

As I said, many of us would be uneasy to make the inner voyage of exploration that David requested of God and that Teilhard described. Most would dare to barely descend beneath the surface. Excuses might include "not enough time" and "it seems so morbid a project." But the thing that makes us most likely to resist David's "search-me" prayer is the dread we have of finding out too much about what's below. Too painful, too humiliating, too demanding for change. And to the extent that any of us avoid the journey, we invite shallowness of personhood and the ultimate possibility of a broken-world experience.

As Teilhard made the descent, he obviously grew wary of the uncharted territory. One is reminded of the oft-noted fact that medieval mapmakers would write on the edges of their maps where land and seas were unexplored, "Here be dragons and wild beasts."

Inner space was meant to be the territory, an inner temple or sanctuary if you please, in which God our Maker would make His interior residence. Here He would commune with us, give empowerment for us to reflect His image and His glory. Here would be the wellspring for thoughts and deeds showing forth what the Bible calls holiness, life after the character of God.

But in my INSIGHTFUL moments, as I began my journey to discover the mysteries of my broken world, I was quick to affirm that this terrible force called evil had violated the inner temple, seizing most if not all of the space for itself. It was as if the dragons, like modern-day terrorists, had hijacked my soul and were holding hostage all the good qualities and attitudes that God intended for each of us when He made us.

As you can see, I end up resorting to fantasy and metaphors to describe the almost indescribable; I end up going along with the modern hijackers and the ancient mapmakers saying, "Here be dragons and here be wild beasts; they seek to kidnap your world and shatter it." That seems to be what makes up the drama played out in a large part of this dark inner space.

A human tendency is to try to build a security gate near the surface of our lives, a gate to protect us from dealing with anything that might arise out of inner space. And it isn't unusual for us to be reasonably successful in keeping the dragons out of sight . . . for a time.

Individuals with material resources are often capable of building strong and high gates that last for some time. That's why life in an affluent neighborhood seems at first glance not to be as evil in appearance as life in the poorer sections of the city. Where money and opportunity are, the gates will often contain or at least hide the inner dragons of people for a time.

In the inner city, the resources to cover things up aren't available; thus, we often see the ugliness of man's heart for what it is first in those places. But get into the private lives of the uptown or suburban residents, and we see that the dragons are there; they are just being bought off for a time.

But dragons inevitably break through the strongest gates, and they have no respect for our timing or our convenience. When they come, most of us are shocked beyond words at the thoughts, the motives, the attitudes, and the distorted values that they bring with them.

Godly men and women have had the painful experience of discovering deep anger, violent and vulgar profanity, suspicion, and accusation flowing from their mouths when the filtering mechanisms of their conscious minds have been inoperative for a time during a serious illness. Where did the words and thoughts and attitudes come from, they wonder? Answer: from some form of inner space with its dragons.

Earlier I mentioned that I'd had an experience with lower-back pain some years ago. One of the interesting things the physician explained to me about the difficulty of diagnosing back problems was that the point of pain in a back was not always the point of the problem. In other words, a problem in the upper back might show up as pain in the lower back.

How similar, it occurs to me, such elusive pain is to the spiritual ailments of many misbehaving people. We are drawn to the point of the pain and try to address that situation when all the time the point of the problem is far deeper inside, where inner evil spawns its dragon-like influences.

St. Augustine was no stranger to sighting dragons or questioning the origin of pain in his inner space.

> Who am I, and what manner of man? What evil have not either my deeds been, or if not my deeds, yet my words; or if not my words, yet my will? But thou, O Lord, art good and merciful, and thy right hand had respect unto the profoundness of my death, and drew forth from the bottom of my heart that bottomless gulf of corruption: what was to nil all that thou willedst, and to will all that thou nilledst. (*Confessions*)

These were the sorts of discoveries I too began to ponder in my insightful moments. There came a time when dragons, if you please, had come through my gates and had caught hold of my mind and my choice-making mechanisms. And I had translated the evil in my inner space into actions in my outer space.

Jesus was referring to this origin of personal performance when He said to His disciples regarding the heart:

> Don't you see that whatever enters the mouth goes into the stomach and then out of the body? But the things that come out of the mouth come from the heart, and these make a man "unclean." For out of the heart come evil thoughts, murder, adultery, sexual immorality, theft, false testimony, slander (Matt. 15:17-19).

In one of his excellent writings, Lewis Smedes brought the issue into even finer focus for me. He told of a woman in a German prison camp who stood watching a friend being beaten by a Nazi guard. She was filled with rage and hatred toward her friend's oppressor. But insight soon followed, and it neutralized her desire for vengeance, for a voice said, "Remember, there is also a Nazi in you."

As I read of that woman's insightful moment, I was seized with the fact *that there was a Nazi in my inner space too*. Perhaps it's more accurate to acknowledge that there was a "Hitler" in me, and given the right set of circumstances, I was actually capable of doing everything he did *and much more*. It was a frightening revelation, and the effect upon me cannot be exaggerated. So, I reasoned, the dragons really are that bad.

I had always subscribed to the essential teaching that all human beings are born sinners, that our misdeeds are the product of a nature prone to disobedience and rebellion against God. But somehow there seems to be a difference between understanding these things from a doctrinal orientation that you might learn in a Sunday school and coming to understand them through a terrible experience of failure where you discover that this *energy of unrighteousness*—what the Bible calls sin—is capable of destroying everything good within and without you. And that doesn't take into account the destructiveness to the personal worlds of "innocent bystanders."

The wrecking crew that expertly took out the skyscraper in Boston without damaging any other building was far more masterful than we sinners who usually manage to hurt lots of other people when we implode. Sin is indiscriminate as to who it hurts.

With a fresh awareness of myself as a sinner I took the Scriptures and began to read St. Paul's letter to the Roman church. As this experience of personal insight within me grew, I read the book straight through and discovered a simple agenda that I had never quite grasped before. I'd read and studied Romans many times in the past, but this time I read it not as a preacher, a small-time theologian, or even a veteran Christian. I read Romans as it was meant to be read, through the eyes of a prodigal who needed help in finding out what had happened and how to get home.

When I was through, I turned to Gail and said, "I see it now. This book was written by a man who had come to the simple realization that he was a broken-world person, that the people he was writing to were broken-world people, and so his subject had to be personal worlds broken by sin and what can be done about them."

Paul knew by personal experience and by the revelation given to him that evil was a force that had to be dealt with. To ignore it was to court disaster, a personal broken world. And so he began that letter with a careful exposé on the subject. Where did he begin? By suggesting that evil has its origin in the decision of humankind to suppress the truth about God and His mighty acts of creation and redemption. History, Paul observed, is one big cover-up, a failure to face the truth.

The result? The systematic breakdown of civilizations and cultures, the destruction of the orderly life-styles of individual men and women. Hatred, corrosive competition, misuse of bodies, hypocrisy. And so we see it today, just as Paul said it happens when evil goes unrestrained.

He concluded his thoughts on the universality of evil in the heart of every human being by writing:

> What shall we conclude then? Are we any better? Not at all! We have already made the charge that Jews and Gentiles alike are all under sin. . . . Now we know that whatever the law says, it says to those who are under the law, so that every mouth may be silenced and the whole world held accountable to God (Rom. 3:9, 19).

Silenced! No excuse! No plea concerning mitigating circumstances.

What was needed was insight, an awareness that humankind individually needs to come to the Cross wherein God has more than adequately and lovingly provided a remedy for the reality and effects of evil within us. God was choosing to deal with our evil through His grace.

What I've been trying to say here violates the suspicions of many Christians. Those with orthodox views are always ready to affirm the doctrine of original sin, but somehow some of us would like to gloss over the truth about how capable we really are of succumbing to that sin.

St. Paul wasn't lying or being falsely humble when he counted himself as the "chief of sinners." His point was not that he had been or was the worst sinner in the world, but rather that he had no illusions about the potential for evil within himself and that he marveled that God's grace was great enough to choose him for an apostle. In Romans 7 he vividly described the inner battle he had with evil. He admitted to being a desperate man who, apart from the empowerment of Christ within him, would not have amounted to anything.

I don't wish to be unfair to Paul, but I suspect that he had a particular ability to be abrasive, argumentative, and intimidating in certain social situations. His brittleness in turning away from young John Mark and the compassionate Barnabas makes one wonder if poor Paul wasn't often victimized by an unforgiving and judgmental spirit. And did the old Apostle suffer from this character defect? My opinion is that he did and that he often asked God for its removal. Could it have been his famous thorn in the flesh? A problem of character and personality rather than a problem of a physical nature?

THERE IS GOOD NEWS

The predicament of evil in the inner space of Paul and in the rest of us was not the way things were meant to be. Perhaps one of the reasons we do not take evil seriously enough is because we fail to realize that the human life was created by its Maker to be something entirely different. The Bible makes it clear that *a single human being is the most beautiful, the most valuable, and the most potentially powerful thing (or being) that God ever created.*

That may be a strange point to make when discussing a gloomy subject like evil. But the gloominess will not be properly handled until we realize what were the original creation intentions of God our Maker and what we have forfeited by diverging from that original design. So we must make this affirmation: human beings were created to be beautiful and integrated, individually and in community with one another, their mission to discover, enjoy, and reflect the glory of God.

This beauty was violently damaged by evil much as the magnificent *Pietà* was damaged in the Vatican a few years ago by a crazed man who charged through the barriers and slammed away at it with a hammer. With the pieces of the *Pietà* on the floor and the world of art in shock, the question became, can this magnificent work of art be restored? And the great question of the Bible after the worlds of the first man and woman were shattered was, can these worlds be rebuilt? And in both cases the answer was yes.

Art experts have since restored the *Pietà* so that the damage can hardly be detected by anyone but the most knowledgeable. And the genius of the Christian gospel is that the beauty of humankind is also restorable or "rebuildable" no matter how badly one's world has been damaged in one's past experience.

It might be useful to meditate on why the art world could be so devastated when something like a marble sculpture was desecrated, but most people hardly wince at the thought that humanity has been ravaged by this inner and outer spiritual energy called evil.

The restoration or rebuilding process in the human experience, St. Paul taught, is in two parts. A "present-life" part in which our original beauty is slowly reformed but some effects of the damage of evil still can be seen. And a "future-time," the day of Christ, when all effects of the original damage evil caused will be erased, and our humanity will be perfected as if nothing wrong had ever happened. The Bible refers to this two-part rebuilding process as the great hope, and it is available to all who seek it through faith in Christ.

A legend from the sheep counties of England exemplifies the process. Some centuries ago two men were arrested and convicted for stealing sheep. The magistrate sent them to prison for several years and decreed that the letter S should be burned into their foreheads with a hot iron. He determined that no one should ever forget their crimes.

When the jail terms were ended, one of the two left the area and was never heard from again. The second, being greatly sorry for his thievery and having dedicated his life to God, chose to remain in the community and offer himself in service to people. As the years passed, everyone fell into his debt because of the ways in which he freely gave himself to aid them in their sicknesses, their family crises, and their difficulties in their work. Soon no one remembered or spoke of his earlier crime of sheep stealing. They spoke only of all he had given them out of a heart of grace and love.

The legend concludes with the conversation of two small boys who because of their young age knew nothing of the past. Seeing the now aged man pass by, one asked the other, "Why do you think he has an S on his forehead?"

"I'm not sure," the second replied, "but from what my mum says about him, I think it must mean 'Saint.'"

THERE IS ALSO BAD NEWS

My inner-space exploration taught me that the evil within me is not going to go away in the present time. However, with the appropriate energy, a gift from God's Spirit, it can be MANAGED. But while the capability of inner evil to upset things will be checked, it will not be obliterated. I must learn to be aware of evil and vigilant for its attempts to betray me much like I might carefully monitor a chronic infection that can be kept under control if I am careful.

Perhaps it is here that many people calling themselves Christians are most apt to get into trouble. Pinning their hopes and expectations on a conversion experience and the seemingly fast changes that often happen in the first phases of a new Christian life, they too easily forget that evil lies miles deep in inner space. Just because the first "two feet" of our inner space have been sifted and momentarily cleaned up does not mean that the miles below are not going to make their contents known sooner or later.

Where are we most likely to see the signs of evil that roar up from deep within? There are probably many answers to that question. But let me suggest a few common times and places when and where we will probably see a side of ourselves that can be unpleasant.

1. WHEN WE'RE "AMBUSHED"

We are likely to discover what is deep within, first of all, when we react in moments for which we are not prepared. For example, that night in the Garden of Gethsemane Simon Peter was suddenly awakened from a nap he shouldn't have been taking, and he realized that men were coming to arrest Jesus. In the fogginess of the moment, Peter grabbed a sword and started swinging, the very thing he'd been taught for three years not to do. Under pressure he reverted to type; the dragons came up from beneath.

C. S. Lewis in *Mere Christianity* speaks of the sinfulness within inner space that is uncovered in the sudden experiences. When he notes sullenness in himself or he snaps at a person, he admits he is likely to reason at first that his reaction is not a demonstration of evil within; rather, he was just caught off guard. But more reflection tells him that he is wrong. What I've called the dragons within, he calls the rats in the cellar.

If there are rats in a cellar you are most likely to see them if you go in very suddenly. But the suddenness does not create the rats: it only prevents them from hiding. In the same way the suddenness of the provocation does not make me an ill-tempered man: it only shows me what an ill-tempered man I am. The rats are always there in the cellar, but if you go in shouting and noisily they will have taken cover before you switch on the light. Apparently the rats of resentment and vindictiveness are always there in the cellar of my soul. Now that cellar is out of reach of my conscious will. I can to some extent control my acts: I have no direct control over my temperament.

2. WHEN WE PERCEIVE THAT WE'VE BEEN "MISTREATED"

We will also find out what is deep within when we've been put at a disadvantage by others: their fault or ours. Some of us will find a desire for vengeance, to fight back, to defend ourselves with endless protests and explanations. We will fantasize about ways in which we can gain back our due and at the same time discredit the other. And if we have been in the wrong, we will carefully think through the way others have responded to see if there is anything we can expose about their lack of grace and forgiveness that we insist we need.

3. WHEN WE ARE TREATED AS WE DESERVE TO BE TREATED

A friend tells me that you know whether or not you're really a servant by the way you react when you're treated like one. And I suppose that there is a corollary: you know if you have accepted yourself as a sinner when people help you find out just a little bit more concerning your sinfulness.

Stanley Jones speaks of a Brahmin convert who began to live at the ashram he and others had founded in India. Everyone was expected to participate in the community chores, including the cleaning of latrines. At that task the former Brahmin stopped short, claiming the job was beneath him. When Jones insisted that in Christ there were no tasks unsuitable for humble people and that those converted to His lordship should have no trouble cleaning latrines, the Indian responded, "Brother Stanley, I'm converted, but not that far."

I've discovered that I do not mind sharing the fact of my humanity with people; however, I do have problems when people highlight *my* humanity and the evidences of its faults and flaws for me. That's when I'm reminded once again that evil dwells deep within.

4. WHEN WE ARE DRAWN TO THE EVIL THAT OTHER PEOPLE ARE DOING

To the Roman Christians, Paul wrote much about evil, and he did not make the issue easier to accept when he suggested that people who "approve of those who practice [evil]" (Rom. 1:32) are telling on themselves.

Why are we drawn to the amusements and spectacles that portray people in real life or in fiction doing things we do not believe in doing ourselves? Our choices of amusement in sports, the theater and the cinema, and literature may in fact tell on us. The "deep" within us subtly calls out to things of evil about us, and the two entities feed on each other.

In my conversations with secret carriers, I've learned that many people, whose lives appear to be exemplary on the surface, are drawn to pornography (soft if not hard), violence and explicit sex in films, and places where all sorts of illicit activities take place. Cable TV has brought into many homes the information and stimulation that can only couple with the dragons within and hasten choices and values that create implosion and a broken world.

Thus, I came to newly affirm that the evil within is matched by the energy of evil in my outer space. The two forms could be said to attract each other. The inner comes in a spirit of rebelliousness; the outer in the form of attractive temptations, usually appealing to aspects of my emotions, drives, and intellect that will give a hearing. I don't know how to say it any better when I observe that there is a conspiracy between the two sources of evil.

Sometimes the evil from without comes to us through another person or through an appealing goal or objective or the temptation to a pleasurable experience. Samson met his Delilah; Gideon heard the crowd's applause; Solomon grew bored and had to keep pressing out the boundaries of sensation. These things and persons became attractive to these men, and the energy of inner evil provided an impetus to destructive choices. And because they were not on top of the situation, managing what was inside them, each imploded and fell in a heap like the building in Boston.

St. John wrote of Jesus that He trusted Himself to no man because "He knew what was in man" (2:24 NKJV). What did our Lord know? What Jeremiah said: that the heart was deceitful and that no one could figure it out. So I am impressed with the notion that if there is a sense in which Jesus can trust Himself to no one in terms of opinions and whims, then there is a sense in which I should not trust myself, either. I must assume that left to myself, energies within will quite likely betray me and urge me into a pattern of drift in life that will eventuate in implosion, a broken-world experience. G. K. Chesterton must have been thinking about this when he said through the words of his famous character, Father Brown, "The one spiritual disease is thinking that one [is] quite well."

This has been a most difficult chapter to write. And even as I finish it, I'm not satisfied with its contents. The subject of the evil within is far too illusive to handle adequately in a few pages. The unattractiveness of the subject is so clear that one is reluctant to write for fear that the reader will drop the book and not read on. The pessimism of the subject is so awesome that one fears a gloominess of soul. BUT EVIL MUST BE NAMED, not only in its generic presence within the inner space but in its specific dragonlike appearances. It must be acknowledged, confronted, managed, and hated.

I add the last word because I am impressed with the words of a young evangelist I deeply admire. When I asked him at breakfast one day what made him go to the streets and campuses day after day and represent the gospel of Christ, he said very simply, "Because I hate sin, and I have something in the gospel that can do something about it."

I was rebuked by his response to my question. The simple fact was that I didn't hate sin enough. I do now!

I watch that building in Boston collapse into rubble. It wasn't the most attractive building in the city over the years of its life. But because I tend toward the sentimental, I think of the architect who designed it, the builder who built it, and the owner who first cut the dedication ribbon and opened it up. I think of all the people who worked there, made friends there, achieved or lost great fortunes there. The building had a million memories imbedded in its walls. And now it's gone; it has imploded. Like a broken-world person who didn't know that the evil within has devastating power.

PART II
WHY WORLDS BREAK

8

Unhealthy Environments

BOTTOM LINE #8: *Influences and moods, people and atmospheres, pressures and weariness: some or all of these, like a smoke screen, can distort what might otherwise be good thinking.*

In 1952, when I was barely an adolescent, my family and I moved from east to west and settled in Denver, then a modest-sized Rocky Mountain city. Since I had spent my earliest years in the urban sprawls of New York and Cleveland, Denver was a dream come true.

The mountains to the west of the city were almost always in full view; the dry, clear air was part of a very appealing climate; and the city possessed a western, rugged quaintness that fit the image of a Roy Rogers culture. The informality of those early 1950s days can best be illustrated by my recollection of walking unannounced into the Colorado governor's office (we called the governor Big Dan) and spending twenty minutes in conversation with him while he sat with cowboy-booted feet propped up on his desk. I was thirteen years old at the time. Denver was a great town for a boy.

All of that former desirability of climate, clear air, and western folksiness sprang out of my memory recently when my mother called to say that she and her husband were planning to move away from Denver. When I asked why, she told me that her physician said a move would be necessary.

"I have weak lungs," she said.

"But is there a place in the world better for someone with weak lungs than Denver?" I asked, remembering the way we all used to boast about the advantages of the environment.

"Well, the doctor says that Denver's air is now so polluted during much of the year that people with respiratory problems like mine can't live here anymore. It's unwise for us to stay."

Basically, my mother was saying that one's health can be adversely affected if one lives in an environment whose elements weaken the body and make it susceptible to other sicknesses and diseases.

This is ironic, I thought as my mother went on to tell me about moving plans. What had once been a city to which people would come in the *pursuit* of good health was now a place they had to leave to *preserve* good health. That's why many cities, like Denver, now have daily environmental reports. "Today we have an air pollution warning," the radio newsperson often says. "Health officials are suggesting that anyone with breathing problems should stay indoors."

If my mother has become sensitive to the quality of an environment because she has undependable lungs, I wonder if there is some value in giving attention to the kinds of environments that could be beneficial *or* detrimental to our spiritual lives. That thought takes me back to the young man who left home for the big city and the good life and ended up with the pigs and lots to think about.

The prodigal son broods in the pigsty. His world is broken into a thousand pieces, and in that shattered condition he slowly comes to INSIGHT. He has begun to measure his thinking against the truth. What his father had taught him and warned him about was in fact the real story of life. But he hadn't accepted his father's perspective.

Now in his INSIGHT he sorts out his willful blunders: his arrogant, know-it-all attitude; his demanding ways; his choices; his selfishness; his blindness to the occasional warning signs. He sees his inner deceit for what it was and is. Perhaps he occasionally gets up and stomps about in angry frustration as he ponders his own stupidity. Now he can see how much he hurt his father; what he lost by not remaining where the love was genuine and the life-style stable and nourishing; how he has accrued consequences to himself that he may have to live with for the rest of his life. The evil in his heart is apparent now; and the cost of permitting it to go unmanaged is quite clear.

The drilling on the cavity of his heart goes deeper and

deeper, and as always, the process is terribly painful. But for the first time he is thinking with clarity. Eventually the cavity will be clean; eventually it will be time to rebuild his broken world.

Now having admitted to himself that he is not worthy to be a part of his father's family, he may be ready to go back and think through the realities of the spiritual and moral environment in which he made his decisions. Having dealt with his interior situation—the evil in his heart—he is ready to look at the exterior, the contributing elements that may have conspired to make his foolish choices possible.

He will begin to think about the city he chose to live in when he left home. Why that one? He'll look with fresh eyes on the people with whom he chose to spend his time. Why them? The places he chose to go; the things he chose to do when he got there. What was in my mind? he may wonder. Why is something that once seemed so satisfying now so distasteful? He has no good memories. The noise, the glitter, the sensations, have lost their appeal.

My imagination sees the prodigal coming to the realization that he had placed himself in an ocean current of influence and activity much like an undertow gradually sweeping him away until the consequences were out of control. Does he not ask himself more than once as he walks among the pigs and occasionally nibbles at a cornhusk, why couldn't I have seen it all as clearly as I see it now? I was warned about these things. I had seen others implode. Did I really assume that I was the great exception?

I strongly believe that our Christian view of human performance must always take into account the decision-making environments if we are to understand why people have broken-world experiences. Most broken-world people who are terribly remorseful will say that the choices they made are now mystifying even to them. As they look backward, they discern conditions that affected the way they thought and acted. And with such hindsight they see things *now* that they did not look far enough to see then. Influences and moods, people and atmospheres, pressures and weariness: some or all of them, like a smoke screen, distort thinking.

This is an extremely delicate subject, this business of environments. In even raising the topic, I run the risk of seeming to provide an excuse for errant behavior. And so, make no mistake, that is why I wrote of the evil in the heart first. I wanted to make sure that I was not misunderstood. Before God, *there is no excuse for evil choices.*

We do no one a favor when we offer excuses for evil performance. *But we also do no one a favor if we stop at the subject of evil or sin and say nothing about what assists a person in making an evil choice on one day that he or she would never have made on another day.* The evil in our hearts and the environments of our worlds are a combination that must be studied and mastered to appreciate how worlds break up. Unfortunately, there is too often a tendency to pay attention to one at the expense of the other.

Perhaps I can best illustrate this point about environments by taking a few samples and then showing their relevance in a conversation I recently had with a broken-world person.

People who frequently travel for business purposes are quick to agree that they often live with heavy moral temptation while they are away from home. Why? *The environment is different.* The away-from-home environment fairly invites various forms of broken-world choices by the unsuspecting.

In the environs of home life with family and friends, there is a schedule of routines, a set of support systems, and a way of doing things, all of which lends encouragement to responsible living and, conversely, restraint against irresponsible living. Virtually all of these external systems fall away when a person is hundreds of miles from home.

Thus, one may have only internal values and convictions upon which to rely for guidance in choices and commitments. If those have been carefully developed and nourished, they are more than adequate. But if they have been ignored? Then the greater susceptibility.

What are some of the specific external supports the traveler misses? INTIMACY, for one. A strange environment stimulates forceful feelings of loneliness and a desire to be in contact with someone who cares. Loneliness is largely a feeling of valuelessness, a "disconnectedness" in which a person feels cut off from spiritual and psychic forms of energy that make him feel whole and special.

RESTRAINT is often missing. In familiar surroundings, an individual has a sense of responsibility to people and systems that he would not want to violate, perhaps for fear that he would become unacceptable in a community where he has to get along. A child, for example, behaves when he knows that his misbehavior will bring a bad report to his parents. This assumes, of course, that he cares what his parents think and fears (in the right sense) their corrective actions.

A traveler, on the other hand, is very much aware of a high level of anonymity. No one will know or care what I do, a small inner voice, not of God, is liable to say. I won't be found out. This message is tempting to the rebellious part of human nature. In other words, one might wrongly conclude, there appear to be no consequences that I have to fear when I make certain unsavory choices.

A third environmental element the traveler sometimes misses is an ACTIVE MORAL CULTURE. He finds just the opposite culture vying for his attention for its own profit. He walks through the hotel lobby on his way to his room and sees the cocktail lounge. Drinks are available at the bar and in most hotel rooms, which may lower one's level of prudence in responsible choice making. Soft-core pornography is there for the asking on the room's television for only a few dollars. And if one is in the company of others, some of them may be only too ready to urge one another on to activities that none of them would be willing to do alone, much less in familiar surroundings.

All of these elements are apparent when I visit with a remorseful frequent flyer who shares with me the story of an illicit encounter with a woman. It occurred when he was one thousand miles from home. He is absolutely horrified when he recalls what happened. "It's hard to believe that that was me," he says. "I've never done things like that before in my life. There's nothing to justify what I did."

He was maintaining a booth for his company at a trade convention. Each evening he returned to his hotel after twelve hours of what felt like nonstop talking with conventioneers who only amplified his sense of loneliness by their seemingly obnoxious treatment of him.

On the third evening he found himself in conversation with a woman who sat a few feet away from his dinner table in the hotel restaurant. "She said things that got me talking about myself. And I have to admit that I enjoyed the conversation. It was great to talk with someone who was attractive and appeared to be attracted to me. I hadn't had a decent personal talk with anyone, it seemed, for three days."

He tells how they talked for a while and then he invited her to his room. He knew logically that such an invitation was poor judgment. But another part of him seemed to take increasing control and drown out the normal warning signals. In that context, he later found himself involved in a sexual relationship.

"When I came to my senses, I couldn't believe what had happened. I felt as if I was monitoring the behavior of someone else. I can't describe how totally I hate myself. I literally shiver every time I think about it."

Naturally my friend is shaken. What has this all meant? What will it do to his marriage and family if his wife finds out? "I really love my wife," he says. "Can you imagine what this will do to our relationship if this thing is exposed?"

What does it say about his character, his years of Christian living? "I know it sounds stupid in light of what I'm telling you. But I'm really not that kind of a guy. I thought this sort of thing only happened to other men."

And, assuming he can resolve this, what about the future? "I'm actually terrified each time I reenact in my mind what occurred. Could this happen again? Am I that weak?"

And then he'd like to know where he stands with God. "I really am committed to my Christian life; I thought I'd been a believer long enough to avoid these kinds of temptations."

As we try to analyze his experience, I point out that he will never get anywhere in understanding this thing he now so thoroughly detests unless he begins with an acceptance of his own responsibility.

"You have to face the fact that before God you're liable for the choice you made that evening. The core issue is sin, and the acts of that night spring from an inner being that, left to its own instincts, will usually swing away from the laws of God and the personal covenants you have made to those around you.

"But then you have to go on from there to understand that you put yourself into an environment that made it easier for you to make a bad choice, a choice you probably wouldn't have made on another occasion. That's not an excuse I've provided for you, but it does describe the context for a bad choice."

"Explain what you mean," he says.

"Well, let's put it as simply as possible. If you had been at home on a normal workday, what would you have done at the end of the afternoon?"

"Gone home."

"Exactly. And, assuming that you and your wife are on the good terms you describe, you would have had some sort of an evening together that would have reenergized you in terms of your needs for intimacy, for sharing the 'goods' and 'bads' of the day, for relaxation among people you love. Right?"

"Of course."

"And let's throw one more thing in. Suppose that there in your own home community you had indeed been going through some form of sexual temptation. Is it reasonable to say that you probably wouldn't have gotten past the fantasy line because, first of all, within a short time you would have been with your family and, second, you would fear being exposed if you did something wrong?"

"Sure. A guy would be pretty dumb to fool around with anyone where he works or in his community. I wouldn't do that anyway, but assuming your logic, it would be a stupid thing to do. There's too much that can go wrong that hurts everyone."

"So what you're saying," I respond, "is that our normal and routine home life is itself a reasonable restraint against what a lot of men and women might otherwise do if they were somewhere else."

"Yeah, that's what I'm saying."

We go on to discuss the environment in which my friend made his regrettable choice that night. Days of hard work in which he felt isolated. A hotel's strange surroundings that offered no accountability for untoward behavior. A person met at an unexpected moment who had acquired seductive skills in order to appeal to and stimulate the desires and weaknesses of a tired, lonely man.

"Tell me," I ask, "who was the first of the two of you to sit down in that restaurant?"

"I guess she was. She was sitting there when I came in."

"Could you have seated yourself any other place in the restaurant?"

He pauses and thinks for a moment. "Yeah, I could have."

"But you chose to sit there, near her. Level with me. Why?"

"Man to man?"

"Yes, man to man."

"Am I really sounding stupid when I say I thought she was beautiful, and I guess I just wanted to connect with some person who was attractive? But I had no intention of anything happening. I guess I would have been happy if she had just smiled at me. Isn't that the way a lot of men want it to be?"

"We all like the smile of an attractive person. It makes us feel valuable. And apparently you weren't feeling very valuable that evening, were you?"

"No, I wasn't. And I guess you're tempted to feel valuable if you can get a good-looking woman to notice you."

"So it started with a choice about where to sit and went on from the hope she might notice you to a few friendly words and then a longer conversation. By then some kind of line had been crossed. Is that the story?"

"That's the story."

"There is nothing in the world that excuses your behavior," I say again. "That has to be acknowledged before God and perhaps to your wife as your responsibility. You're going to have to take your lumps on that. But we can help each other if we examine that environment in which you made your choice and ask what could have been done to make your choice making different."

"So what could have been different?" he asks.

"The first thing is the most obvious. Before you left on that trip, you could have foreseen what those days were going to be like. The schedule was already there to tell you that the days would offer little more than fatigue and loneliness. So you could have prepared yourself spiritually and psychically for it and reminded yourself that this was an environment essentially hostile toward a man who wants his life to follow Christ's ways.

"Then you could have arranged some specific activities in the evening that would have crowded out negative opportunities. Frankly, you and your wife should have discussed the pressures you might be living with before you left. It would have been good to have a telephone date with each other at a certain time. It might have been prudent to think about altering the places where you ate each evening. One businessman I know takes all of his meals in his room to avoid the very thing that happened to you. He isn't interested in meeting strangers in public places. He doesn't go into the restaurant and deliberately pick a table right next to an appealing woman.

"You could have brought along some projects to work on during the evening. An engaging book or two, for example, that would have given you something to look forward to each evening. In other words, you have to know when an environment is dangerous and how you're going to prepare for it.

"On any given day the best of us can cave in to a bad choice if we fool around in hostile environments. Frankly, it would have been wise to have sought out some Christian fellowship. In most cities these days one can find something going on that centers on a Christ-oriented activity. Perhaps you would have been too tired; but at least that would have been an option."

"I don't know that I could have done all that," he says. "I was awfully tired at the end of those days."

"Probably," I respond. "But you did want to know how you could have avoided what happened, and the only thing I know is that one has to avoid adverse environments and pursue healthy ones. Let me illustrate what I mean. My mother called me the other day and told me that she and her husband were going to have to move out of Denver. You'll never guess why."

He couldn't guess, and I told him my mother's uncomplimentary story about Denver . . . going all the way back to 1952. You might have known I would do that.

9

O-Rings and
Cold Temperatures

BOTTOM LINE #9: *Wise people need to know how their spiritual and mental systems are apt to operate in the various environments.*

When the space shuttle Challenger lifted into the sky and blew up seventy-three seconds into its flight, the world was shocked. Most of us have seen the videotape of that terrible moment many times. And we can re-create the picture in our minds of a deep blue sky marked with twisted trails of smoke and large chunks of metal plummeting toward the ocean. And we know, as we recall the grim specter of the explosion, that among the falling pieces were the bodies of some of America's finest men and women.

Most of us also know that the investigations into the cause of the tragedy pointed out some serious shortfalls in human judgment and materials management. The *New York Times* put it frankly: the ultimate cause of the space shuttle disaster was pride. A group of top managers failed to listen carefully to the warnings of those down the line who were concerned about the operational reliability of certain parts of the booster rocket under conditions of abnormal stress. The people in charge were confident that they knew best and that they should not change the launch schedules. They were wrong.

If the ultimate cause of the explosion was *pride*, the specific cause had something to do with O-rings, circular rubber seals that were supposed to fit snugly into the joints of the sections of the booster engines. Their function was to prevent gases from leaking at the joints during the launch phase when the rocket was under the great strain of lifting the shuttle into orbit.

The O-rings performed adequately on all the flights previous to the day of the tragedy. But on that day something was different. The environment. The temperature had dropped below the freezing mark, and under such conditions, some engineers warned, O-rings were apt to become brittle, inflexible, and therefore unreliable. Either that warning was not heard, or it went unheeded. And thus when the go-ahead to launch was given, pressurized fuel did leak past the O-rings, and there was a disaster.

Again, the story is one about environments, the conditions that can affect the performance of objects or people. As it is with O-rings in cold temperatures, so it can be with human life. History includes many stories of reliable men and women who suddenly seem to have reversed course and engaged in a personal scenario totally out of keeping with what they said they believed, what they might have done in the past, or what their stated goals and objectives in life have been.

Why such a break? Why such a choice? We've already established as firmly as possible that the ultimate answer to those questions focuses on the evil in the human heart. Not one of us, in the past or the present, can shirk our responsibility for the dark side within our private worlds. Unmanaged and unrestrained, evil can run amok, confuse and distort thinking, and affect our choices.

But there is the follow-up question of environments that we looked at in the previous chapter. What part do they play in the process of broken-world choices and consequences? A lot, I believe, and I feel strongly that most of us probably do not pay enough attention to these conditions surrounding us and affecting us. *If we did, we might be able to predict those times in which we ourselves as well as others are more likely to struggle and face the full onslaught of battles of the spirit.*

The friend who shares with me his grievous experience in a far-off hotel clearly understands in the aftermath of his terrible moral choice that the chances of his misbehavior happening in "home" territory would have been considerably lessened. He would have been on much more solid ground if he had been sensitive to the fact that the restraints and accountabilities of home were absent while he was away, that he would have to take care to monitor his thoughts and needs to make sure they were not susceptible to untoward influences. He didn't, and his world broke.

On the day of the space shuttle tragedy someone should have said (and somebody probably did but was ignored), "It's cold enough at the launch site to jeopardize the reliability of the O-rings. We can't be sure what might happen, but the margin of risk is too high. Abort the launch!"

Cain made his choice to kill his brother in a time of great anger. Abraham made a choice to impregnate a servant-woman, Hagar, in a time of anxiety as he considered the aging process of his wife, Sarah. In a mood of righteous indignation Moses killed a man. Saul, the first king of Israel, made his choice to disobey God when he was in an agitated state of impatience.

A fascinating successor to Saul a few generations later, King Uzziah, made a broken-world choice when he resisted the warnings of the priests in the temple that he was not qualified to approach the altar. He became a leper and died in disgrace. I can only assume that he made his choice in an environment of boredom and pride.

Study the tragic moments in many lives, and you will often discover that a secondary set of conditions was right behind the reality of embedded evil. Those conditions weakened the resolve of a man or woman to resist temptation and make decisions that were not right or true.

Later on I'll briefly note some more positive environments, the kind that protect personal worlds and provide opportunity for growth and development. But because our theme centers on broken worlds, my objective is to point out samples of negative environments, the kind that contribute to disasters.

Why should we highlight what some will certainly see as the pessimistic side of these milestones in life? I can think of five reasons:

1. We should become more sensitive to the reality of environments so that we can acquire the habit of internally

asking questions such as, what are the conditions inside and around me today that are liable to play havoc with my thinking processes, my values, my responses, my choices?

2. We can make decisions about environments we'd like to avoid and ones we'd like to enhance whenever possible.

3. Knowing something about environments may help us to surround ourselves with various forms of resolve and defense when we know we are in an environment we cannot change.

4. An awareness of environments will make us more sensitive to others around us: what they are facing and whether or not we can, as Christian brothers and sisters should, offer protection and mutual accountability for superior performance.

5. Finally, if we think through environments, we may be able to understand more compassionately what has led to the failure of others and give the sort of mercy and encouragement that might make the rebuilding of their broken world possible.

So I offer some sample environments. Five of them. There are doubtlessly many more. And as I write about these environments, I write with the pen of a Christian man taking a look at life through my own experience and those I've shared with others. There is nothing new here; only the familiar described as succinctly as possible so that we can take a fresh look at ourselves.

The point is simple. If the people at NASA need to know how their O-rings will operate in various temperatures, we need to know how our spiritual and mental systems are liable to operate in the various environments we are likely to face.

THE ENVIRONMENTS OF OUR AGE GROUPS

1. THE ENVIRONMENT OF INFANCY

Gail and I sit on an airplane for the six-hour flight from Los Angeles to Boston. The computer, bless it, has assigned us seats near the bulkhead, as they call it, and that means the odds have increased that we will be near young families with babies. On this flight we have three of them. Now, we like young families; we used to be one. But young families mean babies who cry. Frankly, I don't remember (although Gail strongly disagrees) that our children ever cried in public.

Predictably, soon after the plane takes off, a baby begins to cry—no, scream would be a better description. Perhaps rage might be even better.

Whatever it is, it continues across Nevada, Utah, Colorado, and well into Nebraska. I have sensitive ears, and after 1,050 frequent-flyer miles of screaming, my ability to ignore the matter wanes considerably. I know my question isn't going to gain a satisfying answer, but something in me just needs to ask Gail, "Why doesn't that mother do something for that child?"

Gail knows the answer and says exactly what I knew she would say, "Honey, the child is obviously overtired. They had to get the child up unusually early this morning to make it to the airport, and now the poor thing is simply saying that this is not a pleasant place to be." That explanation settles the matter for Gail; I try to pretend that it settles it for me. And the baby goes on affirming Gail's interpretation of its behavior.

Over Illinois, Indiana, and most of Ohio, another child begins to make its presence known. I look at Gail, and before I can even pose the question, she answers, "You can see, can't you, that the child is hungry? The mother is out of milk, and the flight attendants don't have anything to offer her." Again, Gail is satisfied with her analysis. I am rattled but manage to hide it.

Over Albany, New York, the plane begins to descend toward Boston. A third baby notes this and begins to out-scream the other two. Now Gail doesn't even wait for my signal. "Can you imagine how that child is feeling?" she says. "She's got a cold, and her ears are reacting to the changes in altitude. She's probably going to cry all the way down to the ground. I hope her mother and someone sitting beside me realize the problem. You'd cry too if you had those ears."

We may not like the sound or the performance of a screaming child, but we try (at least Gail does) to understand what might contribute to such behavior. *Environments* of course: fatigue, hunger, altitude changes. And if we believe that, we suddenly become merciful.

I don't wish to belabor this matter, but the very simplicity of the problem of a crying baby may help when the issues later become more complex. On one or two occasions I've watched angry parents spank a toddler for violent crying in public. They seek to end what they perceive to be a misbehavior caused by pain or discomfort, and they do this by causing more pain. They are not happy with the misbehavior, but neither is the child. Wise parents in the airplane situation make a decision: when to be tough and disciplinary and when to be merciful and comforting. They know which alternative to choose not because of some all-encompassing rule about how to treat crying or misbehaving children but because they are there at the moment and sense something of the conditions the children are facing.

2. THE ENVIRONMENT OF ADOLESCENCE

Just as babies do, *adolescents* face the issue of environments. Years ago when our son, Mark, was entering his teen years, he would often sit on the edge of his bed on a Saturday morning and stare out the window for hours if I would permit him to. I would pass by his room several times and wring my hands at the apparent waste of time. "Son," I wanted to ask and frequently did, "how can you squander so much valuable time? What are you doing?"

"Oh, I don't know . . . thinking, I guess."

"What are you thinking about?"

"Oh, ah, I dunno . . . just thinking."

My physician friend, also the father of teenaged boys, tells me that Mark at twelve and thirteen was like any other boy his age. He was the victim of overdosages and underdosages of valuable hormones that were just becoming activated in his body. "That's one of the major reasons why he could be so active one moment and so frustratingly inactive at another moment. Hormones!"

At the time I gained this insight about teenaged boys, I saw my need to be more understanding of my son. I realized that his choices were often influenced by things going on in his body that he knew little or nothing about. Could he control them? How could he listen to them, monitor them, know when to say no to them? That's in part what fathers and mothers are for: to back off when their children are in good control and managing life responsibly and to assert authority when they are not. I had to be sensitive, for example, when Mark's choices were being influenced by energies inside himself that he could barely manage. And sometimes I wasn't.

When she was a teenager, our daughter, Kristy, had more than her share of friends, all of whom seemed to have great plans for her life. Come here with us; go there; do this; do that. More than once I saw her eyes tearful under the weight of trying to be everything and do everything that the group wanted. It was a social environment that could be hazardous at times, a context of life and action in which she could much more easily make bad choices that she might not make if she was around individuals with stronger and sounder judgment.

As I watched our teenagers grow up, I realized and took into account the fact that they were often affected by environmental factors within their bodies and in their social connections. Knowing that caused me to respond differently from ways I might have otherwise responded when their behavior was not what I wanted or expected. It wasn't that their mother or I ever compromised the standards in which we believed; rather, we tempered our reactions with an understanding of their pressurized environments.

If teenagers have made choices that shattered their personal worlds, it's likely that they made their choices when peer pressure was at its highest, when they felt unloved by significant people in their lives, or when their inner drives and passions were stirred up and they were in situations with others where there was minimal restraint. The choices were theirs, of course, but the choices were more easily made to the destructive side in certain environments than in others.

Knowing that our young son and daughter would be vulnerable like all others at the ages of thirteen and fourteen, I sat down with them when they were eleven and said, "You need to know that your mom and I believe that boy-girl dating should not begin until your sixteenth year. Now you're going to find it hard to accept this at times, but we believe that we should not permit you to date until then. It would be wise if you didn't accept any invitations or extend them without remembering this rule. I'm not going to compromise it when you come home and say you'll be humiliated if I don't change my mind. I won't."

And I didn't. Well, perhaps I did compromise at fifteen

and a half. It wasn't that I mistrusted our children; rather, I felt I understood that some environments offer options and pressures that young teenagers are not ready to handle. Better for our kids to be a bit frustrated with their father and mother for a short while than to be crippled for years to come with consequences of choices they weren't yet prepared to make.

The point is this: adolescence offers a whole array of possibilities for misbehavior. But those can be effectively checked in most cases if proper loving authority and accountability exist between family members. If what I am saying is true, by the way, then one has much to think about in terms of the consequences when families adopt separate lifestyles where there is no influence whatsoever across the generations.

3. THE ENVIRONMENT OF YOUNG ADULTHOOD

A *young adult* is not as likely to be controlled by physiological hormones as by emotional needs. *Intimacy,* for example, is the need to enter a circle of personal relationships where there will be the chance to give and receive love. *Identity,* the need to fit in as a useful person in one's society, and *functional value,* the need to prove oneself in a vocation or career, become critically important.

Frequently, young adults will make decisions and choices that seem to make little sense as they try to meet these needs or drives. Broken-world consequences can be just around the corner, and the onlooker wonders how a vibrant young person with a whole future ahead can jeopardize it all with so little wisdom or restraint.

I visit with a woman in her forties who has come to discuss a marriage that has exploded after fifteen years, leaving two people with worlds so broken that they will probably take years to recover. She speaks of a relationship that soured almost before the end of the honeymoon. Of two people who seemed adept at inflicting maximum emotional damage on each other.

"Didn't you see this sort of thing coming before you walked the aisle?"

"Perhaps I did," she answers. "I remember my parents expressing strong reservations about the wisdom of the relationship even up to the week of the wedding. They pressed me pretty hard, but I didn't listen."

When I ask why, she says, "I had a terrible fear of loneliness and couldn't bear the thought that I might go through adult life as a single person. And even though I realized that he wasn't the perfect man, I told myself we could solve some of these problems after we settled into the relationship. You can do that, you know. But maybe I've discovered that there's a set of problems between two people that can't be solved. I wish I'd listened to my parents."

Why the poor choice? The overwhelming emotional environment of the need for intimacy. It spoke louder than wisdom. It should have been controlled, but it wasn't. As you ponder the loss of a marriage, the years of domestic strife, you wonder why there wasn't a stronger opportunity for better decision making.

The fear of living an unmarried life may be the very emotional environment capable of leading a young woman to compromise her moral standards in order to attract the attentions of a man she likes.

In the environment of ambition, the desire to establish oneself and one's dreams, there is the greater likelihood of compromise. The desire to establish a career, get a foothold in an organization, might make it easier for one to turn one's head in the moment of an unethical decision or to ignore an injustice being done to a fellow worker. "Making waves," as some put it, is not the most judicious thing when you're young and vulnerable in the marketplace. There's always someone ready to step in and take your place, one hears. Pressure mounts, and a person finds it much easier to take the first steps toward choices and decisions never before thought possible.

These are just a few reasons why young adults badly need mentors or sponsors, older couples who come alongside and offer supportive wisdom, encouragement, and models of godly behavior. Young adults can thrive in these difficult environments when they renounce the youthful tendency to want to go it alone and seek relationships providing guidance and accountability. In no other phase of life is it more important to establish clear, routine spiritual disciplines than in young adulthood. The temptation to rely on abundant energy, youthful charisma, and inner enthusiasm will lead many to ignore the necessity of quiet, solitude, reflection, and listening. And that temptation has to be checked and countered with the prayerful and receptive life-style. In these ways the danger points in the environment are all but neutralized.

4. THE ENVIRONMENT OF MID-LIFE

The *mid-life person* is in a time of life in which the feelings of gradual and inexorable loss can become very real: loss of time, of opportunities, of energy, of youthfulness. And the person may be sensitive to the fact that a large part of the world gears itself to the values and tastes of a younger generation.

Relationships are changing for the mid-lifer. His parents are aging, his children are leaving, and his peers may seem to be passing him by in their various pursuits of success. His marriage may have lost some of its charm if he hasn't been vigilant in its maintenance; his body may be letting him down because he hasn't taken good care of it. It's a scary time because it suggests that more than half of life is ended and the last half is not as likely to be as kind as the first.

The mid-lifer may experience the pressurized environment of having major responsibility for parents and children. How is he going to handle his kids' college tuition, the needs of his aging parents, and the monthly bills he has to pay? Then one day he has the choice to enter an elaborate kickback scheme that promises to ease the burden. This person would never have thought to do such a thing. *But*, he thinks, *times are different now. Everyone seems to be doing it; I'm not fairly treated by the organization anyway.* The choice, once very clear in its rightness and wrongness, is now not so easy to make.

There may be a great temptation to slow life down by trying to return to young adulthood and all of its perceived glamour. Or there may be a temptation to speed life up and grasp for things that have great promise on the surface but rarely deliver.

"I like you a lot, but I have to tell you that you look awful," I say to a man I know when we bump into each other at a gas station.

"I have a right to look awful," he says. "Everything is coming unglued."

We go for coffee, and I learn that he is deeply in debt and that an unexpected government cut in a weapons systems program on which he has been working is going to cost him his job.

"Carrie (not her real name) and I went way out on a limb this past year. We put an addition on the house, bought a much nicer car than we should have, and credit-carded our way into a lot of stupid debts for clothes and trips we shouldn't have accumulated. I've used up all our savings, and we're broke. The job market stinks—at least in my specialty."

Knowing this man as I've known him, I'm surprised. It's out of character, it seems, for him to have taken such financial risks.

"We got tired of controlling ourselves so tightly, I guess. We saw all our friends taking skiing trips to Switzerland and said to ourselves, 'Why don't we go too?' I got fed up with driving a Chevy when all our friends were into BMW's and Audis. Do I sound unspiritual when I say that I think we were bored? So . . . it seemed rather easy to sign for all that stuff. A lot harder to pay for it later on. Especially when they call you in on a Friday afternoon and tell you that nine years of a good job are over."

After further conversation, I leave my friend and think about bad choices we mid-lifers make when we panic at the passing of our lives. I think about his attempts to cope with perceived boredom by acquiring glittering, expensive things. I'd like to think I wouldn't do what he has done, and I find little reason to excuse his choices. But I do understand his age-group all too well, and I remind myself that the environment makes it quite easy for a man or a woman to do some strange things out of character with previous performance. It's easy to reason that you're missing out on things. And the temptation becomes rather large for some to take risks and make decisions that have great broken-world possibilities.

Mid-life is a time for the building of peer relationships, friends who covenant to walk through the remainder of life together. Their relationship needs to be built on the mutual sharing and exploration of their faith in God, what it means to support one another as the challenge of change comes their way, and what it means to protect one another from foolish choices based on false premises.

Mid-life is a time to dream new dreams, determine to invest oneself in the younger generation as a mentor, and press for quality of life rather than quantity of things or experiences. In athletic terminology that means taking the offensive and not settling for the defensive decisions my friend at the gas station made that cost him so dearly.

5. THE ENVIRONMENT OF SENIOR ADULTHOOD

Even our *senior generation* is quite capable of misbehavior. And when one asks what might be behind certain poor choices, it becomes important again to ask contextual questions about how aging people think and act.

For example, the senior person may be tempted to think that he is losing his value as a person. Rightly or wrongly, he perceives that younger people are more than willing to take his place and often even more capable. He struggles with self-esteem when he discovers that it takes longer to do simple things, and that the mind may not always be hospitable to change although everyone seems to be calling for change. An aging man or woman is tempted to anxiety about sicknesses and diseases, broken limbs, and systems of health care that seem very impersonal and increasingly expensive.

The possibility of bitterness also arises. One finds it very easy to get angry at a world that seems bent on shoving older people aside and not caring that they have feelings too. Add to this the difficulty in covering up negative feelings that used to be "suppressible": words slip out that one used to be able to control; sharp emotional reactions may show themselves before one is able to put a cover over them.

The aging person is frequently reminded of death. Good friends and loved ones slip away, and funerals are frequent occurrences. Children may hardly ever be seen, and young people aren't interested in hearing another's memories or even in finding out what wisdom the aged might have to offer.

It's a difficult time for many senior people. It's easy to sink into despair, and the environment of the senior makes it too easy to choose selfishness as a way of life. One sees it happen with increasing frequency. Good men and women decide that they have given enough and it's time to live only for themselves. They rather easily make a choice that they might have formerly called ungodly because their feelings and needs have ascended over convictions. This is no excuse, mind you, but something that needs our sensitivity.

A Florida man in his seventies watches as his wife slowly succumbs to the effects of Alzheimer's disease. The lovely woman to whom he has given himself all of his adult years, with whom he has shared the raising of a family and a volume of memories, seems no longer to be the person he once married. He sees her suffer and lose her dignity, and when he perceives that he can do nothing more to help her, he murders her, thinking it to be an act of mercy.

His terrible act represents in the extreme the misbehavior that can happen when one has reached a lonely and confused end of the rope. What support systems for him might have prevented what happened?

If babies and adolescents need parents, and young adults need mentors, and mid-lifers need friends, aging persons need almost everyone. We could say that they deserve everyone. They do not deserve what so many aging people get: isolation. And when we permit our aging generation to step out of the mainstream of daily life, we leave them vulnerable to broken-world choices, and we who are young lose a major asset to our lives also. When we understand that our elderly brothers and sisters need to be touched, thanked, respected, and consulted, we will have neutralized some of the negative effects of their environment of age-group.

Put simply, there are five environments of age-groups: infancy, adolescence, young adulthood, mid-life, and the elder years. Each one offers opportunities for people to make choices leading to broken worlds, choices opposed to God's laws and their best interests. But each environment properly understood provides rich opportunity for growth and wholeness. When we explore the upsides and downsides of each, we know how to act, what to choose, and where to be wary of the evil that can come from within or without.

And that kind of wariness is what you wish might have happened the morning the space shuttle lifted off. You wish that the people in the launch control center had asked a few more questions about how the parts of the rocket might act in an unprecedented climatic condition of coldness. But, as the *New York Times* says, there was too much pride in the space agency. Too many self-assured people thought that since they'd already put fifty-five people into space without a mishap, nothing would go wrong that day.

And perhaps nothing would have if it hadn't been for a unique environment. Would that we all knew that about life. Broken worlds might be less in number if we did.

10

When Mud Slides and Floods Take Their Toll

BOTTOM LINE #10: *When the body and the emotions and the mind are stretched to the limit, the risk of sinful choices climbs out of sight.*

Friends of ours recently took us on a tour of famous Catalina Island off the coast of California. As we walked one of the island's many valleys, they noted the seasonal danger of serious mud slides and fast runoffs of water if there is a prolonged rainy period.

"What makes it happen?" I asked.

"The ground can absorb only so much water," someone said, "and then there comes a moment of total saturation when the hills become destabilized. You can't ever tell when that moment is going to come. But when the soil is saturated and the hills are destabilized, the next rain, no matter how light it is, will set off a slide of mud and a raging flood down through the valley that will destroy everything in its path: buildings, livestock, and roads."

Saturated and destabilized! That could be a description of an inner life-style down deep where the emotions, the mind, the heart, the instincts, and the appetites vie for control of one's values and choices. As I stood there imagining the devastation of a mud slide and flood, I could see some personal worlds breaking up in the same way I had seen implod-

477

ing buildings, exploding booster rockets, and meteors hitting the earth.

I began to imagine the pressures, stresses, and sensations of the marketplace, the conflict-ridden home, and anxiety-producing events beating on a person like an endless rain. Suddenly, saturation and destabilization; slides, floods, destruction. A broken world. Everyone in the path affected in one way or another as hearts are wounded, reputations are jeopardized, trust is shattered, and security is lost.

I found myself in a pensive mood that day as I tried to visualize the effects of slides and floods. Here and there in the valley I could see the signs of such damage from former years. *It completes my word picture,* I thought. *The destruction caused by slides and floods doesn't go away in a short time.* The effects can remain for a lifetime whether we're talking about a valley or a personal world.

On that day I came up with a name for an environment of choice making that many of us frequently share. I simply called it the *Saturated and Destabilized Environment.* It includes many possible components, and I couldn't begin to list them all. They would probably not be scientifically or psychologically (let alone, theologically) defined anyway, for we're talking about experiences that can differ from person to person. And what affects one may not even touch another.

Perhaps that's one reason we do not spot saturation and destabilization in others so easily. And it may be why we're sometimes unsympathetic when someone else is struggling with an issue in the personal world that seems rather uncomplicated and quite manageable to us.

The saturated and destabilized environment describes those times in our lives when events and their results have tumbled in upon us to such an extent that we are in overload (as they like to say in our high-tech times). These are the periods of life when we feel that we have lost the initiative, that we no longer control the events around us. We feel as if we are spending all our time responding to the issues and problems other people create. And we sense that our effectiveness is quickly diminishing.

My physician friends tell me that this is exactly what they are testing for when teaching hospitals make medical students work thirty-six-hour shifts. They wish to induce overload, an experience of saturation and destabilization, so that they can see how a man or woman is going to perform under duress. They are anxious to see if the student's ability for diagnosis and treatment is as good at the end of the shift as it may have been at the beginning.

Gail and I know the saturated and destabilized environment well. Individuals who deal in temperament types and know us personally frequently warn us that this environment is our greatest personal threat to well-being.

Like many others, I've spent a large part of my adulthood in a vocation that knows no hourly bounds, no seeming limit to the number of things to do, no point where one can walk away and refuse to see another person. I'm not complaining; I've always liked my work. But I've grown increasingly aware that it can exact an enormous toll on spiritual and physical energy reserves.

Add to this that I am by nature a feeler and an "absorber"; I feel the struggles, the pain, and the aspirations of people around me, and I tend to absorb the anger of others and reveal none of my own. I am likely to accept more responsibility that I can adequately handle because I do not wish to hurt or disappoint people. I find it hard to erect protective fences around myself, assuming that there will be time and strength enough to get everything done that people expect of me. That's why the disciplines described in *Ordering Your Private World* were and are so important to me. They are my "fence" against saturation and destabilization.

Not long ago a young man expressed frustration with *OPW*, as we call the book, saying that he was not as organized as I was and therefore couldn't live up to its standards. I think I surprised him when I said that I wasn't naturally organized or disciplined either and that the book generally described what I found necessary to make my private world work.

Sometimes traits like the ones I've just described appear to look like virtues to some people. But they may not be virtues at all. They are simply facts of temperament and personality. I hope God has seen fit to baptize them into usefulness on occasion. But if these tendencies aren't properly managed, they backfire and lead me and those like me into the saturated and destabilized condition.

One obvious result can be weariness; another can be the feeling that I cannot please people enough. Sometimes having said yes to too many people, I'm liable to let someone down and seem not to have kept my word or followed through.

That's one of the many reasons why I thank God for a wife like Gail who, knowing this temperament of mine, will often say to me as she listens to me make one more commitment or promise, "Now I know you want to do this; but are you being realistic? Can you possibly meet that deadline?" Or make that call? Or have that appointment? Or write that article? Or travel to that meeting? She, more than anyone, knows the signals when I'm headed toward saturation and destabilization.

I sit one night with a friend at a National Hockey League game. The teams are warming up, and I watch the Boston Bruins stand on the blue line and shoot dozens of hockey pucks at the goalie. They shoot them one after another in machine-gun fashion. The goalie must spot each one instantly as it skims the ice or cuts through the air, and then he must catch it or deflect it with his stick, his pads, or the back of his glove.

I watch him respond to every hockey puck and then say to my friend, "I think I know exactly how he feels; I've just had a day like that. Pucks coming at me every minute. If he and I aren't alert, one of those things is going to get past and into the net or in the face, his or mine." Many people in our busy world know what I'm describing.

What sort of conditions might make up the saturated and destabilized environment? Let me name and comment on a few as samples. If we learn to be sensitive to their existence, perhaps we can do a better job of containing and managing them. And if we cannot, we must understand that here we are likely to open the door to the work of evil.

WEARINESS

Weariness, like the relentless seasonal rains on Catalina, certainly leads to saturation and destabilization. Weariness is that deadening fatigue of the body, the mind, and the spirit.

We can assume the presence of weariness when we do our work from obligation and not from challenge, when we seek to escape every time we see another person coming toward us, when cynicism, negativism, and the low fever of bitterness possess our minds. In a check for weariness we might want to look for irritability, the inability to quickly renew energy, the feeling that life no longer includes fun, or the panicky feeling that nothing we do is ever good enough.

Why be overly concerned about weariness? Aren't all busy, productive people always tired to some extent? Of course. But the wise person knows a danger zone when it appears on the screen of life, and he acts accordingly.

My father taught me to ski when I was a young boy. I recall one of his first pieces of advice on the slope: "Remember, Son, that more accidents happen in the final hour of the day than at any other time." I now know that he was correct.

Trying to get one more downhill run in before the ski tow closes, some skiers will rush down the slope forgetting that their bodies are tired and that their reflexes are no longer sharp. Shadows are long; icy and bare spots are hidden. The combination of a depleted body and obstacles not easily seen creates conditions (environments, if you please) in which accidents are far more likely to happen.

My dad was right; at the end of the day one should ski much more cautiously because the good skier knows himself and he doesn't trust the terrain.

Many men and women trying to follow the Lord make their world-breaking choices in similar times of extreme fatigue. Again, not necessarily the physical fatigue after a long day's work; but the fatigue of the spirit and the emotions that occurs after a lengthy period of time when frustration and difficulties have increased to an intense pitch.

I spoke of weariness when I wrote *Restoring Your Spiritual Passion* because I had experienced firsthand what it was all about, and I had become sensitive to the number of people who were signaling that they had the same problem. I did not say in that book what I might have: in the context of weariness I made a series of very bad choices that led to falling flat on my face into sin and hurting many people. Weariness is never to be construed as an excuse. It simply suggests that a person may make certain choices in one environment that he would probably never make in another.

Weariness often leads to something called burnout. One simply loses the will to pursue dreams and senses of mission.

I'm reminded of the comments of a champion boxer who described the other day how he had worn down his opponent and positioned him for the winning blow. "I just kept pounding on his arms and body until he became tireder and tireder. Then when he lowered his arms in fatigue, I put him away with a left to the side of the head." I can identify with the fellow he hit.

It's not a delicate description, but it's an accurate one for a boxer as well as for a man or woman with a broken world. More Christians than any of us know have made decisions that they will regret for the remainder of their lives under the influence of fatigue.

And what do we learn from this? How to monitor the times and circumstances in which such weariness and its ultimate product, burnout, are likely to occur. And then we learn either to avoid that extreme condition or to ask others to help us. In relationships of accountability others can protect us so that we are less prone to hurt ourselves with actions or attitudes leading to broken worlds.

In 1982 we bought a car that included a device that actually speaks to us when something is amiss or needs to be checked. We came to call the computer-generated voice Hilda because it is female in sound.

Hilda says, "Your right door is open" when the door is not properly shut, "Your parking brake is on" when I forget to release it, "Your keys are in the ignition" when I try to get out of the car without taking my keys, and "Your lights are on" when I forget to turn the headlights off.

Hilda's most helpful reminder comes when we have less than fifty miles of gas left in the fuel tank. "Your fuel level is low," she announces, and we begin to search for a service station. Hilda has saved us from some inconvenient moments: from dead batteries, from possible theft, and from being out of gas.

Some of us need to ponder where the "Hildas" are in our lives—the external Hildas, people with enough insight and courage to acknowledge that they see evidences that our tanks are running dry, and the internal Hildas, who send up unavoidable signals that we are suffering from a weariness that is abnormal and potentially destructive.

Weariness may have been a key to the poor performance of Jesus' disciples in the garden. It had been a grueling week, the tension high on every one of the holy days. Debates, accusations, threats, and the ups and downs of the public's response to their Master's message must have worn them down. When they got to the garden that night, their only thought was to sleep. And when Jesus was arrested, they tried to get their wits about them but could not emerge from that fog of weariness. Thus "all the disciples forsook Him and fled" (Matt 26:56 NKJV).

I've written in other places that I believe weariness is a spiritual and physical plague of our time. Modern men and women are choosing to live in constant emotional and spiritual deficit. Most of us are expending more energy than we are taking in. Only a certain number with unusual resilience can maintain such a pace. The rest of us try to measure ourselves against these superperformers and then wonder why we lapse back again and again into weariness and guilt because we cannot keep up with them.

We must be candid with one another that this is a reality of not only the marketplace but also the church and nonprofit institutions of our times. Expectations are increasingly raised, glittering programs and opportunities promoted, and in the excitement of it all, we try to go one more round. In the aftermath of such processes we are most likely to make the initial choices that lead to a broken world.

We may need to be sensitive to how some of us inadvertently create conditions that bring weariness to others. An older woman, now childless, may unwittingly intimidate a young mother absorbed in child raising by making her feel guilty that she is not as active as someone thinks she should be in a community or church program. One man may be coaxed into more and more public activities by another man whose temperament or flexibility of time makes it possible for him to be more active.

I see Jesus dealing with weariness. He appears to have kept long hours, and He frequently went the second mile to meet the needs of people. But we cannot miss the fact that sooner or later He always broke free of the crowds and withdrew into the refreshment of quiet. And He did it without the paralyzing "guilt" that so many of us carry today. When He was alone, He looked heavenward, inward, and only then outward to the world. We never see the Son of God operating from a prolonged environment of weariness.

ADVERSITY AND FRUSTRATION

At other times I have written of a short period of our lives when we lived in western Kansas. Then it was necessary for me to drive our inexpensive Volkswagen "beetle" to Denver twice a week for classes in graduate school. The 176-mile trip was straight westward, and I often encountered powerful headwinds that swooped across the plains from the Rocky Mountains.

Headwinds meant a very slow trip to Denver, and they meant, of course, a relatively fast trip back home. If the winds were powerful enough, I often had to drive most of the trip in second or third gear rather than the fourth gear normally used for cruising. The car was blown all over the road, but I always reached my destination.

Naturally, one could drive the distance in second or third gear, but it meant much slower speed, poor gasoline economy, and some wear and tear on the engine. And the wind gusts often came as a surprise and created dangerous driving conditions.

I came to see that we can begin to encounter certain headwinds in life that offer the same kind of challenges I experienced on the road to Denver. Instead of living in fourth gear, with an economy of motion and emotion, we find ourselves living in second or third gear: working harder to accomplish less. We can do it, but like my Volkswagen, the wear and tear and the slower speed of achievement will be our lot.

I think of such headwinds when I think of *adversity* and *frustration*, great sources of saturation and destabilization. When I use the word *adversity*, I'm thinking of our dealings with abrasive, unlikable, or unpleasant people. And when I speak of *frustration*, I'm thinking of tasks that seem to offer no fulfillment or satisfaction. These are second- and third-gear conditions: dangerous and time consuming headwinds. I meet a lot of people who are living in second or third gear.

These will be no problem at all for those of us who do not let people get inside our skin or for those who enjoy a challenge and remain unflappable no matter what the degree of difficulty on the job.

People who are sympathetic toward the brilliant title of Harvey McKay's book, *Swim with the Sharks without Being*

Eaten Alive, will be able to name some adversity-producing "sharks." A shark can be a boss or manager in the workplace whose leadership style (if there is one at all) runs counter to the way we like to be motivated and evaluated. A shark can be a family member who makes our lives absolutely miserable: a mother who cannot be pleased or an uncle who incessantly whines and complains. Sharks can be nasty students if we are teachers or grouchy teachers if we are students. The list of potential sharks is long and scary.

The sharks wear us down. They consume large amounts of our mental time as we try to think through ways to defend ourselves, maybe even how to get back at them. Even if we get up every morning determined that they will not get the best of us, it's likely that the sharks may break through our defenses more times than we would like to admit. We pray for patience, wisdom, and even supernatural love. And we feel good about ourselves when they come. We feel ill about ourselves when they don't.

A long-time friend of mine works every day with a man whose managerial style creates confusion, mistrust, and joylessness. My friend comes home on the majority of workdays with an intense dislike of his job. When I'm with him, I'm very much aware of how wearing this is on him. Realistically, my friend can do nothing about his situation. And knowing his pain causes me to pray for him regularly because I know that he is often near the point of saturation and destabilization because of that adversity.

I'm reminded of the Greek myth of Sisyphus who was condemned by the gods to the endless job of pushing a gigantic boulder up a steep hill. Every time he reached the top with his stone, it rolled back down to the bottom and had to be pushed back up again. Sisyphus, the Greeks said, was compelled to perform his task for an eternity.

Many people share Sisyphus's imposed vocation. The young mother with two or more preschool children who rarely hears from anyone that her work with them has immense value. The salesperson in a slump who gets only what-have-you-done-for-me-lately questions from his manager. The clergyman who leads a church where no one in the congregation seems to cooperate except in maintaining the status quo.

Frustration is a common experience for the people who

face long-distance commutes or heavy traffic jams every day, the individuals who encounter problems getting things done in a massive bureaucracy, and the vast military establishment if one is assigned to a post where a supervisor seems not to care about excellence or development. You'll find frustrated people in the marketplace, the church, the school, and the home. In their frustration as well as their adversity, there is usually the possibility of saturation and destabilization. And that is an environment for broken-world choices.

GRIEF, LOSS, AND ANGER

Recently a well-dressed, middle-aged man walked into the offices of a New England brokerage house and shot his boss. Police and reporters quickly discovered that the previous day the assailant had been dismissed from his stockbroker's job by the man he killed.

Everyone who knew the two men was in a state of disbelief. Fellow employees observed that the suspect had not been a productive worker, but on the other hand, he had been likable, gentle and, as far as they could see, incapable of such violence.

Something obviously snapped; thinking became confused; feelings exploded; all normal restraint was neutralized. The loss of a job, the humiliation of a personal failure, was apparently more than the man was able to accept. Thus, he made a choice to punish the symbol of all that had happened to him.

What happened? Evil in the heart conspired with a saturated and destabilized environment of the mind. We're not talking about a man with a lifelong record of violence. We're not looking at a man who had a history of temper tantrums or vindictiveness. We're looking at a man who slowly came to a breaking point. And environment and evil conspired to make possible a choice entirely out of line with what others might have expected.

The incident of the man who shot his boss reminds me of a dramatic moment in the movie *Network* when a saturated and destabilized newsman suggested to his TV audience that they should open their windows and shout to no one in particular, "I'm mad as hell, and I'm not going to take it any longer." It would make them feel better, he said.

My first reaction was to laugh as people in the movie began to shout as they'd been told. But then I realized that the film was probably only a short distance from reality. In their grief, loss, or anger, many people are often on the edge of making broken-world choices.

We see this anger in traffic jams when people often exhibit enormous rage at being cut off. We hear of occasional shootings on freeways. We witness anger in supermarket lines and at professional athletic events. And at town hearings when planning and zoning decisions are made that cost someone some money, anger is a prevalent mood.

A common kind of grief is that of losing a loved one in death. As a pastor I've had the responsibility of walking through part or all of the grief process with many men and women. I quickly realized that many of them in their sadness were capable of enormous errors of judgment as they lived in a formidable amount of death-induced confusion.

Grief is a strange inner energy of the mind. We were never created to grieve since we were not made to die or sustain great loss. So grief happens, as far as I can see, when all of the internal systems of the mind and heart scream out, run amok, and try to make sense out of something that seems to have no meaning.

In a state of deep grief and loss, some will withdraw, become almost antisocial. Others will become angry and unconsolable, blaming God or even themselves for the death of a loved one.

Some widows and widowers have fallen into immorality in the aftermath of the loss of someone they have loved and with whom they've shared life. Their loneliness and emptiness seem greater than they can bear. And when friends do not understand the extent of their anguish, they are tempted to turn in whatever direction there is an offer of intimacy.

I've seen good people make unsound financial decisions, choices to move to different parts of the country, and unwise job changes because they were in an environment of loss and grief that led to saturation and destabilization.

Having visited Third World countries on several occasions, I've watched people of more primitive cultures go through loss and grief when a family member has died. I am impressed with the fact that they understand this environment far better than most of us. They take time to grieve, time to think about and resolve their losses. I've heard their wailing and groans. Some people have criticized this process as pagan and bereft of hope. Perhaps there can be an element of that. But more important, these people understand that if we do not give vent to our grief in healthy, acceptable ways, we are quite likely to channel that grief toward the creation of an environment where world-breaking choices will be made.

SUBSTANCE ABUSE AND PHYSIOLOGICAL STRESS

Not long ago three young Boston medical doctors were found guilty in the rape of a nurse. As one might expect, with their convictions and sentences also came the loss of their reputations and their careers. Four worlds were quickly broken in one night. Four lives marked by excellent educations, extraordinary skills, and optimistic futures were destroyed.

The environment? Alcohol. All four had attended a party earlier in the evening, and the heavy drinking while they were there had exacted its toll. Minds were clouded; restraints were cast aside; and animalistic behavior took over. The result? Destabilization and bad choices. Broken personal worlds.

An Amtrak train derails sending a number of people to the hospital with serious injuries. An engineer is killed. Subsequent investigations reveal that half the railroad men involved in the accident showed traces of illegal drugs in their blood.

A small commercial plane crashes in southeastern Colorado. The FAA reports that the pilot tests positive for cocaine use.

A star basketball athlete headed for a professional career dies from a cocaine overdose the night after signing a multimillion dollar contract.

What's happening here? Why are the best and the brightest destroying themselves and others with these broken-world choices? What are individuals who use drugs and alcohol seeking? Psychic liberation? Pleasure? Relaxation? Escape? Social acceptance? Is the risk really worth it?

Most of us are used to identifying these problems with the inner city, with the poor and the undereducated. But if we do, we stick our heads in the sand. It is probable that 10 percent of the people sitting in a suburban church congregation on a Sunday morning have drinking problems. It is also likely that more than a few in the pews have dabbled in the use of drugs that the government has declared dangerous and illegal. And it is frighteningly possible that on the way home from church we will pass and be passed by more than a few whose level of drunkenness or drug-induced state makes them a serious threat to us and our families.

The Bible recounts a somewhat obscure story in the life of Lot in which alcohol played a dominant role.

> One day the older daughter said to the younger, "Our father is old, and there is no man around here to lie with us, as is the custom all over the earth. Let's get our father to drink wine and then lie with him to preserve our family line through our father" (Gen. 19:31-32).

Their plan succeeded. Lot in his drunken state lost management of himself, and his two daughters were impregnated. With that incident Lot's biography ends, and we get the picture of a beaten man whose personal world had broken to pieces. The choices to go to Sodom and to intertwine his fortunes with the people of that city had been bad ones. And this is one more bad moment like the others. This time the choice was made "under the influence."

What can we learn from all that we see going on around us today? The murders, the gang warfare, the arrests, the violence. We can at least learn that men and women jeopardize the last inner restraints against the evil in their hearts when they turn their minds over to substances that alter the perception of reality. A lack of concern for this problem probably creates as much possibility for broken worlds as anything we can think about.

Gail and I walk with our friends through that beautiful Catalina Island valley, and I listen to the frightening descriptions of mud slides and floods that level everything in their path. When does it happen? When the soil becomes saturated and destabilized.

When are men and women liable to get themselves into

trouble big enough to break apart a personal world? The same kind of answer applies: when life becomes saturated and destabilized. When the weariness is numbing, the frustration and adversity intolerable, the grief and anger unconsolable, and the mind uncontrollable. In the accumulation of draining experiences like these comes the increasing danger of broken-world choices.

11

Carrying the Baggage

BOTTOM LINE #11: *Misbehavior may often be rooted in the undisclosed things of our pasts.*

It has been ten years since I had the conversation, but I never forgot it. He was a young man, a relatively new follower of Christ, hardly in his twenties. The subject matter of our talk: the struggle he said he was having finding success in his commitment to Christ.

As we visited, I read resistance and hardness, even anger, in his words and in his face. I sensed these things also in his physical posture and in the angular nature of his gestures. But even though I read those signals, I wasn't quite sure I understood exactly what they meant.

When he said he'd come to discuss the dwindling vitality of his young spiritual life, I responded by trying to provide an academic sort of response for each of the problems and objections he raised. It was kind of like a tennis game: he would serve up a question or a difficult situation he was facing, and I would try to react with the right answer. But the conversation was going nowhere. His "serves" seemed amateurish and my "returns" were no better.

The breakthrough to the real issue came during an interlude of small talk. "What do you like to do for fun?" I asked.

"Sing" came the answer.

"Sing?" I said. "Are you good?"

"Yeah, I have a very good voice."

"Well, why aren't you in the choir?"

"I can't stand the director."

"What's wrong with the director?"

"Nothing as far as I know. I just don't like choir directors."

I'd heard critiques of choir directors before, but nothing as sweeping as this. So I urged him to go on.

"I get angry anytime someone up in front waves an arm and tells me when and when not to sing. I tried singing in two or three choirs but usually ended up so agitated that I just walked out in the middle of rehearsals."

I couldn't believe what I was hearing; but he went on, and I listened.

"Singing in a choir is the least of my problems, really. I have those sorts of feelings every time someone tells me what to do or expresses an opinion about me. I get mad at cops, at signs that tell me what I can and can't do; I even get mad at you."

"At me? What would you get mad at me for?"

"I get mad at you when you're preaching along and start telling me where I'm wrong and how I need to get my act together. I even walked out on you one time. Hey, I know it's probably weird, but I fight these feelings all the time."

What was supposed to be an interlude, small talk, to get us unglued from our conversational impasse suddenly became the real agenda. My visitor may have had a spiritual problem in his relationship with God, but the solutions did not lie in a serve and return-serve volley of questions and answers.

"Tell me about your dad and mom," I said.

"Not much to tell. What do you want to know?"

"I'm interested in knowing something about your relationship with them. Did you feel close to your dad? Do you have good memories of your childhood? Was your mother a warm person? Stuff like that."

"So what we're really talking about here is a lifelong struggle with anyone in authority. Someone tells you what you should or shouldn't do, and you hear your father all over again."

"Exactly."

"Has it ever occurred to you that you might have the same problem with God? If you don't like your father and therefore all choir directors, cops, and sometimes people like me, why should you like God? Doesn't He present an authority problem too?"

"I'd never thought of that. Are you saying that every time I think about the place of Christianity in my life I'm coming up against those feelings?"

That's exactly what I was planning to say to him. But I was glad that he said it first.

I re-create that conversation as I remember it because it describes a psychic environment in which evil is very likely to exert itself with diabolic power sooner or later. My visitor of more than ten years ago may have expressed himself in a rather interesting way, but his problem was not unique to him.

He carried what I like to call *heavy baggage from the past*. Baggage that had never been properly identified, sorted, and discarded, but should have been. Now, because he had waited so long to enter into the process of handling his baggage from the past, he had a difficult challenge on the journey ahead of him. But he made it, and within a reasonable amount of time he was a free man, able to "travel" lightly.

What I have likened to a journey, the writer of Hebrews likened to a race, and in his encouragement to men and women to run as Christ did, he said, "Let us throw off everything that hinders . . . and let us run with perseverance the race marked out for us" (Heb. 12:1). Throwing off everything includes the luggage from the past that bogs down our present and jeopardizes our future. Our inner private worlds are capable of storing up enormous amounts of these unfortunate pieces and permitting them to become influences in present attitudes and motives that can easily produce broken-world performances. Thus, a vigorous identification and disposal of these pieces is an important personal exercise.

There is such a large assortment of this baggage from people's pasts. Much of it is heavy and bulky. It takes a lot of energy to carry it, and the fatigue of carrying it brings out the worst in many of the baggage handlers. I'd like to name three pieces of luggage of the past as examples. They are the "suitbag" of *unresolved relationships*, the "overnighter" of *unaddressed guilt*, and the "attache case" of *untreated pain*.

By giving each a name and identifying it, perhaps we can see some of those areas of one's personal world where there are likely to be seeds of potential brokenness.

The "Suitbag" of Unresolved Relationships

My young visitor of ten years ago had come to hate his father. And neither he nor his father had ever done anything to address the issues between them and bring them to peace. We call that an *unresolved relationship*. Two sisters carry on a lifelong feud; they are filled with resentment toward each other and seldom speak. That's also an unresolved relationship. Two men have a business partnership that dissolves in conflict and acrimony. Each feels cheated by the other and inwardly seethes at every thought of the former association. That's obviously an unresolved relationship too.

Unresolved relationships are most often connected with family situations, for it is within the matrix of family experiences that we are given some of the most important "gifts" that help us form our sense of personhood. If those gifts are not given in a timely and orderly fashion, relationships will be injured. And if we receive something other than those gifts, the injury may be even worse.

What kind of gifts am I talking about?

There is a gift of *well-being* that comes from being loved. God has created us with a hunger to be loved, and if that hunger is correctly satisfied, we will go on in life to love and give self-value to others. We receive this gift through physical affection, verbal affirmation, and a tenderness of contact that stands out in contrast to most other social contacts.

There is a gift of *competence*. Our parents and family are the first people to build into us a confidence that we can learn, create, serve, and make a difference in our generation if we want to. They give it by assigning positive value to things we do.

There is the gift of *security*. As vulnerable children, we must receive security, and if we do, we will learn to produce it later on for ourselves with God's help. We receive this gift IF we live in a home where a mother and father openly love and respect each other; IF we live in a home without destructive conflict; and IF we live in a home where there are the assurances of a set of restraints and routines that give life order and consistency concerning what is expected and allowed. As a result, we learn to feel safe.

Then there is the gift of *becoming*, the gradual freedom that wise mothers and fathers provide so that children might learn how to make choices and determine directions in life. Under ideal conditions we are not overshielded from challenges nor are we unprotected from things too big for us to take on.

Finally, there is the gift of *modeling*, the exemplary life that provides a vision for a boy as to what it means to be a man; that provides a vision for a girl as to what it means to be a woman. It wasn't long ago that most boys hoped to grow up and be like their fathers and most girls like their mothers. It may be different now.

In times past, these gifts could be given to children not only by their parents but also by members of their extended families: grandparents, uncles and aunts, and others who usually lived nearby and who intersected regularly. What one parent might not be able to provide, another individual in the larger family could.

But recent decades have brought the dissolution of the *extended* family as mobility has become a way of life. And in more recent times most children had only the *nuclear* family (parents and children) from which to receive their necessary gifts. Today more than half of America's children grow up in *single-parent* families, and 60 percent of mothers of preschool children have joined the work force. Perhaps this trend suggests the era of the *nonfamily* is just around the corner.

What happens when children do not receive these necessary gifts? Or what happens if they live in homes where the gifts are decidedly hurtful? Instead of the gift of *well-being* there are constant assertions of worthlessness. Instead of the gift of *competence* there are put-downs or reminders that their efforts are futile and noncontributive. And instead of the gift of *security* there is a sense of never knowing what is going to happen next. Children of alcoholics know this experience well.

Instead of the gift of *becoming* there is smothering or its opposite, apathetic freedom. And instead of the gift of *modeling* there is an absence of anything for which to aspire.

When these gifts are not given, inner anger and resentment will grow. And they are liable to surface again and again in adult experiences that are faintly reminiscent of childhood disappointments.

In Brazil a radioactive isotope from a medical laboratory

was carried to a public dump and discarded. Some poor people found the dangerous substance, and not knowing what it was, they handed it around. One child spread some of it on her body; another even tasted it. Before anyone discovered what had happened, a significant number of people in the town were contaminated with radiation.

The anger that some of us carry from childhood is like a dosage of radiation. It will not go away until it is named and properly disposed of. Anger is like nuclear energy; it can have useful purposes, or it can become destructive. We must know the difference.

The Scriptures are not critical of all anger—only of unresolved anger in relationships. Jacob had an unresolved relationship with his brother Esau, and it brought the worst out in both of them until they dealt with it. Absalom was angry with his brother Amnon, and because their father, David, did not force a resolution of the relationship, Absalom killed his brother.

We can begin to deal with our anger only when we acknowledge its existence, find its source, and engage in whatever forgiveness is necessary in both directions between the giver and the receiver of bad gifts. In families where there is anger, some of us have a lot of forgiving to do with our parents, and the longer we wait to do it, the more we are injured and the more we permit an environment that makes misbehavior more possible in our present and future lives.

The "Overnighter" of Unaddressed Guilt

Similarly, we encourage negative environments when we live with *unaddressed guilt* from the past. Now we are talking not of what others may have done but of what we have done that has generated shame and regret.

By using the word *unaddressed*, I'm thinking of those occasions when a significant wrong or harm has been done, and the offender has refused to acknowledge the misdeed and to make whatever restitution is necessary: perhaps a confession and an apology, an untangling of the unfortunate events, or a return or replacement of something taken.

Guilt is usually experienced as a feeling, but it is actually spiritual pain. Real guilt is the result of the inner spirit, created in God's image, crying "foul." God's laws have been violated; His honor diminished. Something deep within us shouts in protest. We feel the shout as guilt.

Guilt can be constant or intermittent. Sometimes it can lie dormant for long periods of time only to surface when we talk with someone who shares a similar situation to ours or when we see something with which we can identify on the movie screen or in a news report. Or as we shall see in a moment, unaddressed guilt may resurface when there is a later pressure or stress that seems somehow mysteriously related to an earlier incident.

It's hard to quantify the full effect of guilt from person to person. Some seem more sensitive to it, actually driven by it. Others appear to have a higher threshold and seem able to ignore the messages. We do know that it is possible to squelch the entire guilt-producing mechanism. That can happen if a young person's conscience is not sharpened by adults who maintain discipline and order, and it can happen when one simply refuses to listen to the inner voice long enough so that the voice gets drowned out by other noises. The biblical writers referred to this as "searing the conscience." Apparently one can turn off the immediate consequences of guilt, but it will take lots of emotional or psychic energy.

Jacob's sons, the brothers of the Older Testament Joseph, seem to have wrestled with unaddressed guilt for more than fifteen years. If you know the story, you'll remember that they were incited to rage by their young upstart sibling, Joseph, and plotted his murder. But just before they implemented their plan, they were appeased by Reuben, the eldest. Relenting, they sold Joseph as a slave to a passing caravan. Out of sight; out of mind. Problem solved.

They covered the disposal of Joseph with a lie to their father. Joseph was dead, they said, killed apparently by a wild animal. The old man accepted the story and lapsed into grief.

It appeared as if the secret of their conspiracy was safe for at least fifteen years. But the guilt lay unaddressed deep in the private world of each brother. And when they later journeyed to Egypt to purchase food during a famine, they trotted out their lie once more.

It came when they bowed before the governor of Egypt not knowing that he was actually Joseph. But he recognized them and put them off balance with harsh interrogation. To his accusation that they had come to Egypt as spies, they said: "Your servants were twelve brothers, the sons of one man, who lives in the land of Canaan. The youngest is now with our father, *and one is no more*" (Gen. 42:13, emphasis mine). In other words, Joseph is dead. A believable story, perhaps, if it wasn't for the fact that Joseph himself was standing right in front of them.

The not-so-dead brother, Joseph, increased the pressure, and the brothers felt it immediately. The interface between the past murder plot and the present sticky situation in Egypt was established in their minds. And even though they were still unaware of who they were dealing with, they replayed the crime of years ago. Unaddressed guilt suddenly was corkscrewing its way back to the surface. It wasn't out of sight or out of mind after all.

> They said to one another, "Surely we are being punished because of our brother. We saw how distressed he was when he pleaded with us for his life, but we would not listen; that's why this distress has come upon us."
> Reuben replied, "Didn't I tell you not to sin against the boy? But you wouldn't listen! Now we must give an accounting for his blood" (Gen. 42:21-22).

Joseph overheard these words. In their ignorance, the brothers remained unaware that he, the governor, could understand their language. And while they panicked, Joseph secretly wept.

Even after the brothers reconciled with Joseph and were assured of his grace and forgiveness, they lived the entirety of their lives waiting for the roof to fall in. They couldn't quite believe that Joseph wouldn't seek vengeance for what they had done. And their fear of retribution was only exacerbated when Jacob died. Then they were sure that in the wake of his death, Joseph would have his revenge. But Joseph's forgiveness was authentic and unwavering. The brothers' long-lived fear was an example of how powerful guilt unaddressed for long periods of time can actually be.

Unaddressed guilt makes for unstable choice making. It distorts perspectives, twists meanings, and undermines the confidence we need to press forward in the present. We cannot expect to live healthily in the future when the baggage of the past keeps banging away at the trapdoor of our minds demanding attention.

Stanley Jones was thinking of the awfulness of unaddressed guilt when he wrote:

> In the book of Revelation are these words: "It was in my mouth sweet as honey: and as soon as I had eaten it my belly was bitter" (Rev 10:10). Is that the total picture of sin? In the mouth it is sweet as honey, in the beginning sin tastes good, seems good; but when life tries to assimilate it, it can't—it turns bitter. For life does not and cannot assimilate or digest sin; sin and the body are not made for each other—they are allergic to each other. A Hindu youth said to me: "After committing adultery with that woman I went up the mountainside trembling." Trembling at what? At the sourness in his stomach. "I was a ninny to do it," said a woman to me in America. Her stomach turned sour.
>
> Everybody who sins, east or west, begins to turn sour. They sour against this, that, and the other; everything and everybody is wrong. They are soured on life because life within has soured. They are trying to assimilate the unassimilatable. Sin is sour business. (*Song of Ascents*)

Our own unaddressed guilt often creates suspicion of others' behavior. It makes us struggle to like ourselves. We wallow in self-accusation. And in this environment of suspicion, self-perceived cheapness, and general bad feelings we are apt to make commitments and choices that will further break our worlds.

Guilt is dispelled only when the truth is told, when the cover-up is exploded away, confession made, and restitution accomplished. Only then will guilt like a block of ice melt away.

Perhaps you've seen an ice sculpture in an elegant restaurant. Once I had an occasion to remain in one of those restaurants for several hours while a meeting was in progress. It gave me time enough to watch the ice figure slowly melt into formlessness and then disappear.

If anger is like a piece of radiated material in a dump, poorly identified and improperly shielded, unaddressed guilt is like a huge block of ice. Kept in a dark, cold place, it remains hard. But brought into the light, identified, and confessed, it begins to melt, and soon it is gone. And free is the soul that no longer is frozen by unaddressed guilt.

Thus, the man or woman who wishes to prevent broken-

world choices monitors the inner self for the signals of guilt.
These people seek to prevent the choices that lead to a broken
world, and they will not carry the heavy baggage of guilt.
They leave it at the Cross where Christ affirmed that He
would handle it in His grace.

THE "ATTACHE CASE" OF UNTREATED PAIN

Among the other things that hinder us as we seek to keep
our personal worlds strong is the problem of *untreated pain*.
These are the open wounds created and sometimes perpetu-
ated by others in our worlds.

When I was a pastor, I often talked with young couples
who wanted to be married. Like many other pastors, I always required a series of conversations with a bride and
groom as a condition of my participation in the wedding.

One of the first questions I usually asked was: would both
of you like your marriage to be like the one your parents
have? I remember well the answer of one bride, "If I could
have a marriage like the one my parents have, I'd be the
most fortunate woman in the world."

Unfortunately, I didn't often hear such an enthusiastic and
positive response. More often the answer came in the negative.
But one negative sticks in my memory more than any of the
others. When I asked that question of one couple, the soon-to-
be-bride seemed to freeze. It was as if death (or was it hatred)
swept across her face. I was sure I'd said something that was
completely misunderstood and taken badly. But I could produce nothing in my memory to suggest that possibility.

"You're very disturbed about my question," I probed.

"Why do you say that?" she said with a distant stare.

"I read it in your eyes, your facial expression. You're telling me in every way possible, except with words, that you're
angry."

"Let's just drop it," she said. And I did, for the moment.

A few days passed, and then a call came with a request for
another appointment. This time the woman came to see me
by herself.

It was my first acquaintance with child molestation. As
she unfolded her story, it included details with which most of
us are now familiar: a father who had made sexual advances

to which she had yielded, a mother who had been aware of what was happening but lived in denial of it all. Having nowhere to turn—"who would believe me?"—the now-adult bride-to-be had endured what she had to until she was old enough to leave the home.

"Now do you see what your question meant to me? You brought back a memory I thought I'd buried. It took me a day or two to be willing to face it myself. Why would I want a marriage like that of my parents?"

A later visit with her and her fiancé resulted in a postponement of the wedding for a few months until some counseling could take place. It was a case of untreated pain, which had engendered hatred, a distaste for sexual intimacy, and a hidden resentment for men in general. All of that might have exploded, broken-worldlike, in the subsequent marriage.

Untreated pain can exist far below the surface of our conscious minds. Smoldering like an underground coal fire seeking oxygen, it simply awaits a distant moment when it can explode.

We are living in a time when the issue of child molestation and abuse is receiving heavy attention. We are learning that many men and women are walking about with the pain of exploitation and humiliation deep within. And as that pain surfaces, it leads to unhealthy present relationships and decisions in which the wisdom and value are not solid.

Untended pain may include failures and humiliations that have never been properly understood. Romances that dissolved so suddenly that one of the parties was left with a lifelong scar of rejection. A death in which one has never fully grieved or faced the loss. A betrayal in a marriage that is never worked through to forgiveness and reconciliation, just swept under the rug.

Again, as with guilt, some of us feel pain longer and deeper than others. The threshold of psychic or emotional pain seems very high for some individuals; they find it easy to forget moments when they've been slighted and embarrassed, when they've been exploited or badly defeated. For others, the threshold is low, and they remember almost everything: a slap in the face, a forgotten line in a school play at which everyone laughed, being stood up for a teenaged date, or being fired from a summer job. For some, these seemingly trivial incidents can be as devastating as a Fortune 500 company CEO being fired by a board of directors or the breakup of a marriage. The pain is measured by the one experiencing it, not by an objective observer.

What does untended pain leave us with? Sometimes a struggle with self-confidence. Sometimes an inability to trust others, especially anyone who reminds us of the one who may have caused hurt in the past. Or we can be left with an expectation that we will be mistreated again, so we resist participating in a relationship or a task that might raise the risk of a repeat experience.

Our memories are deep, seemingly bottomless. And unless we search them in a time of dis-ease, they are liable to betray us when unresolved relationships or unaddressed guilt or untreated pain tap into our spiritual circuitry.

Gail and I enter a hotel carrying our suitbags and our attache cases. We're worn out, my back is sore, and I'm getting tired of traveling. A uniformed attendant comes alongside.

"Let me take those things for you," he says.

"No," I answer. "We can handle them by ourselves." As much as I'd like to give them to the young man, we do not have any cash in our pockets (only credit cards), and I'm ashamed to admit the real reason.

"You sure? I'd like to help," he says.

"I'm sure. Thank you," I say back.

We reach the hotel desk, register, and turn toward our rooms. "Let the bellman bring your bags up in a little while," the desk clerk says.

"No thanks," I respond, again ashamed to admit that I'm short on tipping change.

"Please let him do it," she says. "All the gratuities are added to your bill anyway. You don't have to tip him."

Has she read my mind? Have I carried these bags for fifty yards when someone was there, already paid in effect, to handle them for me? I have the brain of a bird.

Carrying bags when someone is there, paid to carry them for me, is almost as incomprehensible as carrying baggage from the past, be it unresolved relationships, unaddressed guilt, or untreated pain, when Someone *has already paid* to lift it off me. And that's exactly what happened at the Cross. As the hymn writer put it so well: "Jesus paid it all."

12

Tiptoeing on the Spiderweb

BOTTOM LINE #12: *A disrespect for the power of evil is a major step toward a broken personal world.*

While I was in graduate school, Gail and I moved to St. Francis, Kansas, where I became the weekend pastor of a small country congregation. The pastor's study was located in the basement of the church building. It was a rather damp and musty room, and that meant bugs.

That's why I wasn't surprised one day when I discovered a large, magnificently designed spiderweb on one end of a bookcase. I was about to brush it away when my curiosity took control and caused me to sit back and watch what happened if and when some creeping thing got caught in the web.

For several days, I permitted the spider to enlarge his web (I assume it was a male spider), and soon he had managed to take over half a shelf of church history books: all the way from the first-century church fathers to Martin Luther.

When I wasn't concentrating on my studies, I found a certain amount of amusement locating insects and depositing them in the center circle of the spider's silken prison. They were instantly trapped, of course, and a huge black spider would emerge from behind a copy of LaTourette's *History of the Christian Church* and make a quick end to the

503

insect's resistance. I never detected any hint that the spider was thankful for my meals.

One day I became annoyed by a large fly buzzing around the study. Occasionally, he would land near the spiderweb, and each time he wandered closer and closer, even venturing onto some of the outer strands much like someone might test the ice of a frozen pond in the early days of winter. But always after a few tentative steps, the fly would dart away, returning again a few minutes later.

I had the impression that the fly was driven by curiosity about the spider's web. Or perhaps he was playing I-dare-you games with the spider or with something within himself. Did the fly have something to prove?

If he did, the fly didn't get the job done. He made one visit too many to the edges of the web. This time the fly tiptoed too far out on the strands and suddenly became entangled. He struggled mightily but unsuccessfully. The well-built web held its prey, and soon the spider was out of his hiding place behind LaTourette pouncing upon the hapless fly. The contest was over swiftly, and the study was silent; no buzzing any longer.

I think of the spider and the fly every time I reread the Older Testament story of Samson. A man of unusual strength, he had known the favor of God as he had led the oft-beleaguered Hebrews out from under the domination of the Philistines. The enemy blanched, then ran, whenever Samson took to the field because they came to know by experience that it was no contest when he was there.

But Samson liked "spiderwebs," one could say. For him, the spiderwebs were the women of Philistia. And despite the warnings of his father not to get involved, he chose to do so. On both occasions—he consorted with a woman of Timnah and with a woman of Gaza—he made a fool of himself. He never learned from one bad experience to another that while there might be pleasure, there was no love to be found. Only entrapment; only ultimate disaster. It was a matter of tiptoeing one time too many out on the Philistine spiderweb. And finally he became entangled.

It's a strange but instructive story about God's acts in a person's life. In spite of Samson's stupidity a first, a second, and even a third time, God kept giving him the necessary strength to fight battles. We might think that one mistake would have been too many for God. But divine patience and kindness lasted for a longer period than human patience and kindness might have.

What drives a Samson? Is it the love of danger? The unique and the unusual? Does a Samson get a thrill out of testing the outer limits? Or does he simply assume that there is no situation he cannot handle? Is his physical strength to him like the words of a smooth talker? Like the money of one who thinks he can buy his way out of any tight spot? Like the brains of a thinker who presumes he can outwit all competitors?

When men and women get drawn into Samson's game, thinking they can take on anything or anybody, they usually do not think seriously enough about three things: the strange *curiosity within* that draws one toward the web, the *entangling potential* of the web itself, and the *spider* who uses the web for its own selfish designs.

We've been looking at the environments in which evil is most likely to break forth in human behavior. We've looked at the vulnerable moments in our age-groups, observed those times when people become saturated and destabilized, and glanced at the past and how it can affect the present.

But no discussion of the environments in which evil is most likely to show itself would be complete, no matter how cursory the treatment, if we did not take a look at something the Christian church has traditionally called spiritual warfare. This controversial topic cannot be discussed at any length without considerable disagreement and diverse opinion. But I need to take a deep breath and venture into the subject because I believe that a biblical understanding of broken worlds would be incomplete if we did not ask what it has to teach us about ourselves and our human vulnerabilities.

Temptation is a key word at this point. Temptation suggests the notion of a seduction of sorts, a drawing of the fly to the spiderweb through whatever means necessary. The purpose: neutralization and then destruction.

Sin, of course, is another key word. It is usually used in two different ways. A sin can be an act or an attitude that is incompatible with God's standards of right. Or sin can refer to the spiritual disease of the innermost being. Some have likened that disease to cancer, for left unchecked it grows and chokes off what is good. I prefer to use the word *evil* in this second definition because the overuse of the word *sin* has led to a tendency to disregard its destructive nature. It's reasonable to observe that sin isn't taken very seriously by most of us until it has a clear effect in some part of our lives.

The Bible is clear in its teaching from beginning to end that people live in an environment of temptation that seeks to draw them away from the pleasure of the Creator and toward the condition of sin, which is alien and antithetical to Him.

The first temptation and the first sinful acts occurred in the garden, which the Genesis account describes. A being in the form of a serpent approached Eve and proposed that she reconsider the Creator's prohibition on eating the fruit from a certain tree.

Temptation came first from the serpent and then, second, from within. All the serpent did was get the ball rolling. Eve's reasoning process took over from there.

The serpent did his job through deception. He distorted the words of God until he had effectively lowered Eve's concerns about disobedience. Then the writer says:

> When the woman saw that the fruit of the tree was good for food and pleasing to the eye, and also desirable for gaining wisdom, she took some and ate it. She also gave some to her husband, who was with her, and he ate it (Gen. 3:6).

Eve's broken-world choice was built on an evaluation of the issue as seen through her eye, her appetite, and her intellect. Somehow she turned off the deeper part of herself, the spiritual, where she might have measured her choice against the word of God. And that's why it all went wrong. The biblical writers clearly trace the emergence of evil in the world from this one simple but very profound act.

A study of this interesting and tragic encounter might suggest that temptation can come from at least two sources: from without and from within. And so it has ever been.

Why do men and women commit sins, acts that singularly or in clusters can break a personal world into pieces? Perhaps for the same reasons that Samson headed for the women of Philistia. Apparently we aren't perceptive enough to realize that we cannot beat the system that evil has targeted against us. Like Samson, we keep thinking that we possess the capability to do what history says cannot be done: overcome sin and evil on our own.

The temptation to sin can come, most Christians believe, from one of four sources.

SATAN

The first might be a temptation that comes from the devil, or Satan as he is known in the Bible. Among the nouns used in Scripture to identify this strange creature are *deceiver* and *slanderer*. The words themselves tell us that the principal strategy of this evil enemy is a distortion of the truth.

We have a number of biblical references to Satan as a distinct personality. Christian theology has drawn from biblical sources the insight that Satan, once named Lucifer, was an angel of the highest order who chose to rebel against God and, as a result, was expelled from heaven.

We read of a strange Older Testament conversation between Satan and God regarding the integrity of Job. From that conversation came a puzzling agreement that Job's faithfulness would be exposed to a series of "stress tests," including illness, tragedy, and material and human loss. What tests they were! One inference in the story of Job is that Satan is sometimes permitted to initiate a certain amount of suffering in the world. But the follow-up inference is always that it is a limited freedom and will not exceed bounds determined by God. These truths are hazy, at best, to our finite minds. But one thing rings clear and true: the God of Job is not limited in His power, and He can act when He chooses to do so.

In the New Testament we hear of Satan attempting to draw Jesus into impulsive decisions by making Him promises that he wasn't equipped to keep. It was almost as if Satan was saying to Jesus, "You're on my turf; let's play by my rules." But our Lord powerfully resisted Satan's enticements.

Later we are told that "Satan entered Judas" (Luke 22:3 NKJV), and this becomes a curious observation to ponder. What is the connection between Judas's responsibility for his choice to betray Jesus and Satan's apparent commandeering of Judas for his own designs? We aren't given a clear answer to this question. We can only assume that Judas reached a point in his life when he was so much in personal rebellion against Jesus that, without realizing it, he made himself available as an agent for Satan's designs.

Both Paul and Peter warned the early Christians that Satan plots to neutralize Christians and congregations. They pointed out his shrewdness and aggressiveness. He is like a lion, Peter wrote, roaring about, searching for someone to devour. He masquerades as an angel of light, Paul observed. In another place Paul noted Satan to be a schemer and affirmed, "We are not ignorant of his devices" (2 Cor. 2:11 NKJV).

Will most of us be directly tempted by Satan? My own opinion is, probably not. Satan is not omnipresent, as the theologian likes to use the word to signify someone who is everywhere at all times. Only God is omnipresent. Thus, Satan's activities have a primary limitation in that he can be in only one place at one time.

The Bible seems to suggest that Satan's favorite place is somewhere near the throne of God so that he can level accusations at the heavenly family. I take that to mean that Satan rather enjoys trying to spoil God's pleasure in His children.

Perhaps there are occasional moments when Satan directly controls a person. A Hitler? A Genghis Khan? But is it always a mass killer? Could Satan have other disguises should he tempt a person? To outrageous materialism? Sensualism? Nihilism?

A few years ago a comedian employed the line "the devil made me do it" in a set of humorous characterizations. As with most humor, the laughs came because most of us would indeed like to put the blame for our actions on someone else, and the devil is an excellent candidate. He's bad anyway, and a bit more blame won't tarnish his image.

But the biblical truth is that the devil enjoys no control at all over anyone under God's care. He may be permitted to cast his most powerful seductions in our direction; he may be permitted to whisper his most convincing lies; he may be permitted to order certain events so that they seem in the present to be adverse to our interests. But at no time will he ever be permitted to make us do anything. As W. L. Watkinson once wrote: "Hell does its worst with the saints. The rarest souls have been tested with high pressures and temperatures, but Heaven will not desert them" (*Streams*).

THE DEMONIC HORDES

The Bible proposes a second source of temptation: demonic beings. Christian theology suggests that there are large numbers of demons who are invisible, destructive, and aggressive. They too are fallen angels. We are made quite aware of their existence during Jesus' public ministry.

In a dramatic passage in Bunyan's *Pilgrim's Progress* the traveling Christian is faced with enormous despair over his sinfulness. He is besieged by temptation that seems to come from without, perhaps from the very demons we mention in these paragraphs.

> I took notice that now poor Christian was so confounded that he did not know his own voice; and thus I perceived, just when he was come over against the mouth of the burning pit, one of the wicked ones got behind him, and stepped up softly to him, and whisperingly suggested many grievous blasphemies to him, which he verily thought had proceeded from his own mind. This put Christian more to it than anything that he had met with before, even to think that he should now blaspheme Him that he loved so much before. Yet if he could have helped it, he would not have done it; but he had not the discretion either to stop his ears, or to know from whence these blasphemies came.

What we know of demons in Scripture suggests that they may affect people physically, mentally, and spiritually. We have descriptions of men and women possessed or controlled by demons.

The man of Gadara is a prime example. Filled with a legion (more than a thousand) of demons, he was said to be supernaturally strong, a serious nuisance to the community. Every day he ran naked about the countryside, screaming and making himself a general menace. We can imagine that he had parents, a wife, and children who watched this process of human degradation and could only remember what once had been.

Did this thing called demon possession happen all at once in this man's life? Or was it the product of a life-style always positioned on the edge of moral risk? Did he consciously or unconsciously open himself to darknesses deep within? Was there a discernible moment when powers deeper than he'd ever known simply seized control of his psychological and physiological processes? And what of the attitude of the people in the community as they had to find a way to restrain him? He is the ultimate broken-world person. He is a picture of environments and evil at their very worst.

In a newspaper report on the thousands of American students who go to Florida for their spring break from classes, one young man commented on why there was so much drunkenness associated with the event: "There's a time to be serious and a time to be out of control. Spring break is my time to be out of control." You get the feeling that he may have described the worldview of the man named Legion who ultimately became controlled by demons.

Whatever happened, we have the picture of a spiritually captive man the day Jesus encountered him. Half-crazed, he approached the Son of God, and almost immediately he was freed from his captivity. When Jesus expelled the demons, they are said to have entered a herd of two thousand swine that self-destructed by running into the lake.

We learn something of the man's transformation when we are told of his healed condition: he was "sitting there, dressed and in his right mind" (Mark 5:15). "Sitting there" suggests a new tranquillity; "dressed," a new dignity; and "in his right mind," an ability to reason and feel.

I am forced to take the issue of demon activity seriously, first, because I take the Bible seriously. I think I have seen evidences of demon activity in some I've helped as a pastor, but I am not comfortable with those who find demon instigation behind virtually every broken-world failure. This is a matter for us to treat with caution and respect.

It should not go unnoticed that Christians in the non-Western world regularly testify to demon activity, and the stories are so consistent from culture to culture that they have credibility. In the more developed countries, it's possible that demon activity takes on different, seemingly sophisticated, forms. In many instances, we may not be aware that violent and antisocial behavior of people is directly tied to this kind of supernatural evil possession.

The value of the tragic and then beautiful story of the man

of Gadara lies in its candid description of what demon activity is all about. But the key to the story is the fact that demons are always impotent in the presence of Christ's power. "Even evil spirits obey his orders!" (Mark 1:27, TLB) was the observation of the disciples when Jesus demonstrated absolute control over the world of evil. And that trust is as sound today as it was then.

The message is clear: demon activity, even possession, may be a real matter, but the overwhelming power of Christ is just as real. No one who has made a personal commitment to Christ need fear being destroyed by this source of evil. Perhaps some people have felt the oppression of demonic attacks, but they can never be possessed as long as their lives have been placed under Christ's Lordship.

SYSTEMS OF EVIL

If evil has been generated in terms of temptation by Satan and in terms of a possible possession by demons, then according to the biblical writers, a more generalized form of evil energy pervades the systems of our times.

St. Paul warned the Ephesians that the Christian's struggle is not against human beings but "against the rulers, against the authorities, against the powers of this dark world and against the spiritual forces of evil in the heavenly realms" (Eph. 6:12). Paul wasn't more specific in identifying this "enemy," but he obviously wanted people to be alert to such oppression. He seemed to be saying that creation is temporarily sated with the spiritual force of evil and that it would be totally devastating were it not for the restraining hand of God. Be alert, he advised. Be constantly in a state of armored vigilance. Do not take this enemy for granted, he begged.

One does not have to look across our civilized world for very long to believe that Paul was absolutely correct. The evil that seems to pervade the machinations of nations and peoples today defies credulity. In his book *Modern Times* Paul Johnson records and analyzes the history of the twentieth century and the multimillions of people killed by the violence of political action. He finally asks, "What has gone wrong with humanity?"

A spiritual plague fills the air, St. Paul might answer. And only the power of God holds back the full potential of its devastating effects.

Does this form of evil play a role in the spawning of racism, nationalism, and materialism? Do institutions like governments and multinational companies become so driven with self-interest that they slowly become corporate versions of the demon-possessed man at Gadara? Does this form of evil often account for the breakdown of communication in organizations and the failure of people in disparate places such as Northern Ireland, the Middle East, and central Africa to solve their conflicts? Does this evil infect the mind of the terrorist who coldly goes about blowing up people in the name of political goals?

Does this evil affect you and me as we walk the streets of our towns and cities? Is it beating upon us through the news and entertainment media, through the pressure of society's trends? Does this evil even enter the church and cause it to become bogged down with property acquisition, organizationalism, and fund raising? Maybe.

The answer? Paul's warnings to the Ephesians. Be alert. Be armored. Be prayerful. This environment is most dangerous, and it can bring out the worst in us just when we didn't know that it was possible.

THE HUMAN HEART

The final source of temptation comes from within the human heart. But this is not an attractive thing to think about. Nevertheless, the Scriptures are quite clear that inner spiritual sicknesses can plague us all and will always, given a chance, draw us away from intimacy with God.

We human beings are paradoxes. We love the fruits of commitment, love, and order. Yet a dark side of us is often anticommitment, antilove, and antiorder. We would prefer to receive these things; we have to be taught and we have to deliberately choose to give these things. This is a fundamental testimony to the evil within.

One could say that a barbarian is in each of us. To some extent the barbarian can be temporarily tamed in the best situations. And one needs only look at the deteriorating moral situation in many parts of the Western world to understand that the barbarian in us is very much alive. That man loves darkness rather than light.

Many of the temptations to sin first come from this source within. Paul had several lists of these, which included "sexual immorality, impurity and debauchery; idolatry and witchcraft; hatred, discord, jealousy, fits of rage, selfish ambition, dissensions, factions and envy; drunkenness" (this one from Gal. 58:19-20). Jesus of course noted that the motives and designs for man's worst behavior come from within the heart and often find a receptive climate in the public world (see Matt. 15:16ff).

We are on safe ground when we listen to this carefully, when we conclude that each of us is capable of the worst sort of behavior that will eventually break a personal world to pieces. No environment is more vicious, none more dangerous, than the dark side of the human heart and its capacity to promote evil.

Alexander Whyte quotes John Bunyan:

> Sin and corruption would bubble up out of my heart as naturally as water bubbles up out of a fountain. I thought now that everyone had a better heart than I had. I could have changed heart with anybody. I thought none but the devil himself could equalize me for inward wickedness and pollution of mind. I fell, therefore, at the sight of my own vileness, deeply into despair, for I concluded that this condition in which I was in could not stand with a life of grace. Sure, thought I, I am forsaken of God; sure I am given up to the devil, and to a reprobate mind.

Even as I write these words, something within me wishes I could delete this chapter from the computer disk upon which it is recorded. The subject is depressing, and were it left without the hope of preventing and rebuilding in the chapters to come, it would deflate the spirit. But sometimes there is good news amidst the bad news. If the conditions of evil around us and in us are bad news, the good news is that we can be alert to them and appropriate the power of God to defend against them. Christianity is not a gloomy faith; it is a brilliant and powerful strategy against all else that is gloomy.

This warfare in the spiritual realm is real; it must be recognized and prepared for. But before we look away from this environment, we might be wise to ask ourselves this: when is spiritual warfare most likely to make itself felt?

There are occasions when spiritual warfare is most likely to be at its peak in our personal worlds. For example, I call one of these occasions "Going Beyond the Fences."

GOING BEYOND THE FENCES

In early 1988 Charles and Diana, Prince and Princess of Wales, and some friends took a skiing trip to Switzerland. The shocking news came one afternoon of a terrible accident caused by an avalanche in which one of the prince's life-long friends was killed and another seriously injured. It seemed sheer chance that the prince himself was not killed or hurt.

How did it happen? A day or two later the press reported that the prince's group had chosen to ski out on slopes that were closed to the public. The avalanche warnings had been posted, but they had chosen to go beyond the fences because, as one of them observed, that's where the optimum fun and excitement were to be found. Most likely, they found a brand of pleasure that was indeed more than attractive. But it went beyond the margins of what was wise and prudent. And the avalanche exacted its price among those who went beyond the fences. The result? Several broken worlds.

Like the prince and his party who could not stay inside the fences, all of us become curious enough at times to edge out to the fences and see what's on the other side. Perhaps we become curious to see how far we can sneak away from God and not suffer the consequences.

Going beyond the fences has to do with outright disobeying the will of Christ and neglecting the spiritual disciplines given to us for our maximum protection. When we cross the fence line, we open the gate to increasing possibilities for broken-world choices. We invite more intense spiritual warfare. And we are likely to have insufficient "weaponry" to handle the oppression.

Our God takes no pleasure in the disobedience of His people or in the consequences that often result. Rather, He mourns this errant self-confidence that will not bend to the lesson of history: those who go beyond the fences are at the mercy of temptation and will inevitably be overcome by the energy that lies deep within or the spiritual enemy without.

DOUBT

I'm a doubter by nature. And so I speak from personal experience when I say that spiritual warfare increases to a feverish pitch when people like me find it hard to trust.

Asking questions and admitting confusion are not necessarily wrong things for Christians to do when we are trying to grow. Nor does our God expect us to have all the answers sorted and defined.

There are understandable moments when, from the human perspective, events do not make sense and we wonder what these things mean. At times we are keenly disappointed when something does not happen according to our expectations. Suffering, death, loss: they can smash our resolve and our confidence for a time. And in their path some of us might doubt that we are grounded in truth.

I see no place where God condemns doubt. Gracious Father that He is, He seems not to be offended when we speak out in momentary anger to Him, when we frankly disagree with Him, or when we acknowledge that somewhere along the line we've missed His signals altogether and wonder if there were any signals.

But we must remember that while there may be nothing wrong with doubt, it is a dangerous time in which spiritual warfare can increase. At such a time our resolve to be alert to the evil in and around us can be diminished. When you see a Christian make a choice that leads to a broken world, you may be seeing a person who was in a time of great doubt and was caught in spiritual impoverishment.

THE COUNSEL OF THE WICKED

You could be rather blunt in the days when the psalmist wrote what we call the First Psalm. And he was blunt when he noted the tendency of some to walk "in the counsel of the wicked." That's not a complimentary description of some people in our world, but the psalmist was aware that there is no "blessedness" when we continually expose ourselves to the influences of people who have little or no use for God or for spiritual orientation.

Earlier we spoke of Lot, and his misfortunes again provide us with a powerful lesson. He was always being influenced by people around him.

As long as he was under the influence of his uncle, Abraham, his life and choices seem to have been exemplary. But somehow he one day assumed that he could get along without his uncle and so purposed to move to Sodom. Lot learned a sad lesson in that city: you cannot expect to be spiritually strong if your fellowship is constantly with those whose values and commitments are anti-God.

Lot's personal world and those of his family suffered total catastrophe because Lot didn't know this. He lost his wife, his extended family, his assets, and his dignity. The explanation is simple. Lot could not expect to be successful in spiritual warfare when he surrounded himself with people who had no use for his relationship with God.

This is a precedent for Christians to consider. Can we expect to acquire and maintain the spiritual strength and ardor that we want if the predominant influences in our lives are people who are alien to the faith? This is why the Scriptures urge the Christian on to supportive fellowship and accountability with men and women of like commitment.

The fact is that we increase the chances of succumbing to the spiritual offenses of the enemy within and without when we place ourselves in these situations: disobedience, doubt, and a pervasive non-Christian influence.

This subject of spiritual warfare is an awesome one. The thinking person is uncomfortable with it. The emotional person is frightened by it. The activist is sure that there is a conspiracy against him.

But that spider does spin his web. We are by our very nature tempted to explore the outer edges of the web, sure that we can handle at least that part. But every once in a while, someone wanders too far toward the middle. The result? A world breaks. And one again wonders why we did not learn history's lessons.

PART III
THE REBUILDING PROCESS

13

Freeing the Bound-Up Heart

BOTTOM LINE #13: *The freest person in the world is one with an open heart, a broken spirit, and a new direction in which to travel.*

In past centuries, it was a custom in many parts of China to keep the feet of young girls tightly wrapped. Small feet and short steps were considered a mark of feminine physical attractiveness in the Chinese culture. Only in modern times has this discomforting and deforming practice been scuttled.

I have the principle of bound feet in mind when I ponder how we get on with the process of rebuilding a broken world. How do we take the pieces of life and begin the process of putting them back together again?

We've looked at myths and case studies and environments of choice in an attempt to trace the origins and consequences when worlds break into pieces. That is an important foundation for the most important part of this book. How are broken worlds rebuilt?

WHERE DO ANY OF US BEGIN?

My initial thought is to go back to the starting point of all broken-world choices: the inner being; the private world; the

517

heart, the core of the person that Jeremiah said was deceitful and beyond full comprehension. But why go there?

Because the biblical writers almost always start there. They assess the performance of a person or a people by saying something first about the condition of the heart when they record and analyze the broken-world choices of individuals and nations. Favorite adjectives for describing the heart when personal worlds are breaking are *stiff-necked; resistant; darkened; blinded; afflicted; rebellious.* The Bible speaks of the hardened heart of the Egyptian Pharaoh, the cold hearts of the people of Israel, and the violated or penetrated heart of Judas.

On the other hand, when the writers speak of one who has moved into the rebuilding phase, the adjectives describing the heart turn to *broken; turned back; clean; undivided; contrite; new.*

David, the man who constantly struggled with deceit and personal integrity, said to his son, Solomon, as he pointed him to the future:

> And you, my son Solomon, acknowledge the God of your father, and serve him with wholehearted devotion and with a willing mind, for the LORD searches every heart and understands every motive behind the thoughts (1 Chron. 28:9).

In a few words David put the issues of faith into a capsule. We have a God whose view of us begins with the heart, and we are called to serve Him beginning from the heart. The heart is behind the mind; it produces the motives behind the thoughts. And out of all that come the actions that break a personal world or rebuild it.

Two extreme "heart conditions" are a distinct displeasure to God. Both attract His anger and judgment. In their extremes these hearts are bound by evil just like the feet of a nineteenth-century Chinese girl, and they therefore suffer from discomfort and deformity.

One extreme is typified by the personal worlds of the people of the earliest civilization in the Bible: "The LORD saw how great man's wickedness on the earth had become, and that every inclination of the thoughts of his heart was only evil all the time" (Gen. 6:5). This is a brief description of people whose hearts had become so oriented toward the production of evil that nothing of any value could be seen in

them. These people apparently made no attempt at even a
pretense of good. This unbelievably bad condition was the
prelude to the flood of judgment from which only Noah and
his family escaped.

At the other extreme is the heart absorbed in organized
religion with the hope of mounting an impressive performance of human goodness designed to placate God and intimidate people. No one seems to have known this condition
better than Paul. Once a Pharisee, he had been numbered
among those for whom outward appearance was almost
everything. Robes, gestures, routines, verbiage, intellectual
life: from the tiniest detail to the most flamboyant ceremo-
nies, the Pharisee's life was one big attempt to make an
impression for God, for one another, and for the world in
general. But in what order?

I think one of the sources of Paul's overwhelming joy in
Christian faith was his sense of being freed from a formerly
bound heart. In earlier days, impression making had meant
at least three things. First, always living with the inner
realization that he wasn't MEASURING UP to what he set
as external standards. And, second, COVERING UP substandard feelings, thoughts, and desires when he was with
others so that he wouldn't be found to be the imperfect
person that he really was. And, finally, the Pharisees' style
must have meant LOOKING OUT in suspicion and accusation to pinpoint what was wrong with other people. Only in
that way could some sense of superiority and false security
be maintained.

And when he chose to follow Christ, all of that discomfort
and deformity in his bound-up heart was suddenly gone. No
wonder he was exasperated with the Galatians when they
showed signs of wanting to go back to the bound-up life: "It is
for freedom that Christ has set us free. Stand firm, then, and
do not let yourselves be burdened again by a yoke of slavery"
(Gal. 5:1).

George Regas has provided a marvelous illustration of the
repentant man:

There is a moment in Leonard Bernstein's modern opera, MASS,
with which I identify in the most profound way. The priest
celebrating the mass puts on one priestly vestment after another,
one elegant robe on top of another. Then the priest staggers

under the weight of all that tradition. There is a sense of violence in the scene, as if all that religiosity is about to destroy him. Finally the priest tears off all the vestments and stands in his blue jeans and a T-shirt before the altar. He sings, "Look at me. There is nothing but me under this." (*Kiss Yourself and Hug the World*)

And that's what happened to Paul when he found the key to an unbound heart on the road to Damascus. He could never understand why anyone in his right mind would want to go back to the old ways any more than a modern Chinese woman would wish to return to the tradition of bound feet and their discomfort and deformity.

A broken world will never be rebuilt until we learn this principle of the unbound heart. It must be unwrapped and exposed to the light. The light will show some unattractive evil, but then something wonderful will happen. The love of God will be free to flood into the dark recesses, and rebuilding will begin.

The Bible calls this unbinding process REPENTANCE. It is an old word, usually associated with revivalistic religion. And so, frankly, many people find the word repugnant. But as some say, they throw the baby out with the bathwater. They do not understand that behind an oft-misunderstood word is an action that must precede all attempts at rebuilding.

Repentance is a Middle Eastern word. It describes the act of turning around when people realize that they have been going in the wrong direction. It was most likely used in nonreligious settings, such as when a traveler asked directions of someone who knew the countryside and was informed that he'd taken the wrong road and was moving away and not toward his destination. In such a conversation, it would be appropriate for the one to say to the other, "You're going to have to repent and head for that road."

And so the practical word *repent* became useful to describe a moral and spiritual act also. Used by Older Testament prophets, then John the Baptizer, Jesus, and finally the apostles, it meant to change the direction in which the heart was inclined.

John the Baptizer made repentance the theme of every public talk. He spoke of a repentance that took place first in the heart and then in the moral performance patterns of the individual. The latter he called "the fruits of repentance."

When repentant men and women stepped forward and said, "What kind of fruits are you talking about?" he would speak to them about their clear concern for the poor, their renunciation of violence, and their commitment to justice. These things, he said, would clearly indicate that something in the freed-up heart was different.

When the people heard St. Peter's famous sermon on the street in Jerusalem, they "were cut to the heart," a graphic description of people coming to insight about their bound-up private worlds. "What shall we do?" they asked the preacher. "Repent," he told them. They needed to change directions. (See Acts 2:14-40.)

The act of repentance is actually a gift from God in at least two ways. First, repentance is a gift in the sense that insight into our own broken-world need and awareness that something has to change is undoubtedly initiated by God's Spirit. Need and change are issues we simply would not see or appreciate on our own. Jesus said that was the task of the Holy Spirit, who would convict and point out sin, stimulating insight and the desire to change. (See John 16:8.)

This is not a pleasant aspect of God's activity in us, but it is a necessary one. Similarly, physical pain is not pleasant when it sends messages concerning our bodily affairs. But without pain signaling danger or without God's Spirit convicting when evil is on the loose within, we would be vulnerable to every hostile element there is: physical and spiritual. When pain speaks, we stop doing what we're doing, or we immediately seek to rectify whatever it is that is causing the discomfort. When the Spirit of God speaks, we repent: we renounce what we are doing or thinking and choose to replace the evil behavior with a godly one.

Second, repentance is also a gift in the sense that God has made it possible for us to turn back from broken-world directions. He didn't have to.

In a sermon at Harvard University Chapel, David H. C. Read told of his World War II experience as a POW. Standing next to a German guard as a destructive allied air raid took place nearby, they commiserated over the horror of war. "Die menscheit ist verrueckt!" the guard said, "Mankind is mad." And he went on, "The good God should destroy us all and begin again."

But God did not destroy us all. He set in motion the act of repentance: the way back, the way of rebuilding a broken world. I have never forgotten the words of the chief of a small Brazilian jungle tribe who told me of his view of God before he ever heard of Jesus Christ. "We always assumed that our Maker was so disappointed with us that He went off and left us. Now we know that He came to us and made a way for us to come back to Him."

It is relatively easy for us to see this principle of repentance when someone has made a broken-world choice demanding confession and accountability. "If only Nixon had said he was sorry," many used to say, "the country (or most of it) would have most likely forgiven him and let him get on with his presidency." We look for people who have made terrible errors to repent, to acknowledge a change of directions, and we are sad, sometimes even angry, when they do not.

It is more difficult to understand that repentance is not a one-time act; it is actually a spiritual life-style. To live in a constant state of repentance is to acknowledge that the heart is always ready to drift into wrong directions and must constantly be jerked back to control. This is not a call to a morbid kind of introspection that is always on a sin-search, putting ourselves down. But it is an honest recognition that the inward part of us is inclined toward rebellion and disobedience against our Maker. And it will always be that way until the end of time. That's why the hymn writer, Robert Robinson, observed:

> Prone to wander, Lord, I feel it,
> Prone to leave the God I love;
> Here's my heart, O take and seal it;
> Seal it for thy courts above.

And it's why Isaac of Nineveh, an ancient mystic, said,

> He who knows his sins is much greater than he who makes someone rise from the dead. He who can really cry one hour about himself is greater than he who teaches the whole world; he who knows his own weaknesses is greater than he who sees the angels.

The act of repentance can be broken down into several steps. The first was something referred to in earlier chapters: INSIGHT. It usually comes, as we saw in the experience of the prodigal son, when there is a revelation of the state of the acts of evil either by consequence or by confrontation. The prodigal came to insight through CONSEQUENCE; David came to insight through CONFRONTATION.

It would be helpful to recognize a third possibility for initiating insight, and that would be the experience of the prophet Isaiah who came to insight through an EXPOSURE to God in a vision of heavenly glory. What he saw and attempted to record exceeds the mind's ability to comprehend. All we know is that the man was overwhelmed by what happened. And rather than use it as a pretext for religious power grabbing or as something to boost his notoriety, he tells us frankly that the whole thing broke him. In the contrast to God's glory, he came to insight about himself: he was a broken-world person in need of rebuilding, and he lived among lots of other broken-world persons who had a similar need.

If insight has done its work, the result will be something that can be described only as BROKENNESS. As I noted before, variations of this experience are presented throughout the Bible. Broken men in the Older Testament could become very dramatic about their display of sorrow. They might tear their clothes in tatters, daub themselves with ashes or wail loudly. All of these were outward expressions of deep remorse over their own sins or those of their families and people. We might find such public displays rather amusing to think about, but they were serious matters in those days.

One king of Israel reflected brokenness as he moved among the people of his city and saw them starving to death and so desperate that some were even eating their children. After an encounter with a woman who had cooked her own child, "he tore his robes. As he went along the wall, the people looked, and there, underneath, he had sackcloth on his body" (2 Kings 6:30).

Nehemiah expressed what one might call a macro-brokenness when he, like others, confessed not only his sins but those of previous generations. He represented thinking somewhat unknown to people in Western culture that people shared a mutual responsibility for evil in their own generations and in those of their forefathers.

Job also seems to have understood this mutual responsibility for repentance from the other generational direction when, as the Scripture says, he offered sacrifices on behalf of his children saying, "Perhaps my children have sinned and cursed God in their hearts." The writer added: "This was Job's regular custom" (Job 1:5).

Brokenness implies an acceptance of full responsibility for what has happened, a genuine sorrow reflecting an awareness that one has grieved God and those who have been affected by the broken-world choices. We see indications of that kind of emotion and grief in the prostitute who kneeled at Jesus' feet and washed them with her tears. Simon, Jesus' host that day, took one look at the weeping woman and said to himself: "If this man were a prophet, he would know who is touching him and what kind of woman she is—that she is a sinner" (Luke 7:39).

The irony is that Jesus knew exactly who and what kind of person she was. Simon didn't realize that Jesus was most drawn to that kind of person: THE BROKEN KIND. A study of the people with whom Jesus spent His time and gave His compassion might suggest that He was not as concerned about what one had done in the past as about whether or not there was expressed brokenness in the present.

The woman had apparently committed all sorts of immoral acts, but she was broken. Simon had committed nothing in life that his generation thought worthy of an accusation, but his heart was proud and stiffened. He received a stunning, a rather embarrassing, rebuke; she received forgiveness for her sins.

The gospel writers seem to highlight two kinds of people as representing the worst sin in the times: immoral women and tax-collecting men. The former represent a corruption of personal life; the latter a corruption that gouges and exploits others. We have at least three specific encounters with immoral women and three with tax collectors (one is a fictional encounter in the parable of the tax collector and the Pharisee). On each occasion the writers point up the scorn, the judgmentalism, and the feelings of superiority of the upper class. And on each occasion, the grace and the tenderness of Christ are revealed as He reaches out to give hope for a rebuilt broken world.

This is significant. It is not that the Bible is in any way

diminishing the seriousness of the sins of immorality and greed; rather, it is pointing out to us that Christ looks past the sin to the point of potential brokenness. And when He sees it, an immediate rebuilding process begins. But when He does not see brokenness, rebuke, anger, and frequent confrontation result.

Resistance to brokenness caused Paul to be harsh in his critique of the Corinthian church. Paul's own cry of brokenness—"What a wretched man I am! Who will rescue me from this body of death?" (Rom. 7:24)—modeled what individuals do as they come to insight and realize that their performance is beneath the standards of God.

Most outstanding men and women in the Bible seem to have had some sort of experience with brokenness. In fact, it seems to be the absolute essential before God is willing to work with any of them. Having read and reread their biographies, I've come to the conclusion that we might have disqualified the majority of them from ever holding appointed Christian leadership.

Had we lived in Joseph's lifetime, we would have seen him as a convicted attempted rapist. Jacob would have been set aside as having a serious character defect in the area of truthfulness. David would have been considered a poor manager of his home, an adulterer, and a murderer; Moses, a murderer; Simon Peter, a coward; and Paul, a volatile enemy of the church probably not to be trusted, let alone listened to.

St. Augustine never forgot the broken-world performance of his past and how it drove him to confess faith in Christ. In his *Confessions* he wrote often of the constant life of brokenness:

> For what am I without thee, but a guide to mine own downfall? Or what am I even at the best, but an infant seeking milk, and feeding upon thee, the Food incorruptible? But what kind of thing is any man, seeing that he is but a man? *Let now the strong and the mighty laugh at me, but let us weak and needy souls ever confess unto thee.* (Emphasis mine)

Like Augustine, we must live as perpetually broken people. Those who are broken only in the crisis will soon grow cold, and other kinds of broken worlds are liable to follow. Brokenness is a way of life, the realization that the recovering alcoholic carries all the time: I'm licked if I think I can beat this alcoholic enemy alone. And so the man or woman broken before God lives.

Not long ago one of the world's greatest violinists, Isaac Stern, was playing Mozart's Violin Concerto no. 3 in G with Zubin Mehta and the New York Philharmonic Orchestra. Midway in the first movement, Mr. Stern had a lapse of memory and forgot his music. Immediately he ceased playing, walked over to Mehta, the conductor, and asked him and the orchestra if they would prepare to begin the concerto again. Then turning to the audience, this remarkable musician apologized for his mistake and started from the beginning.

Donal Henahan, writing of the incident in the *New York Times*, noted that "the performance began again from the beginning, allowing the audience to hear Mozart unmaimed. Though Mr. Stern could have vamped for a while until memory got back on track, his was surely a more honest and more musically satisfactory solution."

Indeed, a professional like Isaac Stern could have fooled his audience and covered his mistakes. But his fidelity to Mozart and his music demanded of him a clear accounting of his error and a desire to start over. A simple and straightforward way of doing things, something all of us—beginning with me—need to remember. In the spiritual realm, we'd call what Stern did brokenness and repentance, admission of error and desire to start over.

The final phase of repentance, the UNBINDING OF THE HEART, is that of the specific change of direction. *Behavior must not only change; it must be renounced, repudiated.*

R. T. Kendall in an inspiring book on the life of Joseph has a fascinating insight on the relationship between the governor of Egypt and his brothers. They had become broken men through their confrontations with Joseph and had made their initial repentance quite clear.

He instructed his assistant to hide his personal cup in the baggage of Benjamin, the youngest and most beloved of the brothers. Then soon after the brothers had headed homeward to their father, Joseph's men caught up with them and insisted that the cup had been stolen by one of them.

The brothers were horrified and quickly offered their baggage for a search. Soon the cup was discovered in Benjamin's bags. This would have been the time, Kendall observes, for the brothers to revert to type if there was no brokenness. Just as they once discarded Joseph, they might have said to the governor's assistants, "Take him back to face his penalties; we are innocent."

But they didn't. They insisted on returning with Benjamin to face the situation. Kendall writes:

> They all loaded their donkeys and returned to the city. All of them. They didn't say, "Goodbye, Benjamin. Tough luck, but goodbye." No. They all went back. Repentance had truly taken place. (*God Meant It for Good*)

In so doing they proved beyond a shadow of a doubt that they were different men on this side of repentance from what they had been on the other side.

On my bookshelf is an old book of stories D. L. Moody loved to tell. Most of them are outdated now, but one has caught my attention and affection. Moody writes:

> Dr. Andrew Bonar told me how, in the Highlands of Scotland, a sheep would often wander off into the rocks and get into places that they couldn't get out of. The grass on these mountains is very sweet and the sheep like it, and they will jump down ten or twelve feet, and then they can't jump back again and the shepherd hears them bleating in distress. They may be there for days, until they have eaten all the grass. The shepherd will wait until they are so faint that they cannot stand, and then they will put a rope around him, and he will go over and pull that sheep up out of the jaws of death.
>
> "Why don't they go down there when the sheep first gets there?" I asked.
>
> "Ah!" he said, "they are so very foolish they would dash right over the precipice and be killed if they did."

Moody concludes his story by saying:

> And that is the way with men; they won't go back to God till they have no friends and have lost everything. If you are a wanderer I tell you that the Good Shepherd will bring you back the moment you have given up trying to save yourself and are willing to let Him save you His own way.

Bound-up feet create discomfort and deformity. It is no different with hearts that have never been unwrapped by repentance.

14

The Peace Ledge Principles

BOTTOM LINE #14: *The process of rebuilding requires some temporary operating principles by which to navigate through the dark times.*

When my world broke, it happened in three painful stages. The first stage was contained deep within myself as I came to the experience of insight of what I had done. There are no words to describe the inner anguish of knowing that you have disappointed and offended God, that you have violated your own integrity, and that you have betrayed people you really love and care for. There are moments in the life of one whose world is so broken when death would seem a merciful experience. Like others with broken worlds, I lived with that stage for a long time, secret carrying, hoping that I could contain the consequences within my inner life.

Strangely enough, while it was a time of inward anguish, it was also a time in which I became increasingly sensitive to the needs of others. I didn't need many words from men and women who visited with me to know what they were going through; it wasn't hard to identify. And if I gave a public talk during that time, it wasn't unusual for people to speak privately to me and remark about my seeming sensitivity to personal weaknesses. Of course when I would respond by saying that we were all sinners, that we all had weaknesses,

528

they would smile. It was clear that they were thinking how nice it was of me to be so gracious and kind when in fact (as far as they were concerned) I had my own "act all put together."

The second stage of my broken-world experience began when I came to the conclusion that I had to open my troubled inner being to my wife, Gail, and to a few trusted spiritual advisors. The good news was that there was someone with whom to share the grief over what I'd done; the bad news was in hurting those who had trusted me so completely.

Others knew and shared the burden of the grievously heavy baggage. And there was a period of time when they had to catch their breath and wonder how to react to what I had told them. In each case the ultimate reaction was one of remarkable grace and the beginning of the extension of forgiveness.

Gail had spent the better part of a year studying the Bible and the available Christian literature on the subject of grace and forgiveness, and when I opened the dark side of my heart and shared my secret, she knew that her study process had been something more than an academic or a theological exercise. The material she had accumulated on paper and in her heart from the year's study was quickly put to work in a magnificent way. It wasn't done euphorically or automatically. Sometimes it was hard going because our lives were lived in heavy public activity; but the progress was always forward. Both of us embarked on a partnership of giving and receiving grace and discovered that our marriage relationship was rugged enough to stand the shock of a major injury.

The key friends—we came to call them the (ministering) angels—were likewise gracious, but firm! The story of their involvement will be told later. But what should be said now is something about the way they poured their lives and love into Gail and me. We were limping people, the result of my self-inflicted wounds. They came alongside to assist in the process of rebuilding. Our son and our daughter and her husband were drawn into the loop of knowledge, and their support and encouragement brought strength to us that we never thought possible.

Many months later the third stage of the broken-world experience came. And that happened when the secret of what we had hoped was a resolved past became a public piece of information in some parts of the Christian church. Gail and I and our "angels" had faced the possibility of that moment, although we had hoped it would not happen. But when it did, we were prepared to accept the moment as a directive from the hand of God, and we knew what we had to do.

Our worlds were broken. A dream had turned into a nightmare of loss, humiliation, anger, and a sense of a very dark future. There was the terrible realization that many who had trusted me were now disillusioned. There was the knowledge that some people were talking, with or without a knowledge of the facts.

At each of the three stages I had to wrestle with a decision. Would I become defensive, hardened, or resistant? Would I run, quit, or try to rationalize? All of these were tempting, and a part of me—not made of God—would like to have experimented in each category. But I had several things going for me that prevented me from doing so: the partnership of Gail; the encouragement of our children; the pastoral oversight of those we called the angels; and the constant prodding and poking that came from my readings in the Scripture. God clearly used each of these to rebuke me and restrain me.

That's when we withdrew to Peace Ledge, a simple home we'd built years ago in New Hampshire. I will never forget those first days. It was almost impossible to ward off the feeling that life was over, that all the brightness and joy that we had known for more than forty-five years had come to a screeching halt. But those are feelings, and they move quickly into one of the most dangerous moods: self-pity. We had made an early decision to renounce self-pity at all costs.

As the days became weeks, the rebuilding process picked up speed. I began to discover that a set of principles had come into play. We had not devised them; they were a gift to us from God, and they had been mediated to us through our reading, through our friends, and through the dynamics of our personal discoveries. I came to call them the Peace Ledge Principles because they surfaced here on the hill where I write today.

The principles appear over and over again in our journals. Each morning we would arise very early and ponder what God might say to us that day. Who might call? What would the mail bring? Was a visitor coming? Would there be something in the Scriptures or in the spiritual classics we were reading?

In some ways I began to appreciate the alcoholic's view of life. Make it for one more day. Don't think in terms of months and years ahead. Just brood on today and what tiny thing God may have as He orchestrates the rebuilding process.

Now as I study the journal that carries the record of each of those days, these are the principles I see that we followed. They are simple and workable.

Be Silent; Withdraw

The broken-world person who lives with self-inflicted damage faces a heavy temptation to defend himself and his "territory." If he cannot escape responsibility for his misbehavior, he is tempted to do at least three things to ease the embarrassment.

First, he is tempted to spread the blame for his deed. The mind sharpened by this pain of humiliation is adept at looking at all involved in the tragic events and trying to see what they did and did not do. Second, the person with the broken world may try to complain about how poorly he perceives he is being treated by his accusers and critics. And third, he is liable to diminish the seriousness of his own choices by concentrating on the sins of others. *This way,* he thinks, *I don't have to feel so badly about myself. They're as bad as I am.*

Such thinking never brings rebuilding. It retards and usually defeats the process.

In a sermon on the parable of the Pharisee and the publican Helmut Thielicke said,

> When a man really turns to God with a burdened conscience he doesn't think of other people at all. There he is utterly alone with God. It would never have occurred to the publican to say, "Sure, this Pharisee is a man of a different stripe from me, but he too has plenty of blots on his scutcheon; he's a sinner too." This would have been true, of course. But when a man is utterly alone with God and dealing solely with him, then many things that are true are completely immaterial to him. He has something else to think about. And that's why the publican's attitude is completely genuine and radically honest. He measures himself "upward." God *himself* is his standard.

Thielicke went on to remind his congregation that the German people had "had some conception of our guilt after the collapse at the end of the last war and many of us had uttered the prayer of the publican, 'God be merciful to me a sinner! Remove not thy grace from our sunken people.'"

> But then came one of the most dreadful moments in the spiritual history of our nation when suddenly we began to say, "Others are just as bad as we." Then suddenly our aloneness with God vanished, then repentance and spiritual renewal were gone, then began that fateful measuring of ourselves by looking downward and comparing ourselves with the hypocritical democratic Pharisees among the victors. (*The Waiting Father*)

St. Paul made it clear that there is only one useful posture when we come to insight about ungodly choices in life: the posture of silence before God and before the world. We may lessen the impact of the sorrow for ourselves in the short term if we try to avoid the full effect of the responsibility. But we do nothing for the rebuilding the Bible says God wants to make happen if we do not become silent so that we can listen.

Gail and I learned not only that silence implied no defense, but that it meant withdrawing into quiet places. For us, that was Peace Ledge. I am not so much thinking, however, of a *place* as I am of activity. When the broken-world person is living with great wounds he has brought on himself and perhaps also inflicted on others, a season for slipping into a quiet place is necessary. This is no hour for plotting what the politicians call a comeback.

The deeper and wider the hurt, the more important this withdrawal. It is a time to take stock of what happened and why; a time to realign and recharge spiritual resources; a time to probe deep within the inner world to understand where the blind spots were. This cannot normally be done in a matter of weeks. If it is unwisely hastened, there may possibly be a recurrence of misbehavior later on.

Oswald Chambers wrote, and we took his words seriously:

> At times God puts us through the discipline of darkness to teach us to heed Him. Song birds are taught to sing in the dark, and we are put into the shadow of God's hand until we learn to hear Him. "What I tell you in darkness,"—watch where God puts you into darkness, and when you are there keep your mouth shut. Are you

in the dark just now in your circumstances, or in your life with God? Then remain quiet. If you open your mouth in the dark, you will talk in the wrong mood: darkness is the time to listen. Don't talk to other people about it; don't read books to find out the reason of the darkness, but listen and heed. If you talk to other people, you cannot hear what God is saying. When you are in the dark, listen, and God will give you a very precious message for someone else when you get into the light. (*My Utmost for His Highest*)

DON'T DEFEND YOURSELF

The second Peace Ledge Principle was a difficult one to handle. And I had to learn to submit to its charge on almost a daily basis.

When the broken-world person hears of a rumor concerning him that some have not bothered to check out, he has a desire to find every possible medium of communication that might be used to squelch it. When some people think they can explain the broken-world person's behavior on the basis of generalizations that work fine for them, there's a temptation to sound out and let people know of the exceptions.

I have studied Jesus' defensive strategies. They only operate when the issue is truth or the rights and needs of another person. But Jesus never defended Himself. The corollary to this principle, of course, is the mandate we all carry to defend one another. This seems to have been the instruction of the Spirit of God when I looked for direction. If there is to be any defense or advocacy, let it come from others, from friends and colleagues, not from me or from my family. The friends were there, and the principle vindicated itself.

ENJOY THE AMUSEMENT OF GOD'S MESSENGERS

Peace Ledge is a beautiful place to Gail and me. It is our home. But in another sense it became a wilderness when my world broke. A lovely, quiet wilderness. In the past other men like Moses, Elijah, John the Baptizer, Jesus, and Paul went to the wildernesses of their day when they were hunted, when they had something to learn, when it was time to be tested. And when a busy life comes to a screeching halt, broken persons suddenly find themselves in "wildernesses." That's where we were.

In such places you become aware of little things, things that aren't immediately noticeable when schedules are complicated and crowded. For us, the little things were birds, chipmunks, squirrels, deer, raccoons, and even skunks. The flowers, trees, and forest trails all furnished the theater and the scenery for their antics.

The living things at Peace Ledge became our friends, close friends in a strange way. We laughed at the chipmunks who chased one another mercilessly back and forth across the stone walls that lace the Peace Ledge property. The birds with their glorious colors and their individual personalities delighted us with their visits to the feeder. The dignified mourning doves always arrived in pairs. The hyperactive chickadees flew together as if in an airlift grabbing one seed at a time. And the arrogant woodpeckers and the stealthy hummingbirds put on a grand show as they came to Peace Ledge to pay respects.

The squirrels spent literally hours trying to invade the birdfeeder and usually succeeded until we daubed the pole with Vaseline. The raccoons visited regularly and insensitively at 3:30 A.M. All of them, our friends, were God's messengers.

We call them God's messengers because one day at the peak of their performances for us, Gail recalled a description of Jesus' time in the wilderness of temptation. "He was with the wild animals, and angels attended him," Mark wrote (1:13). Did they amuse Jesus also?

We lost all interest in television, world news, professional sports, and scandals. Strength came from everywhere around us. It was as if God had chosen the impersonal elements of His creation to form a fortress about us, a place where we could think and pray, talk and share.

The living things, the trees and flowers, the sky, all became God's messengers of endurance and empowerment. They were our amusement, our inspiration, our reminders of His presence. Each day we offered up thanks to God for the special gift of Peace Ledge and the "messengers" He sent to us.

Assume the Ministry of the Interior

Sometimes the most stunning reality to hit the broken-world person can be the loss of primary function. *What value do I have to anyone any longer?* one might ask. *What can I do?* These were burning questions to me, ones that I probably asked God several times each day. Soon He provided a preliminary and very significant answer.

It came one morning as Gail and I read Oswald Chambers's *My Utmost for His Highest*:

> Enter into the ministry of the interior. The Lord turned the captivity of Job *when he prayed for his friends*. The real business of your life as a saved soul is intercessory prayer. Wherever God puts you in circumstances, pray immediately, pray that His atonement may be realized in other lives, as it has been in yours. Pray for your friends *now*; pray for those with whom you come in contact *now*.

Would you be surprised if I told you that we were astounded by this challenge? It was as if God had prepared a word specifically for us seventy-five years ago, and we were ready to hear it in its fullest force. We felt as if we had lost every opportunity to serve people in the exterior world. But here was a ministry that can never be lost, "the ministry of the interior," Chambers called it. It's a work that can be performed if one is banished to a desert isle or a prison cell. It cannot be stripped away.

That morning I wrote in my journal:

> Chambers challenges us to enter into the ministry of the interior. He points out that the work of intercession is the highest work. Only after Job prayed for his friends was he restored. The Lord seems to be saying to me this morning that I should focus on the ministry of the interior: intercession for my friends. If there is ever again to be a ministry of the exterior, that will come later and in His good time.

I went on in my journal:

> A ministry of the interior, it seems to me:
>   a. Worships in God's presence
>   b. Roots out personal impurity
>   c. Broods upon eternal truths

    d. Offers thanksgiving
    e. Prays for the world
    f. Intercedes for friends

Gail and I made a commitment to each other that day that we would accept God's call to the ministry of the interior, a ministry we had merely dabbled in by contrast up until that time. If we find no other way to serve the Lord in the coming years, we determined, we will do the one thing no one can take away from us. We will learn the discipline of intercession.

And so we started. We were fascinated with how quickly our intercession list grew. Each morning it became a habit to go to our knees in the living room of our Peace Ledge home and lift friends to the throne of God. When people shared their personal concerns and challenges with us, we immediately took it upon ourselves to make them daily issues of prayer.

Intercession became a marvelous instrument of ministry. And we gained the conviction that we just might accomplish more for people on our knees than all the speaking and writing we might have ever done.

Intercession doesn't come easily to most of us. Many husbands and wives do not find it easy to pray together. Although we had learned to do that long ago, the extended intercessory discipline taxed our willpower. But we were determined to seek God's rebuilding of our broken worlds the way Job had sought it—by getting our minds off ourselves and praying for our friends.

Today it would be an uncompleted day if we did not make our appearance—as it were—before the seat of our Father where we can pray for our friends. Our prayer list includes many pastors, especially younger ones who are carrying the responsibility for large congregations and need much wisdom and protection. It includes our children, our parents, and our brothers and their families. The list includes many friends across the world; some of them we do not know personally but God has laid them upon our minds.

It became my activity on the many nights when I couldn't find sleep after midnight. Tempted to lie awake and worry about the past and the future, I learned to dismiss the anxiety by entering into intercession from a global perspective.

Putting my junior-high-school geography class to good use, I would start around the world beginning with Argentina to the deep south of Peace Ledge, praying my way through the countries of Latin America, seeing how many cities in each country I could remember and pray for. I'd pray for national church leaders I'd met or heard of. After Latin America came the island countries of the Caribbean and the nations of the Central American isthmus. Through the states and provinces of Mexico, the USA, and Canada. Over to Europe, down to Africa, then to the subcontinent and on to Asia and down through the Pacific. I rarely made it past Egypt before the Lord provided a quiet sleep.

I have no doubt that this Peace Ledge Principle of intercession has played a key role in the rebuilding process of our lives. Now we know what it is like to be prayed for and to pray for others and to be trusted with their prayer needs.

15
More Peace Ledge Principles

BOTTOM LINE #15: *Listen; receive; give; and then anticipate. No time in the wilderness is ever wasted for the one who intends to return what grace has given.*

At Peace Ledge we were alone with our heavenly messengers and our questions. "When a man is to be hanged in a fortnight, it concentrates his mind wonderfully," Samuel Johnson said more than two centuries ago. Although I wasn't due for a hanging, I sometimes felt like it was what I deserved. And in that prevailing mood the mind was concentrated. It was time to search for more substantial truths about God and about self than we ever had before. We determined to do it.

Out of that came a fifth Peace Ledge Principle:

LISTEN TO THE DEEP THINGS

Somewhere in those early days we equated the principle of being silent with listening. We wished to be listeners to the deep sources where certain kinds of heavenly truth are tapped only by those who have a heart to be attentive. Usually those are the hearts of the suffering or the hearts of broken-world people in search of a rebuilding effort.

We wanted to look at pain the way Joseph looked at it when he scanned the many years of slavery, imprisonment, and ill-treatment and said, "You meant evil against me; but God meant it for good" (Gen. 50:20, NKJV). Our questions were another version of that. How do you take an evil event and its consequences and squeeze good out of it? Is that really possible? Can the worst that human beings do be forced to render something good? Can God play a trick on evil?

For answers to those questions we turned to the Scriptures and browsed through both Testaments. We searched out the biblical biographies of every man and woman whose world had broken for one reason or another. As I've noted elsewhere, we discovered that almost everyone in the Bible was conversant with some kind of broken-world experience. And we came to understand that in almost every case the broken-world moments were the turning points to great spiritual insight, development, and godly performance. That was both a comfort and a marvelous promise.

We also turned to the spiritual classics. Here, our friends became women and men such as Amy Carmichael whose personal world broke through no fault of her own when she suffered a series of accidents and spent the last twenty years of life bedridden. Oswald Chambers whose life was probably shortened through his enormous intensity and physical exertion in serving the Lord during the World War I period. William and Catherine Booth who plowed through powerful ridicule and discouragement to establish the work of the Salvation Army.

I twice read the *Confessions* of St. Augustine and gained insight into the deep struggle of this early church father as he learned what it might mean to give his life to God. John Bunyan, an early Puritan pastor, opened up his life to us in his spiritual autobiography *Grace Abounding*. Only after reading Bunyan's account of his battle with evil did I come to appreciate what I read as I later went through *Pilgrim's Progress* and Alexander Whyte's two-volume *Bunyan's Characters*.

Mrs. Charles Cowman's *Streams in the Desert* and Chambers's *My Utmost for His Highest* became a daily spiritual feeding trough, never failing to provide a word from God to nourish our hearts. The prayers of Quoist, Baillie, and François Fénelon, the words of Tozer, and the liturgical worship of the Book of Common Prayer became our spiritual lines to the deep. And out of them all, words came from heaven itself each day to help in the rebuilding process.

Because we had more time here at Peace Ledge, we read more. And both of us came to a similar conclusion as we discussed the books we were reading. Books written by people who had sustained some sort of a broken-world experience—debilitating illness, humiliating failure, intense persecution, conflict with evil, numbing disappointment—were powerful in their ability to reach into our inner spirits. But books written by people who had little to offer but advice and pithy stories were no more nourishing than cotton candy. Genuine Christianity is a faith of the suffering, we learned. In the broken-world moments, deep calls to deep; pain reaches out to pain; failure searches out failure. And Christianity talks of better, more hopeful days when night ends.

Listening to the deep things also meant spending time in quiet meditation and thought. Our journals filled more quickly than ever as we tried to record everything God was whispering into our spirits through the Scriptures, the classics, and the impulses entering our hearts. There were the early evening conversations as we compared notes from our quiet moments and taught each other what we were hearing.

The themes? The ugliness of *sin*, not only in terms of its sad consequences but also in terms of offensiveness to God and His church. The *grace* of Christ, the *tenderness* of the heavenly Father. The *hope* held out for all who come with the broken pieces of their broken worlds asking to be put back together again. A growing *sensitivity to the fact that scores upon scores of people are seeking hope and rebuilding all the time and that many are not finding the grace and compassion they need.*

And what were we learning personally? How insignificant in God's eyes is the applause that comes with organizational leadership and public recognition. How relatively empty the overly busy life no matter how good the goals and objectives. How cheap the mountains of words we pile up in public talk after public talk. Not that these are bad or inconsequential things. But they are fruitless if one operates from a spiritual baseline that is not richly fed and nourished in communion with the deep where God speaks.

Gail had often wondered aloud in earlier days what it would be like if we were driven to a point of no resources but those God provided. Although financial resources and a place to live were not the problems of those dark days, encouragement, meaning, and security were. And we began to learn as we listened to the deep things that when you are on the bottom, God does indeed speak in ways that would have been otherwise incomprehensible.

Peace Ledge provided a place to listen carefully. Soon we became aware that God has much to say that we had not been hearing. We were usually too busy and in places where the noise levels were too high. God will not shout; He whispers in the deep. Only those who stop long enough or who are STOPPED long enough hear the text of the message from the deep.

RECEIVE THE MERCY; LIVE LIKE A FORGIVEN PERSON

This may have been the most difficult of all the Peace Ledge Principles. It was difficult because I came to see that the greatest accuser of the person with a broken world is the broken-world person himself.

With alarming frequency, the circuitry of accusation activated somewhere deep within. It would replay the past and remind me of past feelings: cheapness, failure, wreckage. There was no way back, the "accuser" would say.

It was actually a challenge sometimes to be among a few select friends and loved ones who were trying as hard as they could to give grace and kindness. The tempter might occasionally suggest that their affection was not genuine; that they were patronizing me; that sooner or later they would have done with me. Their very success seemed to accentuate my failure.

But then a stronger voice would emerge from the deep and say: you never were valuable on those terms anyway. You said you were a sinner; and now you've proved it to everyone. The truth about you used to be subsurface. Now you are what you are, and the evidence is clear for people to see. But you've been to the Cross, and it's time to put your performance where your mouth is. Either you believe in the capacity of Christ's atonement to make you a new person, or you don't. If you do, then start living like a forgiven person should live.

And how is that done? By being a lot more quiet, humble,

thankful, sensitive, and anxious to serve than you ever were before. Forgiven people basically live like that.

I listed a series of short-burst guidelines that I thought sounded like what a forgiven person might be and then committed to them, with God's help, one day at a time:

- Be quiet, don't push yourself.
- Don't be defensive; keep your fists unclenched.
- Serve every chance you get.
- Be as thankful as you possibly can be.
- Affirm everyone you can; build in their lives.
- Keep your new acquisitions to a minimum.
- Be the first to repent.
- Be quick to pray with others.
- Be orderly and dependable about your life.
- Accept and learn from defeats.
- Leave each place a bit better than when you first arrived.
- Watch for addictions to busyness and excitement.
- Don't enslave yourself to people's approval; say the appropriate noes.

Don't Dodge the Pain; Walk Right Through It

That was the seventh principle we learned at Peace Ledge.

When I was an athlete in track and cross-country, I learned that the champions spend a large amount of time dealing with the matter of pain. Mediocre runners like myself made pain the termination point of our performance. But champions made pain the threshold of performance. They knew what the rest of us resisted: you are only beginning to move into the possibilities of your best performance when you refuse to let pain become your termination point.

I had resisted pain as an athlete. For me it was the signal to stop or slow down. At Peace Ledge, we determined not to repeat that principle of mediocrity. We were going to face every ounce of the pain: whether it came from the rebukes, rumors, harsh criticism, or silence; the hurt that we had to face together; or the pain of inactivity.

What are the options in handling the pain of a broken world? Some turn off the emotional and spiritual nerve endings. Some stave off the pain with return anger or self-defense. We came to believe that the best response was to accept the pain, to permit the hurtful consequences to have their effect on us. This is not masochism; it is a process that purifies and calls one to greater alertness. It also resensitizes one to the awfulness of evil and creates a reaction toward sin much like antabuse causes a physical reaction in a problem drinker should he be tempted to take a drink.

The rebuilding process demands that one accept the pain. The bulk of the pain has an ending point, although I am presently convinced that the broken-world person may live with a certain amount of heartache for the rest of his life. That's part of the consequence of sin.

LOOK FOR THOSE WHO NEED GRACE AND AREN'T GETTING IT

Within a short period of time at Peace Ledge, Gail and I realized that we were receiving enormous amounts of understanding and affection from our friends and from many with whom we had never been acquainted. They made themselves known through the mail and through other forms of communication. We came to see that the Christian church is capable of pouring out grace in great quantities. And this is frequently not noted. It's much easier for all of us to talk about Christians *not* being forgiving or compassionate. But that was not to be our experience. Rather, we were startled at how powerful are the winds of encouragement that come from followers of the Lord.

But we were aware that here and there were people who had not experienced the affection and kindness shown to us. And we determined that even though we were in quiet, we would find ways to give grace whenever our spirits witnessed to someone who was suffering from a broken world.

Who might it be? The man who sells us our newspaper? The service manager where our car is maintenanced? The pastor who has been removed from his church in a controversial manner? The person struggling with homosexuality? The one whose business has failed? The mid-lifer suffering under a load of temptation he can hardly bear? The couple whose marriage totters on the brink of disaster?

Where could we send a letter of encouragement? When could we make a phone call that would lift spirits? Were there chances to invite someone to Peace Ledge for an over-night visit and turn our home into what we came to wish it to be: a home of grace?

Of all the Peace Ledge Principles, this became the most creative. We can step aside from positions of leadership that are offered in the Christian community, for those are offices in organizations. But we need never step aside from the actions of grace giving. To serve, that is true biblical leader-ship anyway. There is always someone in more trouble than I am; always someone who can profit from a probing question that will bring frustration or feelings of failure to the sur-face. There is always a chance to press a bit of value into the life of someone who perceives himself to be worthless. There is always a way to give if we want to get our minds off ourselves.

Grace giving and intercession began to go together. Those for whom we pray often become those to whom we give.

JOIN WITH THOSE WHO KNOW HOW TO PRAISE GOD

Some would say that we are meant to praise our Maker just as the stars in the heavens are meant to honor Him by their brilliance. It's possible that human beings reach a point of nobility when we gaze heavenward and direct our thanks-givings and affirmations to the God of Jesus Christ. But it's also quite possible that when Christians enter into praise, we set in motion a healing process for broken-world people.

In one of the darkest hours of my broken-world condition, I found myself one day in the front row of a Dallas church where I had been asked to give a talk. I had made a long-term commitment to be there, but had it not been for my hosts' hard work of preparation, I would have tried to cancel my participation. Frankly, I was in no mood to speak to anyone. But I felt constrained not to cancel, and so there I was.

When the service began, a group of young men and women took places at the front of the congregation and began to lead with instruments and voices in a chain of songs and hymns: some contemporary, others centuries old. As we moved freely from melody to melody, I became aware of a transfor-mation in my inner world. I was being strangely lifted by the music and its content of thankfulness and celebration. If my heart had been heavy, the hearts of others about me were apparently light because, together, we seemed to rise in spirit, the music acting much like the thermal air currents that lift an eagle or a hawk high above the earth.

I not only felt myself rising out of the darkness of my spirit, but I felt as if I were being bathed, washed clean. And as the gloom melted away, a quiet joy and a sense of cleansing swept in and took its place. I felt free to express my turbulent emotions with tears. The congregation's praise was a therapy of the spirit: indescribable in its power. It was a day I shall never forget. No one in that sanctuary knew how high they had lifted one troubled man far above his broken-world anguish. Were there others there that day feeling as I did? Perhaps they would have affirmed as I did: *God was there.*

During that period in my life, I had similar experiences on many occasions in a small Episcopal chapel when I attended what is called Morning Prayer. Unlike in Dallas, praise was highly structured liturgy: written prayers, spoken creeds, the reading of much Scripture, the Eucharist offered at the altar. But there was something else I looked forward to each time I went. High above the altar was a cross upon which hung the figure of the suffering Christ. In my broken-world hours, I found it consoling to sit beneath that cross and look up at the face of the dying Savior. While there was trauma in that visage, there was also an affection and kindness that could be visualized and absorbed but not described. Somehow I gained a remarkable sense of Jesus' presence. If in the free-form worship in Dallas I had been spiritually bathed, there in the liturgical worship I came to peace, order, and healing. Simply put: *Jesus was there.*

Then there were my black friends who know how to praise with their hands, their marvelous gospel rhythms, and their unrestrained expressions of unspeakable joy. Probably no group knows more about a tradition of pain and bondage and the healing message of liberty than our black brothers and sisters. They have learned the hard way that if there can't be liberty in the circumstances of one's public world, nothing can stop the acquisition of liberty in one's private world. Sadness simply cannot endure for very long when music and testimony emanates from the soul tradition. When my black friends included me, I felt free to love and be loved. Rarely have I ever left a time of praise in the black community that I didn't affirm to myself: *the Spirit was there.*

All three traditions of praise—free-form, liturgical, and soul—taught me there is a place of rest and wholeness in the congregation that praises God. It is a place for a broken-world person to be. There is no place like it.

Who knows how many broken-world people enter a sanctuary on a Sunday morning? My guess is that there are a lot more than anyone could guess. And what might they find? Do they find a lifeless liturgy of empty prayers, tired singing, and endless announcements? Or do they find men and women with hearts open to God's Spirit, thankful for God's blessings, and compassionate in the face of human pain? If they have found the latter, they will have discovered one of the principal elements of rebuilding.

Here at Peace Ledge Gail has captured much of the music of those traditions on stereo tape. Often on a Lord's Day morning before we leave for worship, we have sat for a couple of hours listening to the voices and the instruments of praise. And when the time of reflection ends, we know that praise has once again done its great work. Where God is honored, the broken and tired spirit is rebuilt.

LOOK FOR NEW THEMES

That was the tenth and last of the Peace Ledge Principles.

As one seeks to rebuild a broken world, one is tempted to move quickly to the question of future function.

"What are you going to do?" friends frequently have asked. And there was a time when that question rattled about in our minds. I wanted badly to give an answer. Not because I wanted to satisfy their curiosity but because I was tempted to want to make myself feel and sound important again. And in such a temptation I realized that we often want to establish our identity and value on the basis of some defined function.

I wonder what John the Baptizer said that he did for a living. Would his business card have said, "A voice crying in the wilderness?"

Slowly I understood that to worry about what I was going

to do was to worry about the wrong thing. The better issue was: what have I learned that I didn't know before, and how am I going to manage the information and the experience for the glory of God and the serving of others?

When there has been a broken-world experience and the rebuilding process is under way, one should take an inventory of what God has been saying. Paul told the Corinthians that when comfort came their way, they should study it carefully because it would most likely be a kind of comfort that they could give away to others. (See 2 Cor. 1:3-4.)

For us, nothing that God said became more important than what He said about hope and rebuilding. Day after day I heard my heart say: think hope; talk about hope; give hope wherever you can. And we determined to take that from Peace Ledge wherever we went in this world. Find the hopeless and tell them that rebuilding is possible.

Recently, a Texas man was painting the bulbous side of an extraordinarily high water tower. When the scaffolding on which he was standing collapsed, he fell fifty feet before the safety rope broke his fall and left him suspended 150 feet in the air.

Television cameras recorded the drama as rescue workers ascended to the top of the tower and one man was lowered to the dangling painter. Finally, the rescuer and the painter were lowered to the ground. As I watched the rescue process take place, I saw one more picture of how we give hope and value to another who has lost it, who dangles, as it were, helplessly in space. And I knew that giving hope and value to others had to be an important part of any future function of mine. Having been given hope, it might be my chance to give it to others.

Peace Ledge became the wilderness where God spoke to us. For other broken-world people the wilderness may be somewhere in the middle of a city or a desert or a jungle village. God knows where He wishes to place us broken-world people during the time of our rebuilding. And He makes no mistakes.

When we are in the wilderness, it is time to make sure we know how to act. That's why principles like these were so important for us.

A deacon in Alexander Whyte's Edinburgh church came to the pastor's office one Sunday morning to tell him of a visiting evangelist who had preached the night before in another part of town.

"Dr. Whyte, the man said that Robert Hood Wilson is not a converted man."

Robert Hood Wilson was at that time the pastor of the Barclay Church and a friend of Whyte. Whyte was outraged at such a false accusation. For several minutes he spoke in Wilson's defense out of his personal knowledge of the minister's deep spiritual life.

When he was through, the deacon said, "Dr. Whyte, the evangelist also said last night that you are not a converted man."

Suddenly the anger left Alexander Whyte. He became silent and thoughtful. Finally he said to the deacon who waited for a response, "My brother, please leave me alone; I must examine my soul."

These are the reactions of a man who had principles of performance built into his soul for the difficult moments. When a brother was falsely accused, he sprang to his defense. When he was falsely accused, he became silent and searched for the kernel of truth that might be hidden in such unjust and unkind remarks.

Whether or not we have experienced a broken world that is our fault or someone else's, it may be a time for the wilderness. But it is not a time for fear. Even though the pain might be great, life on the other end will be full of hope.

PART IV

THOSE WHO HELP REBUILD

16

Giving a Summer Purse

BOTTOM LINE #16: *The granting of restorative grace is among the greatest and most unique gifts one Christian can give another.*

I could not write two chapters in this book—this one and the concluding one—if a gift had not been given to me that I could not offer to myself. I regard these chapters as the most important ones. The gift is *restorative grace*, and its objective is TO REBUILD A ONCE BROKEN PERSONAL WORLD.

At one time I had the privilege of being a pastor at Grace Chapel in Lexington, Massachusetts. The church started as a small group of people meeting in weekly Bible study. Later it constituted itself as a regularly worshiping congregation and called a pastor. Many years later Gail and I spent twelve wonderful years with those remarkable men and women.

The founders of Grace Chapel chose to celebrate the Christian understanding and experience of grace in their selection of a public name. What's in a name—especially in a name like *grace*? Sometimes in the moments of a congregational struggle, I found myself wondering if we knew anything about how to live up to the name. Then in moments when blessings seemed to pile in on us, I was convinced that we did. But did we really understand the full implications of this heavenly quality with which we dared to identify ourselves? That's an important question.

One day soon after I had announced my resignation from Grace Chapel, a friend of ours, Ken Medema, a gifted poet and musician, sat at a piano and sang to the congregation about its wonderful name and the implications of living up to it:

Grace. . . .
I knew it would be this kind of place.
I knew the people I would face
Would be loving and full of grace.

Time. . . .
I haven't been here for a long, long time,
And I have missed the place.
It's different now from the days
When I was here before,
And it's going to be different more.

Frontier.
You're on the edge of a new frontier.
I wonder what we'll hear;
About the things that go on here.

New. . . .
Some things in your life will be new.
What in the world are you going to do?
And how will you make it through?

It's my prayer that you will be
Open to the spirit-wind that blows
And it's my prayer that
You'll be open to the river of grace that flows.

Name. . . .
Grace is your name;
This is your claim,
Satan-chained,
Made new each day by grace.

Well, I pray that whatever happens in this place
Will be a wonder work of all-miraculous grace.

I'm not sure the surrounding community ever fully comprehended the meaning of our church name. That was apparent the day I handed my Grace Chapel credit card to a service station attendant, and he smiled and said, "Thank you, Mr. Chapel; please come again." I'm sure he wondered what my wife, "Grace," was like.

Our Catholic friends, familiar with churches named after saints, sometimes said, "How are things at St. Grace these days?" And our Jewish friends said, "It's a nice name; why did you name your church after a prayer?"

So you see, it was easy to permit our special name to become nothing more than just an identifying symbol on our signboard, our checks, and our membership applications. We probably even signaled our immunity to the significance of our name when, in our hurried-up language forms, we referred to our church not as Grace Chapel but simply as "G.C."

Most of us are liable to think deeply about grace only when we really need it. For example, I thought positively about grace the afternoon I was motioned to the side of the road by a policeman with a portable radar device. After studying my driver's license, he radioed its number to some central location and then turned to me and said, "Mr. MacDonald, you've got a clean driving record. I'd like to help keep it that way; you help too. Have a good day." I guess that was a form of grace.

I think about grace if the insurance premium payment is overdue. And I think about it when I mail my son's income tax in a day after the deadline: his grace and that of the IRS. Obviously, those of us not good with details may have a lot of thinking to do about grace.

But you think most about grace when it seems as if it is the only thing left that might provide a "tomorrow." When there's nothing else. And, rightly or wrongly, many of us have had times in life when we wondered if there was a tomorrow that would be of any value.

It came to me one day as I walked along to a New England beach that I'd seen life-saving rings hanging on poles before, but I never really paid serious attention to them *because I've never come close to drowning.* Assuming that I might have such a traumatic experience one day, I'm quite sure that I would take a much keener interest in the availability and performance standards of life-saving rings.

Let me tell you: grace to me is like a life-saving ring. It was thrown out to me in the darkest hours of my life when my world was breaking in tiny pieces, and I was sure I would never have an opportunity to rebuild.

The grace to rebuild came first from God. It was there all the time for the asking, ever since the Cross guaranteed its availability to anyone who sincerely asked. The challenge for me was in receiving it appropriately.

Grace also came from people close to me: family, friends, and a host of men and women I'd never met who found ways to say they wanted to be counted among the givers.

And then grace came from the church in the form of a congregation (the Grace Chapel congregation) whose spiritual leadership decided to extend it for the purposes of restoration. Grace indeed was their name.

Probably a few did not wish to extend grace. It wasn't that they were antigrace; but they just weren't in a mood to give it. We who have broken our own worlds and have inflicted damage and hurt in the personal worlds of others must not ignore the fact that we disillusion and anger some people; that some are not going to recover from what has happened very easily.

On the occasions that I heard or thought about people who were not prepared to act in grace, I confess that I was tempted to nurse a defensive spirit. But then something inside would remind me rather pointedly that broken-world people are in no position to demand grace or even to deserve it. They must merely be appreciative receivers; and if some people do not wish to give it, broken-world individuals must accept that as part of the consequences of the situation. What some people may or may not do with the grace there is to give to others is between them and their God.

History records many ugly moments in which human beings have subjected one another to cruelty, exploitation, and vengeance. But history also records some brilliant moments when human beings have given grace to one another. Ah, what a difference!

Several such brilliant moments of grace giving are noted in the Scriptures. Take, for example, the grace that David gave to Saul. David's sins are so often pointed out that we forget he also was a man of grace. As many others have observed long before me, David had every reason to act vengefully toward Saul. The king of Israel cultivated a love-hate attitude toward the young shepherd boy. In his down moments Saul threw spears at David that the young man never threw back. Saul chased David into and through the wilderness on a number of occasions and would have gladly ended his life had he been smart enough to catch up with him. And Saul burned with jealousy toward David whenever he heard anyone praise him for anything. It did not help that

Saul's own son felt more loyalty for David than he did for his own father.

But David never fought back. He never returned the thrown spears; he never took advantage of Saul's vulnerability when he could have killed him in the wilderness. And he never taunted Saul when he could have made him appear the fool. He responded by giving grace.

David's greatest moment in grace giving came at Saul's death on the battlefield. David's grievous lament for Saul is startling. I paraphrase his words when I quote David's cry to his troops at what must have been a memorial oration:

> Don't talk about Saul's death, and don't gossip about what has happened. This is not news to be published among our enemies lest they use it as a pretext for laughing at God. Saul and Jonathan were loved . . . they were swift and strong men . . . how the mighty have fallen in battle (2 Sam. 1).

It would have been understandable for David to have said something like this:

> I want you to take a hard look at how this man has died. He had a great start, and he failed miserably. This is a good example of what happens when you make serious mistakes. This is how you end up. Feel free to talk about it all you want to your kids. Maybe we will all learn a lesson from it.

One sees great models of grace giving at the time of St. Paul's conversion and almost three years later when he was introduced to the Jerusalem church. The grace was given by two men: first Ananias the prophet and later Barnabas.

Ananias of Damascus received a message from God that he should go to a particular house and call on the newly arrived Saul of Tarsus whom he would find blinded and praying. Ananias's reflex reaction was to protest, to inform God about the terrible reputation for killing and imprisoning Christians that Saul had. But God was already informed and urged Ananias on his way with the notice that He had great plans for Saul.

Ananias did as he was told. The Scripture says that he entered the house and placed his hands on Saul while he exclaimed:

> "Brother Saul, the Lord . . . has sent me so that you may see again and be filled with the Holy Spirit." Immediately, some-

thing like scales fell from Saul's eyes, and he could see again. He got up and was baptized (Acts 9:17–18).

I've often wondered what it cost Ananias to reach out and touch the greatly feared man and address him as "Brother Saul." The laying on of hands, the familiar greeting, and the baptism were the gifts of grace from one member of the Christian family to another. Grace at great risk and at great cost.

The opposite of grace might be *retribution*: repayment in kind or punishment or the demand for reparations. It wouldn't have been surprising to some if Ananias had refused to go to Saul and had instead sent a note saying:

> We hear you may have had a change of heart about Christians. If that's true, get back to me in a couple of years. If there has been no further hostile action on your part between now and then, we might meet in a neutral location. In the meantime you might wish to think about repayment for all the damages you've caused because if there is nothing done, we're going to sue your socks off. Our church's attorney's name is. . . .

Church history is different, of course, because Ananias chose the grace option and eschewed the retributive one.

Barnabas entered the process of grace giving almost three years later when he learned that no one in the Jerusalem church was in a mood to receive Paul and give him a hearing. Barnabas became the giver of grace, endorsing Paul and bringing him into fellowship with the Jerusalem church leadership.

Ironically, some years later the same Barnabas would try to graciously mediate in a moment when Paul—who should have known better—rejected the notion of a second chance for John Mark, a previous failure on a missionary venture (see Acts 15:36ff). There was no way Paul would bend in giving grace to Mark; and there was no way Barnabas was going to allow the young man to feel ungraced. So Barnabas became graciously tough, splitting with Paul and heading out on a missions project with Mark. Barnabas's advocacy of Mark is a powerful precedent for giving men and women who have failed a second chance. Many years later Paul seemed to acknowledge that Barnabas had been the more correct of the two of them. From that long-range perspective, he wrote of John Mark, "He is helpful to me" (2 Tim. 4:11).

Like David and Ananias and Barnabas, the good Samaritan in one of Jesus' stories was also a giver of grace. A nameless man, the victim of a brutal mugging, lies in a ditch on the road to Jericho, Jesus told a crowd. He is ignored by dignitaries with clerical and theological credentials, and it appears that he will die alone in the ditch. But a Samaritan (as far as the Jews were concerned, a good-for-nothing) comes along, assesses the situation, and provides everything necessary to bring the man to wholeness: food, bandages, clothing, and hospitality. Everything is given from the generous hand of grace. It was not a story designed to make Jews feel good; rather, it was to provoke them into understanding that real neighbors are those who give grace, not those whose sole preoccupation is with right doctrine and impeccable theology.

Without restorative grace, broken worlds cannot be rebuilt according to God's standards. Unfortunately, there are many stories of men and women who in their distress felt so abandoned and so ostracized that they put their own worlds back together in whatever fashion was possible. But this kind of rebuilding process was fueled perhaps by anger or by the need to survive or by the energy that comes from wanting to stubbornly prove oneself. The results of such rebuilding are usually something like my attempts to rebuild an appliance. Several pieces are left over, and the thing doesn't work very well.

And usually such people have subsequently chosen to go elsewhere, lost to the Christian community where they perceived they were no longer welcome. I think that's a waste. It's also an indication that sometimes we misunderstand one of our central purposes: to rescue the perishing and grace the failing.

We might be startled by the large number of people in our world, now outside the active Christian community, who think of their earlier Christian experience as a bad dream. I know this is too simple an observation, for it does not always take into account those who were willful and seemingly unrepentant in broken-world days. But we must consider what might be possible if repentance and grace were retrieved as prominent activities in the modern church. What might be possible if we deliberately set out to challenge the sin that has captured too many people and snatch back those whose worlds are breaking?

Why do we talk about spiritual warfare and then show surprise when there are casualties? And why, when there are casualties, are we not more active in sending out the "medics" whose task is to apply the healing and restorative medicines of grace? If we are to find this healing and wholeness again INSIDE the church, it will be only because people believe that grace is a gift from God to be given.

In its primary sense, *grace* (literally meaning "gift") is the power of God in the form of forgiving and healing love; it comes to men and women despite the fact that they have done nothing to deserve it. Like the facets of a lovely diamond, grace seems to have many forms. For example, I've found it helpful to talk about RECLAIMING GRACE as the energy that brings a state of peace between a person and God. Traditionally, we may refer to this moment as being born again, accepting Jesus Christ as Savior, or confessing faith in God.

I've used the term REFORMING GRACE to describe the often slow but certain reshaping of one's life into what the Bible calls Christlikeness. This process also is a gift from God, and we are told that God sends His Spirit into the life of the follower of the Lord to make this possible. The gift of His Spirit is part of that grace.

Then there is RESTORATIVE GRACE, and that is what this chapter is about. This kind of grace comes to a broken-world person who comes to insight and acknowledges misbehavior in attitude or deed. Restorative grace is God's action to forgive the misbehavior and to draw the broken-world person back toward wholeness and usefulness again. It is God's response to the acts of repentance and brokenness. Restorative grace doesn't mean that all of the natural consequences of misbehavior vanish, but it does point toward a wholeness of relationship between God and the one who has returned in repentance.

Karen Mains, using beautiful language of her own choosing, is talking about the effects of restorative grace when she writes:

> Nature shouts of this beginning-again-God, this God who can make all our failures regenerative, the One who is God of risings again, who never tires of fresh starts, nativities, renaissances in persons or in culture. God is a God of starting over, of genesis and

regenesis. He composts life's sour fruits, moldering rank and decomposing; he applies the organic matter to our new day chances; he freshens the world with dew; he hydrates withered human hearts with his downpouring spirit. (*With My Whole Heart*)

How big must a sinful act be before restorative grace becomes an important matter? In principle, restorative grace is necessary EVERY time a misbehavior of attitude or action occurs. It would appear that on most occasions a person is dealing with the necessity of restorative grace every time he becomes aware of a personal offense against God and His law. That's what David was seeking when he called out, "Search me, O God, and know my heart; [and] . . . any offensive way" (Ps. 139:23–24).

But if the misbehavior is great enough in consequence that others are also greatly affected or offended, it may become necessary for restorative grace to be received also from those involved.

The father of the prodigal son gave restorative grace when the boy came home. Expecting to be received as a second-class citizen, he was instead received as an honored son with a robe, a ring, and a celebration. That's restorative grace.

One day our local newspaper carried this classified ad: "[Name]: I know you are in [city]. Please call your father (collect). I love you son." (Home and work phone numbers were included.) It was, as far as I could see, an offering of restorative grace.

Grace in any of these forms cannot be purchased; it can only be given and received. Grace is the "glue" that takes the pieces and bonds them into something new again. Grace is the "welcome mat" that lets a person know that having repented and demonstrated the fruits of brokenness, he or she is bid back to a privileged place in the family just as the father welcomed his lost prodigal son. Grace is the "scrubber" that cleans the blotched record and says that some things will be remembered no more. Grace is the "rubber stamp" that says CANCELED and acknowledges that the account is paid for. And (may I go around one more time) grace is the "electric current" that energizes virtually everything of value in the life of followers of the Lord.

An old gospel hymn says: "Mercy there was great, and

grace was free." Four biblical words seem to come together when the subject of grace is under consideration. They are *grace, mercy, peace,* and *kindness.* We act out of grace; we give mercy; we extend peace; and we treat one another kindly.

The person receiving grace cannot be patronized. The granting of grace does not give one Christian an opportunity to "lord it over" another. It does not suggest that the grace giver is a first-class citizen of the kingdom and the grace receiver is a second-class citizen. In our human condition we all too frequently give off that sort of signal.

In truth, I was as much a sinner in need of *grace* before my sin as I was after. But that is not quite believable to many Christians, and unfortunately our treatment of one another shows it. The giving of grace merely extends from one sinner to another.

When we act in *mercy*, we are carrying out the feelings of grace. We have chosen not to belittle or demean the person in need. Jesus never looked down with disdain on the adulteress brought to Him by the religious leaders. He treated her with dignity and showed deep concern for her future.

When we act in *peace*, we show that although we may have been angry about or hurt by what the world breaker has done, a state of peace exists between us.

And when we act in *kindness*, we are going the second mile. We are generously giving to the broken-world person, doing the unexpected thing: giving encouragement, giving hope, giving generously whatever is needed.

Gail and I will never forget two visits on the day our world publicly broke apart. Each visit was from two people. The first visit was with a young man and a young woman who had worked as my assistants for the two previous years.

They sat and listened tearfully to what I had to tell them: how our lives were about to be abruptly changed and how—as a result—their lives would be changed. And when I was through, they instinctively came across the room, laid hands upon Gail and me, and struggled through a prayer for us. These two, in their early twenties, gave more grace and kindness than we could have ever imagined.

The second visit came from two much older people: also a man and a woman. Their gift came in their insistence in reflecting on a number of specific things they felt we had done for them and their colleagues. They insisted on going into detail so that we would not forget for a moment that, as far as they were concerned, history was not a black hole. Grace, mercy, peace, and kindness filled the room that day. And we lived off it for several days that followed.

Restorative grace came through scores of letters as people sat down to express not only their sorrow but also the promise of their prayers. Those with whom we had personal relationships usually tried to remember something positive that one or both of us had done that had made a difference in their lives. If the present sorrow could not bring much value, they seemed to be saying, let's look back into the bank of memories and remember days that did make a positive difference.

There were those who managed to gain our phone number and called to pray or to read Scripture, to assure us of their love and their certainty that God would exchange this time of pain and humiliation for something useful.

And some came to visit. Gail and I will long remember the day-long visit of a well-known pastor who flew across the country, sent by the board of directors of an evangelical organization to share their concern for our welfare. He sat and wept with us, prayed for us, and took us to dinner. A couple, long close to us, came to Peace Ledge for a day and insisted that we permit them just to share the routines of life on the hill: shopping, changing the oil in the car, answering the phone.

A special grace came from my father who flew across the country to meet us as we traveled to Peace Ledge. As we drove the endless miles, he sat and listened. He wept with us, and he made us laugh. After years of living very separate lives, grace drew a father and son into an intimacy that we had never known before.

And then there was the grace that came from a specific group of men I will describe later. They enveloped us as Styrofoam packaging might protect a breakable item being sent through the mail.

All of this was grace: restorative grace. Its eventual hope: restoration. A broken world rebuilt.

More than a hundred years ago D. L. Moody lashed out as a loving critic to certain parts of the church of his time for its misappropriation of energies. The church reminded him, he said, of firemen straightening pictures on the wall of a burning house. In a single sentence he drew a vivid picture of what any of us can become in any generation when we forget the basic activities given to us by the Lord of the church.

I can hardly think of a more important function than the giving of grace: to the man or woman who has never learned of the love of Christ and His reclaiming grace. To the young or struggling believer who seeks a Christlike faith and the joy of experiencing reforming grace. And to the broken-world person who has so disappointed his brothers and sisters in faith and needs restorative grace. Where there is grace, there is hope, hope for a broken world to be rebuilt.

In the *Journal of the American Medical Association* a few years ago Jane McAdams told the story of her sixty-nine-year-old mother who had lived a life deeply marked by the Great Depression of the 1930s. The evidence showed in her frugality and utterly practical perspective on all material things. The only extravagance she had ever permitted herself, McAdams wrote, was a frilly nightgown kept in a bottom drawer, "In case I should ever have to go into the hospital."

That day had come. All the symptoms that made her visit to the hospital necessary spoke of a serious cancer, and McAdams feared the moment when she would have to tell her mother that the prognosis for the future was very poor.

The daughter wondered, "Should I tell my mother? Did she already know? If not, did she suspect? . . . Could I give her any hope? Was there in fact any hope?"

As she wrestled with these questions, McAdams noted that her mother's birthday was approaching. Perhaps she could brighten her mother's days by purchasing a new nightgown because the one that had been in the bottom drawer was yellowed, limp, and unattractive. So she purchased and presented a new nightgown and matching robe. "If I could not hope to cure her disease, at least I could make her feel like the prettiest patient in the entire hospital."

McAdams described how her mother studied the gown after the package was opened. And after a while she pointed to the wrapping and the gown and said to her daughter, "Would you mind returning it to the store? I don't really want it.' Then picking up the paper she pointed to a display advertisement and said, 'This is what I really want, if you could get that.' What she pointed to was a display advertisement of expensive designer summer purses."

My reaction was one of disbelief. Why would my mother, so careful about extravagances, want an expensive summer purse in January, one that she could not possibly use until June? She would not even live until spring, let alone summer. Almost immediately, I was ashamed and appalled at my clumsiness, ignorance, insensitivity, call it what you will. With a shock, I realized she was finally asking me what I thought about her illness. She was asking me how long she would live. She was, in fact, asking me if I thought she would live even six months. And she was telling me that if I showed I believed she would live until then, then she would do it. She would not let that expensive purse go unused. That day I returned the gown and robe and bought the summer purse.

That was many years ago. The purse is worn out and long gone, as are at least half a dozen others. And next week my mother flies to California to celebrate her 83rd birthday. My gift to her? The most expensive designer purse I could find. She'll use it well.

The gift of restorative grace to a broken-world person is the gift not of a nightgown that announces death but of a summer purse that says there is life after failure. That is the message of the Cross and the empty tomb. And it must be the message of the church to the broken-world person.

PART V
PREVENTING A PERSONAL WORLD FROM BREAKING

17

The Bradley Tutorial

BOTTOM LINE #17: *We must assume the inevitability of attacks by an enemy hostile to our spiritual interests and build our defenses in the places he is most likely to attack.*

In his autobiography, *A General's Life*, General Omar Bradley writes of the first time he met William Westmoreland, who many years later became commander of the American forces in Vietnam. On the occasion Bradley describes, Westmoreland was a cadet first captain in the West Point class of 1936.

The encounter between the two occurred during summer maneuvers: war games in which Westmoreland commanded a battalion defending a hill. The young captain and his men performed so poorly in the mock battle that the attackers succeeded in overrunning them.

General Bradley (then a major) had been an observer that day, and when the exercise on the hill was ended, he took the young field officer aside and said, "Mr. Westmoreland, look back at that hill. Look at it from the standpoint of the enemy."

"Turning," Westmoreland later wrote, "I became aware for the first time of a concealed route of approach that it was logical for an attacker to use. Because I had failed to cover it with my defense, he [Bradley] as umpire had ruled for the attacking force."

"It is fundamental," Major Bradley said firmly, "to put yourself always in the position of the enemy." He was speaking of course about those moments when the soldier plans for battle and determines how he will prevent the enemy from seizing positions that are his to defend.

I think Bradley's point is also useful for thinking through how broken-world experiences might be prevented. I'd like to call it the Bradley Tutorial: *put yourself in the position of the enemy*. It's a place to start when you ask the question: *how can broken-world misbehaviors be avoided?* During the past year, I've received many letters from young men and women who pose one form of this question or another. Letter writers are usually polite and respectful as they ask, "Can you tell me anything out of your experience that will help me to avoid major (misbehavior)?"

Although this is a worthy question, I'm not always comfortable being considered an expert on the subject. But pressed to answer, I usually begin with a version of the Bradley Tutorial. Take a look at yourself, I might say, and then put yourself in the position of the enemy: the source of evil that relentlessly comes at you from without and from within. Where will evil find the "crevices" in the defenses of your personal world that can be overrun? The answer is likely to be a different one for each of us.

When we face evil, it is as if we are facing a smart enemy. It is as if we are being carefully studied by a perceptive foe in order to discover the places where we are most likely to make broken-world choices. *The objective of this enemy is to deny God the pleasure of His glory being reflected in us and to deny us the pleasure of being what God created us to be.*

There is an obvious danger in becoming so obsessed with the possibilities of sin that we become morbidly introspective and defensive, adopting what some have called a fortress mentality. It is admirable to be deeply concerned lest we fail, but it can be just as dangerous to forget that the *Christian is called to enter the world and advance the authority of Christ's kingdom. That means the inevitable risk of wounds and casualties.* One would hope few need be self-inflicted wounds.

Everyone knows of the fortress mentality with which the French began World War II. Standing behind their Maginot Line, the French were convinced that their country was impregnable. But they had deluded themselves into a false security, and things didn't work out the way they'd planned. In short, they didn't put themselves in the position of the enemy and take note of its unprecedented mobility. What was needed was a mobile defense system to prevent the invasion of a very mobile army. The astounding part about the French failure to recognize this fact is that their enemy, the Germans, had made no secret of their strategy and capacity to move over the ground and through the air at blitzkrieg speed.

And that is what I have in mind when someone asks me how to defend against the possibility of a broken world. I want to talk about a defense that respects and notes the movements of the enemy, one that is flexible and imaginative enough because of the power of God.

My idea for a mobile and flexible defense of one's personal world comes in seven parts. None of the points are new, but they tend to indicate areas in which the possibility exists for broken-world kinds of failure. Each proposition is centered on what I'll call a PERSONAL DEFENSE INITIATIVE (PDI). This takeoff on a modern military defensive strategy suggests that an effective defense also requires initiative, an aggressive or positive element in our lives that just doesn't stand around waiting for something bad to happen.

PDI #1: ADOPT A REPENTANT LIFE-STYLE

When our son, Mark, was in his seventh and eighth years of life, Gail and I noticed that he often had a difficult time admitting that he had made a mistake or that he was wrong in a conclusion or an opinion. No matter how hard we tried to get him to admit to being wrong occasionally, we could see that a terrible battle in his inner being caused him to slip and slide out of such admissions with excuses or rationalizations.

This trait worried his mother and me because we believed that if he carried it into adulthood, it would adversely affect his personal relationships or his work with teams of people. On many occasions I tried to point this out but never seemed to succeed.

One day Gail and I seized upon a new approach to the problem. Whenever we made a mistake, we would exaggerate our statements and feelings of contrition. For example, when Gail pointed out that something I'd said or done was wrong, I would cry out in mock dismay: "WHAT? ARE YOU SURE? YES, BY GOLLY, YOU'RE RIGHT; I AM WRONG; I'VE MADE A TERRIBLE, HORRIBLE MISTAKE." And turning to Mark, I might say, "SON, DO YOU REALIZE WHAT HAS HAPPENED? YOUR DAD HAS MADE A MISTAKE. I'M WRONG, WRONG, WRONG!"

This reaction usually generated much laughter among all of us. But we were delighted when repetitions of this performance had a positive effect. Mark began to see that his parents had no trouble acknowledging mistakes and that it was OK to be less than perfect. And when he might quietly admit to an error, we made an effort to treat his admission in the same jovial manner. A dance. A song. A loud round of applause. Soon there was no need for the hilarity. We had a son who found that it was safe to be mistaken in his home with those who loved him. Today, many years later, Mark is a man I greatly admire for his skills in developing people. Now he's the one helping others to be more honest with themselves.

This is the pattern of the repentant life-style: the daily awareness and admission that misbehavior, small or large, is an unfortunate reality of our lives. It is probably unhelpful that many of us assume the first mark of growth in the Christian life to be better behavior. I would like to propose that the first mark of maturity is actually *the ability to identify and admit to bad behavior*. A consciousness of God's presence is much more likely to make us aware of things in need of renunciation than anything else.

Some veteran Christians who have shown healthy concern for holiness in their lives have shared with the rest of us the startling news that the closer one walks to the light, the darker the shadows become; the closer one draws to the presence of Christ, the greater the realization of one's indwelling evil.

Thus, the repentant life-style. Maturity, according to this PDI proposition, suggests not that we become more perfect but that we become more willing to face up to what we are within and without and name what is offensive to God and to others. In naming our misbehaviors, we begin to gain control over them. We have a handle with which we can renounce them and throw them away. We have an identifying symbol that we can carry to the Cross when we confess our sins and ask for forgiveness.

John wrote lovingly to relatively new Christians: "My little children, these things I write to you, so that you may not sin. And *if anyone sins*, we have an Advocate with the Father" (1 John 2:1 NKJV, emphasis mine). It is preferable, John acknowledged, not to engage in sinful misbehavior. But when it happens—and John clearly assumed that it will—there is advocacy available before the offended God in the person of Christ. But he would not advocate for those items in our lives that we will not name in repentance. He said at another point: "If we confess our sins, He is faithful and just to forgive" (1 John 1:9 NKJV).

Corrie Ten Boom suggested that the person with a repentant life-style has developed the habit of telling the Lord his sins five minutes before his accuser does. That makes sense. She also coached her listeners to "keep short accounts with God."

The repentant life-style means that I acknowledge my misbehavior to Christ and to others who need to know that I am not what my image or persona often tries to say I am. "In every Little Nell, there is a Lady MacBeth trying to get out," James Thurber wrote. We would do well to acknowledge that fact to God and to others whenever necessary and possible.

The phrase *repentant life-style* is simply another way of referring to brokenness or humility, which I've discussed throughout this book. Brokenness is not only an immediate experience when we come to insight about misbehavior; *it is a way of life*. It is an attitude of spirit, and it is built on the conviction that left to itself, evil is liable to break out in almost any form in our thought life, our words, or our actions. Therefore, we must be ready to name it, acknowledge it, and repudiate it. No excuses; no rationalizations; no denial.

Watchman Nee writes:

Our spirit is released according to the degree of our brokenness. The one who has accepted the most discipline is the one who can best serve. The more one is broken, the more sensitive he is. The more desire to save ourselves, in that very thing we become spiritually useless. Whenever we preserve and excuse ourselves, at that point we are deprived of spiritual sensitivity and supply. Let no one imagine he can be effective and disregard this basic principle.

And a few sentences later, Nee remarks: "The way of service lies in brokenness, in accepting the discipline of the Holy Spirit. The measure of your service is determined by the degree of discipline and brokenness."

This most obvious of spiritual principles would hardly be debated by most evangelical Christians. Yet the practical failure to act the principle out privately and corporately is probably at the root of small and large choices ultimately leading to broken worlds.

It was his understanding of what I have called a PDI principle that made John Bunyan the great man of God we know him to be. In his spiritual autobiography he modeled the repentant life-style with these comments:

> I find to this day 7 abominations in my heart: 1) inclinings to unbelief; 2) suddenly to forget the love and mercy that Christ manifesteth; 3) a leaning to the works of the law; 4) wanderings and coldness in prayer; 5) to forget to watch for that I pray for; 6) apt to murmur because I have no more, and yet ready to abuse what I have; 7) I can do none of these things which God commands me, but my corruptions will thrust in themselves; when I do good, evil is present with me. (*Grace Abounding*)

Although some of us may express great discomfort at such morbid introspection, Bunyan understood that if we do not seek out and name the impurities within while they are small and manageable, we can expect one or more of them to become oversized and, in a weak moment, turn into the stuff of which broken-world choices are made.

PDI #2: PAY THE PRICE OF REGULAR SPIRITUAL DISCIPLINE

Some people have called it the quiet time; others, devotions; still others, personal worship. But my favorite term is *spiritual discipline* because that's what it is. Spiritual discipline is to the inner spirit what physical conditioning is to the body. The unconditioned athlete, no matter how naturally talented, cannot win a world-class race.

John Sculley, CEO at Apple Computers, writes of the corporate culture in which he once worked at Pepsi Cola. There the discipline of the body was held in high esteem. Note the passion for discipline he describes:

The culture demanded that each of us be in top condition, physically fit as well as mentally alert. At lunch time, the glass-walled corporate fitness center was packed with the rising stars of the corporation. Like me, they were the kind of people who would rather be in the Marines than in the Army. Even our exercise regimens became part of the competition. Placards on bulletin boards charted each executive's progress against his colleagues. (*Odyssey*)

It's not my intention to glorify this description of a rather driven lifestyle. I simply want to point out that there are people who believe enough in what they are doing to pay the price. These people understand that their bodies are part of the whole-person effort leading toward vocational and corporate success. *Thus, they see the importance of taking the time to discipline and condition the body.* They may prefer to do other things, but if it takes time to keep the body in shape, these people will come up with the time.

My observation is that many men and women in the Christian community desire the blessings and maturities of the Christian life-style in much the same way as Sculley's associates desire success at their jobs. And they fervently desire that they will never fall prey to temptations or motivations leading to major misbehavior.

Interview them, and I'm sure they would confess that they desire the "well done" of the Master more than anything else. Call it a heavenly brand of success. But we need to ask ourselves sometimes, how badly is that "success" desired? There can often be a long way between confession of what we desire and performance of what we're willing to make happen. Do we want "success" quite as badly as Sculley and his friends appear to want theirs? One test might be the amount of time we put in disciplining the spirit, the core of our private worlds, the first line of defense when it comes to the enemy's attacks.

I'm convinced that paying the price for prevention probably means a substantial period of time set apart every day to condition the spirit. This was the burden of the book *Ordering Your Private World,* and I haven't changed my opinion at all about the principles set forth in that book.

Spiritual discipline means the cultivation of Scripture study, intercession, meditation, and general reading on spiritual subjects. That's easy for some of us, hard for others.

When we do this, we are stepping aside from all the noises of the public world that claw at our souls. We are asking for a "divine" noise, really a comforting whisper, to restore our sense of balance and guidance, to reaffirm our personal value in heavenly terms so that we will not have to seek value from other sources. And we are seeking empowerment to check evil and release the best we have so that we may give to those about us. The discipline of the spirit should result in putting us in touch with Jesus.

Again John Bunyan. In the most famous of all his writings, *Pilgrim's Progress*, Bunyan described a fierce battle that Christian fought against the lion Apollyon. Before and after the rugged contest, Christian was aware that his strength for battle came directly from God:

> When the battle was over, Christian said, "I will here give thanks to him that hath delivered me out of the mouth of the lion, to him that did help me against Apollyon." . . . Then there came to him a hand with some of the leaves of the Tree of Life, the which Christian took and applied to the wounds that he had received in the battle and was healed immediately. He also sat down in that place to eat bread and to drink of the bottle that was given him a little before; so, being refreshed, he addressed himself to his journey with his sword drawn in his hand; *for he said, "I know not but some other enemy may be at hand."* (*Pilgrim's Progress*, emphasis mine)

Bunyan wrote much of Christian's journey from an auto-biographical perspective, and he was clearly saying something about his own PDI program at this point. The discipline of the spirit was his only hope for preventing his own broken-world experiences.

The man or woman who is not taking a premium amount of time each day to look within and draw from the hand of heaven through the Scriptures and intercession takes great risks.

PDI #3: CULTIVATE KEY RELATIONSHIPS

If we are to successfully defend against bad choices resulting in broken-world experiences, it will also be because we have set out to develop some significant personal relationships that offer mutual accountability.

A glance at a major automobile race on television one day caused me to think of this issue of key relationships in a new way. In the middle of the race a car and its driver pulled off the track and into the place they call the pit. Instantly, a team of five men swarmed over the car. One poured gas into the tank; two others checked and replaced tires; one seemed to be checking engine fluids while another talked to the driver about racing strategy as he gave him water (or something) to drink.

The pit crew, the TV sportscaster said, is often the key to the driver's victory. If their work is speedy and complete, they can gain several seconds of advantage for their driver over the competition. They can send their driver and car back to the track with the energy, the strategy, and the capacity to win.

As I watched them work, I came to an appreciation of the fact that we all need to be part of one another's pit crew. I need those who will inspect the tires and the fuel in my life. I need others with whom to discuss "racing" strategy. And, just as badly, I need to join the pit crews of others. In each case the objective is simple: help one another win.

As we saw earlier, our modern world's way of life has all but stripped us of personal relationships where people provide balance, nourishment, and preventative maintenance for one another. Most of us live apart from our extended families, and we move at such a pace that hardly anyone knows the full breadth of our lives. The people in our church may see one side of us; our families another; our working associates still another. There is little pressure apart from what is inside ourselves to make sure that these three sides of ourselves (and there are probably other sides) coincide, that there is integrity in our personal performance.

We must keep reminding ourselves that the inner being is marked with a spirit of rebellion and deceit. Only the strongest of us is liable to maintain the sort of integrity we need by ourselves. Frankly, we need the help of others.

And that is what Christian fellowship is supposed to be. It's also why Paul wrote "love protects" (see 1 Cor. 13:7), a phrase scarcely acknowledged, let alone understood, by most of us. It suggests that we are called to stick close to one another much in the same way that a wingman flies close to his partner as they pilot their combat planes in an air battle. I am charged to protect you; you are charged to protect me.

This little phrase—"love protects"—sums up the meaning of accountability. We are accountable to look out for the spiritual interests and development of our brothers and sisters in the faith, and they are called to do the same for us. And how is it done?

By encouraging us and affirming us when we show growth. By rebuking us and holding us to the standard of godly character when we show the evidence of substandard performance. The friendship that stretches us to grow toward Christlikeness is perhaps one of the most valuable things we can ever have in life.

May I turn to Bunyan and his *Pilgrim's Progress* one more time to reflect on the companionship of Christian and his friend Hopeful? It isn't a coincidence that much of Christian's pilgrimage is in the company of others. Bunyan was anxious to point out, in the words of John Wesley's mentor, that Christianity is not a solitary religion.

In their mutual journey Hopeful is overtaken by a state of numbing fatigue and is in great danger of attack if he cannot be kept awake. Christian keeps him from sleeping, and when Hopeful realizes the danger he was in, he says in appreciation of his friend:

> I acknowledge myself in a fault; and had I been here alone, I had, by sleeping, run the danger of death. I see it is true that the wise man saith, 'two are better than one.' (Ecc 4.9) *Hitherto hath thy company been my mercy*; and thou shalt have good reward for thy labour. (*Pilgrim's Progress*, emphasis mine)

I can think of certain friendships where I feel that I completely failed someone by avoiding the hard questions when I saw signs of stress. And, thank God, I can think of times when I sucked in my breath and, at the risk of losing a friend, made observations that cut to the heart and caused behavior to change. I would write endlessly if I were to record the times when friends have done the same for me.

I am often asked what sort of things friends in accountability might ask of one another. Having found little if any helpful literature on this subject, I put together a list of twenty-six questions, some of which friends might wish to consider if this personal defense initiative is to be effective.

1. How is your relationship with God right now?
2. What have you read in the Bible in the past week?
3. What has God said to you in this reading?
4. Where do you find yourself resisting Him these days?
5. What specific things are you praying for in regard to others?
6. What specific things are you praying for in regard to yourself?
7. What are the specific tasks facing you right now that you consider incomplete?
8. What habits intimidate you?
9. What have you read in the secular press this week?
10. What general reading are you doing?
11. What have you done to play?
12. How are you doing with your spouse? Kids?
13. If I were to ask your spouse about your state of mind, state of spirit, state of energy level, what would the response be?
14. Are you sensing any spiritual attacks from the enemy right now?
15. If Satan were to try to invalidate you as a person or as a servant of the Lord, how might he do it?
16. What is the state of your sexual perspective? Tempted? Dealing with fantasies? Entertainment?
17. Where are you financially right now? (things under control? under anxiety? in great debt?)
18. Are there any unresolved conflicts in your circle of relationships right now?
19. When was the last time you spent time with a good friend of your own gender?
20. What kind of time have you spent with anyone who is a non-Christian this past month?
21. What challenges do you think you're going to face in the coming week? Month?
22. What would you say are your fears at this present time?
23. Are you sleeping well?
24. What three things are you most thankful for?
25. Do you like yourself at this point in your pilgrimage?
26. What are your greatest confusions about your relationship with God?

Never before have I been more convinced that adult Christians need to form personal friendships with those sharing our commitments and values. And yet whenever I have talked about this, people—especially men—have acknowledged that they have no relationship quite as intimate as what I am describing.

One returns again and again to Jesus' forbearing statement to Simon Peter: "Simon, Satan has asked to sift you as wheat" (Luke 22:31). It was a warning that Simon did not heed, but it came from the lips of a Friend who knew what was likely to happen. The PDI principle was in motion; it simply wasn't heeded.

How do we protect one another? We watch a friend's eyes. Abnormal fatigue? Anger? Avoidance of truth? We listen to a friend's words to lovingly discern inconsistencies, attitudes, and negative criticisms of people. We watch spending patterns. Too excessive? Trying to prove something? We note the respect and affection with which he or she treats others. Loving toward a spouse and children? Too harsh? Disdainful? Disrespectful? Too familiar with others? We are sensitive to questionable habits. Substance abuse? Sleeplessness? Workaholism?

I'm not advocating the adoption of a KGB-like stance toward one another. But men and women who truly love one another protect one another from broken-world possibilities. I know of only one way I can protect my friend: stick close enough to him so that we are transparent to each other, so that we can spot the aberrant patterns before they get out of control.

Friends take time. And most of us do not have that time unless we make this cultivation of Christian fellowship a major priority.

PDI #4: RESIST THE "APPLAUSE" THAT BELONGS TO CHRIST

> I am the LORD; that is my name!
> I will not give my glory to another
> or my praise to idols (Isa. 42:8).

The Lord spoke these words through the prophet Isaiah warning kings and religious leaders that it would be fatal for them to permit people to give them honor belonging only to God.

Of all the places where broken-world choices are likely to begin, this may be the most subtle and the one to which we are the most insensitive. Few things kill the soul faster than becoming addicted to the applause of people.

All of us are guilty of helping others fall into the clutches of the enemy when we offer praise that belongs only to the Son of God. We almost guarantee their fall when we do this. This is not to say that we should not express appropriate appreciation when someone has served us well; but it does suggest that we need to exercise greater care as to how we set out various leaders and praise them.

Perhaps we are in danger of permitting that today in the Christian community. Not just to those in the pulpit ministry or in organizational leadership, but in every sector of the church. Like the rest of the world, we always run the danger of creating our own heroes whether they are preachers with unusual communicative talents, musicians, business people, or artists.

We must not dare to ruin these people with undue praise. And we must not permit it to come to us. The temptation is too great to believe the nice things people tell us in the good moments. Such acclaim has a narcotic effect on our perception of the reality of our sinful predicament and our daily dependence on the operating grace of God. When we are praised, we are wise to accept it with graciousness, but to renounce it quickly in the heart lest it lodge there and become believable.

PDI #5: TAKE TIME TO HAVE FUN

Perhaps this personal defense initiative is more for people in leadership than anyone else. But I'm convinced that the enemy within and without uses this strange area of life as much as anything else. Some will grimace at my use of the word *fun*; perhaps they would prefer the word *diversion*.

Modern Christianity is often considered to possess a very serious view of life. Work seems never to be finished; the issues are perceived as too grave; the world is labeled as a dangerous place. These are some of the watchwords by which we approach life and do our work. Our sensitivity to criticism, sometimes our limited funds, and our perceived guilt are all likely to conspire to cause us to take a very serious view of life and feel uneasy about doing things purely for the pleasure of life.

Fun might be called the exercise of the mind and the emotions. It is diversion that takes us away from the pressure of the intense needs we are likely to encounter every day as we do our work in the church and in the marketplace. I'd be hard-pressed to give an instance of fun in the New Testament. The biblical writers were not writing to inform us of the private lives of the apostles, and so we are not likely to hear that they occasionally stopped somewhere for a refreshing beverage or that they enjoyed moments of humor. Is it possible that Paul was a player of practical jokes or that Barnabas occasionally enjoyed an afternoon of quiet reflection under a tree?

It is reasonable to assume that diversion came on long walking trips, on shipboard, and in the homes of people where the apostles stayed. With the pace of modern travel we have all but squeezed those kinds of relaxing moments out of our schedules and almost feel guilty if someone suggests that we take the time to relax and play.

The ambitious, hard-driving leader is quite likely to go weeks and weeks without ever taking the diversionary time off that renews the body and mind, that introduces laughter and positive sensation back into one's life. We often admire people who seem to have squeezed fun out of their schedules, and then we are shocked if they burn out or succumb to various temptations. We need to make sure that we are not complying with a system that has caused them to never let up and find freedom from all the pressure.

PDI #6: HOLD THINGS LOOSELY

We don't have to study the New Testament characters for very long before we see that they held all things loosely: their material possessions, their jobs, their security and, finally, even their lives. They seem to have seen all things as on loan, ready to be recalled at a moment's notice. There is no protest in them.

This loose holding of all things did not come easily. The struggle was hinted at when Simon Peter said to Jesus, "We have left all we had to follow You!" (Luke 18:28). Several similar comments suggest that the disciples expected at first that they would get a lucrative payback in one form or another for their loyalty to Christ. But the wealth would be computed in forms other than what they expected.

John the Baptizer watched the crowds slip away from him as they followed after Christ. He lost his life to the executioner at the behest of a vengeful woman.

Simon Peter left his business and ended up traveling the world until he was martyred in Rome. St. Paul laid aside his position in the prestigious Sanhedrin when he was converted to Christ and spent his life planting the church in Asia Minor and Europe. He apparently died penniless and might have had reason to wonder if all of his efforts were going to last.

We are very much aware that we follow a Savior who was little more than a pauper during His entire public ministry. He had no home, no wardrobe, no income, no investments. Our faith has little to say about things except to challenge us to hold them loosely and be willing to part with them without warning.

That thought seems to militate against a large part of modern Christianity, and it may be a key reason why men and women end up in broken-world experiences. In fact, it might also be why many churches end up in trouble. When individual Christians and congregations begin to accumulate property, payrolls, and other forms of assets, they increase their vulnerability to conflicts and choices that can lead to broken worlds.

Sin flourishes when people hold on to things tightly enough to compete, to protect, or to covet. And sin flourishes when people become obsessed with the acquisition of things so that their focus moves from the objectives of faith to the goals of things. And in that refocusing, people open themselves for a hundred evils to break forth.

What are the snares that lead toward broken-world choices about material matters? *Debt* and its ability to put us into financial captivity; *pride* and its ability to move us toward measuring ourselves against others; and *greed* and its ability to engender within us a sense of dissatisfaction. We have put a personal defense initiative system into place when we choose to live out of debt, within the confines of our income, and in obedience to the biblical standard of generosity as we give to others in need or in ministry.

PDI #7: Be Filled with the Spirit of God

I left this initiative until last because it is the most important. In the Bible, being filled with the Spirit of God always meant that a person was given extraordinary power to achieve something, or wisdom to discern something, or unusual force of character to be a leader or a prophet.

In the Old Testament, these strange and wonderful experiences occured only for short periods, but the Bible always pointed toward an era when ordinary people would have access to them. And that era began on the day of Pentecost when a group of simple men and women entered the streets of Jerusalem speaking in strange languages and were able to connect with a large crowd of people speaking similar languages who were on pilgrimage from other parts of the world.

From that time forward, the fullness of the Spirit in one's personal world became an issue for Christians. What did it mean to have the life of God within in this special way?

It meant to the New Testament Christians special gifts and capacities, discernment of things not ordinarily understood, and strength to do things that ordinary human beings were not able to accomplish. In other words, people were lifted beyond normal capacity and character.

Jesus spoke of this Spirit who would enter the lives of Christians as One who would guide us into truth, who would bring to mind the teaching of Christ, who would empower us to be spokespersons about faith. At the base of all this was the certitude that when the Spirit of God was at work in believers, He Himself would be the most powerful "weapon" in preventing broken-world choices.

This Spirit could be ignored, squelched, or resisted, St. Paul warned the Thessalonians. And that's what we broken-world people are aware that we did. For a time, we found a way to ignore warnings and rebukes.

The fullness of the Spirit is available to every Christian who simply asks for it on a regular basis. It may ebb and flow in strength and vitality with the follower of the Lord as he or she is conscious of asking and submitting to its direction. And that may be the chief item on the agenda of anyone who pursues spiritual discipline every day.

Among my many friendships is one with an older leader in

the Christian church who, when he calls me on the phone, always asks this question: "Gordon, are you filled with the Holy Spirit today?" The first time I heard his question, I recoiled. Was he being nosy? Was the question not a bit trite? But after further thought, I came to realize that it was one of the most important questions anyone might ever ask me. His question was a gesture of Christian affection.

"Are you filled with the Holy Spirit?" is indeed a caring question. And it is a challenging one. I wonder if I should not resolve to ask it of my friends with greater frequency and welcome it when they ask it of me. The question forces an inward look: a quality-control check to see if the life within me is energized by God's purposes or by issues that are less than best.

"Look at the hill from the standpoint of the enemy," Major Bradley told Cadet First Captain Westmoreland. Good advice to a young officer who wants to prevent the enemy from gaining a foothold on the hill he must defend. And it's good advice for believers who wish to prevent the foothold that leads to broken-world choices. Prevent we must, or broken our worlds are likely to be.

And where are the crevices on the hill the enemy is most likely to exploit? The crevice of the *unrepentant heart*. The crevice of the *undisciplined spirit*. The crevice of the *isolated Christian*. The crevice of *undeserved applause*. The crevice of the *tired, overworked mind and body*. The crevice of the *materialistic man or woman*. And the crevice of someone who has never come under the *indwelling power of God*.

How do we prevent worlds from breaking? We seize the Bradley Tutorial: we put ourselves in the position of the enemy. He's likely to attack at one of these points of vulnerability.

PART VI
REBUILDING YOUR BROKEN WORLD

18

Rebuilt

BOTTOM LINE #18: *The grace that helps to rebuild a broken world is something given: never deserved, never demanded, never self-induced.*

I have imagined the scene on Lake Galilee more times than I could ever estimate. It is early morning, and the sky above the Golan hills to the east hints at a pending sunrise. The lake is dotted here and there with fishing boats, and if you have good eyesight, you can pick out the figures of men working their nets in hopes of a final catch before they have to quit.

One boat holds a group of men who seem tired and depressed. In charge is Simon Peter, and with him are John and several other men who have more recently been known as disciples of Jesus. What could you learn if you could pick their brains? What feelings and what explanations do they toss about in their private worlds as their thoughts keep snapping back to that night not long ago when they utterly failed the Lord? At a moment of supreme test they had simply cut and run when the more valorous thing would have been to take the same bullets the Master was taking. They hadn't, and they were escaping their embarrassment by working hard at something else.

Simon Peter has to be the most thoughtful. In his mind he has to account for absurd promises that never came close to being kept, the drawing of the sword in the garden, and the three-time renunciation of any association with Christ. The cowardice of the others was bad enough, but if there was a prize for the greatest fool, Peter would win it.

Suddenly a voice calls from the shore. "Friends, have you any fish?"

"No," the answer roars back with more than a little irritation. It's been a bad business night.

"Throw your net on the right side of the boat, and you will find some."

They did! And fish fairly leaped into the nets. So many in fact that the net was too heavy to pull over the side of the boat. Some numbers-crunching member of the crew would later determine that they had 153 fish.

John put the sound of the voice and the success of the strategy together and concluded that the Man on the shore was the Lord. "It is the Lord," he said. Was it a triumphant shout or a frightened whisper?

No matter. It was all Simon Peter needed to hear. In seconds he was over the side of the boat swimming with all of his strength toward shore. Again, what went through his mind as he swam? What was he looking for? And what did he anticipate that Jesus might say to him when he arrived?

Did he ponder the possibility that Jesus might say, "I've come to say good-bye?" Did he think that he might hear the Lord say, "Peter, I really tried hard to make you into an effective performer, but I'm afraid you don't have what it takes in you?" Perhaps he might have expected Jesus to say, "We need to sit down and talk about where you went wrong the other night."

But none of those comments were uttered. Instead, when Peter dragged himself on shore, he found the Lord preparing breakfast over a charcoal fire: bread and fish prepared to serve some hungry, cold, and tired men. Think of it: the Son of God cooking breakfast for a group of failures. *That is grace!*

No, Simon Peter heard none of the possible negative comments that any of us might have been prepared to say to him. Rather, he heard a question asked three times: *"Do you love me?"* And three times Peter struggled with the truth that came from insight. No promises this time. Only the truth. "Yes, I love you." *I don't know how that translates into action,* I can sense Peter thinking, *but I will tell you where my heart is.*

Each time Peter responded, he heard words that perhaps he had never thought he would hear again: feed my lambs; take care of my sheep; feed my sheep. *The original call was still in place.* Peter had not been dumped. HE WAS BEING RESTORED. His broken world was being rebuilt.

Every reader of the Bible has a favorite story. This one is mine. It is down to earth; it is emotional; it offers hope. It is a model of what it means to take the gift of restorative grace and press it into the life of a human being who has caused his world to be broken and now needs help in putting things back together again.

I find it insightful that the last chapter of the book of John concludes with the story of the restoration of a close follower of the Lord and that the first chapter of the following book picks up with the story of the evangelization of the world. It all suggests to me that God is in the business of taking broken-world people like Simon Peter and sending them forth to be His agents in kingdom expansion.

Three important things happened that morning on the beach. First, *Jesus came to Peter in his world.* The rebuilder went to the broken-world person knowing, perhaps, that Peter was too wounded to take the initiative himself. Second, *Jesus gave Peter a chance to replace his earlier three denials* with three honest attempts at a reaffirmation of his love for the Lord. And, third, *Jesus reissued His call.* When the beach scene was over, there were no longer any second-class citizens in the community of Jesus.

Among the most precious gifts the church has to offer is restorative grace to the broken-world person. We are talking about a community where one can confess failures, find forgiveness and counsel so that there will not be a repetition of earlier broken-world choices, and then begin to experience usefulness in serving God again. That's what Peter found on the beach, and that's what broken-world people need to find today in the congregation.

In talking about restoration we begin with the assumption that the broken-world person has acknowledged actions and attitudes that have led to consequences and offenses grievous to the Christian community. That is confession and repentance, and no one can do that for the sinner. But conversely, the repentant person cannot restore himself or herself; he or she must be restored by others. Again, I must say that I feel free to write on this subject only because I have received such restoration personally.

Many examples of restoration appear in the Scriptures. The great theme of restoration laces itself throughout Israel's history. Jeremiah could be called the great prophet of restoration; his sermons are saturated with calls for "faithless Israel" to return to the Lord,

> for I am your husband [God says]. I will choose one of you from every town and two from every clan and bring you to Zion. Then I will give you shepherds after my own heart, who will lead you with knowledge and understanding (Jer. 3:14–15).

Again Jeremiah mediated the word of God to adulterous Israel:

> If you repent, I will restore you
> that you may serve me;
> if you utter worthy, not worthless, words,
> you will be my spokesman (Jer. 15:19).

Some of the most wicked kings in Israel's time learned something about God's restorative grace. Manasseh, the king of Judah, probably had more to learn than anyone else.

> Manasseh led Judah and the people of Jerusalem astray, so that they did more evil than the nations the LORD had destroyed before the Israelites. The LORD spoke to Manasseh and his people, but they paid no attention (2 Chron. 33:9–10).

Result? A broken world.

> So the LORD brought against them the army commanders of the king of Assyria, who took Manasseh prisoner, put a hook in his nose, and bound him with bronze shackles and took him to Babylon (2 Chron. 33:11).

But Manasseh repented.

> In his distress he sought the favor of the LORD his God and humbled himself greatly before the God of his fathers. And when he prayed to him, the LORD was moved by his entreaty and listened to his plea; so he brought him back to Jerusalem *and to his kingdom*. Then Manasseh knew that the *Lord* is God (2 Chron. 33:12–14, emphasis mine).

Consequences for Manasseh? Absolutely. But restoration? Absolutely.

St. Paul reflects this theme of a restorative God in several familiar passages as he instructs new Christians on the way of life that is unique to followers of the Lord.

> Brothers, if someone is caught in a sin, you who are spiritual should restore him gently. But watch yourself, or you also may be tempted. Carry each other's burdens, and in this you will fulfill the law of Christ (Gal. 6:1-2).

The key word is *restore*. In other parts of the New Testament the same Greek word speaks to the idea of fixing or repairing or refitting something so that it can become useful again.

Nowhere do we have a better view of what Paul had in mind than when he wrote to the Corinthians about a man in the congregation who had committed a gross immorality. Originally, Paul was greatly upset over the church's failure to surface this sin and discipline the guilty man. But when they acted in discipline, Paul turned to the matter of restoration.

Aware that the man had expressed sorrow and repentance for his act, Paul said,

> The punishment inflicted on him by the majority is sufficient for him. Now instead, you ought to forgive and comfort him, so that he will not be overwhelmed by excessive sorrow. I urge you, therefore, to reaffirm your love for him (2 Cor. 2:6-8).

Forgive and *comfort* appear to be Paul's two-point program for restoration. Forgiveness seems to have been a specific act of declaring that the past would no longer be remembered. Comfort appears to have been an ongoing procedure to provide the man with a defined pathway of reconciliation to those he offended and to help him regain his place of service and fellowship in the congregation.

It looks like *everyone* was called to participate in the restoration process. It was a priority great enough that Paul made it a major issue in his writings. It was important because not to have done it would have permitted the enemy of the church to neutralize the congregation.

> If you forgive anyone, I also forgive him. And what I have forgiven—if there was anything to forgive—I have forgiven in the sight of Christ for your sake, in order that Satan might not outwit us. For we are not unaware of his schemes (2 Cor. 2:10-11).

This would have been a most appropriate time for Paul to say that the man, though forgiven and reconciled, should not be permitted to serve in certain capacities in the church. I find it important that Paul never said anything of the sort. Restoration means full return to congregational life, period.

I am also impressed with the fact that Paul clearly trusted the actions of the Corinthians. I hear him saying, *you have obviously done the right things; I affirm your actions and agree with your conclusions. Count me in as a fellow restorer.*

Stanley Jones writes of a group who understood this process at a crucial moment in his life when he found himself on his way to what could have been a broken-world experience:

> For months after [my] conversion, I was running under cloudless skies. And then suddenly I tripped, almost fell, pulled back this side of the sin, but was shaken and humiliated that I could come that close to sin. I thought I was emancipated and found I wasn't. I went to the class meeting—I'm grateful that I didn't stay away—went, but my music had gone. I had hung my harp on a weeping willow tree. As the others spoke of their joys and victories of the week, I sat there with the tears rolling down my cheeks. I was heartbroken. After the others had spoken, John Zink, the class leader, said: "Now, Stanley, tell us what is the matter." I told them I couldn't, but would they please pray for me? Like one man they fell to their knees, and they lifted me back to the bosom of God by faith and love. When we got up from our knees, I was reconciled to my heavenly Father, to the group, and to myself. I was reconciled. The universe opened its arms and took me in again. The estrangement was gone. I took my harp from the willow tree and began to sing again—the Song of Moses and the Lamb, especially the Lamb. The cross was my refuge and my release.
>
> That was a very crucial moment in my Song of Ascents, the moment when I lost my music. *My destiny was in the hands of that group.* I was a very bruised reed; suppose they had broken me? I was a smouldering wick; suppose they had snuffed me out? Just a criticism: "I told you so. Too good to be true. He was riding for a fall." *But they never uttered a criticism, or even thought of one, as far as I could see. The reaction was nothing but redemptive love.* That group became redemptive. I saw and experienced the power of redemptive love incarnate in a group. (*A Song of Ascents,* emphasis mine)

This extraordinary description of a restorative group is beautiful to read. It oozes with grace. It's not a complete story, of course, because there are times when confrontation and critique must take place for the well-being of the broken-world person. But this is a story of the healing dimension that happens when a team of people determine that a broken-world person should be rebuilt. In restoration there are things that only the team or the church can do. The broken-world person's hands are tied.

A number of elements of a full restorative process are helpful to think about. Each fits with the others like pieces in a jigsaw puzzle, and when they are complete, we may see a broken world on its way to rebuilding.

Restoration first requires confession by the broken-world person. The secrets of the heart and of past actions have to be put into the light. That's what David was doing when he finally stopped holding out and admitted to Nathan, "I have sinned." David went further in his confession when he wrote Psalm 51 in which he pours out his heart both to God and to the people about his remorse over what had happened and his desire that his broken world be rebuilt.

This is a confession of guilt and responsibility. It avoids all excuses and rationalizations. It makes no attempt to blame others or to shirk responsibility for what has happened. Until this happens, the healing process has no chance to begin.

A second aspect of the restoration or rebuilding process takes place when the broken-world person and a restoration team take time to go into the history of the events that led to misbehavior. This is an important process, like the drilling of that tooth before the dentist can fill the cavity and rebuild it to former strength. But it isn't a process for a large number of people—perhaps a group of three who are mature enough to sit with someone who has been in trouble and wants to bring the truth to the surface. There is no need for the public to know the details of one person's failures. If there is to be full restoration, however, a few need to come alongside and affirm that the issues have been dealt with.

When I faced a moment like this in my broken-world failure, the three men who formed my original restoration team met with me and engaged in a formal session much like a court. We kept a detailed set of minutes of what we said to one another.

As honestly as I knew how, I opened my life to them.

Having heard everything I said, they then knew something of how they could go about helping me find a process of rebuilding. That session ended with a remarkable experience of prayer and forgiveness, the beginning of a healing that goes on until this day.

I must underscore the significance of counseling at this point. Although we may give or receive forgiveness, that is no guarantee that all the roots of misbehavior have been discovered. Counseling from a gifted therapist can go a long way to making sure that the "decay" is treated.

Third, *restoration requires discipline.* The broken-world person cannot take this into his own hands. He needs to trust in a body of mature, godly people whose agenda is rebuilding. Along the way some painful steps must be taken to regain the confidence of others and to experience healing, and the members of the restorative body should determine how much time to allow.

Discipline usually means restrictions: being relieved of certain responsibilities, being asked to account to others on personal spiritual activities, and being required to submit to pastoral oversight or counseling. In some cases, discipline may even require the act of restitution—the formal seeking and granting of forgiveness to offended parties, repayment of monies that have been taken, or agreements that there will no longer be verbal attacks or slanders. As much as possible, discipline will require that damages and offenses are recognized and settled. This is not punishment; but it is a recognition that, for everyone's good, a time of withdrawal is wise so that the rebuilding work of Christ and His church can take place. We do no favors to one another if we rush a wounded soldier back to action.

Then restoration involves comfort. No one but the broken-world person knows how painful can be the humiliation and loss following misbehavior and its consequences. If the Christian community desires to restore an individual, regular attempts have to be made to pour courage and confidence into him.

I have strong memories of the almost daily phone calls that came to our home for Gail and me from the men who set out to help me rebuild my broken world. When they called, they read the Bible to us, having selected passages that they believed would offer hope. They often prayed with one or both of us over the phone, interceding to God in our hearing about our needs. Through the mail came notes, articles, and books for us to read. In every way possible they set out to say, "There is a tomorrow; wait for it."

Samuel Logan Brengle, an evangelist in the Salvation Army, was once called to give such comfort to a colleague serving with him who had hit the bottom in spiritual despair. The man to whom he wrote had been overcome with the conviction that he no longer had any use to Christ. Watch Brengle pour encouragement into him with this letter:

My Dear Troubled Comrade: "Absolutely useless to God and man!" You must please excuse me for breaking in on your rest with this note, but I'm still laughing and rejoicing—laughing at that ridiculous idea born in your tired brain, and rejoicing to think what a black eye the Devil is likely to get.

You say in your note to me: "I was born to the fight"; and now that you are in a real fight you feel that you are absolutely "useless!" No, no, you have often been on dress parade when you thought you were fighting. When you were at the head of a lot of shouting men and women, cheered by thousands, the Devil may have sat down, crossed his legs and watched it all as a pretty performance. But he is on the job now. I imagine that I hear him hiss: "Now I'll crush him! Now I'll smash his helmet of hope! Now I'll rob him of his shield of faith! Now I'll break his sword of the Spirit! Now I'll quench his spirit of prayer;"—and what a Devil he is.

Don't imagine that you are out of the fight. You are in it, and you must fight the good fight of faith now, in loneliness and weakness. But you will triumph.

We Salvationists exalt the active virtues, not too much, but too exclusively. The great battles, the battles that decide our destiny and the destiny of generations yet unborn, are not fought on public platforms, but in lonely hours of the night and in moments of agony.

You were indeed "born to the fight." (*Portrait of a Prophet*)

A *fifth aspect of restoration is advocacy.* The process of rebuilding always has a stated objective, which is healing and a return to service or usefulness. Those involved in the rebuilding actually take on the responsibility to speak for the broken-world person, to represent the possibilities for his rebuilding to others.

I have heard little in the church about the subject of advocacy. Yet Barnabas, the favorite New Testament character for many of us, was an advocate on at least two occasions we've already looked at. He advocated the interests and growth of Paul before the Jerusalem church when no one wanted to trust the man. And he advocated the interests and possibilities of John Mark before Paul when the old apostle didn't want to trust the younger man.

Who will advocate for the broken-world person? Who will make sure that news about his or her personal world is truthful? Who will stand with the repentant sinner and assure that he or she receives the forgiveness and grace the Scriptures tell us God wishes to give? Having experienced all of this from those who determined to rebuild my personal world and having known its hope-giving value, I wish it for every broken-world person.

Finally, *restoration requires an official declaration when it is accomplished.*

A specific time must come when one is released from discipline. Perhaps this is a public occasion, a time when the advocates of a person's restoration are prepared to say to the world or to those who care: this person is ready once again for responsibility. This can be a small or large service for Christian people. The news of what has happened should be widely circulated since it is usually true that bad news travels far and wide, but good news crawls. It needs to be declared.

I must not dare close these comments on restorative grace in action without saying once more that broken-world people will almost always live with heartbreaks and consequences that inevitably flow from wrong choices. Some, remembering the plight of Jacob who always walked with a limp after he dared to wrestle with God's messenger one night, will suggest that broken-world people will also always walk with a limp of sorts. For the most part the restorative team cannot remove this. But they can ensure that, to the best of their ability, no soldier is ever lost to the fight; no gifts ever wasted; no call, if possible, ever terminated.

There is a sense in which Jesus seems to have done all of these things for Simon Peter when they met on the shoreline of Galilee. What a moment it must have been as Peter stumbled on shore and saw the fire and the food. Was that a hint to him that he was walking not into harshness but into hospitality? Did the three questions—"Peter, do you love me?"—slowly bore into Peter's humiliated private world with the assurance that he was being given a second chance to affirm what he had originally denied? And what must it have meant when he heard the Son of God say, "Feed my lambs?" In a flash he must have known: *the call was still alive*; he still had a chance to go forth and die for this One who had died for him. Grace was real; restoration was an accomplished fact.

> Peter,
> had I
>   followed him as eagerly
>   served him as loyally
>   loved him as utterly
>   agreed to die with him as willingly
> as you,
> and then denied him as dastardly,
>   thrice,
> I would weep when roosters crow.
> But
> because I have done all things
> conservatively
> and have faced death not at all,
> I have neither wept
> nor been tenderly restored
> and called a rock.

(Gerald Oosterveen, *Decision* Magazine)

PART VII
SOME PERSONAL COMMENTS

Epilogue:
Finishing the Race

BOTTOM LINE: *When you have been pushed or have fallen to the ground, there can be only one useful resolve: GET UP AND FINISH THE RACE!*

I began this book with the stories of two runners who sustained terrible falls in the middle of races. One got up; the other didn't or couldn't. I might have mentioned a third well-known trackman of recent years who also once took a fall: Jim Ryun.

Ryun was a favorite in the Olympic 1,500 meters the day he fell. As a massive crowd in the stadium and on television watched, Ryun made his way around the track in a pack of finely conditioned runners. And then, just as it had happened to the others, he crashed to the ground. In a race of that sort, a fall virtually guarantees that it will be impossible to win. And Jim Ryun must have known that as he lay there on the track.

What were the options Ryun sorted through his mind in that moment? Quitting and heading for the locker room and a hot shower? Anger at having trained for so long for this event and now missing the chance for the gold medal? Self-pity over the seeming bad deal he'd gotten by being jostled in the pack?

None of these, apparently. Rather, he seems to have had only one thought that eclipsed all of these possibilities I've mentioned. Getting up and running again; FINISHING, even if he couldn't win. AND THAT IS WHAT JIM RYUN DID. He got up and ran again. Others won medals, but Ryun won a large measure of respect when he determined to finish the race.

Many biblical challenges call us to a performance in the Christian life worthy of a medal. But underlying all of those encouragements is an even more important one: FINISH THE RACE.

This metaphor is also a challenge to the church, to the fellowship of men and women who have found the life of the Cross the only way to live. To them goes my plea: help broken-world people get up and finish the race. Confront them like Nathan confronted David; seek them out like Hosea did his wayward wife, Gomer; forgive them like Paul did the jailer; pray for them like Stephen did for his executioners; rebuild them like Barnabas rebuilt John Mark; and restore them to usefulness whenever possible like Jesus did for Simon Peter.

In recent years we've spent enormous amounts of energy asking how the church in the West might find renewal. We've sought the answers in the pursuit of powerful preaching, evangelistic marketing programs, group dynamics, and upbeat, contemporary public services. Perhaps there is virtue in all of that. But I would like to propose that if we were to rediscover the ministry of restorative grace, we might find an enormous number of people crowding forward to receive what God has offered to give through Jesus Christ. There, in the ministry of restoration, may be a key to renewal.

Both inside and outside the church are broken-world people, and they are there in no small numbers. They yearn for an understanding and wise ear; they dearly wish for an amnesty that would provide the chance to make things right and new. If their spirit is right, they are not asking that their sins be diminished or overlooked; they are not asking that people pretend that nothing has happened. What they seek is what the cross of Christ offered: grace freely given; healing fully applied; usefulness restored.

And to the broken-world people: my brothers and sisters in that worldwide fraternity of those who know what it is like to feel useless and hopeless, there are great things to learn when the heart is sweet and open to the disciplining voice of

God. Charles Spurgeon looked back upon dark hours in his own life and said:

> I bear willing witness that I owe more to the fire, and the hammer, and the file, than to anything else in my Lord's workshop. I some times question whether I have ever learned anything except through the rod. When my schoolroom is darkened, I see most.

The objective of rebuilding a broken world is not returning life to business-as-usual as if nothing had ever happened. That could never be. No, the objective is to come out of a dark time and finish the race with a depth of grace and humility that might not have happened under any other circumstance.

We broken-world people live with a strange irony. Not for one moment would we ever wish to repeat what caused the original collapse. But we cannot ignore the fact that when restoration has had its way, we may be in a better position to offer insight and grace to others than we ever were before. We should never imagine ourselves heroes or worthy of special attention. But we do have a stewardship: a responsibility to testify to the pain, the grace, and the joy of reentering the fellowship of God and His people.

Broken-world people are equipped now to understand other struggling people. We know how to give grace because we have received it. We know how to spot the earliest signs that someone is headed in the wrong direction, and if we are wise and caring, we may be able to help others in ways we wish we'd been able to help ourselves.

All of these things and much more come to individuals who choose, when they have fallen, to get up again and finish the race. Many of the saints in the Scriptures who hit the infield grass can testify to this great grace.

For each broken-world person who has to make the choice to get up and run again, the circumstances of rebuilding will probably be unique to some extent. There will be different kinds of support structures, different kinds of "angels," and different time frames. For me the most important single factor in the rebuilding process was the partnership I share with Gail. We lived through the darkest days *together*; we pursued the Peace Ledge Principles *together*; we walked through the restoration process so graciously overseen by others *together*. Day by day, *together*, we searched the mind of God and we built a refreshed love for one another, stronger than we had ever known before. This partnership we share today is really an uncommon bond: unbreakable and resilient. I would wish for every broken-world person a champion like the one with whom I have shared this dark time.

When I fell to the infield grass and the news later became public, Gail and I were flooded with loving letters from all over the world. Some of them were difficult to open because the envelope was marked with the name of a special person I knew I'd especially let down. But each envelope contained a message of love, and it had to be read.

One such letter came from an old, old friend, a professor from graduate school days of whom I've often spoken because of his modeling of character and godliness. Dr. Raymond Buker had been an Olympic athlete, and strangely enough, he had run in the 1924 Olympic Games where Eric Liddell had made his mark on athletic history.

When Buker wrote to me in some of my darkest hours, it was as if he had been reading my mind because he said:

Dear Gordon: Back in 1923 I once ran an invitational race (one mile) with Joey Ray and Ray Watson.

We three were members of the relay team that set the world record for the four mile relay held for over twenty years. These two had a better time than I by three or four seconds. They never beat me in a race; I never did well without competition.

Anyhow in this race we three were running along at a mile rate together—the first lap, then the second lap. I suddenly hit a branch of a tree, a solid branch, (with) my left shoulder. It was a terrible blow and stopped me cold. The blow almost knocked me out. For two or three seconds I could not think. I cannot remember whether it knocked me on to the ground, but it knocked me out of my running place, stopped me cold.

I remember trying to figure out what I should do next. How could I ever catch them—should I bother to stay in the race. Everyone would understand that the blow by the tree branch knocked me out.

Somehow I staggered back on the track and stumbled along. I can see them (now) many, many yards ahead of me.

But I remember one clear conclusion. "I must keep going—even if I come in long behind. I must not quit." So I kept going. I won the race.

This then is the lesson I learned: whatever the difficulty—the blow—we must keep on. God will lead to the result that will glorify Him.

It was powerful advice, and I seized it. If you are on the ground today, I hope you will too.

And some who are the most gifted in the things of God will stumble in those days and fall, but this will only refine and cleanse them and make them pure until the final end of all their trials, at God's appointed time (Dan. 11:35 TLB).